# Comparative Educational Systems

## Edward Ignas
University of Chicago

## Raymond J. Corsini
and contributors

F.E. PEACOCK PUBLISHERS, INC.
ITASCA, ILLINOIS 60143

To Helen, Mary Beth, Mark and Chris
from whom I learned the most about education
and
To Evelyn Ann, Jon, Roberta, and Mike

Copyright © 1981
F. E. Peacock Publishers, Inc.
All rights reserved
Library of Congress
Catalog Card No. 80-52449
ISBN 0-87581-260-0
Printed in the U.S.A.
Fourth Printing, 1988

# CONTENTS

# PREFACE

There are two apparently contradictory professional conclusions about American education:
It is the best of all systems in the world.
It is a dismal failure.
Certainly the educational system in the United States is the world's most expensive. Its teachers are the best trained. It produces more professionals—engineers, doctors, lawyers, scientists—than any other country. Most Nobel Prize winners are Americans. And yet eminent students of education declare that the American educational system is a failure. Of the children who come out of our schools with 12 years of education, a high percentage—about one fifth—are unable to read or fill out a job questionnaire. Their attitudes are autistic, their beliefs unfounded, and their assertions unscientific. Such eminent observers of the educational scene as James R. Conant, Rudolf Dreikurs, Nathan Hentoff, Jonathan Kozol, R. D. Laing, Hyman Rickover, and Charles Silberman have independently given evidence that the U.S. educational system deserves a failing grade.

In this book, as well as our previous one, *Alternative Educational Systems*, our major intention has been to alert decision makers to the need for the traditional American educational system to examine itself and consider alternative methods of preparing our children for the 21st century. In *Alternative Educational Systems* we examined the traditional U.S. system critically, as well as nine alternative systems. In *Educational Systems Throughout the World*, we take a new critical look at our present system and examine a number of the educational systems employed in advanced countries. In both books our overriding concern is not the relatively trivial purpose of examining 20 systems in pursuit of knowledge for its own sake, but the urgently important purpose of improving education to improve the chances of the next generation of Americans.

H. G. Wells said that the future history of humans would be a race between education and destruction. That his prediction could be coming true is becoming increasingly evident. Only a truly well educated citizenry can think logically, act sensibly, and survive in an increasingly complex, dangerous world. Perhaps only education can save it.

In editing this book we have taken pains to locate the most knowledgeable and most articulate writers on each system. With some difficulty, we have persuaded them to cooperate in preparing their chapters according to the same format employed in *Alternative Educational Systems,* in order to provide a complete a comprehensive survey of all important aspects of each one. After reading both books, the reader should be within reach of a truly comprehensive understanding of all major educational systems.

A number of individuals have been of assistance during the lengthy process of planning and editing. We wish to thank the following professors and colleagues for their assistance: C. Arnold Anderson, Edward Beauchamp, Jerald L. Gutek, George M. Gazda, Carol Iboshi, Wallace G. Lonergan, Anthony F. Munger, Paul Pedersen, Jennette Rader, Harold G. Shane, Dan N. Simon, Alan Simpkins, Cecile T. Small, and Thomas E. VanDam.

Our thanks and appreciation are extended above all to the authors of the chapters, all busy professionals involved with their own affairs, who were willing not only to write the chapters but to follow a highly restrictive format, and who graciously accepted our editorial suggestions.

Edward Ignas
Raymond J. Corsini

# Outline of Book

*West German education, holistic in structure, does not fall into the specified categories of the Applications entry.

CHAPTER 1

# The Traditional American Educational System

## EDWARD IGNAS

## DEFINITION

The approach that elementary and secondary education has taken in the United States since the middle of the nineteenth century can only be described as "eclectic." This eclecticism has been the result of the ongoing search for a single "best" educational system, as the systems of yesterday incorporated the "best" system of the moment.

Rather than one utopian system, what has evolved is a monolithic bureaucracy that spawns and then reabsorbs countless variations of itself. The variations are like children, a few of which occasionally survive and reach a degree of autonomy, but far more often they are short-lived mutations into a species that soon loses its distinct form and merges again into the body of the parents. The parental system bears the scars of all these births but remains readily recognizable through a set of remarkably stable, even fixed hallmarks. These include the following characteristics: (1) children are assigned to a school within their geographical area and then to a specific classroom at a specified grade level; (2) children enter a grade level usually on the basis of age and are expected to advance at the rate of one grade per year; (3) students are expected to learn a core of knowledge and skills apportioned throughout a preestablished curriculum; (4) instruction is generally teacher-directed, and student progress is determined by the teacher's judgment; and (5) instructional activities center on academic subjects and are heavily dependent on textbooks and other print resources.

In the democratic tradition, schools accept individual differences among students and, within the age-graded classrooms, make an attempt to diagnose individual needs and offer some degree of individualized instruction or ability grouping. The premise is that education must be directed toward children at their present level of achievement and move them toward the development of their full potential. However, realization of this ideal is hindered by the teachers' limited diagnostic skills and by the lack of a valid or effective model for individualization. In practice, the system is structured best to disseminate a basic body of knowledge and skills, which all children will hopefully be able to learn at roughly the same age, in the same school environment, and under essentially similar instructional conditions.

## INTRODUCTION

### Objectives of Education

American society's expectations of its schools have consistently taken two major themes: (1) that the schools produce citizens with the necessary skills, knowledge and attitudes to function in the nation's social, political, and economic structures, and (2) that every child be given the opportunity to learn whatever is needed to carry out basic life tasks. The objectives of the American schools have always been drawn from this context. However, there has never yet been a single universal, functional statement of educational objectives in the traditional American educational system.

In colonial America, schools were viewed as sources of literate, moral members of society. The school's authoritarian atmosphere bespoke the subordination of individual needs and preferences to society's norm. Instruction centered on reading and interpreting the Bible. As the country grew and the population shifted from agrarian to urban and industrial settings, the religious emphasis of the schools gave way to other needs. Schools were now expected to produce a work force trained for industrial jobs and citizens enlightened enough to function as the democracy's electorate. There were masses of immigrant children to be Americanized. As the mastery of the basic subjects of reading, writing, arithmetic, social studies, and science became standard objectives, schools were also expected to inculcate patriotism and enough discipline for students to exercise basic social skills.

The establishment of democracy strengthened the nation's commitment to individual freedom and opportunity. In the schools, this commitment translated into the school's objective of actualizing individual students' potential as fully as possible.

The occasional efforts to articulate the objectives of education in the United States reflect attempts to balance concern for the needs of the individual with those of society.

In 1918, the Commission on the Reorganization of Secondary Education issued its Cardinal Principles of Secondary Education. These seven principles or goals were: (1) health, (2) command of fundamental processes, (3) worthy home membership, (4) vocation, (5) citizenship, (6) worthy use of leisure time, and (7) ethical character.

Twenty years later, the Educational Policies Commission of the National Education Association (NEA) delineated four categories of objectives: (1) self-realization, (2) human relations, (3) economic competence, and (4) civic responsibility.

Both earlier statements were reaffirmed in 1961 by the Educational Policies Commission of NEA with the addition of one other goal: "The purpose which runs through and strengthens all other educational purposes—the common thread of education—is the development of the ability to think." With the exception of this addition in 1961, statements of educational objectives have remained relatively unchanged.

These goals have remained stable over time, not because everyone agrees with these objectives, but because disagreement and controversy are so common that there is little chance of any new consensus. Especially since World War II, various pressure groups have demanded that the schools address themselves to objectives like reducing poverty, promoting racial integration, bringing about social justice and equal rights for disadvantaged groups, providing sex education, encouraging the preservation of minority cultures, and developing the individual student's mental and emotional health, to name only a few. These and other objectives remain largely rhetorical. The pressures their advocates can bring to bear on educational policy making are uneven and fragmented. Proposals for the curricular implementation of these objectives are poorly defined or nonexistent. Controversy over new objectives, which may conflict with one another or be mutually exclusive, neutralizes their impact even on the theoretical level. Even when the objective gains theoretical acceptance, the impact in the classroon is slight. Educators discuss affective education and personality development, but few classroom teachers accept explicitly any objectives beyond the three R's. In certain isolated situations, an individual teacher can be found who is implementing an effective, though highly specific, curriculum in affective areas of learning. Although there is room in the system for these initiatives, the objectives that the teacher is pursuing are far more likely to be his or her own than to be derived from the traditional educational system. Usually, this isolated teacher has gone to a workshop or been influenced by a college professor and thus learned techniques for using a particular curricular approach. The objectives of the overall system remain general and vague. They impart little information about the teaching and learning that takes place in a particular school or in traditional schools in general.

### The Reasons for This System

In a number of respects, the traditional system has responded well to the perceived needs of American society at various stages of social development. The system has given Americans of all races and classes comparatively ready access to more prolonged and higher quality schooling than was or is available to the citizens of other countries in any era. The United States has developed a tradition of pride in education. Every generation of parents places a higher value on their children's schooling. Rising expectations on the part of parents have led to demands for more years of schooling for children. At first, mass education on the elementary level was considered the public right, then mass education on the secondary level. Today, a majority of young people are expected to attend some college.

The successful implementation of these expanding social goals has ironically led to a rising discontent with the schools' performances. Although the schools are educating a greater proportion of the nation's children for longer periods of time, the popular outcry that the schools are failing to educate our children grows louder. Criticisms, though vocal, are not unanimous and are even conflicting. One group of critics' charges indict the schools for abandoning the three R's and urges a return to "the basics." Advocates of educating the "whole child" urge both cognitive and affective education in the schools. From whatever point of view they come, the calls for reform are urgent. Books with inflammatory titles like *The Literary Hoax, Why Children Fail, Crisis in the Classroom,* and *Why Johnny Can't Read* have enjoyed widespread popularity over the past two decades.

Yet the system continues basically unchanged. The system is gigantic, yet diffuse and subject to no centralized national control. The system lacks within itself any capacity for its own reform. The various reform lobbies are plagued by fragmentation, compete among themselves, and neutralize one another. The ultimate reason may be quiet but widespread consumer satisfaction. In recent national polls, the majority of parents report that they are satisfied with what children are learning in schools and that their children like school. Although the polls also show some decline in the positive attitude of the public toward the public schools, the majority of parents with children in the public schools continue to be satisfied with the schools' performance.

## HISTORY

### Beginnings

In their infancy, well over 200 years ago, American schools were generally nonpublic and often church-affiliated. They were usually located in small one-room buildings where one teacher instructed children of all ages. Attendance was voluntary and often considered a luxury. A sense of elitism sometimes led to the intentional exclusion of certain populations.

Most of the very early colonists placed little value on school. The majority never attended and did not expect their children to do so. By 1800 the average attendance of an American citizen was less than half a year by today's standards. A century later the average attendance had increased to five of today's academic years. No one individual can be credited with founding the traditional system, but among the early colonies, the colonists of Massachusetts probably deserve mention for their pioneering efforts toward public education, starting with the 1647 law requiring that any town of 100 families or more must establish a school. Two centuries later, in 1852, the first law requiring compulsory attendance was passed, again in Massachusetts. The measure required all children aged eight to fourteen to attend twelve weeks of school per year. About the same time, perhaps the single most revolutionary change in the early years of American education took place: the shift from the one-room schoolhouse to the age-graded classroom in Quincy, Massachusetts, in 1848.

Once elementary education became readily available and expected, laws for compulsory elementary schooling followed. Twenty-seven states had such laws in 1890; in 1918, Mississippi became the last state to pass legislation for compulsory elementary school attendance.

Universal secondary attendance gained acceptance far more slowly. In 1900, only about 10 percent of the teenage population received any secondary schooling, and few of those graduated. By 1940, over half the nation's youth enrolled in high schools, and about 40 percent graduated. Today, approximately 90 percent are enrolled and nearly 75 percent graduate from secondary school.

As American society learned to view education as a necessity, compulsory education spread. The traditional educational system grew and evolved into a massive complex of age-graded, multi-roomed schools in large bureaucratic public school systems, each of which is held responsible for educating all the school-aged children and youth within its geographic district. It is a system at once fragmented and monolithic, straining under increased pressures and demands and yet highly resistant to change.

## Current Status

Over the last decades (1950–1980), the traditional American system has undergone tremendous growth, becoming an ever larger target for its critics. One might question whether the mounting disillusionment stems partly from rising expectations and a more sophisticated understanding of human development and social systems, which schools should reflect —and often don't. Did the traditional American schools ever really address the majority of students' or society's needs? Certainly the schools seemed more effective three or four decades ago, when they appeared to be meeting more of society's expectations.

With the launching of the Soviet satellite Sputnik in 1957, there began a series of intense criticisms of the flaws in the system. Concern over the nation's strength and well-being prompted federal leadership to unprecedented levels of financial and legislative support for the schools, particularly for mathematics, science, and technical education.

A host of other new demands followed, as vocal laymen and educators called on the schools to become relevant to various social needs. In the 1960s, schools were expected to develop programs to prepare students for participation in civil rights movements and the war on poverty.

In the 1970s, disconcerted by the ethical erosion evident in our national leaders, the public demanded that the schools focus on moral development. Later in the decade and at the dawn of the 1980s, other widespread, serious concerns posed challenges to the system. The need for new sources of energy, the continuing world population explosion, the evolution of new communication systems, changes in the speed and modes of transportation, changes in life-styles, the advent of cultural pluralism, and scientific and technological advances were accompanied by demands for the public schools to respond with new programs for systematic change. Viewed against the background of these expanded expectations, shortcomings of the traditional system are even more evident than they might otherwise be.

When over one quarter of the population became involved in education in one way or another, as student or as employee or both, education became the nation's biggest business. During the 1960s, the rise in spending for education in the United States increased 50 percent faster than the rise in gross national product and is still accelerating. Educational spending annually exceeds $100 billion—more than is spent on defense.

Commitments of large sums of federal money over the years have brought about substantial physical improvements in the traditional system in the form of well-stocked libraries, more abundant and sophisticated teaching aids, and audiovisual materials. At the same time, demographic trends eased the overcrowding of schooling. A decline in the population of school-aged children brought about smaller classes, a more desirable student-teacher ratio, and in some areas, an oversupply of qualified teachers. Increased costs and inflation have eliminated most of the fiscal advantages of a declining school-aged population.

Throughout these changes, the educational system continues to be financed primarily through local property taxes, a source of support developed during the old local, one-room-school era. The inadequacy of this funding base and the increased expenditures have led to severe financial problems in many major cities where strikes, early school closings, and severe cutbacks in programs became common during the late 1970s. Athletic programs, extracurricular activities, and programs for the gifted, the culturally disadvantaged, the physically handicapped, and learning disabled children have all suffered.

Any close scrutiny of school budgets will reveal large amounts of money spent each year for the replacement of school property destroyed by vandals, for the purchase of electronic alarm systems and other protective mechanisms, and the employment of security guards. Urban school districts with over 25,000 students spend an average of $135,000 annually on costs of vandalism. Over a six-year period, annual assessments of the losses of public schools from vandalism increased from $200 million in 1971 to roughly $600 million in 1977.

In the face of society's rising expectations, soaring budgets, and the concurrent problems of vandalism, violence in the schools, dropouts and truancy, educators and members of the general public have been forced to question what these serious problems mean. Are they results of the failures of the schools, of the family, of society, or all of them? Certainly other factors contribute, but the increasing vandalism suggests widespread student dissatisfaction with educational programs and the people who run them. At the same time, there has been a marked decline in achievement test scores. Over a fifteen-year period, scores on the Scholastic Aptitude Test of the College Entrance Examination Board have shown a steady decline. Other surveys including the National Assessment of Educational Progress have discovered similar declines in the areas of mathematics, science, and social studies. Only in the area of reading have scores generally improved or held constant. A flood of books and articles during the 1960s and 1970s voiced public concern over the decline of the school system. Publication of *The Tyranny of Schooling, Up the Down Staircase, Robots in the Classroom, Our Children Are Dying, Why Children Fail,* and *The Literary Hoax,* among many others, expresses mounting public concern over the failure of the schools. A series of more than a dozen national reports analyzing the traditional educational system during the 1970s unanimously concluded that major reforms were needed in schools.

The criticisms of the schools took one of three major forms. Evidence that the schools were failing to teach students the three R's generated a demand for a return to the basics and elimination of so-called frills from the curriculum. Another set of critics focused on the failure of the schools to offer programs relevant to pressing social problems and their indifference or hostility toward needed social reforms such as desegregation and equal opportunity. Still another approach was characterized by an increasing demand for a comprehensive strategy for the development of life skills. This approach stressed not only the importance of the three R's but also the importance of other functional competencies such as decision making, problem solving, ability to clarify values, understanding of personality development, a grasp of the nature of the world of work, health maintenance, group dynamics, and parenting. The underlying assumption of the competency-based approach is that schools not only need to teach the basics but also need to teach children how to learn and how to be prepared for lifelong learning. Studies of large samples of American adults indicate that many members of the adult population lack basic competencies needed to perform some essential life tasks.

The back-to-basics movement, which surfaced in the middle of the 1970s, developed partly in response to parental demand and partly in reaction to the studies and statistics revealing declining achievements. In 1975, there were twelve schools established in the country devoted specifically to the return to basics. By 1978, this number had reached 200 and was still climbing.

Alternative schools have been another remedy frequently suggested during the 1970s. Some alternative schools are relatively or almost entirely autonomous of the traditional system and center on methods for giving children and youth opportunities to learn outside the schools, in the community itself. The community orientation addresses the persistent criticism that traditional schools isolate youth and children from participation in the rest of society for so many years (Coleman, 1974, *Youth: Transition to Adulthood*). Other alternative schools are established as a part of the traditional system. About one third of all public schools had alternative schools in their system by the end of the 1970s, and two thirds of the larger systems had them. These schools were attempts to provide options for meaningful education to the youth of an area. The magnet school, which developed largely in the last half of the 1970s, exemplifies one form of alternative school within the traditional system. Magnet schools often served as a desegregation strategy in cities carrying out court-ordered integration. The magnet school represents an attempt to offer high-quality education in special programs to students of diverse ethnic backgrounds, drawn from a much larger geographical area than the average school district.

Another reaction to the traditional school's failing has been the movement toward competency-based programs and the institution of the competency testing in the traditional schools. Over half the states had legislated some form of competency-based testing requirements by the end of the 1970s. However, these programs have as yet addressed only the most basic skills such as reading and have not yet had much more than an academic impact on the overall educational effort.

Regardless of the approach, most alternative schools still rarely address the issue of the responsibility for learning. Rarely do these programs bring the teachers, parents, administrators, and children all together into the collaboration necessary for a successful educational system.

The educator working with students in the next twenty years—the remainder of the twentieth century—must realize that decisions and educational expenses will be different from those of the preceding age. Every educator of high school youth is keenly aware of the "glut" of youth since the 1950s. The unusually high birthrate from 1950 through 1965 resulted in this "youth culture." From 1954 through 1965, there were more than 4 million births each year, the largest number of births ever recorded. Between 1965 and 1970, the number of births decreased about 20 percent and has held steady at approximately 3.1 to 3.3 million births a year during 1970–1980. The projected increase of the fifteen- to twenty-four age-group between 1960 and 1980 is shown in Table 1-1. This group reaches its high point in 1980; thereafter it decreases between 1980 and 1990, first slowly, then much more rapidly. Educators accustomed to increasing enrollments will have to readjust their roles and expectations.

Educators of the future must be keenly aware of these population statistics; they cannot rely on stable demographic trends. Already, the federal government has taken measures to provide socially useful opportunities for youth. The government will take further steps to develop socially useful employment to youth and will encourage business and industry to employ young individuals throughout the next critical decade of the 1980s. Teachers, too, must be trained so that they can adapt their teaching skills to other career orientations.

**Table 1-1**

**U.S. Population Projections from 1960 to 2050**

**(in millions and percentages)**

| Age-Group | 1960 | 1970 | 1975 | 1980 | 1985 | 1990 | 2000 | 2025 | 2050 |
|---|---|---|---|---|---|---|---|---|---|
| *Population in Millions* | | | | | | | | | |
| Under 15 | 56.5 | 57.8 | 53.6 | 51.2 | 53.9 | 58.1 | 58.9 | 62.6 | 65.4 |
| 15–24 | 24.1 | 36.5 | 40.2 | 41.5 | 38.5 | 34.8 | 38.8 | 40.9 | 43.3 |
| 25–39 | 35.0 | 36.5 | 42.5 | 50.2 | 57.0 | 60.3 | 54.9 | 59.7 | 63.2 |
| 40–54 | 32.7 | 35.2 | 35.0 | 34.3 | 36.5 | 42.5 | 57.6 | 54.8 | 58.9 |
| 55–64 | 15.6 | 18.7 | 19.8 | 20.8 | 21.5 | 20.5 | 22.9 | 34.1 | 36.2 |
| 65–74 | 11.1 | 12.5 | 13.8 | 15.4 | 16.4 | 17.5 | 17.1 | 30.1 | 29.1 |
| 20–64 | 93.6 | 107.6 | 116.6 | 126.5 | 135.5 | 141.3 | 152.6 | 168.4 | 179.6 |
| 65+ | 16.7 | 20.2 | 22.3 | 24.5 | 26.7 | 28.9 | 30.6 | 48.1 | 51.2 |
| 75+ | 5.6 | 7.7 | 8.4 | 9.1 | 10.2 | 11.4 | 13.5 | 18.0 | 22.1 |
| All Ages | 180.7 | 204.8 | 213.5 | 222.8 | 234.1 | 245.1 | 262.5 | 299.7 | 318.4 |
| *Population Percentages* | | | | | | | | | |
| Under 15 | 31.3 | 28.2 | 25.1 | 23.0 | 22.9 | 23.7 | 22.3 | 20.8 | 20.5 |
| 15–24 | 13.3 | 17.8 | 18.9 | 18.6 | 16.4 | 14.2 | 14.8 | 13.6 | 13.6 |
| 25–39 | 19.4 | 17.8 | 20.0 | 22.5 | 24.3 | 24.6 | 20.9 | 19.9 | 19.8 |
| 40–54 | 18.1 | 17.2 | 16.4 | 15.4 | 15.5 | 17.3 | 21.9 | 18.3 | 18.5 |
| 55–64 | 8.6 | 9.1 | 9.3 | 9.4 | 9.2 | 8.4 | 8.7 | 10.4 | 11.3 |
| 65–74 | 6.1 | 6.1 | 6.5 | 6.9 | 7.0 | 7.1 | 6.5 | 10.0 | 9.2 |
| 65+ | 9.2 | 9.9 | 10.4 | 11.0 | 11.8 | 11.8 | 11.7 | 16.0 | 16.1 |
| 20–64 | 51.9 | 52.5 | 54.5 | 56.8 | 57.8 | 57.7 | 58.1 | 56.3 | 56.2 |

*Source:* U.S. Bureau of the Census, *Current Population Reports*, Series P-25, No 601, October 1975. Table 8, Series 11.
*Note:* Assumptions: Fertility rate at 2.1 (replacement level). Immigration, 400,000 per year. Slight decrease in mortality, 1970 to 2000.

Current approaches to reform are most often reactions to the traditional system, which, as soon as they gain acceptance, tend to be caught up again into the traditional system, often diluted and distorted. Promising innovations are evaluated before they have had an opportunity to be proven successes or failures. Often teachers have not yet had time to become thoroughly comfortable with new techniques or programs, but an impatient public judges them prematurely and usually finds fault. The average life span of an educational innovation in the United States is three years.

For this reason, the primary outcome of the reform efforts of the 1960s and 1970s has been to increase skepticism about the ability of the schools to educate our children and the ability of the schools to reform themselves. This paradox is illustrated by the conclusion of Martin Meyer. After thirty months of interviewing, observing, and reading about the current system, he commented "the higher one's view of human potential, the more one will dislike the schools as they actually exist." Paul Goodman has suggested "that perhaps we already have too much formal schooling and that under present conditions the more we get, the less education we get." The system continues to work, but needed reforms falter. And so the current status of the schools is this: (*a*) general parental satisfaction with the schools and, ironically, a simultaneous widespread public dissatisfaction and virulent criticism of the schools, (*b*) lavish spending on the educational system coincident with serious financial problems and cutbacks, and (*c*) widely acknowledged urgent needs for sweeping reforms of the system but apparent immobility because of some intrinsic incapacity of the system to reform itself.

## THEORY

The traditional school is the pervasive educational model on the American scene, but it usually exists in some modified form, as schools experiment sporadically with various innovations. In a survey of elementary schools in one large Middle Western city in the late 1970s, in only one third of the schools studied could the staff apply to their school any labels at all, such as "open," "continuous progress," or "traditional." Two thirds of the schools studied corresponded so little to any of the described models that they were not classified at all (Goodlad, 1979). The traditional school exists, then, primarily in its mutations rather than in any pure form. This is a result not only of the eclecticism that characterizes the system, but also of the gap between the commonly accepted learning theories and the actual practices of the schools.

In fact, the absence of a coherent learning theory may account for the presence of not only different but even conflicting approaches to learning being used within a single school or in a single classroom.

Depending on norms within a school district or within a given school, one school may combine several approaches to education. For example, an elementary school might have nongraded open classrooms in the primary grades and a departmentalized approach to the upper grades. Another school might combine open classrooms with self-contained classrooms and some amount of individually guided instruction.

### Learning

Perhaps partly as a result of the eclectic nature of the traditional educational system, no coherent statement of the system's learning theory has ever been made. Theories that are commonly espoused are frequently resisted in practice, while others that are unacknowledged may form the basis of widespread practices. The only consistent characteristic of learning theories operating in the traditional system is that they are rarely used in their "pure form."

Various popular theories are accepted in whole or in part and used in combination with one another, whether or not they are compatible. Innovations are generally set into the matrix of the traditional system; this usually weakens or distorts the new approach to learning from the start. For example, most learning theories today contend that students learn in a variety of different styles and manners and at different speeds, and that student readiness will vary greatly for students of the same age. Educators have found countless ways to implement this concept, from programmed learning and individually guided education to ability grouping and the track option.

Yet the structure of most traditional schools still requires that twenty or thirty students of the same age in a class study the same thing at the same time in the same way. Students who learn too fast or too slowly or differently are punished by low grades that brand them as failures or are punished by being confined to boring or irrelevant classroom activities.

Although it is difficult to generalize about such a multiform system, certain aspects of learning theory seem to be relevant to more traditional schools. Not all have had a positive influence on the schools, but they have been accepted as key concepts in the conceptual framework of the traditional system.

> *(1) Despite favorable reception as theory,*
> *cognitive psychology has had little positive effect*
> *on the schools.*

Since the early 1960s, the cognitive psychology of Jerome Bruner and others had been widely acclaimed and used as the basis of significant attempts at curricular reform. Bruner suggested that the structure of an academic subject indicated what the appropriate heuristics of the teaching-learning experience should be. Thus, in learning mathematics, students would be placed in situations in which they could make the same discoveries as mathematicians, but on a more elementary level. The new mathematics of the 1960s was an application of Bruner's concept of the "spiral curriculum," which was based on this process of discovery, experimentation, and development of perceptual and cognitive skills. New curricula based on Bruner's thoughts were developed in various disciplines but, in most cases, were poorly implemented on the classroom level. Traditional teachers and schools generally lacked the ability or willingness to trade their knowledge-based approach to learning for the new process-based curricula. Traditional educational rhetoric continues to allude to cognitive psychology, but thus far the theory has had very little application in classroom teaching.

> *(2) The assumption that education ought to*
> *impart to every student a core body of*
> *knowledge has been repeatedly discredited; yet*
> *this assumption continues to serve as a basis for*
> *most traditional schooling.*

The traditional system incorporates in its theoretical construct the belief that there exists some body of knowledge that is meant to be passed on to continuing generations. The natural result of these assumptions is the heavy dependence upon teacher lectures and presentations and on reading textbooks. Students engage in rote learning and recalling and are expected to give evidence of their learning by being able to remember and restate the information they have received. Although other cognitive skills are not totally neglected, a disproportionate emphasis is placed on recall.

Even if the body-of-knowledge approach was once desirable, it is not now because there is too much knowledge to cover. It is no longer merely difficult to select a few of those most important bits and pieces of knowledge to pass to students, it has become impossible. Consequently, especially in the elementary grades, the trend is to stress learning how to learn. Recent curriculum reforms center more on the structural elements and methods in the subject disciplines and on knowing and the nature of knowing. The new mathematics was more than just an attempt to incorporate upbeat content into the curriculum; it also implied learning by discovery and induction rather than deduction.

Advocates of process-based curricula or competency development agree that there is a narrow core of content necessary to teach but that this content could be taught in far less time than the current traditional curriculum takes. New curricula, if well designed, would integrate reading and mathematics skills into the teaching of other competencies and life skills. Proponents of competency-based education would determine what these competencies should be by asking what skills people need in order to accomplish their life tasks with respect to work, interpersonal relationships, and their own individual growth and development.

The implications of such an approach to learning are vast. It is becoming commonplace for theoreticians to challenge the concept of teaching as telling and instead to encourage teachers to provide opportunities for students to explore, test, inquire, and make discoveries for themselves. Practice takes a while to catch up to theory, however. Traditional schools continue to rely heavily on lecture, teacher-led discussion, rote learning, and recall.

*(3) Behavioral psychology, while rejected in its more extreme forms, is the basis for a large number of practices within the traditional system.*

The behavioral psychology espoused by B. F. Skinner has met with an amalgam of acceptance and rejection in the traditional educational system. On the level of rhetoric, traditional educators are generally resistant to extreme forms of behavioral modification and would claim to disavow its use. Yet the stimulus-response theory has been a cornerstone of traditional educational psychology throughout the twentieth century, and it is the unacknowledged basis for many of the methods used in the schools to bring about behavioral change. Rewards and punishments such as grades, honor rolls, detentions, and suspensions are used commonly to control and modify student behavior in terms of both academic learning and social skills.

With the behavioral psychological approach used in traditional schools, motivations for learning are generally based on competition. The use of reward and punishment for motivation has always been deeply ingrained in American society, and teachers who employ rewards and punishment generally do so without connecting their instructional techniques with learning theory. Often they are unaware of the extent to which they are using rewards and punishments. Some effective teachers may be found who give students appropriate support and encouragement, either deliberately or out of a natural warmth toward children. However, a number of studies have shown that positive reinforcement such as praise and verbal rewards are often administered infrequently and are not clearly designed to attract the student's attention to the close relationship between the effort and some goal he or she is pursuing. In its most negative form, the behavioral approach consists primarily of punishing undesirable behavior, which has been found to be of little use in eliminating the unwanted behavior and far less use in helping the learner discover what behavior is desired.

Competition in the traditional school is usually between individual students or between one group or another. Rarely does it take the form of the individual student competing with his or her own prior achievements. Both rewards—teacher and peer approval and good grades—and punishments—disapproval and bad grades—focus on facts extrinsic to learning itself. Being designated as a winner or a loser is nonessential to the intended learning. The student may not actually learn the desired material, but he or she will quickly absorb this learning process. Monitoring and evaluating one's achievement by the use of external standards becomes a lifelong habit for many students who pass through the traditional system.

Competition, which permeates classroom activities and extracurricular activities on all levels, has been unquestioningly accepted as an American virtue. Yet, the benefits of competition have not been adequately defined, whereas its drawbacks in the learning process are quite definite. Competition leads to the labeling of winners and losers, softened with terms like *bright, clever, achiever, advantaged,* or *dull, underachiever, disadvantaged.* Labels are generally detrimental to learning because they discourage children or confuse children about the relation of achievement and human worth. The stress on scholastic competition has been justified as a "preparation for life." However, the life skills needed for functioning in our society involve cooperation at least as much as they do competition. Most schools need to give students more experience in learning cooperation. Warnings to "do your own work" without help from anyone else may encourage self-reliance, but they also give some students the impression that cooperation or collaboration is somehow wrong.

> *(4) Educators acknowledge that students learn most powerfully from the interpersonal relationships, the ambience, and structure of their school experience; yet schools take little responsibility for the quality and outcome of this learning.*

Probably the most profound and lasting learning that takes place in the school is not part of any planned curriculum, but the rather incidental learning that takes place in any life setting. Through such unplanned and often unintended learning, children quickly perceive how they are valued by their teachers and peers and form their self-images accordingly. Regardless of the academic subjects being taught, each day in the schools children learn about the American social and political structures. They absorb certain moral values and expectations; attitudes and biases with respect to race, sex, age, and life-styles; and the relative value of both academic and nonacademic achievements. Students learn about living up to the demands of persons in authority or about how to get around the rules or the system. In many cases, the traditional schools teach children that they are not responsible for their own learning but are dependent on others for their progress. The authoritarian structure of the school teaches them that someone else is in charge of their education.

The importance of this so-called hidden curriculum is evident, and most schools in the traditional system have just begun to acknowledge their contribution to this powerful cultural conditioning of the students who pass through the system. The positive utilization of these factors needs more active encouragement by those who make school policy.

### Teaching

Most of the teaching done in the traditional system bears no direct relationship to theory of teaching. Teachers who have passed through an array of education courses absorb certain principles. Among these is the need to reach a child at his present level and pace teaching so that the student progresses at his own speed toward his own self-actualization. Teachers know that children learn more by doing than by hearing. It is also commonly believed that children learn better if they are taught through subject matter with intrinsic appeal—a theory supported by educators including John Dewey, William H. Kilpatrick, and Alfred North Whitehead since the early twentieth century.

In spite of the popularity of these enlightened approaches to teaching, actual classroom instruction is rarely grounded in any substantial teaching theory, and the traditional system has not yet developed a coherent theory of instruction. Within the classroom, the individual teacher has considerable autonomy and is held ultimately responsible for how teaching will be done. Students play an essentially passive role in their own education. The individual teacher's talent, training, and temperament, as well as tradition and the prevailing norms of local educators and parents, have far more effect on teaching than any theory.

It is commonplace to observe that most teachers teach the way they themselves were taught. The predominant modes of instruction are lecture, class discussions, recitations, and occasionally demonstrations or modeling, especially in areas such as science or foreign languages. In the majority of these modes, teacher talk is dominant, that is, the teacher talks from 60 to 90 percent of the time during periods when there is any form of verbal interaction in the classroom. There is relatively little use of peer teaching, student presentations, or student-led discussions. One-to-one contact between teacher and student during regular class time is not common: Tutoring or individual conferences are usually conducted outside of class time. Individualized instruction often takes the form of using programmed materials or individual learning packets and usually means that the students all learn the same material but at different rates. Most classroom teachers do not diagnose needs prior to or in the course of instruction. Application of the concept of individualization must be more systematic.

While teachers are constantly bombarded with evidence that even students on the same grade level vary widely in abilities and learning styles, the structure of the traditional school has usually been set up for teaching a whole class of thirty students the same material, at the same time, and in the same way.

Within this structure, some attempts to accommodate individual differences are made, usually by dividing students into subgroups. The most widely used approach to grouping is on the basis of ability—assigning students to classes based on their previous performance on intelligence or achievement tests, grades in prior schoolwork, or a teacher's judgment of a student's ability. In some schools, students may be placed at random or by a voluntary sign-up system, but most traditional schools group students in some way, either through counseling or through administrative decisions.

The purpose of ability grouping is to make classes more homogeneous so that instruction can be geared to students who are on the same level. The difficulty is that students within a homogeneous group have such a wide variety of cognitive skill levels that this goal is rarely accomplished with any degree of success. Furthermore, it has frequently been observed that even when students are grouped homogeneously, teachers do not always modify their presentations accordingly.

Certain ill effects can be observed with ability grouping. Damage to the self-esteem of students in the less able groups and a narrow-minded elitism among students in the more able groups may result. There have been some legal challenges to the concept of ability grouping on the basis that it is a form of de facto segregation. This controversy has not yet been tested thoroughly in the court system, and many schools are still using ability grouping.

APPLICATIONS

## Curriculum, Academic

Generally, the academic curriculum of the traditional educational system has evolved in response to changing social expectations. Classical education served as the core of the traditional system during the eighteenth century, when education was thought of primarily as a means of preparing an elite who would run the country or as the means of preparing a certain segment of the population for college. Later on, those who thought of the purpose of education as the Americanization of immigrants from other countries also saw the classical curriculum as the primary means of achieving those goals. The so-called progressive education of the 1930s and 1940s began to pay more attention to the education of the masses in view of the fact that over 60 percent of the high school students of those decades did not go on to college. At this time, one common view of the school was as a custodian of youth, a means of guarding and keeping youth out of the labor force until a certain age. Subjects that were added to the curriculum at this time included such practical subjects as vocational education, mechanical drawing, and modern languages (rather than Greek or Latin).

As criticism of the traditional system gained momentum in the 1950s, 1960s, and 1970s, demands for change became more intense, frequent and at times violent. Many new trends in the curriculum evolved as reactions to these criticisms. Critics of progressive education, which focused on the education of the average child, reacted with a demand for more basic skills. For a while, in the 1950s, the liberal arts curriculum was dominant as a possible means of providing youth with a sense of values and of philosophy of life that would enable them to live in a modern world. The late 1950s, the advent of the Sputnik era brought a renewed emphasis on the need for science and technological education. The schools were supposed to turn out highly trained manpower for a technological society. Huge sums of federal money were pumped into the curriculum through the National Science Foundation. The concept of educating an elite was no longer seen as something schools would admit to as a goal.

The next wave of demands for curriculum reform sprang from research on how children learn, particularly the work of the cognitive psychologists such as Jerome Bruner. Another force was the growing perception of the atmosphere in schools as inhumane and a demand for a more humane environment. Because of the implications of learning theory and the desire to liberate children from the oppressive structures of the traditional classroom, the curriculum began to reflect the influences of the open classroom, the development of alternative schools, the use of the community as a resource for learning and for gaining work experience, and vocational education. New interdisciplinary subjects entered the curriculum. Originally, subjects in the academic curriculum corresponded to the various disciplines: literature, mathematics, reading skills, history, geography, and civics. Each would be a separate subject. The trend toward interdisciplinary subjects led to the entry into the curriculum of ethnic studies, women's studies, black studies, sex education, consumer education, and drug education. The various disciplines were refined for curricular purposes more as methods of thinking rather than as bodies of facts. Physics and mathematics, in particular, began to be taught by the so-called inquiry method. Students were taught not a body of information that would eventually become obsolete, but rather a way of thinking and solving problems that they could use to master the fast-evolving, new knowledge in the various disciplines.

The original American curriculum centered around the three R's, and the high school curriculum was primarily a college-preparatory curriculum, focusing on the classics. The curriculum was organized around the various academic disciplines, each of which consisted of a body of content that defined the amount of knowledge students were thought able to absorb. The purpose of the curriculum was the transmission of knowledge within each of these discipline areas.

Within each discipline, the specific items to be learned over the years have often been stated in the form of behavioral objectives. A behavioral objective is overt, observable, and measurable and therefore makes it easy to determine when learning has actually taken place. Although the behavioral objective has been in use for many years, it gained impetus in the 1960s, especially with the advent of certain nationwide agencies or clearinghouses, which would collect and exchange behavioral objective statements. While some proponents of behavioral objectives saw them as a step toward specific and concrete mastery learning, others debated their value and questioned whether simply knowing answers amounts to actually being educated.

By the late 1970s, a new set of pressures brought a new set of curricular reforms. Nearly 90 percent of the high school population now went on to some college; yet standardized achievement tests showed the general overall learning level was falling steadily. Attempts to teach students methods of thinking rather than a specific body of knowledge seemed to coincide with a decline in basic skills, especially in the areas of reading and mathematics. The new math is an excellent example of this cyclical pattern. In the early 1960s, the new math stressed grasp of scientific concepts. It was not important whether students could actually get to the right answers as long as they knew how to go about looking for the answers. However, achievement levels dropped and basic skills suffered. By the late 1970s, a blend of the new math and a fundamental approach became more commonly used. Mathematics was being taught with less technical language and with more relevance to real-life situations. Mathematics textbooks were often written on a more elementary level to allow for poor reading skills on the part of many students.

The finding that about one quarter of the nation's eighteen-year-olds lack skills to be employable led to a resurgence of interest in vocational and technical education. Career education, as it is currently called, is far more commonly seen as the schools' responsibility. Proponents of career education urge every teacher to stress career implications within his or her discipline. The career education program also involves vocational skills training, as well as providing opportunities for observing work in real work settings. Opportunities for work experience, which allow the student to negotiate the interaction among school, home, and society, are intended to give students marketable skills, attitudes, and the knowledge and motivation to make appropriate career decisions.

One of the most powerful forces to shape the evolution of curriculum, especially in the last thirty years, is the heavy dependence of the school system on textbooks and other printed materials. Although theoretically the local school districts and schools are free to design their own curricula, in fact, a national curriculum has evolved as determined by the choices of a few major publishers. While there is some local flexibility in the selection and use of textbooks, the overall content of textbooks nationwide is determined by a few major publishers. Within specific states or school districts, textbooks are selected from those available, and normally in the actual classroom each student is provided with a textbook on each subject studied. Opinions vary as to exactly how much a textbook determines the curriculum, but most observers agree that it determines a major portion of the course development. Within the actual classroom, the individual teacher has considerable latitude regarding how he or she will or will not use the text, but the end result of the competition among textbook publishers is the de facto existence of a national curriculum within a traditional system.

In the late 1970s, a concern about the apathy and disaffection of students within the system in general have led to some revival of interest in the humanities as a way of giving youth a greater sense of meaning, purpose, and beauty in life. The humanities have included the study of literature, language, history, art, music, philosophy, and even the study of religious thought and culture. Various other less established subjects have entered the curriculum such as death education, moral education, or values clarification. Study of the future and futurism and even relaxation or transcendental meditation techniques are included. Each of these trends is an attempt of the schools to address certain needs of youth for basic life skills beyond the four large R's of education: Responsibility, Respect, Resourcefulness, and Responsiveness (Corsini, 1979). Nevertheless, these innovations generally do not permeate the entire traditional system and have not altered it drastically. They are spawned in response to the deficiencies of the traditional system, often rise up on the fringes or outside the traditional system, survive an average of three years, gradually are absorbed in part into the traditional system, often are then swallowed up by it, or are watered down, and may survive only in vestigial form. Curricular revision needs to take place in the context of the entire curriculum and its implications for students' overall needs. In spite of the sporadic attempts to incorporate reforms into the traditional curriculum, the traditional system remains basically conservative and highly resistant to change. Even with all the discussion, experimentation, and innovation, most of classroom activities going on and subjects being learned would be similar to those used in the schools of several decades ago.

### Curriculum, Nonacademic

The nonacademic curriculum in the traditional school is not clearly distinguished from the academic curriculum. Traditionally, the academic subjects would include everything under the broad heading of arts and sciences, and nonacademic would include everything else. Nonacademic curriculum includes both classroom and outside-of-class, or cocurricular, activities, often referred to as student activities. Many people would classify physical education, vocational training, and general business courses as part of the nonacademic curriculum. Journalism or physical education might be classified either way, as academic or nonacademic. Extracurricular activities such as speech, debate clubs, athletics, and student government are commonly considered part of the nonacademic system or curriculum. Many critical kinds of nonacademic learning in the life skills and affective area are really not assigned to any specific or nonacademic class or extracurricular activity. Values clarification and the development of attitudes are acknowledged as an essential part of learning, and yet may never be directly addressed in either academic or nonacademic activities. The appropriate expression of feeling, self-motivation, self-esteem, and the full range of affective learning that determine success in life needs to take place.

Much of the nonacademic learning that happens in schools is derived from the actual structure of the classroom and of the school itself. Too great a stress on getting good grades or the division of students into fast learners or slow learners are examples of ways outside the academic curriculum in which the school teaches children concepts and habits. Interfacing with the community through activities such as field trips or work experience programs is another important aspect of the nonacademic curricula in some schools. Schools have tended to isolate children from the society in which they live rather than to prepare them for it. This aspect of the nonacademic curriculum is still far from adequate in most schools.

### Student Evaluation

The individual classroom teacher bears the primary responsibility for student evaluation in the traditional system. Teachers evaluate students on the basis of tests of various kinds, observation, and sometimes grades given on classroom performance or homework assignments. Tests may be purchased from textbook manufacturers or may be teacher-made. Some tests take the form of written essay questions or so-called subjective tests. Others are objective tests of a true/false, multiple-choice, matching, or fill-in-the-blank types, which require students to feed back specific bits of information. Even with testing, teacher evaluations are generally highly subjective in nature. Reports of student progress generally take the form of letter grades, usually issued on a report card. Some elementary schools use parent-teacher conferences for reporting to parents, and in many schools, a combination of report cards and conferences is used. Grades are usually letter grades—A, B, C, D, and F—and determine whether a student on the elementary level will pass on into the next grade. On the secondary level, grades determine whether a student will receive academic credit for class work. Students who do not receive a passing grade in a given course or subject, especially on the elementary level, are required to either repeat the same grade the following year or through summer school or tutoring or to engage in other compensatory education to make up the work that has not been mastered. One disadvantage of this policy is that students repeat a course or a grade and finish with little additional progress toward mastery as compared to what they had the first time around. Sometimes a form of battle fatigue on the part of teachers and students leads to the eventual passing of students to the next grade or course level, even when mastery has not been achieved. This phenomenon accounts for much of the decline in academic standards, so that a great many students who simply hang around a given class or subject long enough eventually pass by teacher default.

In addition to grades for academic or "hard" subjects, many schools require teachers to give students grades on "deportment" or "citizenship," terms for attitudes and behavior students exhibit in school. While teachers try to base their grading of students on so-called objective data, most observers and teachers, in their more honest moments, agree that the entire grading system is riddled with subjectivity.

In most school systems, an attempt to evaluate students objectively and compare them to other students in the country takes the form of a standardized testing program. Standardized achievement tests are generally used about once a year or a little less often to assess the overall achievement level of students in a particular school or school system. Test scores take the form of grade-level equivalents. The test score is norm-referenced, because scores are based on the normal behavior for a given population. Thus, a given test might tell how a fifth grader compares with other fifth graders in mathematics, but it will give little direct information about the particular student's actual level of mathematical skills. Standardized tests are generally used to determine how effective a school district is compared to national or statewide norms. An individual student's test scores may be given to that student or his parents, but they are generally not included as part of the classroom teacher's evaluation of the individual student.

Classroom students are often grouped according to ability as determined by their standardized test results. Thus, students with a low score in a reading achievement test can be assigned to a remedial reading class. One of the risks of the entire evaluation system in the traditional system is that a child can easily misconstrue an F as a value judgment of his intrinsic worth as a human being. The negative evaluations can interfere with student learning by discouraging intellectual pursuit, exploration, and willingness to risk failure.

## Counseling

Over the years, the guidance and counseling personnel of the traditional system have sought to be flexible and responsive to institutional and societal needs and changes. However, during the past two decades, it has been necessary to design intervention methods for larger numbers of specific clients and concerns. Recently, PL94-142 has added handicapped students to target groups with which school counselors are becoming increasingly involved. The multiple roles counselors are asked to assume demand a high level of counselor expertise and endurance. Surveys indicate that most counselors feel that there are too many students and too few counselors to respond adequately to client needs. Schools traditionally have assigned one counselor to several hundred students. This demanding counselor/student ratio has traditionally restricted the amount of individual counseling available to students with more serious problems. As a result, many counselors work with students in groups in an attempt to provide group counseling and guidance activities. Some counselors invite teachers to assist in providing group guidance services. In addition, much counseling and guidance is attempted by classroom teachers and administrative staff on matters relating to discipline, family problems, personal problems, social problems, educational problems, or other counseling needs that the student or staff perceives. Counselors are equally responsible for administering a variety of testing instruments that focus on students' interests and vocational aptitudes, achievement, and general intelligence.

The majority of counselors in traditional schools have completed accredited master's degree programs and have received special training to provide a variety of services. No single theoretical counseling approach is utilized in traditional schools. Most counselors employ eclectic approaches when providing services for students, parents, and staff members. Typically, the services provided by counselors in the middle and high school grades include assisting students with scheduling and scheduling problems, planning college and vocational programs with students and parents, working as a liaison with both colleges and employers, supporting students in their efforts to find part-time employment, making vocational information available and providing individual and group counseling for students and parents. Program structures mostly consist of academic counseling (for example, college selection) and vocational counseling.

Counselors in urban school districts are also becoming involved in helping students and anxious and confused parents respond effectively to the problems arising from the population changes in large cities. The majority of these cities have become cosmopolitan in a sense that is surprising and perplexing both to the long-term residents and to the educational community.

The migration of minorities—black, Hispanic, and Asian—into the largest cities of this country has been a startling phenomenon of major concern to counselors. The extent of this influx was almost imperceptible prior to 1965. Table 1-2 shows the percentage of various minority students in the public schools of the sixteen largest cities in 1976. Of the sixteen cities identified, only three had white student populations as high as 50 percent: San Diego, Indianapolis, and Milwaukee. Cities with less than 30 percent white enrollment include New York, Chicago, Detroit, Baltimore, San Antonio, Washington, D.C., San Francisco, Memphis, and Los Angeles.

The data indicate that counselors in inner-city schools serve mostly minority students. Most of these schools are and will become largely or totally black or Hispanic. Perhaps more than their white counterparts, these students and their parents require specialized counseling and guid-

**Table 1-2**

**Distribution of Enrollment by Race/Ethnicity in Public Schools of Sixteen Largest U.S. Cities, 1976; and Annual Rates of Change in Enrollment, 1970 to 1976**

| City | 1976 Enrollment (Thousands) | Percentage Distribution of Enrollment by Race/Ethnicity 1976 | | | | | Average Percentage Change in Enrollment 1970 to 1976 | | | | |
|---|---|---|---|---|---|---|---|---|---|---|---|
| | | White | Combined Minorities | Black | Hispanic | Asian | Total | White | Combined Minorities | Black | Hispanic |
| New York | 1,076 | 30% | 70% | 38% | 29% | 3% | −1.0% | −4.8% | +1.0% | +0.6% | +1.1% |
| Chicago | 521 | 25 | 75 | 60 | 14 | 1 | −1.7 | −7.3 | +0.6 | −0.3 | +4.4 |
| Philadelphia | 261 | 32 | 68 | 62 | 6 | 1 | −1.2 | −3.5 | 0.0 | −0.1 | +8.4 |
| Houston | 210 | 34 | 66 | 43 | 22 | 1 | −2.3 | −8.5 | +2.1 | +0.9 | +4.7 |
| Detroit | 238 | 19 | 81 | 79 | 2 | ∨1 | −3.0 | −13.3 | +0.7 | +0.7 | +0.8 |
| Baltimore | 160 | 24 | 76 | 75 | ∨1 | ∨1 | −3.1 | −8.1 | −1.1 | −1.2 | b |
| Dallas | 139 | 38 | 62 | 47 | 14 | 1 | −2.8 | −9.7 | +3.4 | +2.6 | +6.0 |
| San Diego | 120 | 66 | 34 | 15 | 14 | 5 | −1.2 | −3.5 | +4.3 | +1.5 | +3.5 |
| San Antonio | 65 | 15 | 85 | 16 | 69 | 1 | −2.8 | −10.0 | −1.1 | −2.4 | −0.8 |
| Indianapolis | 82 | 54 | 46 | 46 | ∨1 | ∨1 | −4.3 | −7.2 | −0.3 | −0.3 | b |
| Washington | 125 | 4 | 96 | 95 | ∨1 | ∨1 | −2.5 | −6.5 | −2.3 | −2.4 | b |
| Milwaukee | 109 | 56 | 44 | 37 | 5 | 1 | −2.7 | −7.1 | +5.5 | +4.7 | +5.9 |
| San Francisco | 68 | 28 | 72 | 29 | 14 | 29 | −4.9 | −9.8 | −2.7 | −4.6 | −4.4 |
| Memphis | 121 | 29 | 71 | 71 | ∨1 | ∨1 | −3.4 | −11.7 | +1.8 | +1.9 | b |
| Cleveland | 120 | 38 | 62 | 58 | 3 | ∨1 | −4.2 | −5.0 | −3.6 | −4.0 | +4.0 |
| Average | 228 | 33% | 67% | 51% | 13% | 3% | −2.7% | −7.7% | +0.5% | −0.1% | +3.1% |
| Los Angeles[a] | 556 | 30% | 70% | 25% | 39% | 5% | −1.7% | −8.2% | +2.5% | −1.4% | +5.4% |

[a] Data for Los Angeles refer to 1978 and 1970-1978 changes.
[b] Rates of growth for Hispanics not calculated for school districts with fewer than 2,500 Hispanic students in 1970.

ance services. At the present time, relatively few school counselors are members of minority groups.

Recent developments in counselor education such as more practical experience, extensive education, competency-based instruction, emphasis on self-awareness, incorporation of new emphases, multilevel training, and more representative selection are indicative of the effort to prepare counselor trainees better for their future roles. Organized approaches have been implemented in areas of continuing education and self-supervision approaches are designed to provide in-service renewal for practicing counselors.

Counselors themselves must take responsibility for changing their roles and the conditions under which they work. In school settings where counselors are not employing active leadership, administrators commonly assign them to lunchroom duty, hall patrol, study halls, substituting, and various administrative duties. Several directions are apparent for the future role identification of counselors. Efforts for planned change are more commonly linked to the counselor's role as consultant. Consumer advocacy and client rights are becoming prominent issues among counselors, and public relations activities are also becoming a more important role. Change agentry is ultimately most consistent with new counseling emphasis on prevention. Finally, individual counselors and counseling organizations are currently planning to develop organized efforts to change institutions and environmental conditions.

The lack of a clear professional role identification, national visibility, internal regulation, and actions of other professional groups have created a distinct movement toward greater professionalization. Recent developments toward counselor licensure, registry, third-party payment, professional disclosure, counselor education program accreditation, and elementary guidance legislation are representative of organized action toward increased professionalization. The central role of the American Personnel and Guidance Association in such organized action underscores the importance of membership and participation of all counselors. Professional organizations encourage the role counselors play in students' learning in affective areas.

### Discipline

Discipline is generally considered the number one problem facing American schools today. Crime, violence, vandalism, absence, and truancy, which are rising at an alarming rate, now cost the system more than $600 million a year, more than what is spent on textbooks or instructional materials. Assaults on both teachers and students are not uncommon, leading to situations in which teachers often carry weapons for self-defense. Extortion by and of students is also typical in large city schools.

The disciplinary problems facing schools seem to exist in all types of schools of all sizes, in all kinds of communities throughout the country. There are conflicting opinions about the reasons for this situation. One opinion is that the outbreaks of violence and vandalism are the result of the oppressive nature of the traditional system and the lack of freedom that students experience. On the other hand, an equally loud faction insists that the problems are the result of too much permissiveness within the schools. Yet a third reaction is to blame the problems on the ills of the society in general and in particular to widespread use of alcohol and drugs within the adult population, practices that are widely emulated by children and youth. The overall response of the public is to desire greater controls and to impose more severe discipline within the schools.

Attempts to meet disciplinary problems have generally been on a policy level, often districtwide. Codes of behavior are developed and the system of due process has been worked out for dealing with offenders. Procedures for suspension and expulsion are often elaborate and detailed, reflecting pressures for the recognition of students' rights. One of the dilemmas of the traditional system in a society in which school attendance is compulsory is that students who misbehave often have no other place to go. In some communities, alternative schools are available, but this is generally not the case. Even when alternative schools are available, children with behavioral problems have difficulty in adjusting to the more inner-directed, less authoritarian environment of the alternative school. The use of alternative schools outside the traditional system as a "dumping ground" for discipline problems has occurred and resulted in little benefit to the child or to the school.

Within the traditional schools in urban areas, there is increasing use of security guards, alarm systems, and other institutionalized attempts to impose discipline. Corporal punishment is legal in all but about five states, and there seems to be an increasing willingness to resort to it on the part of many parents and educators. The disadvantage of corporal punishment, of course, is that it does not provide positive reinforcement for more appropriate behavior. Instead, the use of corporal punishment teaches students that violence is an acceptable way of handling problems in life.

Many disciplinary problems originate in the classrooms and reflect and intensify the frustration of teachers. Teachers in general lack the training and resources for effective classroom management. Some teachers themselves are often the product of either overly rigid structures or excessively permissive education. Few teachers have been prepared to apply research findings on effective discipline techniques such as the response of children to the presentation of the natural and logical consequences of their behavior.

ROLES

With a budget of over $100 billion annually, American education is big business. More than 70 million people, approximately one third of the population, are involved in schooling at some level, from preschool through graduate school, either as student, teacher, administrator, or support staff. Students in the elementary and secondary schools number about 50 million and, of these, nearly 90 percent are in schools that could be classified as part of the traditional educational system.

### Administration

Public school systems are administered by districts within the states. The trend has been to combine districts so that over the last forty years their number has declined from well over 100,000 school districts to approximately 15,000 at present. In some states, local elementary and secondary schools have separate administration and school boards, but in most states, these are combined into one large school district for each geographical area. Each local system is governed or administered by a local school board of education. Local citizens become school board members, usually by election but occasionally by appointment. Board members generally are one of two types, either concerned parents with children in the local schools or citizens without children, who are serving out of civic dedication or a concern about the cost of education. The board's function is to make local policy, to see that the system operates in accordance with state laws, and to hire the superintendent who is the chief administrator of the school. The superintendent is appointed by the local school board to administer the system according to board policy. The superintendent has a staff responsible for such specialized areas as curriculum and instruction, personnel, transportation, food, business operations, and student records. In very large districts, assistant superintendents may be appointed to handle each of these areas. Even in smaller systems, it is common to have at least one assistant superintendent for curriculum and instruction. Directors are often appointed for both the secondary and the elementary system to work closely with principals on curriculum and development and to perform duties such as teaching in-service training.

This bureaucracy has not been proved to be an effective resource for teachers and for the schools. Critics charge that it is simply an elaborate series of bosses who absorb the teachers' power to affect what goes on in the system. Very large districts sometimes are decentralized into smaller geographical districts run by area superintendents with a staff similar to that already described.

Faculty

The most important single unit of the American educational system is the faculty. Many parents and students are totally unaware of the central administration and evaluate the school entirely on the basis of what goes on within classrooms. The principal, of course, is the head of the school faculty, carrying out the role of a supervisor of instruction, a business manager, and the director of relationships with parents and the public. The principal is the leader who needs to make the entire student body and faculty and staff into a cohesive, functioning organization. As the business manager of the school, the principal is ultimately responsible for the budget and all funds handled by the faculty collected from students or parents or any student funds. She is responsible for the school plant and grounds, for all equipment and supplies, and for programming all activities, both the academic classes and the nonacademic and extracurricular activities.

The public relations role of the principal is directed to parents, students, and community at large. In this capacity, the principal is often involved in community activities, even automatically an officer in any parents' organizations in the school, such as the Parent-Teachers Association (PTA), and is expected to attend all school functions. In the area of instruction, the principal's role is to schedule classes, assign teachers, supervise the teachers (the principal may or may not have some say in hiring), and relate to the teachers as a coach and evaluator. The principal is primarily responsible for providing in-service training to teachers and for meeting with teachers regularly, both in a group and on a one-to-one basis to be kept informed of what is going on in the classroom. Normally, in the case of any severe discipline problem or other difficulty, the principal will cooperate with the teacher in handling the problem. The principal's role as nurturer or developer of the teachers conflicts somewhat with the authoritarian aspects of this job, especially because the teachers are directly accountable to and are evaluated by the principal.

In one sense, the principal is theoretically responsible for the total educational program in the school, but in fact, since the hiring of teachers and the budget are handled by central administration, the principal's power is limited. In fact, the principal is in a middle position between the central administration and the faculty. This tends to be a very high-pressure spot, and the principal and the rest of the faculty often relate to one another as adversaries. Frequently the principal has little peer support in his or her job, since there is little occasion for contact with other principals.

Principals are often poorly trained for this very diverse and demanding job, which requires the administrative skills of problem solving and decision making, group leadership, ability to effect an organization's climate, the creation of cohesiveness among the staff, and the ability to be supportive and encouraging to the teachers and the staff. Traditionally in the American system, little preparation has been provided to the principal for developing skills such as the ability to identify infra-group structures and learn how to work with them in order to make the faculty more effective.

The traditional authoritarian structure, which places the principal in charge of the teachers, likewise places the teacher in charge of the students in the individual classroom. The teacher's authoritarian role stems from early days of the American colonies, a concept imported to the United States from the western European schools. Although the United States became a constitutional democracy, most schools in fact have not been run on a democratic principle. The authoritarian system survives. Individual teachers have attempted to incorporate a more democratic process into the classroom by involving students in choosing their learning activities and setting goals in cooperation with the teacher. These efforts are rarely very successful because students and faculty both are accustomed to the authoritarian system. Teachers themselves are a product of this system in which they were taught by lectures, teacher-led discussions, recitations, and supervised study. It is a truism to say that teachers teach the way they themselves were taught, but this is the case in most of the traditional schools. The structure of the traditional school requires the teacher to be a strong disciplinarian, because he or she must keep a class of twenty-five or thirty students occupied for a given period of time each day or week through the school year.

With the increasing onslaught of criticism of the schools and the rise in student violence and crime, teachers have mounting levels of frustration. On the one hand, they have so many demands placed upon them and on the other hand they are often ill-prepared to respond to those demands. Many teachers need more training in the basic life skills. Skills such as basic communications and helping skills, ability to counsel and interview, group dynamics, ability to discipline through the use of logical and natural consequences, and the ability to deal with parents effectively are missing. These are all areas in which a teacher absolutely must be proficient to succeed. Both parents and teachers come out of a traditional orientation of fault finding, blaming, and scapegoating. Addressing problems constructively and solving them cooperatively is not yet the common mode in traditional schools. Rarely are teachers able to consult with parents about problems in a relaxed and constructive way.

Even though teachers are required to study a certain amount of educational psychology and learning theory, most teachers know very little, if any, learning theory. Often teachers are effective, because they are acting empirically or intuitively. Many teachers talk about learning theory, but when researchers observe them in action in the classroom, they observe very little behavior that is founded on valid learning theory. Instead, teachers often exhibit a lack of understanding of basic motivation and personality development.

## Students

The traditional American system has never acknowledged the profound individual differences among students, especially in their rate of development and their learning styles. A certain type of student has always found the system compatible. The student who either likes or does not mind a somewhat passive role that requires him or her simply to be present, to be attentive, to work hard, and to conform to the expectations of the system does well in the traditional system. Certain students who enjoy learning can enter relatively easily into this mode of learning.

Other children and youth find the system less well suited to their needs and temperaments. In the early days of the traditional system, these children were either never found in the schools or attended only for a few years and then were allowed or even encouraged to quit and go to work. As the Industrial Revolution spread and the labor market changed, it became more desirable to keep children and youth in school, and so compulsory education became the norm. There was little basic change made in the curriculum, teaching, or structure of the schools to suit the changed student population. The results of this unresponsiveness of the system to some students can be seen in the increasing crime and violence in the schools, in the decline in achievement test scores, and in the huge number of dropouts from the school—about 1 million per year over the last two decades. More and more of the students who do pass through the system and actually graduate are still functionally illiterate. It is estimated that students forget over 85 percent of what is learned in the classroom, but that their peer relationships of youth are remembered for a lifetime, yet the traditional schools' emphasis seems to be on the 85 percent of learning that will be forgotten. Whether the students absorb the formal curriculum of the schools or not, they are using the school experience to form lasting patterns of interaction with their peers, with authority figures, and with work and learning. They are building for good or for ill their basic self-concept. One of the primary tasks of an educator is to feed the spirit that hungers for learning. Some argue that the structure of traditional schools stifles the initiative to learn and inhibits mastery of learning techniques. In today's American system, too many students emerge from the system with that spirit either damaged or completely dead.

The schools have not only failed to respond to the changing composition of the student body, but also to profound changes in the world itself and in society and in our culture. Students feel, whether they understand it or not, the discrepancy between a world in which knowledge is expanding so rapidly that every forty minutes a new twenty-four-volume encyclopedia could be produced and the type of curriculum their schools are presenting. The all-pervasive presence of television in American culture has changed children and yet has barely been acknowledged by the traditional system.

The civil rights movement and the movement for human rights have begun to have a slight effect on the schools as the rights of students are acknowledged more and more. Freedom of the student press, freedom of student speech, the right to due process, and the abolition of dress codes are some of the signs of the inroads of student rights into the authoritarian school structure.

### Parents

The parents' role in the traditional system is primarily to serve as a source of support and money. Even though public education is funded by tax money, additional requests for funds somehow reach the parents in a multitude of ways. Most schools involve the parents superficially in activities such as the PTA, parent conferences, or serving as room mothers, or participating in school events such as football games, plays, musical presentations, or carnivals. Rather than having any direct impact on the curriculum or instruction that takes place in the school, these activities usually center on fund raising. The parent is usually in a totally passive role.

Schools seem to prefer this minimal interaction with parents. In most cases, both parents and teachers feel guilt and frustration over their children's difficulties with education. Parents are also intimidated and/or alienated by their own school experiences and by the defensiveness of the faculty who fear parent intervention. A few parents attempt to take an active role in their children's schooling, often despite the discouragement of the school personnel. Public relations efforts urging parents to help their children with their homework or to take an interest in their children's education are not congruent with activities that keep the parent outside the school's domain.

The reform of the traditional system will require that parents be led into a partnership with the faculty and the students. Parents must be led to make a commitment to the educational process. They also must be given specific skills and knowledge that they need in order to learn how to listen and respond to their children: how to give encouragement, how to set up family councils, and how to use logical and natural consequences to discipline children. Schools cannot achieve their objectives with children unless the parents are involved. Only a minority of parents are involved at present in the traditional system. Most parents are not passive because they don't care about their children, but because they do not know how to respect and support their children appropriately and effectively. One of the tasks of the school could become to teach parents how to respect their children.

## SYSTEM IN ACTION

How the traditional system really operates can best be seen by looking at the different ways that the local school systems are organized. Around the beginning of the twentieth century, there were only two categories of schools in most school systems: elementary schools, with grades 1 through 8, and the secondary schools, with grades 9 through 12. The addition of kindergarten and even preschool classes is one alteration that has taken place over the years. Junior high schools have been added, and, more recently, the middle school. Today, the most common division within the traditional system is to have the primary grades, kindergarten through grade 3, and the elementary grades, 4 through 6, in one school building. A separate school building would house the junior high school, grades 6 or 7 through 8 or 9 and still another building the senior high school, grades 9 or 10 through 12.

Each student is assumed to take one year to accomplish the learning of any individual grade level. The curriculum to be learned during that year is roughly standardized by state and local curriculum committees, especially on the primary and elementary levels. The textbooks that are available, the input of local school curriculum committees, and occasionally parent-teacher organizations also may influence the curriculum in a given school. Ultimately the individual teacher in the classroom has considerable control over the actual curriculum.

While the curriculum may be more standardized in terms of learning objectives in the lower grades, the actual structuring of the given school day is often looser and subject to the discretion of the individual teacher on the lower levels. This is most true in kindergarten where classrooms are generally far more flexible, open, and permissive than in the other grades. There are two different philosophical viewpoints regarding the education of kindergarten youngsters. On one hand, some kindergarten teachers believe that their primary goal is to provide opportunities for socialization, for play, and for making choices with regard to play. This point of view is usually accompanied by a permissive view toward children's behavior. In contrast, other kindergarten teachers see their function as that of preparing children for the primary grades, and these teachers place a strong emphasis on academic work, especially reading readiness and introductory reading activities.

The exact source of ideas for instruction on the kindergarten level is difficult to determine. Local and district curriculum guides appear to be the major determinants, but teachers draw on much of their own experience and judgment in selecting appropriate learning activities for children. In the primary grades, textbooks begin to play a strong role in determining the academic curriculum, along with state guides and bulletins sent to the schools from county and local curriculum committees. Primary grades are usually taught in a self-contained classroom with a single teacher dealing with the same group of children all day. One third to one half of classroom time is devoted to reading and related activities. In the primary grades, most teachers begin to divide the school day up into time periods allotted to the various subjects with reading periods in both the morning and the afternoon. Ability grouping is very widely used, especially for reading groups, beginning with the primary grades and used throughout both elementary and some secondary schools.

In the other elementary grades, reading continues to be the major part of the curriculum, but the time spent on reading is reduced. More time is spent on social studies, mathematics, science, and spelling. Some amount of art or music or physical education is allotted to time periods throughout the day. Occasionally, some departmentalization begins to occur in the middle and upper elementary grades. Students may be grouped and be under the direction of specialists in such subject areas as science, social studies, and mathematics for a partly departmentalized day, but they may still work with their own homeroom teacher or adviser for the remaining subjects of their curriculum in a still largely self-contained classroom. One trend in the elementary school is toward the nongraded or ungraded system, in which children from several grades are grouped in one large segment of the school, for example, kindergarten through third grade. Within that population, students work individually through the curriculum at their own speed. The same educational experiences are undertaken by each, but students move along through the units of study at different rates of speed rather than at one pace. However, teachers find it difficult to individualize instruction in the ungraded setting. The system calls for a high degree of individualization and at the same time uses uniform evaluation practices such as standardized tests. Teachers frequently protest against standardized testing and the use of uniform evaluation standards. In a so-called highly ungraded school, however, children are still regularly categorized according to their grade-level equivalent.

In the junior high school and especially the high school, the curriculum is divided still further into specific units of instruction, during which a subject is studied for a semester, a quarter, or a year. The amount of learning that has taken place is commonly referred to in terms of this time period as in, for example, saying a student has had two years of biology or three years of Spanish. These designations of course are assumed to indicate a certain degree of mastery of learning but, in fact, have no relevance to the amount of actual learning a student may have done. Middle schools and junior high schools are increasingly departmentalized, and secondary schools are always departmentalized and offer a far wider range of curricular offerings. On the junior high school level, students would typically go through a series of seven to nine class periods each day, each class period ranging from thirty to forty-five minutes in length. Almost every student would have one period a day of studying social studies, science, mathematics, and the language arts (English and reading). Many schools place extra emphasis on language arts by allotting a double period for them. A foreign language may be available to students on this level and some elective courses in art, music, home economics, or industrial arts. Physical education classes are probably required but may not meet every day. The junior high schools and middle schools also offer a range of extracurricular or nonacademic activities, including interscholastic or intermural sports.

Senior high schools are highly departmentalized and offer a wider range of curricular offerings. Students are often tracked according to ability or according to whether they are planning on attending college or not. Students within each track are supposedly homogeneous groups. Individual students have far more choice about the particular subjects, but they still study within their track. Usually, a large school will have separate tracks for college-bound students, for students in vocational training, and for so-called general students, those who will terminate their schooling with high school graduation.

The track system is a logical outgrowth of the tremendous attempts within the traditional system to provide individualized instruction through ability grouping, or grouping children homogeneously. The criteria for such grouping may be reading ability, achievement scores on academic tests, or even IQ, and/or chronological age. The theory behind such grouping is that it allows a more efficient use of teacher time. One major drawback, which was mentioned previously, is that huge individual differences still remain within each so-called homogeneous group.

Furthermore, negative effects of homogeneous grouping have been reported in a number of studies, which find that students in the lower ability groups are fully aware and highly affected by their status as slower or less able learners. The damage to the individual student's self-image and self-concept can be extensive. On the other hand, there is some evidence that the students in the higher ability groups also suffer from a kind of elitism. Students in all groups may be affected by the isolation they experience from students of other ability levels or learning styles. The ability grouping or tracking system in fact results in a form of de facto segregation among students in a given school population.

The philosophy of the traditional school has always stressed giving each student an equal opportunity to learn. This has proved a difficult ideal to achieve. There have been many studies that have found that particular groups of students in the traditional system have been given less opportunity to learn than other groups on the basis of social or economic position, race, ethnic background, geographical location, religion, and so on. In another attempt to respond to this situation, increasing emphasis has been placed on the goal or outcome of education rather than on egalitarian opportunities. There is increasing recognition that children are different and learn in different ways. Teachers are urged to find ways of giving each child the help and encouragement he or she needs rather than treat all children alike. Inequality of treatment may be needed at least at certain ages or stages in the learning process if students are to obtain roughly equal learning outcomes. In this view, the stress is shifted from an attempt to see that each child is treated fairly to an attempt to adapt teacher activity, instructional materials, and procedures to suit the individual level and learning style of the child. However, the classroom teacher rarely has the time, resources, or skills to do adequate diagnosis of individual student needs that such individualization would require.

Throughout most of the elementary and secondary schools, the typical classroom is still arranged much as the classrooms of antiquity were, with rows of desks seating twenty to thirty or even as many as forty students facing the teacher, who presides at the front of the room. Variations on this are found especially in schools where the desks are movable and especially in science courses, lab courses, vocational courses, and other classes that require the use of special equipment or materials. There is also a much greater flexibility in classroom arrangement on the primary and kindergarten levels. Nevertheless, the average adult over forty can walk into any classroom in the country and almost immediately recognize sights that are very familiar from his or her own youth.

The activities taking place in the average classroom would also be very familiar. At all grade levels, the most common activity is the teacher's talking. Teachers ask questions and children respond, often using only a few words or phrases and usually correctly. The response of the child is often acknowledged or approved of by the teacher. A number of studies report that teacher-to-child interaction is the dominant mode in all but perhaps 5 percent of traditional classrooms. In addition to teacher talk or telling and questioning, individual children, especially in the elementary school, spend an enormous amount of time doing what is called "seatwork." This usually involves written exercises in workbooks or on worksheets that have been provided by the teacher on which students fill in blanks, answer questions, and write in short answers. Very little actual writing is done, especially in the elementary grades. Written and oral drills and exercises, however, are very common. The prime medium of instruction is the textbook, supported by textbook-related worksheets and workbooks.

Learning materials and equipment on the preschool and kindergarten level tend to consist of toys, blocks, dolls, and puzzles. Children are involved in a number of independent activities on these levels. Beginning with the first grade and on through high school, the provision for independent student activity is increasingly limited or virtually nonexistent, except for the so-called seatwork assignments that students do on their own. Very often, while a teacher is working with one small group of students in a reading group, for example, the rest of the children in a classroom will be working on "seatwork." Some students complete this work easily and procede to other assignments, but other students find it very difficult to meet these assignments successfully. Children are rarely engaged in self-initiated and self-directed, small-group or individual activities. Even more rare is the involvement of the child with any activity outside the classroom or off the school grounds. Children are exposed mostly to teaching strategies that focus on subject matter, routine materials, and a mode of instruction that is geared to group norms and expectations rather than individual differences in learning rate and need.

Textbooks are virtually absent in kindergarten but increase in number and variety in grades 1 through 12. As textbooks multiply dramatically after kindergarten, so do toys and games decline very abruptly, beginning with first grade. In the first grade, textbooks are primarily readers. Library books are introduced in kindergarten and predominate in subsequent grades.

Chalkboards are available in all classrooms. Either flannel boards or magnetic boards are installed in the lower grades of elementary schools. Bulletin boards on all grade levels commonly display both teachers' and students' work. As one observes the upper grades, commercially prepared materials appear more frequently. At the higher grade levels, there is also a greater correlation between ongoing classwork and bulletin board displays.

Although audiovisual equipment is commonly available to teachers, audiovisual aids are used sparingly. Most traditional schools provide teachers ready access to such equipment as phonographs and records, tape recorders, maps and globes, abacuses, and, less commonly, 16 mm projectors and films. Some schools have videotape equipment and some machines for programmed learning. Nevertheless, the textbook remains the primary instructional material. For a number of years, educational leaders have been warning educators about this overdependency upon textbooks and have urged the use of a wider variety of instructional media. Greater use of tapes and records not only provides more flexibility for individual differences in children and varying learning styles, but also offer the convenience of easy use and storage. Many suburban school systems offer a magnificent array of audiovisual instructional materials and devices, but inner-city or rural schools may be less well equipped. Although the computer is now available for use in the schools, its relative newness and expense still makes it prohibitive even in most well-to-do suburban areas. In the traditional schools today, the most extolled systems approach to instructional materials is still in the planning stages or pioneer stages. The era of the electronic classroom in which an arsenal of instructional materials is readily available to all children has not yet arrived.

Classroom instruction draws very little if at all upon the human resources available from the community. Occasionally, student teachers from nearby colleges or universities or aides from the community are utilized in the classroom. Less often, special resource personnel and supervisors provide consultation and assistance to classroom teachers. Overwhelmingly, the norm is that the individual classroom teacher operates in relative isolation within her self-contained classroom. In spite of the rapid proliferation of available audiovisual techniques, the teacher is still the single most influential factor in the student's learning experience. Since students are taught by teachers normally in groups of twenty to thirty or even forty at a time, it is inevitable that some individuals learn well while others learn less well. In a given class period and sometimes for an entire day, week, or year, an individual student may be essentially at the mercy of a particular teacher. Specific teaching styles and teacher behaviors that may be favorable for some students may be destructive or an obstacle to learning for other students.

Students are typically passed on from one teacher to another at the end of an academic period or year. Errors that have developed in the student's learning during one term are frequently compounded with errors by subsequent teachers in subsequent academic experiences. The errors are ultimately built into the student and only rarely are they detected and corrected. Only in a minority of cases are errors discovered in time for corrective action to be promptly taken. A number of investigators have found that if appropriate corrections are introduced as they are needed, the educational system can correct problems as they occur, before they are compounded with later errors. Normally, however, errors go undetected and uncorrected. This is most common in the area of affective learning. For example, if a student views a particular learning situation as a threat, fails to learn, and believes that he or she is inferior, this blocks the learning process. This would be comparable to an "error" in a computer program or a metabolic pathway. If the situation continues, the student will lack the courage to benefit from the opportunities provided there. If uncorrected, the earlier learning error will undermine or damage all subsequent learning activities.

At most grade levels, individual teachers exercise considerable flexibility with respect to choice of curriculum and, in particular, with respect to selection of activities with which to present certain bodies of content.

Observation of most classrooms reveals a moderate pace of activities with both children and teachers normally working at something most of the time.

## PROSPECT

The traditional American educational system is falling short in educating American youth. Criticisms of the schools; anxiety about declining achievements and test scores; concern over the lack of discipline in the schools, permissive education, and the retreat from the basics; the movements toward back to the basics and toward competency testing are all superficial but significant signs of the profound and growing gap between what the schools are teaching and what students need to learn. There are demands on the part of parents and employers for better reading skills, better writing and arithmetic skills, stricter discipline, more homework, more demanding classroom recitations, and the end of social promotions. All are symptoms of the basic vagueness of the traditional education system's objectives, the inadequacy of a content-based curriculum, and the ineffectiveness of the great bulk of instructional activities. The needs of students for additional skills in areas of citizenship, family life, decision making, career development, consumerism, communications, the arts, and many other areas clearly indicate that the traditional approach to curriculum and instruction needs reform. It is no longer possible to cover all the knowledge that is important for students to have. Selecting a prepackaged curriculum of instruction is no longer possible. Teaching by telling must give way to educational experiences that permit children to explore, try, test, inquire, and discover for themselves. The drive toward widespread educational reform exerts many pressures.

1. *The pressure for improved teacher preparation and accountability.* Seldom has there been such pressure on the teaching profession to justify its

work with the nation's youth. Increasing numbers of states are planning various methods for ensuring that teachers are held accountable for their school performance. The minimum competency test for teachers is the most common method. A recent Gallup poll of the public's attitude toward the public schools reported that 85 percent of those polled said that teachers should be required to pass a state exam in their subject areas and they should be continually retested. Testing alone will not improve the situation unless educational courses for preparing teachers are re-vamped from top to bottom. New emphasis and training must be provided for developing the large repertoire of professional competencies that a teacher needs to meet the challenges of his or her difficult role. This movement calls for a fundamentally different and a more serious approach to teacher education than has existed in the past—an approach in the same serious manner as that currently employed for the preparation of lawyers, physicians, and dentists.

Retraining of teachers currently in the schools is a much-needed but exceedingly difficult task. Many teachers are in the classroom without the skills that they need to enable students to learn. Carefully developed and field-tested models are needed to demonstrate inductively how teachers can utilize a range of instructional media. Retraining is further needed in areas relating to diagnosis and individualized instruction, developing interviewing procedures, motivating and disciplining children, and facilitating learning in which students are actively involved in discovery.

2. *Pressure toward financial reform.* Inflation during the 1970s and early 1980s continues to pose severe problems for education. The cumulative rate of inflation has been much higher than the increase of teacher salaries. This has caused teachers to lose ground in comparison to many other white-collar workers. Partly as a result of economic pressures, today's teachers are organizing to obtain greater power and to determine their destinies. Through collective bargaining, teachers are increasing the pressure on the school system to invest in quality education for youth. Educators have generally accepted unionism and are implementing labor tactics to obtain the right to collective bargaining with their employers in many of the nation's school systems. The main tool for increasing the power of teachers has been the use of collective bargaining contracts.

Ironically, as the cost of education continues to soar, enrollments of students in the nation's schools have steadily declined since the early 1970s. Enrollments dropped off by half a million during 1971 and 1972. The drop in 1974 was closer to 700,000. (See Table 1-1.) A decade of declining enrollment has left schools with problems of too few students rather than too many. Challenges that face administrators now include what to do with empty schools and how to reduce the teaching force. In most cases, school districts resort to reassignments, voluntary retirement, freezes on hiring, and reduction in staffing. Considerable staff anxiety and community discord have accompanied declining enrollments.

Inflation, collective bargaining on the part of teachers, and declining enrollments have not helped to equalize the educational opportunities in the nation. The gap between the poor school district and the rich school district remains, even though more than twenty-five states have attempted to equalize educational opportunities. In 1979, a Rand Corporation study found that school-financed reforms have somewhat loosened revenue ties to local property taxes and state treasuries and have begun to assume larger shares of school expenses. However, the poor schools still remain poor and rich schools remain rich, and the equalization of the two is still a long way off.

3. *Lobbies*. A great number of special interest groups and pressure groups of all kinds have developed during the 1970s and will continue to exercise tremendous influence upon the school systems of the 1980s, the 1990s, and at the turn of the century. Lobbies exist for students' rights, the education of the handicapped, equal education for women, bilingual education, and equal opportunity for people of all ethnic and racial backgrounds. In 1975, Congress passed an act legislating more nearly equal educational opportunities for physically, mentally, or emotionally handicapped children. The law provides for individualized schooling for 5 to 7 million handicapped children. Other lobbying groups have demanded expensive changes in school plants and facilities to make them accessible to all handicapped children. Special federal grants have been made available to the states to serve as an inducement to the implementation of this legislation. This massive, humane educational venture has involved considerable struggle and bureaucratic red tape for meeting federal guidelines. The struggle has raised doubts and generated many complaints among educators. Nevertheless, the special-interest lobbies seem to have become a permanent part of the legislative and educational landscape.

When the need for reform is so obvious, it is equally important to understand why the traditional system is so resistant to change. The system is not centrally administered by any national governing body. It has no direct accountability to individual client satisfaction, no necessary relevance to client need, and no scientific relationship to professional research that can be disseminated and applied to the actual classroom. Furthermore, the traditional system is locked into a certification system, which supposedly guarantees a certain minimum of quality of classroom instruction and student learning. Members of this system have grown up in it, are conditioned to accept it, and hesitate to tamper with the system lest quality be even further damaged.

Furthermore, a long series of curricular innovations and other kinds of academic and nonacademic innovations have led to a certain cynicism and disillusionment among educators. Each new program starts out with great promises, good publicity, and almost always leads to disappointment. Such programs are generally poorly implemented, and too often are evaluated too quickly, before the new technique has had a chance to stabilize and before teachers have had a chance to learn to use it effectively.

The career education programs pioneered by Sid Marland, former head of the Office of Education in the Department of Health, Education and Welfare, are an exception to this rule. Many innovations of the past two decades have been poorly conceived and at best only partially implemented in schools claiming them. Classroom teachers often seem to twist the innovation into a familiar conceptual framework and adapt it to resemble more closely established patterns of instruction. For example, the team teaching innovation approach more often than not was diluted into departmentalization.

At question is whether the drastic need for immediate change in the traditional system can outweigh the massive lethargy, the tendency to self-perpetuation, and the skepticism about innovation, which pervade the traditional system. If anything will bring about the reform that is needed, it is not going to be another series of Band-aid solutions, but rather a re-creation of the entire organizational structure of the schools as they exist. New structures must be evolved that present children both with the three R's and opportunities to learn needed life skills. Schools that are structured in a way that can enable children to learn how to continue learning, learn how to solve problems, learn how to interrelate and cooperate with others, both in school and in the community at large, are a pressing social need.

REFERENCES

Bayh, B. *Challenge for the Third Century: Education in a Safe Environment—Final Report on the Nature and Prevention of School Violence and Vandalism.* Washington, D.C.: U.S. Government Printing Office, 1977.

Bloom, B. *Human Characteristics and School Learning.* New York: McGraw-Hill, 1976.

Bloom, B. S. (ed.). *Taxonomy of Educational Objectives, Handbook I: Cognitive Domain.* New York: David McKay, 1956.

Bronfenbrenner, U. *Is Early Intervention Effective? A Report on Longitudinal Evalua-*

tions of Preschool Programs. DHEW Publications No. (OHD) 74-25. Washington, D.C.: Department of Health, Education, and Welfare, 1974.

Bruner, J. S. *The Process of Education.* Cambridge, Mass.: Harvard University Press, 1960.

Carnegie Council on Children. *All Our Children.* New York: Harcourt, Brace, Jovanovich, 1977.

Clark, David H. *Factors Associated with Success in Urban Elementary Schools.* Bloomington, Ind.: Phi Delta Kappa, 1980.

Chadwick, C. B. "Why Educational Technology Is Failing (and What Should Be Done to Create Success)," *Educational Technology,* 1979, pp. 7–19.

Coleman, J. S. *Equality of Educational Opportunity.* Washington, D.C.: U.S. Office of Education, 1966.

————. *Youth Transition to Adulthood: Report of the Panel on Youth of the President's Science Advisory Committee.* Chicago: University of Chicago Press, 1974.

———— et al. *Equality of Educational Opportunity.* Washington, D.C.: U.S. Government Printing Office, 1966.

Corsini, R. J. "Individual Education." In Edward Ignas and Raymond Corsini, *Alternative Educational Systems.* Itasca, Ill.: F. E. Peacock, 1979.

Cronbach, L. J., and Snow, R. E. *Aptitudes and Instructional Methods.* New York: Irvington, 1977.

Cubberly, E. P. *Changing Concepts of Education.* Boston: Houghton Mifflin, 1909.

Dewey, J. *Experience and Education.* New York: Collier, 1963.

Doyle, Walter. Research on Classroom Realities: Who Needs It? paper presented at the annual meeting of the American Educational Research Association, 1978.

Elam, S. (ed.). *The Gallup Polls of Attitudes Toward Education 1969–1973.* Bloomington, Ind.: Phi Delta Kappa, 1973.

Fantini, M. D. *Alternative Education.* Garden City, N.Y.: Doubleday, 1976.

Glaser, Barney G., and Strauss, Anselm L. *The Discovery of Grounded Theory.* Chicago: Aldine, 1967.

Goodlad, J. I., Sirotnik, K. S., and Overman, C. *An Overview of a Study of Schooling.* Bloomington, Ind.: Phi Delta Kappa, 1979.

Havighurst, Robert J. "Social and Developmental Psychology: Trends Influencing the Future of Counseling," *The Personal and Guidance Journal,* January 1980, pp. 328–330.

Keyes, R. *Is There Life after High School?* New York: Warner Books, 1976.

Kohlberg, L. "Moral Stages and Moralization: The Cognitive Developmental Approach," in *Moral Development and Behavior,* ed. T. Lickona. New York: Holt, Rinehart & Winston, 1976, pp. 31–53.

Luria, A. R. *Cognitive Development: Its Cultural and Social Foundations.* Cambridge, Mass.: Harvard University Press, 1976.

National Commission on Resources for Youth. *New Roles for Youth in the School and the Community.* New York: Citation Press, 1974.

Pietrofesa, John J., Berstein, Bianca, Minor, JoAnne, and Stanford, Susan. *Guidance, An Introduction.* Chicago: Rand McNally, 1980.

Shane, H. G. *Curriculum Change Toward the 21st Century.* Washington, D.C.: National Education Association, 1977.

Smith, V. "Traditional Education" in Edward Ignas and Raymond Corsini, *Alternative Educational Systems.* Itasca, Ill.: F. E. Peacock, 1979.

_____, and Gallup, G. H. *What the People Think About Their Schools: Gallup's Findings.* Bloomington, Ind.: Phi Delta Kappa, 1977.

Task Force on Secondary Schools in a Changing Society. *This We Believe.* Reston, Va.: National Association of Secondary School Principals, 1975.

CHAPTER 2

# Australian Education

## ANTHONY J. SHINKFIELD

### DEFINITION

The Australian education system is highly centralized with each of the
six states administering schools bureaucratically from its capital city.
Unchanged for the last hundred years, this system developed with the
intention of giving equal educational opportunities to all children, no
matter how remotely situated. As a result, uniformity of approach, even
between the states, has characterized Australian education. One quarter
of Australian students attend independent schools, most of which are
church schools and predominantly Catholic. These schools are nonsys-
tematic, and charge fees. In recent years, the commonwealth has entered
the arena of kindergarten through grade 12 education, where its influence is increasing. The traditional British pattern in Australian education,
once so discernible, has faded as distinctively Australian elements have
emerged.

### INTRODUCTION

#### Objectives of Education

It is difficult, if not impossible, to consider objectives of education in
isolation from the society that establishes them. For this reason, systems
of education evolve, each with definite objectives that must be achieved
to preserve its particular society. These objectives are often common to
all societies or, by contrast, may be unique. As an example of a common
objective, all systems of education make provision for social adjustment.

Strong emphasis on work experience for students, however, may be unique to a particular system.

Objectives of education, and the formation of institutions where they can flourish, is one of the important activities of any society. A society must ensure that educational objectives are relevant to its own aims, and that by means of a monitoring process, a nexus between societal and educational objectives is always apparent. Only if this occurs will the educational system preserve, renew, and strengthen a society in ways acceptable to that society.

For any of a number of reasons, discrepancies may exist between society's demands on an educational system and the educational objectives that institutions within the system are trying to achieve. As a general statement, it is true that educational institutions tend to lag behind a society's expectations for training its young. It is equally true to say that the objectives that the educational system sets for itself seldom lead the way to change within society generally.

Schools are formal institutions vested with the responsibility of imparting and developing skills and attitudes essential for an individual to fit into society. This is not to say that the educational objectives of a school will encompass all aspects of the development of a child. Groups such as the family, friends, social and cultural organizations, and peers will play their part, as indeed will the media. Thus the school alone is not responsible for setting objectives in areas such as intellectual, social, physical, and moral development In many aspects of these areas, however, society itself is uncertain about standards and values. Nevertheless, schools must endeavor to develop a set of values and standards that give meaning to educational objectives.

In their broadest context, educational objectives are ideals. Consequently, a gap will exist between objectives and classroom practices and outcomes. Moreover, factors such as the home background of a child will determine the extent to which formal educational objectives may be attained. The approach to objectives that follows is therefore subject to the qualification of the disparity between purposes and practices that is common in any system of education.

While educational objectives are related, it is possible to consider them in broad groupings. An attempt has been made to do this.

### Equal Opportunity

Particularly since the movement toward democratization following World War II, there has been a growing acceptance that education should give all children equal life chances. A prime purpose of schools is to enable every child to develop abilities that will lead toward happier living. This will include undertaking satisfactorily any vocation indicated by a child's aptitudes and interests. The issue of equality in education is an educational objective that overrides all others. At the same time, it is openly acknowledged by most Western countries (in reports and political debates) as the most difficult objective to put into practice.

### Understanding Society and Its Values

Society requires its educational institutions to conserve the heritage of worthwhile things in its history. It also requires its young to accept its major values and conventions (often called *mores*). Expressed in terms of educational objectives, societal values become statements of role expectations. In particular, formal education must help each individual to prepare for adult roles such as worker, parent, voter, leader, follower, and so on. Preparation will lead to an understanding of each role and the kind of responsibility each demands. While these tasks are difficult for schools to assume, formal education can impart knowledge and attitudes about society more cogently and objectively than any other agency.

A proper understanding of society and its values should make children critically minded, but it should also encourage them to be fair-minded. While their analyses of society will show deficiencies in its own purported ideals, their critical skills should also allow them to accept that social institutions and conventions developed painfully, and with good reasons, over many years. As responsible citizens they will seek change, but this will evolve from, not replace, that which time has proven to be worthwhile. Progress, they must learn, is based on honest respect for the distinguished attainments of the past.

### Personal Values

If children are to become socially well adjusted, it is necessary that they develop attitudes and habits that characterize responsible citizenship. Essential values would be strong fellow feelings, including a respect for the individuality of others and a desire to help those who cannot meet society's demands; an honesty in one's dealings with others; an independent outlook on life; and a respect for work.

Clearly, the home will be the dominant force in developing personal values. Nevertheless, the school situation can reinforce them. It can also encourage attributes such as sharing with others, and joining with other children, as leader or follower, in common ventures regardless of thoughts of personal gain. Such activities will encourage students to grasp a basic tenet of democracy: the need to exist within social institutions and conventions observed by the majority while rationally bringing to bear that kind of criticism that will allow necessary improvement.

Most societies are increasingly giving schools responsibilities in ethical areas. While this is a difficult assignment, educational objectives are often delineated to guide personal conduct in moral concerns such as sexual responsibility, drug or alcohol abuse, and interpersonal relationships. At the very least, the school should accept an obligation to help children to acquire factual knowledge and values to overcome ignorance. Out of this should grow interpersonal respect and competence.

### Development of Personal Abilities

The ultimate aim of any system of education is to provide those kinds of experiences that will allow a child to leave school confident in his abilities to cope with problems, well adjusted to societal demands, sure in the knowledge that he can identify with those aspects of a society that are rapidly changing, and competent to make wise decisions. This is a tall order for educational systems. It becomes even taller if the onus is placed on educational systems to make the development of these skills an exciting process for children. It is contended here that a school has failed to a degree if it does not develop in students the desire to achieve to the best of their ability and to enjoy the striving for the kind of success each is encouraged to attain. Tough mental skills cannot be forsaken, and the traditional curriculum has much to offer in this regard.

It is also important that as children are encouraged to make the most of their abilities, they are also brought to a realistic understanding of themselves. Only then will there grow an understanding and tolerance that are essential for the harmonious survival of pluralist societies and a pluralist world.

### Reasons for This System

It has been the vogue among writers on Australian education within the last two decades to disparage schools and education departments. These institutions undoubtedly have their faults, and their faults have become easy pickings for critical academics who are too often out of touch with actual school situations. This chapter will certainly expose weaknesses in Australian education, but it will also endeavor to stress positive elements.

Generally, there is a growing recognition in Australia of the national importance of education, and there is an acceptance of the need for greater equality of opportunity in terms of access to education that will ensure that each individual, irrespective of social and economic status, has the right to an education that will extend innate abilities.

As the section on history will show, Australia developed in the fashion it did to meet the needs of a sparse population scattered over an area the size of the continental United States. But whereas the United States and

Canada have provided a spread of centers of economic life, of government, and of cultural initiative over most of the country, this is not so in Australia. The majority of its citizens have always lived in the capital cities of the six states. Administration of education has become centralized in these six centers, allowing democratic uniformity of educational offerings to most young Australians. It has also allowed the rapid spread of desired changes throughout each of the state systems. With many schools very remote from a capital city, both uniformity of approach and ease of communication have been considered essential elements in a striving toward the ideal of equality in educational opportunity for all children.

Australia's government system is parliamentary and democratic. Resulting from statewide public opinion expressed by local members of Parliament, major educational policies are formulated by state cabinets (consisting of the government's ministers) and by the ministers of education. These policies are then translated into courses of action for schools by senior personnel of each state's education department. There are three main advantages to this process. First, society's desires for modification of the educational system can take effect consistently throughout the various states. Second, provision of resources such as staff, buildings, equipment, and support services can be equitably distributed throughout the schools of a particular system. And third, like the French centralized system, efficiency is an undoubted outcome.

There are, of course, costs associated with the pursuit of uniformity and efficiency in the state systems of education which cater to 80 percent of kindergarten through grade 12 schooling. Approaches to learning have tended to become stereotyped and sometimes lack vigor. Nevertheless, the six state systems have operated to the satisfaction of most citizens for a century. During this time they have developed schools and teaching expertise of reasonable quality throughout extremely large areas and often under uniquely difficult circumstances. Education departments have had to be imaginative and inventive to meet such trying circumstances.

For all the criticism of the uniformity of approaches to teaching and learning, positive gains are apparent by comparison with other countries. Comparing the Australian system with that of countries with local control (such as the United States), Partridge (1968) commented:

> It [that is, uniformity of standards] has helped to avoid the worst silliness of "child-centered education," and the treatment of schools as existing to make children well adjusted and happy rather than to furnish and toughen their minds and initiate them into the important mental disciplines and skills. It has also been a protection against petty, illiberal or obscurantist local interests (Partridge, 1968, p. 69).

By comparison with the United Kingdom, the Australian system appears less stolid. Innovation and change, albeit often uniform, have been readily accepted in Australian education, particularly since World War II. While lacking the academic rigor of the French and German systems, Australia's education makes a greater contribution to the overall develop-ment of every child in the system.

Australian schools are very much a part of the society in which they exist. Despite the fact that little is done openly in schools to inculcate patriotism—by comparison with the United States and Japan—children nevertheless learn indirectly to become proud of their country. Particu-larly in the last two decades the educational system has been responsible for a greater tolerance of reform and a greater realization that Australia is a pluralist society since the large influx of immigrants during the 1950s. Compensatory education programs have been developed to encourage each child to adjust to society and contribute to its welfare.

## HISTORY

World War II markedly affected the Australian outlook and conditions, not the least in its relations with the United Kingdom. For 150 years after 1788, when the colony of New South Wales was founded, and despite the intervening achievement of self-government in the 1850s, Australia remained strongly British socially and culturally. An examination of these 150 years, however, reveals a gradual Australian flavor being added to the educational fare. Today, the system of education in this country is distinctively Australian, although the British influence lingers in the independent schools, and an American influence can be seen in the processes of state schools.

### Beginnings

#### The Penal Heritage

Australia began as a penal colony. The first of the eventual six colonies, New South Wales, began when Captain Arthur Phillip landed a party of 1,030 soldiers, sailors, and convicts where Sydney is today.

From the beginning of settlement in each colony, government and administration were strongly centralized in the capital cities. This in-cluded the administration of grants to societies to provide schools, such as they were. Lacking other sources of funds and an established church with financial resources to provide welfare services, early governors attempted to obtain finances through local tax measures. By the 1840s, when transportation of convicts ceased, Australians had developed an expectation that the centralized colonial governments would provide public services. Local government as it existed in America or England was virtually unknown, and attempts to legislate some local control of schools consistently failed.

### The Religious Question and Early Education

Government initiative and financing for elementary services was most conspicuously illustrated by the development of education in the six colonies. Grants were made to religious societies to assist in paying salaries of teachers and the cost of school buildings. But the Anglican, Presbyterian, and Catholic churches held firm to the belief that the control of teaching was the proper responsibility of the church. Education and moral training were inseparable. Thus the churches, and especially the Church of England, saw themselves as the proper agents of education.

Until the middle of the nineteenth century, provision of education in the colonies was haphazard. With the exception of a few fee-paying schools of the English grammar school type for children of the colonial upper class, schooling was provided in primitive conditions by untrained teachers for some children for periods of time ranging from a few months to several years.

Sectarian bitterness arose for a number of reasons; its effect was to retard the provision of education. The privileged position conferred on the Church of England, which inspired the Church and Schools Corporation of 1826, was opposed by the Catholic church. In turn, the other churches opposed the proposal for a pound-for-pound subsidy system because it was similar to the Irish National System.

During the 1850s New South Wales instituted a "dual" system of education. Under this arrangement, government aid for schools was offered to the various denominations through the Board of Denominational Education. Simultaneously, the Board of National Education was responsible for the commencement of a system of state-controlled, nondenominational schools. This latter board took its duties very seriously and encouraged the establishment of national schools to such an extent that by 1851 twenty-two such schools were operating.

Other colonies labored under much the same problems as New South Wales. A mixture of governmental enterprise, occasional voluntary effort, and state assistance to denominational schools was the general pattern. In the colony of South Australia, however, government interference in education was strongly opposed. Consequently, governmental assistance to the churches, begun in 1847, was abruptly discontinued in 1851. South Australia became the first colony to discontinue support of denominational schools from public funds. A commitment was thereby made to nondenominational, public education.

The "dual" system satisfied no one and after a few years was abandoned by all colonies.

### The State Education Acts

The drive toward educational development from about 1860 was occasioned not only by native-born Australians, but also by immigrants. Following the discovery of gold in 1851, Australia's population almost trebled within a decade. There grew a new sense of freedom, not the least form of which was a sense of equality whereby all could enjoy the benefits of a diminished class-stratified society. This included education for both the urban and the isolated rural child. Discussing this matter, Jones (1974) said, "So strong has this egalitarian sentiment grown, that it may still be distinguished in policies relating to education" (Jones, 1974, p. 19).

In the 1860s and 1870s the provision of education in the six colonies was dismal. Those children remote from the cities and those from underprivileged homes received no schooling at all, buildings were squalid, and teachers were often incompetent. A well-organized educational structure was seen to be essential—and Australian colonial history dictated that it would be centralized, unified, and strongly uniform.

The last three decades of the nineteenth century showed remarkable development in Australia. Bushrangers and wild colonial boys were replaced by astute politicians as a new nationhood emerged. Railways and roads opened the outback, and the winds of change were favoring a federation of the six colonies.

Between 1872 and 1893 all colonies passed legislation leading to education acts. These acts established government-controlled school systems and withdrew state aid to church schools. The schools established by these acts purported to be "free, compulsory, and secular." If there was doubt about the complete validity of this statement, there can be no doubt that the acts shaped the administrative form of present-day educational organization. They gave birth to an Australian system of primary education.

Reluctantly, the Protestant churches accepted public nondenominational education. They nevertheless continued to run their elite fee-paying grammar schools, such as the Anglican Geelong and Melbourne Grammar Schools (in Victoria), St. Peters (in South Australia), and Kings (in New South Wales). But the Catholic church strongly opposed the terms of the acts. This church has continued ever since to maintain and develop its own separate system of schools while agitating for state aid. Developments during the 1960s and early 1970s have almost put to rest the bitter feud between the Catholic section of the community and other citizens over state aid for education. Financial help is now given to all denominational schools by a system of federal grants.

Toward the end of the nineteenth and the beginning of the twentieth century, movements were made to institute secondary education. Legislation provided day schooling in institutions called high schools, which imitated many of the characteristics of the church grammar schools. The state secondary systems took shape and grew after federation in 1901, which formed the Commonwealth of Australia. Following World War II, enormous growth occurred in secondary schooling, as indeed it did in all other aspects of the Australian educational system.

## Current Status

With the burgeoning of education in Australia in the last thirty years it is possible here to relate only the most important events, concentrating on what has commonly occurred within the various state systems. Perhaps the most important development during this period is the change in balance between the commonwealth and the states; this has had a marked effect on educational policy formation.

### The Commonwealth and the States

Like the United States, Australia has seen increasing federal intervention into educational areas once the sole province of the states. The Australian states themselves are predominantly to blame for this situation, as they surrendered tax power to the commonwealth in 1942. Ever since, the states have had tax reimbursements according to a formula that is adjusted from time to time. This situation has given the commonwealth government large policy-making powers not only in tertiary education (which is now completely funded federally) but also in many aspects of kindergarten through grade 12 education.

The most significant incursion by the commonwealth into pretertiary education has been the establishment of the Commonwealth Teaching Service (1973). In effect, the commonwealth has assumed control of education in the Australian Commonwealth Territory (Canberra) and the vast, very sparsely populated Northern Territory. The Australian Commonwealth Territory Schools Authority was established as a result of the growing size of the A.C.T. operation but also because of parental dissatisfaction with the New South Wales education system. The Northern Territory takeover followed South Australia's withdrawal, which began in 1972. In the Northern Territory, the Commonwealth Teaching Service is now providing a more vigorous educational provision for both aboriginal and white children than ever before. This has resulted from a single system replacing a dual system: white schools financed by the commonwealth but administered by South Australia and black schools administered by the commonwealth's Department of the Northern Territory.

### The Commonwealth and State Aid

The commonwealth first entered the field of school support with offers of interest-free loans to independent schools in Canberra in 1957. In 1963 it undertook to provide grants to independent schools in all states for the purpose of building new science blocks. Commonwealth scholarships (instituted to encourage more children to complete secondary schooling) became available to nonstate schools. Toward the end of the 1960s the commonwealth introduced annual per capita grants to independent schools, provided further assistance with buildings (for example, library facilities), and extended these provisions to state educational systems.

These forms of state aid to nonstate schools caused little sustained hostility. There would appear to be two main reasons. First, plurality and diversity have become accepted, and sectarian vituperation has diminished proportionally. Second, it was widely recognized that the nonstate sector, providing education for 25 percent of Australia's youth, faced insurmountable financial problems in the face of the urgency of educational growth.

### The Commonwealth and the Australian School Commission

In May 1973 the Interim Committee for the Australian Schools Commission published its report. This stimulated the establishment of the Australian Schools Commission whose functions have substantially increased the federal government's financing of aspects of kindergarten through grade 12 schooling. According to planning, emphasis in the 1976–1978 period has been directed toward projects that aim to:

- improve learning of basic skills
- explore ways to "open up" the school
- involve students in decision making
- integrate "special" children into ordinary classes
- help handicapped children get employment
- promote cultural pluralism
- meet the special needs of aboriginal children
- compensate for isolation
- bring school and community closer together
- promote the feasibility of recurrent education
- reduce the disadvantage of girls
- cater for children with special skills

Moreover, the commission allocated an initial grant of $6 million for special projects. These must attempt to foster change in primary and secondary schools. Money is allocated to teacher-innovators for any purpose that potentially could advance the progress of education.

The areas of commonwealth intervention into traditional state education discussed so far indicate that the commonwealth's role has grown like Topsy. This view has been expressed well by Johnston (1968) and Gill (1965). Parallels could be drawn with federal intervention in the United States. However, the financial status of the Australian government is considerably stronger relative to the Australian states than is the government in Washington to the state and school district authorities in the United States.

## The Development of Secondary Education

In the last thirty years there has been great development and change in secondary education. The cry of equality for all following the end of World War II has had its effects throughout the Western world. In Australian education, it heralded the introduction of popular secondary education. Retentivity soared during the 1950s, the upper age for compulsory schooling rose to fifteen years, and the percentage of an age cohort who completed secondary schooling increased from slightly over five in 1946 to more than thirty in 1976.

Changes in secondary education have been achieved at a time of unprecedented growth in school population. Such growth no longer occurs. With drastically reduced fertility rates and numbers of immigrant children, both elementary and secondary school populations have stabilized.

There has been a definite trend toward abandoning traditional external examinations, which have been strongly influenced by universities. Consequently, new forms of certificates have developed, necessitating new curricula, teaching methods, and attitudes of parents, employers, and the public generally.

The greatly increased secondary enrollments have resulted in many new, and radically different, secondary schools in line with changing philosophies toward secondary education with its increasing component of less academic children and with the new teaching methods. Gymnasiums, drama workshops, flexible art and craft centers, excellently equipped science laboratories, expansive resource centers, and language laboratories are some notable additions to the traditional concept of a secondary school. The flexibly planned open space secondary (and, indeed, primary) schools in South Australia exemplify all of these facilities. They have been widely acclaimed both for their imaginative design and potential for motivating student learning.

One major movement, in both state and nonstate schools, has been toward comprehensiveness. Earlier divisions, both physical and administrative, between technical and academic high school education have now largely disappeared. Secondary schools are usually comprehensive high schools offering a wide range of courses to students over a period of five or six years.

### Provision for Isolated Students

It has long been official policy in Australia to endeavor to provide equal opportunities for rural children and for city dwellers. The small, one-teacher rural schools (reminiscent of the American little red school-houses) are rapidly disappearing as consolidation has occurred. It has been found more economical to bus children to central, larger schools; more importantly, it is considered educationally more beneficial to children.

Beginning in 1916, correspondence courses have allowed children in isolated areas to be given lessons regularly. Parental help and supervision are essential so that satisfactory standards, at least in basic literacy and numerical skills, are attained. Courses are offered for children at the secondary level, but these are usually supplementary to studies undertaken at remote schools (such as Alyangula Area School, on Groote Eylandt in the Northern Territory). Reference libraries are provided for enrolled students.

A more recent innovation is the School of the Air, which first commenced operation in 1951. There are now thirteen of these schools which operate with the assistance of the Royal Flying Doctor Service. In effect, teachers have "classrooms" scattered over thousands of square miles on cattle stations, mining settlements, and settlements of religious orders. The School of the Air facilities work in conjunction with the correspondence school of a particular state. Occasionally, arrangements are made for classes to meet with their teachers. Such meetings cannot be frequent when travel of up to 1,000 miles is involved!

### THEORY

Until recent years Australian teachers were trained in teachers' colleges, which were under the control of state education departments. Lecturers came mostly from the state teaching force. As a result, Partridge (1968) stated, ". . . almost all teachers from the time of their entry into the teaching service of their State have thus been moulded by the assumptions, policies, traditions and practices of the particular system." (Partridge, 1968, p. 96.)

The effect of this close direction was that learning and teaching theory were largely ignored both by teachers in the field and by teachers in training. Teaching was considered foremost as a matter-of-fact, practical business. Theory was practiced, of course. But its range was narrow, unenterprising; the fact that so many teachers taught the way they had been taught emphasized the extent to which theory was implicit. Within the last five years or so significant changes have occurred. Teacher registration, for instance, demands a minimum of three years of training. As a result, the strength of the teaching force, particularly in the areas of learning and teaching theory, has markedly improved. And encouragement is given to all underqualified teachers to attend relevant in-service courses. The effects of these movements will not become apparent systemwide for some years. At present there is a wide discrepancy between those teachers, often the younger ones, who understand and practice theory of learning and teaching and those who through ignorance or indifference do not.

It has long been a criticism of Australian schools that undue emphasis has been placed on teaching what is definite and examinable. Hallmarks of this approach have been excessive drilling, stress given to the syllabus and textbook, and examinations. None of these has been conducive to the cultivation of experimentation and enjoyment in learning and teaching so necessary for student inquiry and intellectual independence— what Bruner terms "autonomous interests." While these emphases persist in many classrooms, they are decreasingly prevalent. The demise of many external examinations and the growth of interest by many teachers in learning and teaching theory are mainly responsible for this change. In the next section, various broad areas of learning theory being practiced in Australian schools will be examined.

## Learning

Learning theories are concerned with the ways in which learning occurs and with factors that promote conditions favorable for desired outcomes. Various learning theories are likely to define the curriculum differently, support differing teaching practices, and stress a particular core from which other learning may grow.

There are various methods of categorizing learning theories, one of which makes a division by the two most influential families—the behaviorist stimulus-response theories and the cognitive theories. The behaviorists emphasize the following points:

- The learner must be active (S-R theory stresses the significance of the learner's responses).
- Frequency of repetition and reinforcement are important.
- Practice in various contexts is essential for generalization and discrimination.
- Drive (motivational) conditions are important.
- Conflicts and frustration must be recognized, resolved, or accommodated.

The cognitivists emphasize that:

• The knowledge must be organized (as, for example, from simplified wholes to more complex wholes).
• Features of a problem should be easily perceived.
• Learning must be accompanied by understanding.
• Goal setting by the learner gives direction and incentive.
• Divergent thinking to create the novel effect and convergent thinking for logical conclusions play a vital part.
• Feedback confirms accurate knowledge and corrects faulty learning.

Another way of classifying learning theories, and one more appropriate to Australia because of its broadness and generality, consists of five main categories. There are S-R conditioning, the field theories, Freudian theory, self-initiated learning, and motivation for learning theory. Each will be discussed briefly, with comments on its place in Australian education.

### Stimulus-Response Association

*Learning is a conditioning process by which a person acquires a new response; experience is the key word.*

According to S-R theory of learning, a person does not necessarily have to want to learn something in order to learn it. Supporters of this theory maintain that motivation, and therefore behavior, is directed by stimuli from the environment.

The approach to teaching resulting from this theory places importance on learning by doing, reinforcement of desired responses (for example, teacher praise), frequency of repetition, and generalization and discrimination. Regardless of the validity of assumptions upon which S-R theory is based, the process or method of behaviorism derived from it can be valuable in many learning situations where the learner has no intrinsic desire to acquire knowledge.

In one form or another, S-R is practiced widely in Australian schools. Rewarded responses, which vary with individual learners according to what each perceives to be important, has been found especially useful in many aspects of teaching. These include teaching of basic skills, specialized help to slower learners, motivation of children disinclined to the learning task, and planned procedures for those in need of step-by-step learning.

Behavior modification, a product of S-R theory, has been found very useful with children, particularly at the middle primary stage, who are slow to learn or who have lost the incentive to learn through persistent failure. Behavior modification endeavors to reward desired behaviors while ignoring or disapproving those which the teacher considers should be discouraged. Used with understanding and sensitivity, it is an effective, caring way to control behavior in school. When success is the outcome of positive reinforcement, the child's self-image is strengthened, and the need for external rewards diminishes. Although some children with learning difficulties may never reach the point of self-actualization, the S-R process will continue to help them to acquire skills which they otherwise may never have attempted.

Behavior modification is also a useful means of eliminating cases of unwanted behavior in the classroom, allowing a more productive climate for learning to develop. A child's behavior is observed and tabulated. A reward system suitable for that child is invented on a type of contract basis where rewards gained are proportional to desired behavior.

## Field Theory

*Obtaining an overview, or a wholeness, is often
important in learning; without this we often lose
the forest for the trees.*

The various field theories—the gestalt-field, the cognitive-field, and perceptual-field—state that "wholeness" is primary, and that learning should begin with a grasp of the total aspects of a situation and then should move to particulars in the light of the whole. Teacher preparation in Australia has long given regard to field theories. But it has been only recently that teachers have practiced these theories in any except a token way. It is noticeable, also, that Australian textbooks are giving greater recognition to the importance of field theories.

These theories are based on a seemingly solid assumption that human beings wish to understand concepts and that they need to organize their environment in order to deal effectively with it. Children who understand that a basic knowledge of spelling is a necessary component of written communication will have more incentive to learn to spell than those who are told that they must learn to spell. A study of the rainfall of Australia is useful to children only if they are presented with an overview of geographical factors and population needs to see its significance.

According to these theories, knowledge must be organized from simplified wholes to more complex component wholes rather than from arbitrarily meaningless parts to meaningful wholes. It is also generally agreed that learning experiences (in the order suggested) should be made relevant to children's needs and interests. If this occurs, learning will be more permanent and transferable than rote or piecemeal learning. What most affects a child's learning are the generalized meanings that exist for the individual as a result of his unique perceptions. The stronger the grasp of a learning area, the stronger the child's self-concept is.

### Freudian Theory

*An awareness of self—one's own thoughts and feelings—is a vital adjunct to learning.*

Many theories of learning have grown out of the work of Sigmund Freud. There would not be a classroom in Australia where the Freudian influence would not be found, although most teachers would not recognize this phenomenon. Freudian learning theories are used freely and compatibly by exponents of S-R associationist, the perceptual-field, and the cognitive-field learning theories.

There would appear to be three basic units of learning theory arising from the work of Freud. These are awareness or self-understanding, identification, and imitation.

The importance of self-understanding is possibly the most basic premise of Freudian psychology. Students must first become aware of their own thoughts and feelings, their own strengths and weaknesses, before effective learning can occur. A good teacher encourages students to come to an understanding of themselves. Knowledge can then relate to feelings and perceptions and become relevant to an individual; growth can then occur.

Identification and imitation are closely allied. It is generally recognized that much of what people learn in life originates from imitating examples they see around them. Early in life we learn to talk and walk by example. Later, as beginning students of formal education, we learn to read and write by imitation. The stronger the identification of a child with a person, the stronger will be the desire to imitate. Whether consciously or not, teachers are examples or models for learners. Children need the teacher, at least in part, to serve as a model for their own behavior. Blind identification and imitation may nevertheless be defeating to that kind of learning which leads to balanced growth in which self-identity is paramount. Self-knowledge must moderate overwhelming identification and imitation.

### Self-initiated Learning

*Self-initiated learning leads to constructively gained knowledge and to the joy of discovery.*

The advent, and rapid growth, of flexibly planned schools in Australia with their open-space areas fostered the movement toward self-initiated learning in Australia. In many ways, it is the antithesis of traditional teacher-directed learning. For this reason, it has not made significant headway, particularly at the secondary level.

The basic premise of self-initiated learning is that, having been taught basic skills, the learner takes responsibility for learning that leads toward prespecified goals. Individual progression can occur only if the classroom (or school) climate is suitable and if the teacher offers guidance based on an understanding of the individual's abilities and interests.

Proponents of self-initiated learning stress its value in the pursuit of learning throughout life. Habits of knowledge seeking and fascination in discovery, gained at school, are likely to become permanent.

Importantly, for appropriate skills and attitudes, schools must carefully plan stimulating learning situations that will attract children and prompt them to search for knowledge and to discover for themselves. Self-initiated learning helps every child to come to terms with his environment and to identify with it closely when he leaves school by encouraging him to reach his own conclusions. The teacher directs and facilitates; the student systematically seeks knowledge and makes inferences or decisions.

The sudden insights, the joy of discovery, which are associated with the best self-initiated learning, offer dimensions of learning not possible in a classroom where the teacher's influence is dominant. If the knowledge gained by the child's own initiative is related and meaningful to his life-style, it is likely to be applied to a wide range of new life situations.

Planned group work from time to time prevents isolation; and, apart from socializing effects, student reporting to others helps substantiate gained knowledge.

## Motivation

*If the promise and potential are there,*
*motivation brings development to fulfillment.*

Essential to the learning process is motivation, which selects goals deemed to be valuable and gives direction for activity based on these goals. All learning theories state, or imply, as one of their objectives the need to motivate the learner. While the importance of motivation for learning is understood by Australian teachers, some lack the necessary skills to put theory into practice.

In planning learning experiences for individual children, a teacher must take into account many factors. These include maturation, age, readiness for learning, background experiences, and capacity to grasp new concepts. The interaction of these variables determines the goals and activities needed to motivate a child to learn. Some will be satisfied with self-initiated experiences while others will need the security of close direction. But in every case, children will know that they are achieving. This implies that the child accepts both learning goals and criteria for success.

A teacher should be concerned not only with utilizing motives that exist but also with shaping them in certain directions to give increasingly desirable educational outcomes. For instance, it may be recognized that varied approaches to teaching, sensitivity to children's attention span, an attractive array of resource materials, allowance for independent study, and frequent class discussions motivate children to learn. However, it is possible that a different combination of these elements may be more fruitful, or that individual children may profit more from other activities as yet untried. The science of motivation for learning is in its infancy, and therefore, the imagination and flexibility of outlook of the teacher is all the more important. Different things motivate different children to learn.

Motivation is usually associated with the child who is disinclined to learn. It should also be applied to the bright child who needs to be challenged and extended. Teacher perception and identification of exceptional talent is basically important.

## Teaching

### Teacher Instructional Expertise

Teaching theory is the other side of the coin to learning theory. The latter states ideally what should be done, while teaching theory propounds ideally how it should be accomplished.

A phrase that is consistently applied to teaching in Australian schools, unfortunately with a deal of truth, is "mechanical approach." There is nevertheless a wide diversity of teaching theory put into practice, thinly spread throughout the various states.

The fact that so much teaching in Australian schools is stereotyped and unimaginative can be attributed partly to inadequate preparation of older teachers. It can also be attributed to intra- and interstate conformity, strong lingering of the British "chalk-and-talk" tradition, and bureaucratically bred pressures to comply with centralized education department edicts on curriculum. A defence of conformity in teaching principles and materials of instruction often put forward by both teachers and educational authorities is that equality of opportunity (or a "fair go") is thereby offered to all children. Such a view is open to debate.

With vast improvements in teacher preparation since training institutions broke the shackles of state education departments and became autonomous, and with very strong in-service programs in most states (particularly South Australia, Victoria, and Tasmania), teacher instructional expertise is growing. Aspects of teaching theory that have been recognized in Australia as being important are presented next.

### Classroom Environment

*A good climate arises from skillful teaching, and*
*good learning should follow.*

Very few classrooms in Australia have an oppressive atmosphere. Equally few, it would be fair to say, have an air of excitement about them. The large majority between these extremes have a climate influenced, in the main, by instructional skills of the teacher. Clearly, however, the total school climate has a marked bearing on that of individual classrooms. Despite teacher agitation for increased power in state school management, the principal has remained dominant; this person, above all, determines school climate. Thus, the best efforts of a skilled teacher may be in vain if the school generally is indifferent to standards of behavior and academic expectation and if it lacks suitable learning resources.

Whether at the preschool, elementary, or secondary level, the teacher who can encourage students to undertake voluntarily intellectual inquiry and creativity has established a good classroom climate. The varying abilities of students are recognized and catered to. These demands challenge the ingenuity and competence of teachers. Flexibility is essential, and far too many Australian teachers give instruction as if all students progress at the same rate, with the same interests, despite all the theory and research that run counter to this notion. Such inflexibility of approach is least marked at the preschool level and most marked at the tertiary (where lockstep progress is habitual).

The difficulties involved in developing a suitable classroom environment are not to be underrated. George Howie had this to say:

> . . . the task of instructing a group in subject matter is less demanding than providing an educational environment in which children will enlarge their experience and grow in their capacity to understand and recreate the world they live in. (Howie, 1969, p. 154)

### Appropriate Curriculum

*Properly undertaken, curriculum development is*
*scientific; in practice, it is haphazard.*

The theory of curriculum design and development is understood by very few Australian teachers. And it is not, for that matter, particularly well grasped by central curriculum committees which radiate their curriculum guidelines (often little more than subject syllabuses) to schools. Ironically the latest cry is for schools to develop their own curricula.

While the commendable aspects of school-based curriculum development are obvious, one has to wonder where the necessary skills will be found. Certainly teachers more recently graduated from teacher training institutions will be well versed in curriculum concerns; and the same applies to teachers who have returned to these institutions for studies in education. But all these total a small percentage of the teacher work force.

In general terms, it could be said that the minimum requirements for curriculum design and development would be knowledge of:

- needs assessment procedures
- values clarification
- bases and criteria—that is, underlying social forces, human development, the nature of learning, and the nature of knowledge
- design techniques
- evaluation procedures

The new federally funded and sponsored Curriculum Development Centre in Canberra has as one of its functions the task of helping in school-based curriculum development. Its success will be measured by the extent that its influence impinges on individual teachers and individual classrooms.

### Grouping Procedures

*Flexibility in grouping recognizes individual differences of both students and teachers.*

There has been a movement in Australian schools away from the concept of classes of set size primly seated in serried rows. This change, as yet in its infancy, recognizes individual differences among students. It also recognizes that teachers have differing talents.

Flexibility of scheduling should accompany flexibility of grouping. Both acknowledge that the best learning cannot be compressed into rigid situations and rigid time modules. Many primary schools allow approximately two hours each morning for flexible group work in core basic skills areas. Children change groups according to attainments and interests. The principle is that, according to an individual student's learning speed and maturity, a combination is offered of horizontal (more of the same skill area) and vertical (remediation or, more likely, advanced studies) enrichment. With this kind of flexibility in grouping and regrouping, student needs are met by different approaches to teaching. Moreover, teacher skills are utilized to their best advantage with some teachers helping students individually and others guiding imaginative extensions of core subjects. Nevertheless, too many teachers are unprepared to break with traditional practices that insist that students remain in their own classrooms where all are taught at the same pace. Many primary schools, however, are practicing various degrees of "ungrading" or multiple grading. This procedure underlines the fact that instruction is not identical with education and that education is the development of problem solving, creativity, and understanding. Grouping is not for instruction, but for discovery, activity, inquiry, and development of cooperation and interpersonal skills.

A significant aspect, in theory if not always in practice, of the fast-growing flexibly planned schools, particularly in South Australia at the secondary level, is that grouping procedures have differed strongly from the traditional. There has also been a trend toward individualizing schedules as widely as possible to allow for student differences. Teachers and counselors develop these schedules with students in the light of student interests, abilities, aptitudes, personal goals, and achievements. Groupings may then range from the very large, where team teaching is used to impart essential content of various subjects, to tutorial groups. Considerable allowance is made, from this point, for independent study.

### Student-teacher Responsibilities

*A good teacher will be able to make a student*
*want to learn; from that point, the responsibility*
*largely rests with the learner.*

In general terms, schooling in Australia is more structured the older a child becomes. At the upper secondary level, where the influence of external examinations still looms large, there are often discouraging demands made of students. It is unfortunate that students should associate responsibility for learning with demands of examinations whether internal or external. This certainly is the case in Australia. Learning is associated with academic success and measured by examinations and not by understanding and appreciating for their own sake. There are many factors in Australia that militate against valuing learning dissociated from examinations. Chief among these, perhaps, is the low priority given to excellence for its own worth.

Good teachers should be able to make students want to learn. Too many, however, have allowed examinations and all their connotations (favorable and unfavorable) to provide the motivation for student learning. And by so doing, these teachers have rejected what should be a basic responsibility to students and, for that matter, to the importance of the true nature of learning.

A strong component of structured secondary education is homework. A regular amount of home study, increasing by grade level, is set daily, and usually closely checked by teachers. The principle behind homework is that the "learning" of subject content is best done under quiet conditions of the home and that training in self-discipline is an outcome. Clearly, the child from a home background not conducive to learning is disadvantaged. For example, it is futile to expect most aboriginal children, apart from those in government residential colleges, to have home conditions suitable for learning. It could be conjectured that only those few children motivated to learn by independent study strategies gain a great deal from homework. There is a world of difference between learning for a test and learning directed toward gaining knowledge enjoyably. Freedom to learn when a student wishes, in the way he or she wishes, is not characteristic of Australian education.

Classroom management in Australia is the province of the teacher. Children are, however, given responsibilities and allowed to take the initiative in many different ways. These may vary from classroom duties such as organizing lunches to responsibility for sports equipment. Although increasing number of schools have some student participation in advisory committees, their influence is minimal in actual decisions made. Similarly, student representative councils, which have replaced the prefect system in state schools, have had little effect on school management. In nonstate schools, prefects and team captains play a significant role in school leadership. Parameters of student leadership powers are clearly delineated by tradition as much as anything. Nevertheless, the main decisions of an educational nature remain the prerogative of the headmaster or headmistress. There is widespread acceptance of this situation.

### Educational Materials and Technology

*Discreet use of educational materials and technology is an important accompaniment to good teaching.*

In some ways it is fortunate that Australian education lags behind the American example. One of these areas is the use of new educational materials and technology. Only those instructional aids from overseas that have undergone a satisfactory trial period are widely used in this country. There is universal teacher agreement that wise use of such materials as learning kits, resource books, laboratory equipment, and other aids relevant to particular subjects, and technology such as audiovisual equipment are essential accompaniments of good teaching.

Educational materials and technology aid efficiency in education. A very large amount of material can be displayed quickly and attractively. Video and audio tape recordings, television, films, and slides present a scope of experiences to the learner that would otherwise be unattainable in a school. Useful numbers of teacher aides have been trained in the operation of educational technology during the last decade. Many of these are located in resource centers where their contribution to the upgrading of teaching and learning has been evident.

The usefulness of the hardware of communications technology has been advanced by special sections in state education departments. No longer is the new hardware (if blackboard and pencil are the old) regarded as aids to be used at a teacher's whim. Learning is essentially a process of human interaction between the learner and the teacher, and the teacher's tools, sophisticated and unsophisticated alike, depend upon their discreet and skilled employment.

## APPLICATIONS

The history of curriculum development in the various Australian states cannot be considered separately from the development of the six state education departments. Each of these, as we have seen, was situated in the state capital city, from where it bureaucratically administered all aspects of public education. Curriculum was the most important of these aspects.

Following the state Education Acts of the Victorian era, published curricula were entirely prescriptive. They were also modeled closely on the British pattern, but not entirely. Even before the turn of the century, it was evident that public education was responding to electoral wishes and expectations of the various state communities. Much the same situation holds today, the only exception being that external influence has shifted away from Britain to the United States. The American influence is most marked in areas like textbooks (particularly secondary science), learning kits, and educational technology.

The centralized bureaucracy of the various state education departments has been the major cause of criticism by both local and overseas writers. It is seen to be stultifying to imaginative educational action and growth. While some of these writers have been more impressive for their rhetoric than for their complete understanding of the situation, others have not been wide of the mark. The education departments are thoroughly integrated into the states' machinery of government, and all public school teachers are state-employed and subject to bureaucratic constraints. In addition, it is true that secondary education has been unduly influenced by matriculation demands of universities.

Both standard criticisms should, however, be tempered by events of today. Most state education departments (Queensland remains an anachronistic exception) are allowing schools considerable freedom in many directions. This is most obvious in South Australia where many schools have strongly taken up the challenge to make their own decisions in areas like curriculum development in response to the director general of education's watershed document "Freedom and Authority in the Schools," published in 1970. Concerning university influence on secondary curricula, all secondary schools now offer courses alternative to the purely academic. Standards in these courses are maintained by centrally organized moderation procedures. Moreover, secondary schools are succeeding in their demands to have a school-based assessment component as part of the academic external examination. The tendency toward uniformity is decreasing as a consequence.

### Administration of Curriculum

Administration of curriculum by the central authority comes under the direction of senior officers (usually titled director or superintendent) and is made possible by a group of inspectors. The inspectors visit schools these days not with the air of martinets requiring prespecified standards of student attainment, but with the express aim of interpreting curricular guidelines and facilitating course developments. It is usual for central offices to form state curriculum committees in various subject areas (or combined subject areas) to develop curricular guidelines. Inspectors act as links between the central office and schools, communicating in both directions. They facilitate, advise, and encourage.

Inspectors have a wide range of supporting roles in respect to curriculum. Apart from contact with individual schools, they convene subject curriculum committees (composed predominantly of teachers), are members of boards for external examinations, generate and disseminate ideas about curricula from many sources, and evaluate as well as they can curriculum organization and practices. Some inspectors are located in the central office and deal with broader issues of curriculum development, while others are located in regions and are in regular close contact with schools.

Schools are also supported by subject consultants. These expert teachers also give advice to schools, but only by invitation from a school. They help with the planning and evaluation of syllabuses, with teaching techniques, and with the development of appropriate supportive materials. In addition, project teams are set up to plan new subjects, task forces undertake special assignments for limited periods, research sections carry out special studies connected with curriculum design and development, publications sections arrange the issue of completed curriculum booklets, and state educational technology centers offer advisory services in the use of the media in relation to the curriculum.

## The Curriculum in Independent Schools

Almost a quarter of Australian children are enrolled at independent (that is, nonstate schools). Most are associated with one of the churches, and religious faith and teaching play a part, to varying degrees, in the life of the school. This is not so in the secular state schools. Independent schools, at least the wealthier non-Catholic ones, have been in a position to offer educational variety in contrast with the too-standardized state systems. This opportunity has seldom been accepted, however. During the last decade of significant innovation and change in education, it has been the state systems showing the lead and the independent sector following state initiatives if teachers have had sufficient skills.

Many independent schools nevertheless do experiment with curricula, types of courses, teaching techniques, and organizational structures. However, as Partridge points out, "there seems to be little evidence that such experiments are of significance outside the particular school" (1968, p. 105). Held back by traditionalism and habitual shortage of funds, the Catholic schools at the most offer children curricula generated by the state system with only minor variations.

### Curriculum, Academic

### *Primary Schools*

The academic, or formal, curriculum of Australian primary schools has two main elements. One is basic literacy and number skills, and the other is socialization.

Most parents consider that, if a primary school teaches a child to read, write, and develop confidence in number work, then it has done its job well. The informal curriculum, with its creative elements, by comparison rates very low. Consequently, a majority of time, particularly in the early grades, is given to the acquisition of basic skills. The methodology of teaching reading has improved markedly in the last five to ten years, with specialist services instituted statewide to help teachers. For the past decade or more, "new" mathematics (of the American post-Sputnik variety) has been taught throughout the country. This innovation has often had startlingly good results. However, many employers of students who have graduated from the system under the new mathematics approach claim that, if anything, the standard of basic arithmetic skills has slipped.

Socialization encompasses an increasing awareness of the place and importance of social institutions and customs. Australian primary schools undertake this task through formal study. This involves planned activities, discussions, project work, and excursions (including school camps). Social science curriculum guidelines are constantly being revised to keep schools in touch with societal change and emphasis.

*Secondary Schools*

The academic, or formal, curriculum in secondary schools is usually considered to consist of those subjects that are to be studied sequentially (in one form or another) for at least five years and that most likely will be examined for the awarding of final certificates. Thus the academic curriculum generally consists of English, foreign languages, the sciences, mathematics, and social science.

Four of these subject areas, English, science, mathematics and social science, form core (or required) studies for the first three years of secondary schooling. If children pursue an academic course throughout their secondary years, they will study these subjects (and perhaps foreign languages) for their entire schooling. Other "nonacademic" subjects will be dropped when they begin their senior years.

### Curriculum Organization

In almost all states there has been a movement away from the subject curriculum in upper primary and lower secondary schooling. A core curriculum, with some distinctively Australian characteristics, is emerging, the main aspects of which are:

- structured by broad social problems or social themes—that is, stress on cultural values
- required study by all students
- cooperative planning of activities by teachers and children
- flexibility, provision for special needs and interests as they arise
- basic skills taught incidentally (and in addition to "formal" morning sessions in primary schools)

Such a scheme requires teachers to have a sound background in the theory of education. It also demands buildings and grounds suitable for a variety of activities, large time blocks, provisions for flexible grouping, and close liaison with the community.

In secondary schools, the trend toward a core curriculum of the type described is to be expected, since the high school is no longer merely for an academic elite, for whom the subject curriculum was suitable, but for the general education of all adolescents.

### Curriculum, Nonacademic

Australians have traditionally looked upon the nonacademic, or informal, curriculum as being less significant than the academic. As a consequence, subjects such as art, drama, music, and the whole range of manual (craft) subjects has been looked upon as somehow inferior. While this attitude still persists in all states, giant strides have been made recently to give parity of esteem to all curriculum areas. As a result, modern secondary schools have art, drama, music, and craft facilities that can only be described as lavish. As Australia grows toward maturity, there is an evident appreciation for the artistic and the creative aspects of life. Much of this growth may be attributed to the huge wave of immigrants after World War II.

Technical education has largely been removed from the secondary realm and placed under departments of further education (that is, post-secondary). Apart from commercial subjects, vocational training is generally not the province of education departments which maintain that kindergarten through grade 12 schooling should be general. After leaving secondary school, many youths become apprenticed to a trade and attend trade schools or technical colleges part-time for further training.

Physical education and sports are an important part of the nonacademic curriculum. With abundant sunshine, access to excellent physical education facilities (most schools have their own), and a traditional love of sport, young Australians generally need little encouragement to participate in physical education. Health education is often taught in conjunction with physical education; its importance is recognized in a society that lacks physical fitness and which is suffering the effects of drug abuse.

### Special Education

Special education in Australia is designed for children with deficiencies that impair learning. It does not relate, at present, to extremely intelligent children who also require a different curriculum from the normal. Each state education department has a section offering special support for children who are mentally deficient, hard of hearing, blind, physically disabled (for example, spastic), and autistic. Institutions with highly trained staff and excellent equipment endeavor to meet the learning needs of these children. "Mainstreaming"—placing less physically or mentally impaired children in classrooms with normal children—has just begun. Where mainstreaming has occurred, provision is made for teachers to have special training.

There are, of course, dimensions of learning difficulties. Some children can cope easily with aspects of the curriculum while having apparently insurmountable difficulties with others. This very real problem is being faced in Australian schools by the provision of teachers trained in remedial techniques (or developmental, according to one's viewpoint), regional advisers, and centrally located reading centers.

### Work Experience

Increasingly, senior students in secondary schools are being given the opportunity to experience actual situations of the working world. This usually commences at about grade 10.

The purpose of work experience is primarily to introduce students to as wide a range of vocational offerings as possible. Students are released from regular schooling for half-day periods extending over several months (although this varies from state to state). Vocational choice then becomes less haphazard than otherwise would be the case. Development of sound attitudes to superiors, to fellow workers, and the community generally are other important aspects of work experience. Work experience and career education are often the province of school counselors.

## Student Evaluation

The traditional, and still prevalent, concept of student evaluation in Australia conjures scenes of children laboring over tests, and of teachers spending long hours compiling questions, marking, and producing sets of marks and individual reports for parents. This may be true of some schools that persist in giving marks based solely on factual knowledge, and percentages and class positions for reporting. But it is not generally an accurate picture.

### Concepts

Australian teachers usually acknowledge that student evaluation is a two-way process. Classroom assessment indicates to children the nature and extent of their learning and their standing by comparison with teacher expectations or normative values. It indicates to teachers whether they need to improve classroom practices.

Although scholastic evaluation must remain a dominant concern, Australian teachers realize that they spend a far greater proportion of their time observing, forming impressions of the personal traits of students, and assessing social behavior. The sum of these activities is informal evaluation.

There is also a firm belief held by the majority of Australian teachers that formal evaluation does not do justice to the range of the curriculum or to the complexity of the processes involved. It is too easy to measure only the tangibles and allow the subtleties to remain unmeasured. What does a teacher wish to know: whether a student learns scientific facts, or whether the scientific knowledge allows the student to identify with society?

### Applications

In keeping with these concepts, student evaluation procedures are varied. Recorded information usually falls into three main groups, although teacher methods of arriving at conclusions about aspects of any one group may be haphazard. In this respect Australian teachers do not vary from others.

The first group concerns student attainment. Attention is centered upon general ability and performance. Attempts are being made by many teachers to gauge affective, as well as cognitive, aspects of student learning. The characteristics of the second group bear upon classroom behavior and attitudes: courtesy, cooperation, persistence, and attentiveness. And the third group includes interpersonal relationships such as popularity and leadership as well as personal attributes like social confidence.

Australian parents and prospective employers require reports of students' progress in these categories, although the form of reporting usually differs for either audience. Many schools have a committee of teachers, parents, and sometimes students themselves to determine the frequency and format for reporting student progress. School-leaver statements and similar reports for future employers incorporate the ideas and wishes of school system authorities and employer representatives.

In general, teaching, learning, and evaluation are seen to be related, each contributing to the others.

## Counseling

Formal counseling services, as separate from informal counseling of students by all teachers, have been introduced into Australian schools only within the last decade. Most states now provide limited counseling services for secondary students. A significant lead has been taken by South Australia, where 135 senior counselors are available to help students. While the ratio in this state of one counselor to approximately 700 students is inadequate, it is better than other states. Counselors must have a minimum number of years teaching experience (in South Australia it is seven), they must have been outstanding teachers, and they must have displayed strong sympathy with students and their problems. Unlike the situation in America, Australian school counselors usually have had little formal academic training for the position; however, colleges of advanced education are now offering appropriate courses.

### Job Demands

Unlike their American counterparts, Australian counselors give little direction to students on courses of study. Most time is taken up with student problems and concerns, usually on a person-to-person basis but occasionally in small groups. Often a student will be referred to agencies outside the school for further assistance. This necessitates the counselor being in close contact with health, welfare, and general guidance agencies (such as Life-line). Home visiting by counselors is discouraged. However, interviews with parents frequently occur within the school with the agreement of the student seeking help.

Career guidance and employment placement are important parts of the counselor's job. In large schools with more than one counselor, it is not unusual in the present climate of poor employment prospects for one counselor to work full-time on employment placement. Counselors build up an extensive array of contacts for potential student employment both in industry and employment agencies such as the Commonwealth Employment Service.

It is essential that counselors have the complete respect and cooperation of the school administration and teachers. Usually there is little difficulty, as the caliber of the counselors is very high. Counselors are among the busiest school personnel; in today's complex and troubled society, there are increasing numbers of children who either cannot, or do not wish to, cope.

## Discipline

Many Australian parents still consider that discipline and punishment are synonymous terms. Fortunately, this is not so with teachers. From early school years, children are given opportunities to develop self-discipline by being encouraged to adopt a responsible attitude in a variety of situations. Australian school children are amenable to discipline. Indeed, apart from some schools in the inner suburbs of cities like Sydney, indiscipline has not been a major concern of teachers and their unions.

### Methods of Handling Indiscipline

Young teachers, as a group, have more problems with indiscipline than their more experienced colleagues. Uncertainty, usually arising from an inability to establish a comfortable social distance with students, produces an overassertiveness. Moreover, young teachers lack the knowledge of methods to encourage self-discipline, and of suitable methods of control when indiscipline occurs. Appropriate disciplining is one area of teaching where experience and maturity are an advantage.

Corporal punishment, even for the worst cases of defiance and misbehavior, is seldom used in Australian schools. Many parents, only too aware of their own inability to discipline their own children, lament this diminution as if increased corporal punishment in schools would magically solve their own problems of lack of control. By regulations, principals have the sole right to administer corporal punishment; however, they may delegate this responsibility. In secondary schools, the worst violators of school rules and codes of expected behavior are either suspended from school for varying periods of time or, in the most extreme cases, expelled with permission of the minister of education of a particular state. In the case of independent schools, the headmaster has the power to expel. Nevertheless, suspensions are not common, and expulsions are rare in either state or independent schools.

There are various methods commonly employed for handling indiscipline. These include detaining after school (difficult in rural schools because of busing), essay writing on model behavior, and repeated writing of "lines." It is doubtful whether any of these methods achieves anything worthwhile, least of all growth toward self-discipline. The irony is that punishments of these kinds are often inflicted on children by inadequate teachers (experienced or inexperienced). Good teachers capture the interest of children, keep them profitably active physically or mentally, and win their respect; the least concern of these teachers is indiscipline.

## ROLES

### Administration

Each Australian state has a bureaucratic structure of educational organization in many ways similar to that of France. Central controlling offices are located in each of the six capital cities and in Canberra for the direction of federal influences in education. Education departments are organized on hierarchical lines for both professional and clerical staff. Within the departments the following main divisions of systemwide responsibility have emerged: personnel, curriculum, administration and finance, guidance and special education, buildings, and research and planning. Some state education departments have persisted with horizontal divisions according to school type. For example, primary and secondary divisions control their own personnel and curriculum concerns.

Closely defined regulations ensure uniformity of approach throughout each state system. The regular promulgation of documents of various kinds—policy statements, memoranda on procedural matters, curriculum guidelines, budget concerns—reinforce the centralized power of these systems. Moreover, the regulatory influence of the corps of inspectors of schools, although less formidable than in the past, is nevertheless significant. The inspectors undertake the vast amount of professional work necessary to keep the system viable. With greatly increased union negotiating strength during the period of teacher shortage twenty-five years after the conclusion of World War II, the influence of the inspector waned as school principals and teaching staffs have been allowed more professional responsibility. Nevertheless, inspection is still necessary if a teacher desires promotion, which is determined on a statewide basis.

## Decentralization

Those Australian states that have decentralized educational administration have permitted devolution of power in relatively minor organizational matters and not a whit in important decision-making areas. Education is still firmly controlled from the center. For example, regional directors are usually able to transfer staff within their region, place centrally allocated staff in regional schools, instigate urgent minor repairs, and arrange local in-service work. They cannot hire staff, they cannot undertake any major building programs, and they cannot permit extended in-service training of teachers such as annual scholarships. Many important aspects of regionalization of education in Australia are tokens of devolved authority.

Queensland began attempts at decentralization in 1948 and has been followed by New South Wales, Victoria, and South Australia in more recent times. Being close to the scene, regional directors and their support staff of inspectors, advisers, and clerical personnel are supposed to implement policy with clearer judgment, present a less anonymous face of bureaucracy to teachers, and facilitate local problem solving in educational matters. Or so the theory runs. What has occurred is that the central office has been able to delegate to regions many of the unpleasant chores it formerly had to undertake. Many of these tasks, it is true, the regions are able to perform better than the central office.

In principle, regionalization of education has much in its favor, and indeed, outstanding people in the field ensure that it works within the limits of their delegated authority. But until regional directors are given decision-making powers in important areas of responsibility and funds to use at their professional discretion, regionalization remains, in many ways, a travesty of purported intention. Contrary to their intended purpose, regional offices have often become an additional barrier for schools seeking help in areas like major curriculum decisions, buildings, and staffing concerns because decision-making powers in areas such as these have remained firmly entrenched in central offices.

## School Administration

Australian schools follow the hierarchical pattern established by central office example. Principals, deputy principals, subject seniors, teachers, and students all play well-defined roles, and these roles have decreasing status. This is not to say that some schools are not run on democratic lines, with committees consisting of personnel at various levels having decision-making powers. These kinds of schools are few and far between, and even so, their principals alone are finally responsible to the central office for what occurs within the school.

Nevertheless, the sharp divisions that once existed between principal and teacher no longer prevail, and a spirit of colleagueship has become evident with the growth toward professionalism of teaching in Australia. Cooperative planning and the forming of task forces for problem solving and developmental purposes are common practices.

Schools are not held accountable in the American sense of the word. There are several main reasons for this. First, there is no direct tax paid for education. Indirectly, of course, the income tax does pay for the schools, but the feeling of directness is lost by the time income tax is paid to Canberra, states are reimbursed, and monies are applied statewide. Second, school districts, and therefore school boards with their localized demands do not exist. And third, there is an indifference toward education and a belief that schooling is the responsibility of "the government," which is considered monolithic and therefore unchangeable. For these reasons, at present, there are not strong pressures on schools to be accountable. Any pressures that do arise come from employers (usually based on complaints about the inadequacy of basic skills training), the education department itself, which requires reassurance from time to time that regulations are being met, and from principals or teachers themselves who request evaluation of school programs for the purpose of educational improvement.

Regulations cover ages at which children can begin preschool (between three and four) and junior primary school (between five and six). They also cover attendance—regular attendance is required to the age of fifteen in most states—and the keeping of confidential records showing details of attendances, health, behavior, and scholastic attainment. Regulations do not, however, cover class size. The fact that student/ teacher ratios have fallen well below thirty in primary schools and below twenty in secondary schools can be largely attributed to pressure by teacher unions. There is at present strong union action by the Australian Teachers Federation to have noncontact time given to primary teachers; secondary teachers have always enjoyed this concession in the interests of improved lesson preparation, marking, and professional discussions.

*Independent Schools*

About one in four children attend independent schools, and of these 80 percent attend Catholic schools. Each of these schools is self-administered and depends for its survival on fee-paying clients. Federal grants, as mentioned earlier, supplement fees. Per capita and capital grants for new buildings have been directed largely to assuaging Catholic claims that they could not survive without state aid.

The Catholic independent schools have combined within and across orders in the various states to help rationalize resources. For instance, a state's Catholic education office can act as a more effective lobby for federal grants than individual schools or individual orders. Similarly, other nonstate schools find that the formation of state independent school boards is collectively very useful and does not impair the autonomy that member schools enjoy.

With right of hiring and firing staff, independent school headmasters have powers well beyond those of state schools. Moreover, independent schools have carefully preserved the status of various organizational positions; the opportunity to experiment has been accepted no more in administrative areas than in any others. Sharp (1971) commented on this point:

> The old-world authoritarian chain of command—from head down to senior, then to junior staff, to prefects, house officers, monitors and thence to the lower ranks— . . . [is] remarkable evidence of the way social structures can retain a strong thread of continuity despite rapid changes of context (Sharp, 1971, p. 267).

### Faculty

The fact that, in a quickly changing world, all professional people must reorient themselves to the ways in which their profession is facing general change, is firmly established in the minds of educational leaders in Australia. All states now make provision for extensive in-service, including release-time scholarships extending up to a year. All states send teachers and administrators overseas every year to study or to observe. Australia's geographic distance from countries with advanced systems of education makes these visits prudent and beneficial, particularly when thoughtful reporting is given by returned travelers.

### Teacher Development

Despite system-organized schemes for teacher development, it may be contended that the best strategies are those planned and carried out within the school itself. Far too much reliance has been placed in the past on systemwide promotion opportunities to provide the necessary incentive for teachers to improve professionally. In the wave of quick promotions during the last twenty years, teacher unions became very powerful, monitoring promotion procedures immaculately. Importantly, one notable outcome is that terms like "assessment" and "evaluation" have assumed opprobrious connotations in the minds of teachers.

With a stable school population, promotion positions are now difficult to secure. A new incentive for professional reorientation and improvement is now essential. The key word is "professional." If teachers are professional, then they will wish to improve their skills without the promise of external rewards such as promotion. Clearly, schemes of intraschool evaluation of teachers, with teachers themselves cooperating in the venture, must be instituted. One Australian state is seriously contemplating providing schools with the necessary information and support to make such a scheme viable. One thing appears certain. Unless teacher evaluation for professional improvement becomes a reality, teachers are likely to become frustrated and, more important, provide poorer quality services to help student learning.

### Students

There is an interpretation of education prevalent in Australia that children go to school to be turned into socially well-adjusted, typical, and ideally conforming suburban dwellers. If the general population sees children developing this way, many students themselves certainly do not. Suburban middle-class values are not theirs. Moreover, whatever the social needs of these students are, particularly as they reach adolescence, they are not being met by schools. The role of the school vis-à-vis the older child needs urgent research in this country.

It is accurate to say that Australian children generally conform to school rules, even if some may do so somewhat cynically. Dress codes are adhered to (most secondary schools require a uniform), school property is respected, and enthusiasm is generated during interschool contests (particularly sporting competitions). Classroom participation has improved markedly in the last decade or so with the emphasis placed on communication skills and interpersonal relationships.

### Student Roles

The Australian student has few rights; indeed the term powerless is appropriate. There is no Australian legislation to protect individual rights comparable with the Bill of Rights of the United States. It is interesting to note that, in literature on Australian education, what children think about their schooling scarcely rates a mention.

By retaining the prefect and house systems (that is, vertical student groupings that develop corporate spirit for sporting and cultural contests such as debating), independent schools, overtly at least, offer traditional leader and follower roles. State schools have largely discarded the prefect and house systems; leadership roles are offered in student representative councils (which have very limited powers), sporting and other teams, and cultural areas such as school orchestras and drama clubs. One state, South Australia, has allowed student representatives on secondary school councils. However, students have not usually accepted the invitation with enthusiasm, possibly because they feel ineffectual. Nevertheless, the concept of student participation, however meager, in decisions affecting a school, is commendable.

### Student Advancement

Australian schools do not promote students at an accelerated pace. Educational authorities have considered it wise not to place children too far from their age-group if stable emotional growth is not to be impaired.

In primary schools, children are often grouped according to progress in a particular subject for core work and, ideally, each should work with academic peers during these periods. Structures for student academic advancement in secondary schools vary from state to state. Generally speaking, much the same courses are pursued by all students during early secondary years, with the exception of foreign languages which are taken only by those with a special aptitude for these studies. New South Wales, under the Wyndham scheme, offers a student each core subject at three levels, according to aptitude in these individual subjects. This scheme, with much to commend it, has influenced subject structure in other states.

Two major problems remain. Parity of esteem does not exist between academic and nonacademic subjects despite growth in this direction during the last decade. Students taking nonacademic courses at higher secondary levels feel inferior. Anderson is critical of this situation, "Those who don't make it in the professional stream should not feel an inferior breed" (Anderson, 1969, p. 56). The other problem concerns aboriginal students, those from poor socioeconomic backgrounds, and migrant children (particularly Italians and Greeks whose home backgrounds are often nonintellectual). The counterparts of each of these groups can readily be found in America and in other countries, of course. There are enlightened opinions in Australia about how these disadvantaged groups should be educated and, indeed, the federal government has made moves lately to meet policies with bold practices. But the trouble is that the backlog of unmet needs is formidable.

Although the gap of privilege is narrowing, Australian education, particularly at the advanced stages, has traditionally been considered the prerogative of boys rather than girls. Discrimination against females can be seen in most walks of life and has been reflected in many aspects of education. But attitudes are changing and yearly a higher percentage of girls remain at school beyond the compulsory attendance level.

## Parents

It was pointed out earlier that the Australian community has never expressed strong dissatisfaction with its educational system. Education is the business of the government; there is not great concern whether it is state or federal. Parents play an unusual role. They accept that the schools generally meet their expectations (examination results remain the primary value for the majority), they do not seek change nor wish to explore the wide implications of true education (particularly in respect to learning that does not have a utilitarian value), and they strongly support the schools their children attend. Parents win prestige by having their son in a top secondary class gaining academic success in foreign languages, or a daughter dux of the school (with every chance for social mobility, ironically revered by Australian parents). Parents are inhibitors of change in the Australian education system because they accept and fortify the status quo. They do not challenge the system.

### Parental Roles

Parents accept the role of school supporters. Although the door has been opened in two states, at least, for school councils, composed almost entirely of parents, to have more decision-making powers in school affairs, the business of education largely remains with the principal and staff. It should be pointed out that school councils or committees, the equivalent of American PTA's, have never enjoyed wide responsibilities, nor have they sought them. They raise money to purchase special facilities not provided by the education departments, help with ground improvements, find board for teachers in rural areas, complain about trivial issues, organize social functions, and offer their services as voluntary aides two hours a week to hear children read or to re-cover library books. There is no doubt that parents are useful to schools and that they are welcomed as helpers. But schooling is so much a matter for the "professionals"that the whole system would go awry if parents demanded active participation in the workings of the school and in major areas of decision making. Parental acceptance of the status quo in respect to educational practices and their own role in these is strengthened by principals and teachers attributing the same role to parents. Staines sums up these points well:

> Over a long period in Australia, both parents and teachers have come to expect a fairly clear pattern of behavior for parents. They are to provide the raw material for the educational process and not to take too much interest in what happens to it—"the teachers know best" (Staines, 1971, p. 157).

Parents are interested in maintaining standards (which are seldom defined) of schools, both in physical and academic ways. Through formal channels to the central office and by less formal methods such as lobbying through the local member of parliament, parents and parental organizations act to demand physical and academic provisions at least equal to those of other schools. This kind of action, which is both common and continuing, has two differing, almost opposing, aspects. In a commendable sense, it helps ensure that basic educational provisions for all state-educated children are equal (although some critics would justifiably argue that socioeconomic factors forbid true equality). Less favorably, it helps substantiate the uniformity and resistance to change that have often been causes of criticism of Australian education.

## SYSTEM IN ACTION

It is, of course, stretching credibility to depict single events as being typical of systemwide education. Nevertheless, "near average" occurrences can be related. And so a usual school day of a boy (there are more boys than girls in Australia) aged eleven (the average age of children attending Australian schools) in a suburban primary school at grade 6 level will be depicted; his teacher is female and under thirty years of age.

### The Morning Session

Typically, the morning sessions in Australian primary schools are more formal and structured than the afternoon periods. The morning sessions are therefore more likely to be taken up with the formal curriculum.

### Early Morning Procedures

Michael lives a mile from his school and, like many of his friends, rides a bicycle to school. Lessons in road safety, given both by his teachers and by representatives of the Road Safety Council, have made him careful on the roads. He is tidily and lightly dressed; he carries with him his schoolbag containing his lunch, homework books, and sports clothes. Michael tells inquiring aunts that he likes school but confides in his grandmother, whom he can trust, that lessons bore him sometimes.

Michael's school, which has an enrollment of 500 students, is almost 100-years-old, and yet modifications over the years and the addition of a flexibly planned unit, swimming pool, resource center, and attractive lawns and gardens have taken away the forbidding air it held for its students. Before school commences, Michael makes a small purchase from the bookroom where students volunteer their services. Meanwhile some of his friends are ordering their lunch from the canteen while others are helping Mrs. Rogers, their class teacher, arrange the classroom for lessons that day.

The bell rings at 8:50 A.M. for students to assemble. As the school does not have a hall (very few primary schools do), the children gather in the school yard in orderly lines. After the principal has made a few announcements, including praise to the students for their response to a yard cleanliness campaign, classes move to their homerooms. There Mrs. Rogers calls the attendance roll and collects 50 cents from students for a planned excursion. With preliminaries over, the business of the day begins.

*Basic Skills Development*

The grade 4, 5, and 6 children assemble together each morning for two hours in the large open spaces of the flexible planned unit for basic skills development. On alternate days, language arts and arithmetic skills are taught. Today it is language arts.

Children from the three grades work in one of six advancement-level groupings. Those with particular difficulties in areas like spelling, reading, and writing are in small groups of less than ten, while those with advanced skills are in large groups with considerably less directed learning. Many of the more advanced students set their own learning goals in skills development. Teachers are helped by a skills development specialist who also closely supervises the work of the children with the most problems. Occasionally, mothers volunteer to hear children read, but none are present today. Michael is in a middle-level group in language arts (he has some difficulty in expressing himself in writing) and in an advanced arithmetic skills group.

The group of twenty students, of which Michael is one, has a variety of activities during the two-hour period. Some of these are undertaken as a group, as for example, during brief periods of rote learning or reinforcement teaching of spelling. Others are undertaken individually, particularly when children read and write. Others again are undertaken in groups of three or four; examples are reading aloud to other students and discussion of topics in today's news to increase communication and vocabulary skills. Noticeably, Michael is not always an active listener, and he needs encouragement from his teacher to participate in small-group work.

Toward the end of the skills development period, the children help pack away the extensive array of audiovisual equipment that has been used as aids to learning. Small homework assignments are given to the grade 6 students. Michael has a writing assignment that will take him about twenty minutes to complete. Groups are then dismissed for a twenty-minute recess period. Michael kicks a football with other boys on the school oval while others play a variety of games (the boys more robustly and more noisily than the girls).

## Formal Lessons to Lunch Time

Two periods, each thirty-five minutes long, follow. Mrs. Rogers teaches both, the first of which, social science, is held in the homeroom.

Today the class is continuing with the project on mapping skills for the first part of the lesson. Using the overhead projector, Mrs. Rogers formally teaches the next steps in mapping. The children then apply what they have learned to their own project. Several of the students, including Michael, have not been able to grasp what Mrs. Rogers has been teaching and become increasingly frustrated as they attempt the mapping task.

They are particularly pleased when Mrs. Rogers opens the second part of the lesson to general discussion about an excursion to Parliament House planned for next week. Children take notes about busing arrangements, parental consent forms, time schedules, and planned activities while in the house. These notes are based partly on directions from the teacher and partly on majority decisions by the class. It is also planned that tomorrow the class will compose a form containing questions to be answered on parliamentary procedures. Answers will come from reading parts of relevant books in the library and from the actual excursion.

The science lesson that follows is held in the science laboratory, which is poorly equipped by comparison with secondary schools. As the lesson is on the topic of magnetism, the teacher aide has placed magnets, iron filings, and other materials on the benches. A five-minute film is screened showing the form of magnetic fields. Under the direction of Mrs. Rogers students then carry out a series of simple experiments, jotting down their discoveries as they progress. In the discussion period that concludes the lesson, general statements about magnetism are formulated and placed on the blackboard for students to copy into their notebooks. The class is dismayed when Mrs. Rogers reminds them that they are going to have a test in science in two days' time, but they brighten when the lunch bell rings.

The lunch period lasts for fifty minutes. For the first twenty minutes, students are not permitted to play. During this time they collect lunches from the canteen and eat them either in the lunch shed or under the shade of trees. It is Michael's week for road-crossing duty. Having finished their lunch, Michael and two classmates attend the road crossing outside the school (where 25 kilometer per hour flashing lights operate). Armed with orange jackets, whistles, and stop signs, the three quite enjoy their prestigious position as they control the traffic to allow children to cross in safety.

*The Afternoon Session*

The three afternoon periods are each forty minutes long, with the last two separated by a fifteen-minute recess period. Michael and his classmates prefer the afternoon periods to the morning. They usually find the less academic curriculum more interesting and enjoyable. In many ways, they are able to express themselves more freely; they certainly are more active.

Today the first period of the afternoon is arts and crafts, held in a room that is still being developed for the purpose. A teacher aide well trained in aspects of craft work, has materials ready for the class, and as the lesson progresses, she helps Mrs. Rogers in various ways. During their three arts and crafts periods each week, the students are encouraged to take the initiative in a wide range of activities such as enameling, pottery, painting, drawing, and wirework. Today, however, the entire class is engrossed in making a large collage to decorate the school foyer. Most are participating well, and there is evident pride in their collective achievement.

Mrs. Rogers has made arrangements for the class to attend the resource center during the following lesson. This is a new building, impressively equipped, and very functional. Before entering the resource center, Mrs. Rogers reminds the class of the code of expected behavior and the punishment (a one-page essay on good manners) that offenders will incur. Having incurred this penalty two days ago, Michael is determined to set about his library tasks diligently today. He reads about parliamentary procedures and collects information from journals about New Guinea for a class presentation in two weeks' time. During the last ten minutes of the period, the librarian gives the class formal instruction in library reference skills. At the end of the period, Michael checks out a book from the fiction section for reading at home.

The class change their clothes during the afternoon recess period, ready for the final lesson of the day, physical education. Mrs. Rogers' class combines with Mr. Smith's for this lesson. Mr. Smith is the first male teacher Michael has experienced since starting school; he is popular on this count, and also because he is an outstanding footballer. Today the classes continue with circuit training in which ten physical skills are being developed and achievements recorded. Yesterday both teachers spoke about drug abuse as an introductory lesson before the police department's drug squad speaks to the classes next week.

Having showered after an enjoyable physical education lesson, in which he improved his personal achievement in six of the ten skills areas, Michael cycles home feeling that school isn't so bad really. His mother (who works part-time each morning) listens to his chatter about school while she prepares the evening meal. Her mind wanders to what members of the mothers' club will be asked to contribute for the school fete in two weeks' time.

## PROSPECT

There is a great deal that is good, rational, and useful in the Australian system. Its weaknesses are easily discernible and open to criticism. Seldom, however, have critics offered viable alternatives. In this section, an attempt will be made to predict the future of the system and to suggest some directions for improvement.

### Major Issues

Australian education has been accurately characterized by the remarkable administrative and institutional similarity (even to this day) between the states, by its conservative and cautious approach (certainly by comparison with America, Germany, and Sweden), and by the uniformity of its offerings to students. Improvements, particularly in buildings, teacher skills, class numbers, and groupings, and school-community relationships have been marked in the last two decades.

Nevertheless, there are few indications that pedagogical experimentation will leap ahead with inspiring bursts. Change will be slow. Moreover, with individuals and social groups likely to place increasing scrutiny and accountability pressures on schools, unguarded advancement will not materialize.

### Commonwealth Influence

State authorities will continue to view commonwealth interference with distrust and suspicion. The present uneasy relationship, one of undefined compromise, is unlikely to improve with uncertainty from Canberra about the kind or extent of influence the commonwealth should rightly have in kindergarten through grade 12 education. This is most obvious in the attitude of the two political parties toward the Schools Commission. The Labor party saw it as an instrument to improve areas of weakness in Australian education; it adopted a "redemptive" philosophy that influenced policy thinking toward discrimination in favor of the disadvantaged. But the Liberal party, returned to power in 1975, sees the function of the Schools Commission somewhat differently. It has imposed guidelines on the commission, thus limiting its competence and weakening the previous Labor government's philosophy of redemptive egalitarianism.

There is one extremely useful function the commonwealth could undertake in the interests of Australian education. It could direct a close, systematic, objective evaluation of the organization and administration both of the various state systems and of independent schools. Directions for change and concomitant planning would ensue. Such an evaluation could reveal that the main deterrent to change in the public sector is the persistently self-defeating practice of promoting to positions of authority only those who have duly complied with organizational mores.

## Teachers

Very real progress has been made in the preservice training of teachers. Universities and colleges of advanced education, at present consolidating after a period of unprecedented growth, are offering ever-improving courses. Moreover, a minimum training period of four years will soon become the norm.

Teacher development is another matter. The professionally indifferent older teacher, tenured and organizationally secure, must be motivated to improve. Systemwide schemes of school-based teacher evaluation for professional improvement are a critical need in this country.

## Decentralization

Decentralization of educational policy making and financial responsibility beyond the present trends toward limited administrative devolution is unlikely to occur in the foreseeable future. There are two main reasons. First, the traditional pattern of centralized state governments has allowed large political vested interests to accumulate. And second, there is considerable doubt in the minds of those professionally concerned with education that an extension of decentralization has clear advantages over possible risks and losses.

There is, however, little doubt that individual schools will be granted greater flexibility and responsibility in decisions about curriculum and school management. As this occurs, schools will be able to incorporate into their teaching more relevant political, social, and cultural issues of their communities. There are also healthy movements, which are likely to accelerate, toward the development of special schools and classes and specialist assistance to children in normal classes.

## Independent Schools

There has always been criticism, sometimes scathing, of the validity of the two main assumptions for the formation and continuation of church schools—that is, religion and educational experimentation. Certainly the second criticism is justified. Nevertheless, parents will continue to send their children to these schools and federal funding will increase their ability, particularly that of the poorer Catholic parochial schools, to offer reasonable levels of education.

Perhaps the most valuable prospect of the independent schools will occur when they offer credible alternative forms of education to the monolithic state systems with their propensity toward sameness in education.

### Greater Emphasis on Research

The long-neglected area of educational research will receive far more attention in the future. Its place in speeding the momentum of rational change is being realized.

Apart from the well-established Australian Council for Educational Research, the federal government is supporting field-based experiments at school level as well as a national Curriculum Development Centre, and individual states are allocating more money to their own educational research departments. Teacher attitudes to research will determine whether worthwhile outcomes will result from all this effort.

### Final Comment

As a nation, Australia has been compelled by numerous significant events to be self-dependent. If the schools are to play a major part in national definition and growth, educational leaders must be found, and a structure capable of coping with the future must develop. Above all, the individual talent of every child must be nurtured and cultivated. This country needs pride in its national heritage, and it needs distinctive, creative people as the products of its educational system.

### REFERENCES

Andersen, W. E., and Cleverley, J. *Exploring Education.* Carlton, Victoria: Pitman Publishing Pty. Ltd., 1975.

Anderson, D. S. "Equality in Education," in *It's People That Matter,* ed. D. McLean. Sydney: Angus and Robertson Ltd., 1969.

Australian Council for Education Research. *Review of Education in Australia 1955–1962.* Melbourne, 1964.

Baron, G., Cooper, D. H., and Walker, W. G. (eds.). *Educational Administration: International Perspectives.* Chicago: Rand McNally and Co., 1969.

Bassett, G. W. et al. *Primary Education in Australia: Modern Developments.* Sydney: Angus and Robertson Pty. Ltd., 1974.

Borrie, W. D. "Demographic Trends and Education in Australia 1966–86," in *Planning in Australian Education.* G. W. Bassett. Melbourne: ACER, 1970.

Cleverley, J., and Jones, P. "Australia and International Education: Some Critical Issues," *Australian Educational Review, No. 7.* Melbourne: ACER, 1976.

D'Cruz, J. V., and Sheehan, P. J. (eds.). *The Renewal of Australian Schools.* Richmond, Victoria: Primary Education Pty. Ltd. 1975.

Dunn, S. S., and Tatz, C. M. (eds.). *Aborigines and Education.* Melbourne: Sun Books, 1969.

D'Urso, S. (ed.). *Counterpoints: Critical Writings in Australian Education.* Sydney: John Wiley & Sons Australasia Pty. Ltd. 1971.

Fitzgerald, R. T. *The Secondary School at Sixes and Sevens.* Melbourne: ACER, 1970.

———, and Matthews, J. "What Alternatives for Schooling? Some Current Trends," *Overview: A Series of Occasional Reports on Australian Education.* No. 1. Melbourne: ACER, 1973.

Gill, P. N. "The Federal Science Grants Scheme: An Episode in Church-State Relations in Australia, 1963–64," *Melbourne Studies in Education, 1964.* Melbourne University Press, 1965.

Hill, B. *The Schools. Australian Schools: What They Are Like: Where They Are Going.* Ringwood, Victoria: Penguin Books Ltd., 1977.

Howie, G. "The Education of Teachers," in *It's People That Matter,* ed. D. McLean. Sydney: Angus and Robertson Ltd., 1969.

Jecks, D. A. (ed.). *Influence in Australian Education.* Perth, W. A.: Carroll's Pty. Ltd., 1974.

Johnston, G. L. "Politics and Policy in Australian Education," *The Forum of Education,* Vol. 27, No. 1 (March 1968).

Jones, P. E. *Education in Australia.* Melbourne: Nelson, 1974.

Karmel, P. (chairman). *Education in South Australia: Report of the Committee of Enquiry into Education in South Australia.* Adelaide: Government Printer, 1971.

———. *Schools in Australia: Report of the Interim Committee for the Australian Schools Commission.* Canberra: Australian Government Printing Service, 1973.

McLaren, J. *Our Troubled Schools.* Melbourne: F. W. Chesire, 1968.

McLean, D. (ed.). *It's People That Matter.* Sydney: Angus and Robertson Ltd., 1969.

Maclaine, A. G. *Australian Education: Progress, Problems and Prospects.* Sydney: Ian Novak Publishing Co., 1974.

Matthews, J. K., and Fitzgerald, R. T. "Educational Policy and Political Platform: The Australian Labor Government." *Australian Educational Review,* Vol. 7, No. 4 (1975).

Partridge, P. H. *Society, Schools and Progress in Australia.* Sydney: Pergamon Press, 1968.

Roger, T. *The Myth of Equality.* Melbourne: Heinemann Educational Australia Pty. Ltd., 1971

Sharp, N. "Education—The Old School Tie-ups," in *Critical Writings on Australian Education,* (Ed.) S. D'Urso. Sydney: John Wiley & Sons Australasia Pty. Ltd., 1971.

Shinkfield, A. J. "The Development of Teachers Through Positive Appraisal Techniques: Implications for Australia." *The South Australian Journal for Educational Research,* Vol. 1, No. 1 (1978).

Simpkins, W. S., and Miller, A. H. (eds.). *Changing Education: Australian Viewpoints.* Sydney: McGraw-Hill Book Co., 1972.

The Australian College of Education. *New Directions in Australian Education.* Carlton, Victoria: ACER, 1976.

Tomlinson, D."The Liberal Party: Politics and Educational Policy."*Australian Education Review No. 8.* Melbourne: ACER, 1977.

Turney, C. (ed.). *Sources in the History of Australian Education.* Sydney: Angus and Robertson Pty. Ltd., 1975.

Wyndham, H. S. (Chairman). *Report of the Committee Appointed to Survey Secondary Education in New South Wales.* Sydney: Government Printer, 1958.

CHAPTER 3

# Chinese Education

JOHN N. HAWKINS

## DEFINITION

The Chinese word for education in many respects sums up historically how various Chinese governments and officials have defined the pedagogical process. The first character of the compound, *zhiao-yü*, carries the literal meaning of to teach, educate, guide; and the second character (*yü*) means to rear, nurture, nourish. Together, they form the concept of education that contains a cognitive aspect of imparting information, transmitting data, and acquiring skills, combined with the affective notion of moral and value education. Cognitive and affective education has been conducted in China in both formal and nonformal educational institutions. Formal educational institutions have consisted of village schools, academies, and institutes, and today form a network of precollegiate, collegiate, and research institutions. Nonformal efforts in education have included tutoring programs, on-site educational efforts (in the family setting, at the work site), and currently refer to a widespread program of half-work, half-study schools, spare-time schools in factories and communes, and a variety of nonformal skill-transfer projects related to China's industrialization and development. Finally, there has been an intensive effort to infuse political education through all aspects of the educational system. In this chapter, Chinese education will be examined in both the formal and nonformal modes in terms of the objectives, history, pedagogical theory, curriculum, and the roles played by the parties concerned.

## INTRODUCTION

### Objectives of Education

Historically all cultures and societies have provided some form of "education" whether formal, nonformal, or informal. In certain traditional societies in order to become fully functioning members of the culture, a form of rite of passage is necessary to provide the essential skills and values for survival (Scanlon, 1967). Other forms of education are performed in a demonstration manner, as is the case with the Warao tribesmen in Brazil (Wilbert, 1976). More formal and institutionalized educational systems can be observed throughout the world that in some cases seem unnecessarily elaborate and bureaucratic in their goals, structure, and objectives. Whether we are discussing informal education of a demonstration variety or the highly ritualized and formal mechanisms of a doctoral program in the United States, all systems of education operate implicitly or explicitly with a set of pedagogical objectives. Variations are practically endless. Education has almost always been viewed as an instrument to achieve numerous objectives for individuals, families, or societies.

In a broad sense the overall goals of education, formal and nonformal, are to transmit the skills, competencies, and values that the specific culture deems necessary to assure the maintenance of the society. More specifically, we can list some narrower objectives, more practical proposed challenges for education. For some, education is directly related to income and standard of living; the more you have of the former, the more you will get of the latter. For others, education is to provide the basic skills necessary to function effectively under the conditions of a given social system. Then there is moral and values education, or how to be a good citizen, how to be patriotic and loyal. There may be emphasis on health, nutrition, and sex education, the necessity to be fit physically and participate in sports activities. Then there may be stress on more cognitive considerations such as the value of learning facts, acquiring information for the sake of information, and developing analytical skills to learn how to learn. More recently there is emphasis about the need to prepare people early for lifelong education, since schooling will eventually extend forever into one's later years. The purposes of education as viewed internationally are broad and wide-ranging. Depending upon the specific needs of individual nations or cultures, or upon the historical and cultural constraints on an educational thinker, the range of objectives deemed essential for education varies. No single educational system can accomplish all objectives. Societies and individuals must make choices, selecting some objectives as priority items and rejecting others.

One possible conclusion is that all educational systems and objectives are relevant and no single one is necessarily better than another. While this stance is important in avoiding bias and subjectivity, it does not release one from assuming a critical position when attempting to make sense of education in a specific setting. It is perhaps necessary to remain objective but not neutral as we analyze the goals and objectives of education around the world.

## Reasons for This System

The intellectual and pedagogical foundations of China have characteristically been associated with a brief historical period during the latter part of the Chou dynasty (500–200 B.C.). Perhaps the longevity and persistence of Chinese culture and educational practice is the single most compelling evidence cited as the basic value of Chinese educational systems as they have developed and changed over time. Education in China has always concentrated on developing practical skills while at the same time instilling a sense of purpose and value for service to a larger cause. Whether the basic reason for studying was to "become an official" or to "serve the people," the sense of national service or mission was always present. While it is true that historically, until the early 1900s, there were few fundamental changes in educational policy and practice, it is also true that traditional Chinese education performed and functioned very well. It managed to create a widespread bureaucratic network, a system of formal precollegiate and collegiate educational institutions, and to train officials to manage the various affairs of state; and it did this for more than 2,000 years. This long-standing heritage and cultural continuity cannot be ignored when discussing the value of traditional Chinese education. The Chinese may well have invented the concept of a rationally trained civil service and national competitive examinations. The examinations were a major route to social and political advancement; and while social mobility was not widespread on a national scale, there were cases sufficient in number to merit considering Chinese traditional education as a system based on achievement value rather than ascription.

This cultural legacy has been summed up well by one noted scholar of Chinese traditional education:

> There is, therefore, a firm belief in the universality of education, because all the larger organized units of human beings, whether the family or state, are composed of individuals on whose moral rectitude the wellbeing of the larger units depends. It was this belief in the universality of education that prompted Confucius to declare that "in education, there are no class distinctions." Also, it was this belief that distinguished traditional Chinese

education from education in the West, where even today the age-old conflict between the humanist and rationalist philosophies on the one hand and the Christian school of thought on the other, still manifests its influence in many countries (Hu, 1967).

The advantages of such a philosophy perhaps are best revealed in the endurance of Chinese educational forms over time and the persistence of some of these objectives even today.

While current Chinese educational theory and practice are clearly to be distinguished from traditional modes and the brief Republican period (historical summaries of these periods appear in the next section), the advantages of this cultural legacy are still apparent. The Chinese now are seeking to modernize and industrialize, and in this sense the overall goals and objectives of the present system differ from previous practices. The Chinese still, however, reveal a commitment to the power of education to transform individuals and society. The current Chinese educational system continues to stress diligent study, "open door" education, or "universal" education. While the traditional system expressed a desire for universal education, the present system has managed to operationalize it to a degree never before achieved. China's needs as a developing country are being met in a manner that is rare in most developing nations. The reasons for the system have been clearly expressed by the Chinese in terms of both the expert skills needed for the task of political and economic development and the value orientations necessary to maintain a sense of nationhood and develop appropriate international attitudes. This is not to say that the road to a workable educational system has been smooth. The at times violent political struggles associated with educational policy since 1949 are well documented (Fraser, 1971; Hawkins, 1974; Price, 1970). With each struggle, however, the Chinese leadership has consistently returned to educational formulas that have worked in the past, adjusted for new priorities and needs. In this sense we can assert that the Chinese educational system historically and today still exhibits a commitment to "universal" education, the development of practical skills, and the development of positive values toward broader national goals. The system has "worked" to a surprising degree considering enormous historical, developmental, and practical difficulties and perhaps has become a model for a variety of other nations faced with similar difficulties.

## HISTORY

The historical foundations of Chinese education and subsequent development of educational theory and practice span more than 2,000 years. To attempt to encapsulate such a tradition in a few pages presents an enormous selection problem. In the pages that follow, only selected historical highlights will be presented; and it should be understood that we are by necessity glossing over numerous events and developments that are certainly significant but cannot be adequately discussed due to space limitations. For this reason, the following sections will contain a variety of references allowing the reader to pursue individual study of topics, issues, and historical periods that may be of interest.

## Beginnings

We begin a discussion of Chinese education with the period known as the Chou dynasty (500–200 B.C.), although assuredly some form of educational practice and thought existed prior to that time. The moral code of Confucianism permeated Chinese education from Chou to the Ch'ing dynasty, which ended in 1912. This code focused on a set of social relationships such as those between parents and children, brothers and sisters, and subject and emperor. Because the codes involved social behavior, they could be taught; and Confucianism particularly emphasized the power of education to improve society and citizenship in both an intellectual and moral sense. By providing a model that people could emulate, education could transform society. The model had two main functions before the innate goodness (*jen*) of man could be brought forth. It must first "provide peace and prosperity" and second "provide moral training and education" (deBarry, 1960). Thus, the rationale was provided for considering education as a primary goal of the just society; as we have seen, Confucius suggested that "in education there should be no class distinctions" (*you zhiao wu lei*), thus laying the theoretical groundwork for a broadly based educational system (Ho, 1968).

Later, during the Han dynasty (200 B.C.–A.D. 220), intellectuals and scholars assumed new roles as government advisers and officials. During this period scholar-officials grew to become the dominant social force in government. When Confucianism was decreed to be the official ideology, state universities or academies were established, along with a competitive civil service examination, which in turn served as a catalyst for whatever education existed at that time. The establishment of the examination system insured the continual reproduction of the scholar elite, a segment of the ruling group (Ho, 1968; Loewe, 1965). Thus, the Chou and the Han periods set an intellectual pattern that was to dominate and define educational theory and practice until the next major period of intellectual change during the Sung dynasty (A.D. 960–1279).

The Sung period represented in some respects a Confucian revival, as ideas formulated more than a thousand years previously were reaffirmed and discussed anew. Movable type was invented during the Sung, facilitating the widespread use of books, and thus provided an impetus to educational development. Academies were established, and urbanization created a desire for new ideas (deBarry, 1960). With the new emphasis on learning and knowledge, an educational system was designed to prepare students for the more specialized civil service degrees. The idea of education as a social change agent, and the belief that correct knowledge could transform human society, represented another strong trend during the Sung (Dow, 1971). Proposals were formulated for the establishment of a national school system from the district level to the capital, in order to facilitate training of civil servants (deBarry, 1960).

A third major period of educational change and development occurred during the Ch'ing dynasty (1644–1912). This period, which directly preceded the formation of the Republic of China, witnessed many scholars rejecting some of the idealism of the neo-Confucians, thus opening the way for a more scientific approach to examining questions of knowledge and learning. They stopped short, however, of developing the inductive empirical scientific method of Western thinkers of this period. Against this background, education became more involved with problem solving, while retaining the philosophical idealism of Confucianism (Levenson, 1964). As the West and Japan began to threaten the centuries-old internal solidity of the Chinese scholar class, it became apparent that to preserve some semblance of Confucian values and norms, concessions would have to be made to bring about a revitalized education system more conducive to the needs of modernization. From 1860 to 1905, the aim of education shifted from emphasis on the reproduction of a scholar class, well versed in the classics, to a new aim which subscribed some importance to Western learning. Modernization of the school system took place, however, primarily at the top, where some selected Western-style technical schools were established essentially for the purpose of training military personnel (Ayers, 1971; Biggerstaff, 1961; Peake, 1932). The military defeat of the Chinese in the Sino-Japanese War (1894-1895) and the decline and fall of the Ch'ing dynasty in 1911 brought on a period of uncertainty during which the Chinese searched for new social, political, and economic forms while not wanting to discard all the old ones.

When Sun Yat-sen's haphazard 1911 revolution was realized, the social fabric, including the educational system, was already tearing at the seams. As a result of the Sino-Japanese War and the later abolition of the centuries-old examination system (1905), educational thought and practice in China began to undergo significant changes in response primarily to external demands. By 1905, a large number of Chinese had traveled to and studied in Japan, and their pedagogical impact upon returning was profound. Proposals and some policy resulted in efforts by some

Chinese educators to adopt a Japanese, centralized model of education, which included a curriculum composed of classics, history, geography, morals, and sciences (Peake, 1932; Wang, 1966). Following the establishment of the Republic in 1912, educational reformers were convinced that one result would be a complete restructuring of education. Apart from some minor modifications, there was, in fact, little change in the content of educational theory and practice except for a continuing trend of reflecting the current domestic and international political situation. As relations with Japan became more strained, largely as a result of the Twenty-One Demands in 1915 and labor hostilities in Shanghai, the Chinese began searching for alternative educational models (McAleavy, 1967). By the early 1920s, many Chinese had studied in the United States and returned impressed with the American system of public education. Prominent American educators such as John Dewey and Paul Monroe toured China, and they carried with them the spirit of the progressive movement then under way in the United States. By 1922 leadership in educational matters passed to American-trained Chinese, and the government sanctioned a basically American-style educational system. Students were encouraged to "learn by doing," and a generally progressive attitude spread among Chinese educators (Peake, 1932; Wang, 1966). The rise of Chinese nationalism and militarism during the period 1925–1927, however, brought about another shift in educational policy and the subsequent introduction of a rigorous and strict version of German education (Wang, 1966). As full-scale war erupted between Japan and China in 1937 and conflicts between the Nationalist Republican government and the Chinese Communists increased (finally developing into nationwide civil war in 1946), social conditions were chaotic at best, and the power of the government over education as well as other areas of society weakened and declined. The deterioration of the educational system and the Chinese Communists' victory in 1949 heralded the advent of the first truly revolutionary break with traditional or borrowed educational forms.

### Current Status

When the Chinese Communists seized power in 1949, they inherited an educational system devastated by foreign and civil war. Their educational task was framed within the general program of economic and social reconstruction; from 1949 to 1953 schools were reopened, rebuilt, and consolidated. An administrative structure was established to bring the schools under Chinese Communist party (CCP) control, particularly in the cities where the Communists were least experienced. The Ministry of Education was formed in Peking with the responsibility of incorporating into the five-year plan, educational needs and goals. Provincial, city, and county educational bureaus were also established or reformed, bringing education at all levels under a highly centralized system of control.

Primary and secondary education followed a conventional twelve-year cycle, though considerable differences existed between the superior facilities of the urban centers and the peasant-run village schools in the vast rural regions. In the area of higher education, the previously existing standard universities and colleges were reorganized to combine facilities, faculties, and departments, thus separating polytechnical universities from the liberal arts or composite universities. In the early 1950s, limited attempts were made to provide spare-time adult education for the industrial working force, but similar efforts lagged in the rural villages. Curriculum development at all levels was centralized and often simply involved the translation of Soviet texts into Chinese. Teacher and student roles were likewise conventional, exhibiting a teacher-centered classroom retaining many elements of the traditional Chinese teacher-student relationship.

The next major period (1954–1959), dominated by a movement initiated by Mao Tse-tung in 1958 called the Great Leap Forward, witnessed further educational reforms. This period was characterized by an increased emphasis on rural primary and secondary school expansion and a continued regearing of higher education for technological and agrotechnological training. With the Great Leap Forward, a new program for nonformal education also finally received official, albeit reluctant, support. Spare-time primary and secondary schools experienced increased support and growth in the industrial sector, and for the first time the rural areas began to experiment with half-work, half-study schools designed to provide educational facilities for the vast number of illiterate adults. Administrative and curricular control became more decentralized, with increased local participation in decision making. Higher education was likewise affected by the Great Leap Forward, as "red and expert" colleges were established to recruit and train students from among the working class and peasantry in an attempt to break down traditional social class barriers at this level of training. This entire educational program was summed up in the commune movement, which was to encompass virtually all social and economic activities in Chinese society: ". . . our goal is to gradually and systematically organize our industry, agriculture, commerce, culture, education, and military (i.e., militia) into a great commune, making it the basic unit of society" (Mao, 1966b). The commune concept as it related to education would have effectively shifted the delivery of educational services from the more conventional educational institutions to the broader segment of society. However, economic setbacks in 1959 hindered many of the educational experiments of this period.

The five-year period from 1960 to 1966 represented a retrenchment in one sense and the prelude to a major reorganization in another. Many of the previously initiated social and economic programs had been discredited by the failures of the Great Leap Forward, and a more conservative pedagogical position developed. A dual-track approach to education appeared, with a small elite group attending the regular primary and secondary institutions and high quality standard universities and colleges, but with the majority of students attending spare-time and half-work, half-study schools which terminated at grade 9. The majority of students were thus receiving a minimal literacy education buttressed by a small-scale program of vocational education. Further centralization during this period increased controls both for local educational bureaus and the Ministry of Education in Peking. The net result was disaffection between educational authorities and the local communities, increased wastage as students dropped out rather than risk failure, and discontent between and among students and teachers.

On another level, serious political struggles were taking place between such leaders as Mao Tse-tung and President Liu Shao-ch'i over a wide variety of issues, including educational policy. The Great Proletarian Cultural Revolution (GPCR) represented yet another major campaign designed to reassess and regear educational policy and practice. This struggle gained momentum in 1966, and by 1968 significant changes had taken place in many educational programs. Rural development and an emphasis on training middle-level technicians received new priority, and the schools regeared to meet the new challenge. The dual-track system was dismantled and ability grouping of students discontinued. Schooling cycles at all levels were shortened, nine years for the unified primary and secondary cycle and two to three years for the first level of higher education. School management became a local prerogative as "three-in-one committees" composed of teachers, students, and party representatives were formed in the individual schools to take responsibility for administration and curriculum development. The primary goal was to provide a universal, comprehensive educational network coordinated with but not dependent upon the strongly established regular schools (Hawkins, 1973). Examinations were also either reformulated or eliminated, particularly entrance examinations at the university level. A vast network of formal and nonformal educational institutions was established, effectively linking China's skill training programs and political education with overall long-term planning needs. The experience of the past ten years has revealed that the traditional lines between school and society in China are becoming increasingly blurred.

The late 1970s have ushered in another phase of Chinese education. Many GPCR educational programs have been called into question, though by no means has the system been totally restructured as it was in the mid-1960s. Current educational reforms call for an emphasis on science and technology, the enrollment of selected students directly into colleges and universities, the reinstatement of college entrance examinations, and the overall shoring up of quality factors at all educational levels. A series of recent (1977–1978) decisions have been made by the Chinese Communist Party Central Committee and the State Council in this respect. Special commissions have been formed to coordinate and plan for education and scientific development, a new system of higher educational management has been formulated, long-range plans are being drawn up for the development of science and technology, a merit award system has been enacted to encourage experimentation and innovation on the part of technical personnel, a series of academic and professional conferences have been called and are being institutionalized. For the first time standard textbooks are being compiled by the Ministry of Education for the entire country, efforts are under way to import technology and knowledge from abroad, funds for research and education in general have been increased, and educational diffusion efforts have been increased through more efficient use of the mass media (*Peking Review*, 1978).

It is clear that China's educational history is replete with many unique and innovative changes. The system has been a dynamic one and will continue to change and develop in the future.

**THEORY**

As we have noted earlier, Chinese pedagogical theory has historically stressed the notion that the individual can be perfected or molded through formal education and training, provided it is carried out according to the criteria specified by whatever ideological (or philosophical) dictums are current. During the Confucian period classical studies and the observance of proper social relationships were paramount. There was a brief interlude of experimentation with non-Chinese educational theory and learning theory, but this stage was rapidly terminated with the establishment of the People's Republic. While there is clearly some historical and cultural continuity present, current learning and teaching theory bear unique characteristics of the intensive efforts during the past three decades to synthesize Chinese thought and concrete circumstances with European, and to some degree, American educational theory. More specifically, the impact of Marxist educational theory has perhaps been the most significant development in Chinese learning and teaching theory.

Learning

Much of current Chinese learning theory, and particularly its implementation in the educational sector, derives from the theoretical and philosophical writings of Mao Tse-tung, who over the past three decades has been the principle architect of China's educational system. During the late 1930s, Mao and other Chinese theoreticians formulated what were to become the general guidelines for the Chinese approach to the processes of cognition, knowledge, and learning. Marxist dialectical materialism provided the basis for Chinese educational theorists, including Mao, as they struggled with the relationships and linkages between knowledge acquisition and social practice.

In a wide-ranging theoretical document written in 1937, Mao elaborated on the fundamental stages in the acquisition and practical application of knowledge, and this statement formed the basic theoretical underpinnings for subsequent research in Chinese educational learning theory. Five fundamental stages were outlined:

1. *Sense perception:* At this stage only separate aspects of reality are perceived, and more general concepts and logical conclusions cannot be drawn.

2. *Conceptual stage:* At this stage the individual has engaged in practical activities to the point that images pile up in his brain, experiences are repeated enough times to necessitate a cognitive leap after which concepts are formed, thus bringing knowledge to a qualitatively different and higher level.

3. *Application of conceptual knowledge:* The conceptual knowledge acquired in the second stage is now reapplied in a practical setting both for reinforcement and initiation of change.

4. *Theory building:* This stage means that the experiences gained in the previous steps result in a synthesis of concepts and experiences leading eventually to general theoretical principles for understanding social reality.

5. *Adaptation to new conditions:* Although some theoretical principles are now clear to the individual, there are still errors present and the dynamics of change require that the concepts and theories thus far acquired be revised in part or at times totally (Mao, 1965b).

This statement and others that followed were essentially adaptations of Marxist dialectical processes and were summed up by Mao as follows:

. . . while we recognize that in the general development of history the material determines the mental, and social being determines social consciousness, we also—and indeed must—recognize the reaction of mental on material things, of social consciousness on social being, and of the superstructure on the economic base (Mao, 1965b).

Thus the individual's acquisition of knowledge depends on a two-way interaction of mental processes on the material world and the material world on mental processes. Mao has here departed from classical Marxist determinism.

The educational implications of this view are several. First, the Chinese express an enormous faith in the learning ability of virtually every individual. Change and improvement in the individual's acquisition of knowledge is seen as always possible. Recent expressions by Chinese psychiatrists reveal some elements of Pavlovian thought and references to "correct thought leading to correct processing by the mind's second signal system, which in turn leads to correct behavior" (Walls, 1975). On the other hand, Freudian notions of the unconscious are rejected by the Chinese as being excessively concerned with the individual and the self and not compatible with the group-oriented approach currently favored in China. Another important implication is the emphasis on positive reinforcement that dominates Chinese educators' attitudes toward achievement. Although recent (1977–1978) changes will focus more on selection of students according to ability, the overall direction is likely to continue to place greater emphasis on rewarding students for what they have achieved rather than on punishment for failure to acquire certain skills. Finally, classroom observation gives the impression that many teachers and professional educators continue to stress the concepts of learning by doing. The final test of development of learning skills is whether or not an intended outcome can be observed. If problems are revealed in an operational sense, then the fault lies not with individual or group deficiencies but is attributed to the learning process, instructional materials, or teaching strategy. The underlying assumption is that anything can be learned by anybody; there are no natural proclivities. Re-education may be necessary to remove undesirable attitudes or incorrect information, but once there is "correct thought," then all things are possible. Chinese educators are not unrealistic about the rapidity with which such a concept can be completely operationalized, nor are they in total agreement on a unified theory of learning; but the basic principles of cognition expressed by Mao and others are continuing to provide the principle guidelines for educators at all levels.

## Teaching

Teachers in China have historically been revered as an elite class, and for thousands of years the scholar-gentry class dominated the upper echelons of China's social structure. On the one hand, their basic qualification for imparting knowledge was the fact that they themselves had been selected and rigorously screened through the national examinations, which required memorization and rote learning of selected classical literature. It is not surprising then that the basic teaching style of the literati also emphasized rote learning with little analysis and was highly teacher centered. On the other hand, the *xian-sheng*, or teacher, had the moral responsibility of treating students as a father would a son, with warmth and respect. While this model provided the classical heritage, it is obviously a simplification, and other styles appeared and were experimented with during China's long history.

In any case, during the twentieth century Chinese educators and theoreticians struggled with the necessity of developing new goals and objectives toward the teaching process that would better fit overall policies of modernization and skill acquisition and above all promote analytical and critical thinking. One of the first significant documents on teaching style to appear during the early phase of the Chinese Communist party focused on ten points that all teachers were to follow in their educational work.

1. Resort to the method of enlightenment (abolish the more traditional inculcation methods).
2. Proceed from the short range to the long range in analysis.
3. Proceed from the superficial to the deep on a conceptual level.
4. Speak in the popular language as opposed to the complex and abstruse classical statements.
5. Be explicit and to the point when explaining an aspect of the subject matter.
6. Make what you say interesting.
7. Aid speech with gesticulation.
8. Review concepts taught last time.
9. Utilize an outline and organize subject matter well.
10. Utilize group discussions rather than formal lecturing (Mao, 1969).

All these points were designed to address instructional strategy problems that existed in traditional Chinese education and were still plaguing the twentieth-century educational system. Although many early efforts were devoted to changing various aspects of traditional Chinese instructional theory, the Chinese Communists were not totally opposed to other, more positive teacher and instructional practices. For example, in classical Chinese schools the teacher formed a close personal relationship with the students, and ideally the instructional approach was on a friendly one-to-one basis. The rise of more contemporary educational practices had the effect of straining this relationship: ". . . teachers and students do not have any affection for each other. The teachers cherish only money, the students only the diploma; to trade one for the other, to give and receive instruction is merely like a market place" (Hawkins, 1974). This critique does not sound unusual even today. The Chinese Communists experimented with several variations on the ten points before arriving at a policy and practice that satisfied instructional needs for the entire nation in 1949.

It should be noted, however, that during the chaotic years prior to the establishment of the People's Republic there were brief periods of infusion of teaching theories from outside China. It has already been mentioned that American progressive educational theory had an impact in the early 1920s, especially through the visits of John Dewey and Paul Monroe. Ideas and concepts related to ability grouping, individualized instruction, and an emphasis on individual differences appeared briefly in Chinese educational writings. German and Japanese instructional theory also had a modest impact. However, by 1949 the Chinese began training teachers and refining instructional theory on a nationwide scale and in their own unique manner.

During the past three decades, the Chinese have elaborated on the earlier ten points but have not departed from the implied emphasis on practice. Although in the early 1950s special courses were designed for imparting teaching theory, since the 1960s virtually all educational psychology and teaching methods courses have been dropped from the curriculum. An enormous emphasis has been placed on learning teaching skills from actual classroom experience rather than from formal courses or textbooks. Prospective teachers are expected to engage in real teaching experiences early in their training; they are supervised by a master teacher, record extensively all activities and experiences, and finally discuss their teaching experiences with other young teachers-in-training. In this way general teaching methods emerge as well as specific methods geared to the individual teacher and specific circumstances. Since the GPCR, it would be accurate to say that no single teaching theory has prevailed, apart from general commitments to learning by doing and developing teaching skills through practice. Teaching styles and methods thus varied from region to region and city to city. Recent changes, however, suggest that a more rigorous and disciplined approach to teaching may be underway. A retraining program has been instituted primarily for young teachers, specifically to assist them in developing systematic teaching methods. A major effort is underway to intensify the study of basic educational theories and "raise the quality of teaching and learning as a whole." It is charged that previous policies ignored theory and concentrated unduly on practical experiences. The Ministry of Education in Peking has recently held a series of conferences to discuss the development of a national textbook program, national examination system, and therefore, a national program to train teachers effectively in the use of the new materials. The dimensions of this program are too recent to have been formulated precisely, but clearly a more nationally sanctioned "theory" of teaching is emerging.

Another important area of teaching theory involves the differentiated responsibilities and relationships of teachers with students and parents. From the early 1950s to mid-1960s, teachers concentrated on identifying selected class members who then composed a slate of candidates for election as class and row leaders. The class leaders worked directly with the teacher to assist in maintaining class discipline and working with slower students. Because the teacher participated so directly in the selection process, these students clearly expressed loyalties more to the teacher than their peer group. On the other hand, this selection activity was very important in initiating at early stages the concept of peer group tutoring which has remained to the present. During the post-GPCR period (1968–1976), the concept of class leader shifted to allow more direct selection of such students by the students themselves. Student revolutionary committees were formed and students (depending upon their age) elected "red guards" to represent them vis-à-vis the administration, and even on occasion, parents. The red guards had responsibility for maintaining class discipline much as their class leader counterparts did, but they also represented the students and would file grievances to teachers and school administrators if student interests seemed threatened. At this time it appears that there is a swing back toward a more balanced teacher-student power relationship.

The teachers, for their part, had responsibilities in addition to their primary teaching function. Teachers, especially at the elementary grades, were expected to acquire intimate knowledge about the personal lives of their students. Some estimates indicated that teachers at the lower grades actually spent more time making friends with students than in giving formal instruction (Sieh, 1971). Clearly, student-teacher relations have characteristically been close and cordial, with notable exceptions such as the GPCR at which time highly politicized student groups singled out teachers for particularly harsh treatment. Currently there is a move to encourage teachers and students that they should mutually respect each other while at the same time indicating clearly that the teacher has the final authority in the classroom. The slogan utilized to express this new relationship is "respect teachers and love students." Respecting teachers means that students must make a genuine effort to show respect for their teachers and "obey their correct management." The previous emphasis on student organizations and rights has been shifted to a more vague pronouncement supporting student criticism of teachers only when it is done through "correct avenues." Teachers, on the other hand, are to love their students primarily by pointing out their shortcomings and criticizing their "wrong words and deeds." This position is in contrast to the period 1968–1976 when teachers were instructed to concentrate more on positive reinforcement almost to the point of ignoring student difficulties. Previous policies are now criticized for pitting students against teachers and for disrupting the unity (as well as the authority) that teachers had with students. It is theoretically recognized that many teachers are still laboring under traditional notions of teacher "absolute authority." However, it is suggested this is a problem that can be easily solved by the CCP, and students do not need to attack teachers directly for advocating and practicing traditional teacher-student relations.

In summary, we can make several judgments regarding current Chinese teaching theory. First, with regard to instruction it appears that the very strong classical tradition of the integrity and authority of the teacher is being reasserted, albeit in a new form. Instruction in the classroom will depend much upon the strength and positive position of the teacher and less on individual student motivation. It is likely that the previous emphasis on uniform instruction for all students regardless of level or ability will begin to give way to a more individualized approach focusing on ability grouping. Second, the classroom environment and management of the classroom will increasingly emphasize the role of formal administration (CCP committees, teacher committees, and to some degree student representatives) rather than the vague and often ill-defined three-in-one committees. Third, in the area of curriculum and teacher preparation, the current proposal to develop a nationwide, standardized curriculum will certainly influence teacher training, as preservice teachers will be focusing their attention on learning skills and competencies directly related to the curriculum with which they will be working. Whereas during the past decade it was difficult for researchers to discern any one model of teacher preparation or even draw basic conclusions about teaching strategy, the new thrust toward a more centralized educational policy-making body will have an impact on both preservice and in-service teacher training and application. There is some initial evidence that suggests that many teachers are enthusiastic about these changes and believe that teaching as a career will be enhanced by the new, clearer guidelines. One final conclusion is that historically the role of the teacher and the development of attitudes and policies regarding teaching theory has been a persistently critical theme for the Chinese. It has certainly been one of the most dynamic, and we can expect even more changes in the future.

## APPLICATIONS

Chinese educational theory has been implemented primarily through a formal network of educational institutions: The village schools and the academies in traditional China, the "modern" (Western) missionary schools and universities and colleges during the Republican period, and today through a universal program of elementary, middle, and upper-middle schools and a variety of liberal arts and polytechnical colleges and universities. However, it is important to keep in mind that during the past three decades a parallel (and at times intersecting) system of nonformal schools has been developed to focus on educational issues and problems requiring special attention and to compensate for the obvious scarce resources in physical plants and numbers of trained teachers. In this section we will discuss only the most recent applications of Chinese educational theory (1949–1978) with reference to the interwoven mix of formal and nonformal schooling. Statements will be presented on the basic structure of Chinese schooling, the curricula, student evaluation, counseling procedures, and discipline policy and practice.

*Basic Structure*

Over the past thirty years, the formal Chinese educational structure has consisted of basically two models. The first model evolved over a twenty-year period and carried with it features of Western education, early Chinese educational forms, and imported Soviet characteristics. This model consisted of two tracks and covered every level from preschool to universities and research institutes. For the fortunate few (primarily in larger towns and cities) there was a complete schooling cycle of nurseries and kindergartens admitting students from ages three to six, elementary schools up to the sixth grade, junior middle schools of three grades, senior middle schools with an additional three grades, and a tertiary level consisting of technical colleges, universities, institutes, and colleges. This cycle provided a lockstep system, allowing able students to proceed from preschool through university while attending school full time. A parallel track (primarily in small towns and villages) was available for the bulk of China's school-aged cohort. Large day-care centers were provided for working parents, although in many rural families small children were cared for by elderly relatives. The first entry level of formal schooling consisted of spare-time primary schools of six years' duration, junior and senior spare-time middle schools buttressed by short-term worker and peasant adult middle schools, and "red and expert" middle schools initiated during the Great Leap Forward in 1958. For those who completed this cycle, opportunities did exist for further education in a variety of "red and expert" colleges. However, in general this second track was overcrowded, lacking in systematic educational programming, and, it was later charged, discriminatory to the masses of people, especially in rural areas. For these and numerous additional reasons, this system came under criticism during the Great Proletarian Cultural Revolution in 1966–1968 and was effectively dismantled.

The second model that developed in 1969 was designed to merge the two tracks into one universal schooling cycle. Several changes were mandated. An effort was made to expand formal nurseries and kindergartens to all sectors of the population, thus providing an early start to schooling in such critical areas as language learning and computation. A unitary primary cycle was promoted consisting of five years (instead of the previous six) for both rural and urban areas. Likewise, a unitary junior and senior middle school program was initiated for a total of four years, thus bringing the completed precollegiate schooling cycle to nine years (as opposed to the previous twelve years). The school-leaving age was now reduced to sixteen to seventeen (although in some schools it remained at eighteen). At this level the lockstep that was characteristic of the previous model was broken. All students were required to take at least a three-year moratorium, working either in factories, on farms, or in some other productive capacity. In other words, it was impossible for anyone to go directly from the precollegiate level to the collegiate level. There were both practical and pedagogical reasons for this reform. Practically, the labor force, especially in critical shortage areas such as public health and education, was augmented with literally millions of young people who could assist in a paraprofessional capacity. The rural shortage of trained teachers was relieved by young people who, having completed nine years of formal schooling, were literate, knew basic computational skills, and could serve effectively as teacher aides and eventually as full-time teachers. Pedagogically, it was the opinion of some professional educators in China that children were becoming divorced from the practical realities of life in China and were acquiring too much "book learning." In addition, it was charged that students who proceeded directly from elementary and secondary levels to college and university often lacked clear career goals, and that if there were an opportunity to engage in some work-related activity prior to tertiary training, the transition from school to work would be much smoother. In any case, the enforced moratorium remained in effect until early 1978, when some reforms were enacted allowing a selected few students to proceed directly to postsecondary training.

These post-GPCR reforms extended to the collegiate level as well. Universities and colleges shortened their curriculum, reduced courses of study from four and six years to two and three years, and generally regeared to concentrate training programs on middle-level personnel. These actions were followed by increasing the level of political education, encouraging graduates to work in rural or economically depressed areas (rather than the relatively prosperous cities), and gradually reducing the role of the formal university as a training site. Instead, it was suggested that higher education be conducted on site in factories, on farms, and in other production-related areas. This trend was closely connected with an overall emphasis on the important role that nonformal schooling could play in China's educational system and development program.

The nonformal educational system operates in conjunction with the formal system and serves basically two purposes. First, it fills in the gaps in areas where the formal system has not yet penetrated (primarily interior rural areas); and second, it concentrates on providing training facilities and programs for specific problems that for a variety of reasons fall outside the regular formal schooling system (Hawkins, 1973, 1976, 1978a). Some examples at the precollegiate level are mobile teaching centers in the Northwest for seminomadic tribesmen, more stable yet autonomous teaching centers in rural areas where the population is widely dispersed, and mobile schools constructed on boats to serve villages connected by China's internal waterways and fishing villages on the coast. The basic principle here is flexibility—in choice of construction site, curriculum, and financing. A variety of adult nonformal education opportunities exist as well in such critical areas as family planning, minority education, upgrading production skills, and literacy education. A massive program is under way in China's marginal rural regions to introduce new and innovative technical skills to farmers through a complex network of rural educational dissemination centers (Hawkins, 1978b). Finally, in addition to the formal liberal arts and polytechnical colleges and universities, several nonformal models of worker and peasant postsecondary institutions have been established. While the curriculum is similar in many respects to the formal schools, what distinguishes them from the more standard institutions is the fact that they are located on site in factories and on communes, are more specialized to the specific task of the enterprise (primarily at the middle technician level), and are applied in training and output. These institutions were stressed as being critical during the period 1968–1978 but now appear to be in a steady-state situation as the new government in the post-Mao period is again placing emphasis on formal schooling and higher-level training.

**Curriculum, Academic**

Curriculum in China, as elsewhere, has been an area of rapid and radical change. From the rather refined classical tradition of studying the "four books" of Confucius, the twentieth-century curriculum resembled a complicated and difficult jumble of courses. In the rather colloquial and straightforward terminology of Mao:

> In the educational system of our country, required courses are as thick as the hairs on a cow. . . . Speculating on the intentions of educators, one

is led to wonder whether they did not design such an unwieldy curriculum in order to exhaust the students, to trample on their bodies, and ruin their lives (Mao, 1970a).

The Chinese Communists experimented with a variety of curricular modes during the early years prior to the establishment of the People's Republic in 1949. In one sense, their reaction to both the classics and Western education with its proliferation of courses was to concentrate on "basics" (language, mathematics, and science). Educational authorities flirted briefly in the 1950s with Soviet materials and textbooks (many of which were uncritically translated directly from Russian to Chinese), but in the end rejected this outside influence and began a serious program to adapt curricular needs to Chinese political and economic realities. Increasingly from 1958 to 1968, the trend was toward a decentralized approach to developing courses of study, specific materials, and evaluation procedures.

While there has been variation in curricular emphasis during the period from 1949 to 1978, some general patterns are discernible. Chinese preschools and day-care centers have received guidelines both from the Ministry of Education at the national level and from local educational authorities (at the provincial, county, and town levels). However, even during periods of extreme decentralization (GPCR, 1968–1975), most programs deviated little in their major curricular goal, which was the political socialization and ideological cultivation of young children. Five primary curricular goals characterized many preschool programs during the mid-1970s. First, and possibly most important, was the emphasis on "proletarian politicism." Ideological education of this kind mainly took the form of easily read political literature that told a story related to some historical episode (for example, an allegorical story of persistance entitled "The Foolish Old Man Who Removed the Mountain"). A second aspect is termed "current affairs" in China and serves as a news vehicle to communicate to children in simple language the complex political events taking place in China on a daily basis. A complementary course, "internationalism," comprises the third. Cultural education comes fourth and consists of learning to write simple slogans in Chinese (roughly 200 Chinese characters are taught in this fashion), drawing, simple mathematics (addition and subtraction), singing, and dancing. The final area of activity concentrates on physical and productive programs. Students might plant small vegetable gardens, grow medicinal herbs, engage in sports activities, or work on some public works project. In all cases they not only are expected to learn the skills necessary to work successfully on the project, but also learn the significance of the work (the vegetable garden teaches the difficulty of raising food so that children will "not be fussy at mealtimes").

The primary and secondary school curriculum has, since 1949, stressed the acquisition of basic skills. Particularly at the elementary levels, the emphasis has been on basic language, computational, and political competencies. The regular curriculum of many primary schools consists of six subjects: Chinese language (still accounting for more than 40 percent of classroom time), mathematics, politics (about 12 percent of classroom time), music, drawing, and (during the fourth and fifth grades) a course in general knowledge which includes some history and geography, primarily of China. The secondary school curriculum allows the student more flexibility in course offerings, although an emphasis on basics still prevails. At this level there are anywhere from ten to twelve course offerings. In all schools, however, both rural and urban, the majority of the school week is spent in studying Chinese. Despite significant efforts to simplify the written language (the spoken language has now been standardized by adopting a variant of the Peking dialect for the entire nation, in Chinese called *putonghua*, or ordinary language) by reducing the number of strokes necessary to complete an individual character, the language still requires years of study to memorize roughly 2,500 characters. Other courses include advanced mathematics (algebra, geometry, and in some schools trigonometry) and science courses (chemistry and physics). At the secondary level additional social science courses and foreign language study begin. Students can choose to study advanced topics in Chinese history, economics, and the history of other nations (until recently the focus was primarily on developing nations in Asia, Africa, and Latin America). The most popular foreign language is English. Optional "culture" courses are also offered, emphasizing traditional Chinese art forms such as brush painting, calligraphy, Peking opera, and drama. It should be noted that in all curricular areas there exists a decidedly practical bent to subject matter. Often mathematics is taught in relation to the solution of practical problems (geometry for measuring land, calibration and torque calculations for machinery repair, and so on), and science skills relate to some aspect of industrial or agricultural production (pest control, chemical fertilizers, and the like). The intention has been to combine theoretical skills with practical application, and it is important to note that every school day in China includes some form of productive labor in addition to academic programming. Students have established workshops ranging from simple carpentry shops to rather sophisticated chemical works. Both males and females engage in these activities.

Recently announced curricular reforms at the primary and secondary levels are directed toward reducing the previous emphasis on practicality and increasing the development of basic conceptual and theoretical skills in the sciences. A meeting of the Scientific and Technical Association of China has developed guidelines for the study of mathematics, physics, and chemistry, which, it is reported, will comprise the core curriculum for elementary and secondary schools in the future. Educational publishing houses have been instructed to print more articles and books for young people in the sciences, and educational media (films and television) are increasing their programming in these areas. In addition, a variety of enrichment activities (visits to scientific institutions, special courses for students who indicate a strong interest in science and technology) are being established and will play a more important role in education at the precollegiate level than in the past (*People's Daily*, 1977). In summary, both elementary and secondary education in China will likely assume a more standardized appearance, and that such curricular instruments as teacher guides, standardized printed and nonprinted instructional materials, and a variety of special programs will become required for the majority of the nation's schools.

The academic curriculum at the collegiate level in China has also gone through a series of reforms since 1949. During the period 1949–1960, the Chinese government reorganized college and university curriculum and departments five times. The first two reorganizations were aimed at colleges of science and engineering, the next three concentrated on liberal arts institutions and on reducing the total number of institutions of higher learning, and the final reorganization directly affected the curriculum primarily in the area of ideological education. By the 1960s a pattern of higher education emerged that consisted of standard universities (liberal arts and polytechnical) and several alternative higher educational institutions. Teacher education institutes also fall within the category of standard universities. The curriculum of the liberal arts universities and colleges (also called "composite" universities) basically includes language study, history, philosophy, political economy, international politics, law, and library science, as well as specialized courses in anthropology, archaeology, and classics. The polytechnical universities are greater in number and clearly have received priority attention during the past three decades. Here we find a wide range of technological and engineering fields such as civil engineering, chemistry, physics, mechanical engineering, agricultural sciences, hydraulics, marine studies, electrical engineering, computer studies, and mathematics. Again, specialized optional courses are also available (for example, in nuclear sciences and astrophysics, although the more specialized the course of study, the more likely it is to appear in postgraduate research institutes). In general, it is safe to say that the courses of study in all of

China's collegiate level institutions are directly related to national construction goals and aims as expressed in the state economic plans. As was the case with the precollegiate curriculum, the emphasis has shifted during the years depending upon political struggles carried on within the top leadership of China. At this time (1978), the emphasis on quality and expertise, especially in science and technology, being expressed by educational authorities in the Ministry of Education will be reflected in the formal curriculum of China's colleges and universities at least for the foreseeable future.[1]

### Curriculum, Nonacademic

China's nonacademic curriculum includes a vast program of physical, moral-political, and extracurricular programs that fall outside the formal schooling system. Since 1949 these programs have ranged from the highly organized children's palaces located in the major cities to a variety of enrichment programs for semi-urban and rural children. The children's palaces are perhaps the most visible nonacademic programs and provide urban youths with a full range of extracurricular activities. There are both physical and craft activities. In the former category, children may engage in organized sports including basketball, soccer, gymnastics, traditional Chinese calisthenics, and the inevitable Ping-Pong. Art and craft activities include traditional and modern dance, musical instruction, model construction, drawing, painting, and calligraphy. In addition to these primarily recreational activities, practical skills are also introduced, for example, working with tools, experimental agricultural plots, and so on (Fraser & Hawkins, 1972; Gamberg, 1977). It is important to note that the programmatic activities of the children's palaces have fluctuated over the years in line with changes in overall educational policy. But the basic function of providing out-of-school enrichment activities has remained unchanged.

More significant and far-reaching nonacademic programs, however, have operated primarily through China's mass organization network. Basic to the functioning of Chinese society has been the complex system of mass organizations that cut across virtually all levels of Chinese society. A full range of youth organizations has been in operation since 1949, including the Young Pioneer Association and the Communist Youth League (ages nine to fourteen and fifteen to twenty-five, respectively) which focus on the leadership ability of young people and impart ideological education in Marxism-Leninism and the writings of Mao Tsetung. Young people in these organizations have taken the lead in the

---

[1]Not covered in this section are such higher educational institutions as medical schools, political cadre training schools, and so on.

various political struggles that have taken place in China since 1949, and the more successful have been recruited into the Chinese Communist party. These organizations, then, have had principal responsibility for moral and political education in a nonacademic curricular sense. Additional youth organizations exist in other areas (for example, sports, women's groups, neighborhood associations, and so on), but perhaps the majority of nonacademic curricular activities takes place during the periods when Chinese youth are exposed to "productive labor" programs. During the school years, and especially after completion of the elementary-secondary cycle, young people in China engage in intensive periods of practical work activities under supervision of the various work departments in the Chinese government. Until recently (and particularly following the GPCR, 1968–1977), virtually all young people have spent some time working productively at a task often related to their long-term career interest. Students have worked in factories, with dance troupes, in commercial enterprises, and in the rural sector. In 1968 the government issued a directive encouraging young people to "go to the countryside" to gain experience in agriculture (still the dominant productive enterprise in China) and to be "re-educated" by the peasants (Mao, 1970b). Apart from the economic considerations involved in providing communes with educated personnel (many of the students served as teacher aides, paramedical personnel, administrative assistants, and so on), this program contained political, attitude-modification implications. Previous political campaigns involving young people had failed to impress upon them the importance of combining education with productive labor, theory with practice, and the other pedagogical theories discussed earlier. Through working in agricultural production and participating in political meetings and discussions, students are expected to acquire skills in everyday living, transformed attitudes toward labor and the rural sector (still the biggest developmental task facing Chinese planners), and in addition, to contribute more advanced ideas and concepts to rural communes as a result of their relatively high level of training in urban schools. When students have demonstrated their ability to work in difficult situations, they are eligible to apply for further training at the college level. In fact, many have remained in these positions due to the shortage of places at the collegiate level. Recent reforms are directed toward improving the opportunities for youth who have gone to the countryside to continue their education. In any case, these out-of-school experiences have clearly had an enormous impact, primarily in the areas of political education, attitude modification, and the acquisition of basic life skills.

These two programs have clearly had the most impact in a curricular sense over the past three decades. However, numerous other nonacademic curricular activities have been encouraged by Chinese educational officials. They include special programs for introducing young people to traditional Chinese arts and crafts, vocational and manual arts training, specialized military training, and community development projects. In keeping with the overall educational goals of merging formal and nonformal schooling, Chinese educators have perhaps placed more emphasis on nonacademic curricular activities than have educators in other nations. Despite the recent trend toward increasing quality education through a more rigorous formal schooling program, there is thus far no evidence that Chinese leaders are abandoning these innovations and important nonformal curricular activities.

### Student Evaluation

The Chinese quite possibly invented formal examinations. As early as 124 B.C. (perhaps earlier), the Chinese imperial government was conducting official civil service examinations to recruit personnel into government service. The examinations were geared to formal university-level instruction and represented a national effort to assess objectively the knowledge level of individuals who had passed through various stages of formal schooling. Although several modifications in the examinations were instituted during China's long history, the basis for student evaluation remained with the mastery of selected portions of the classical literature which students would memorize and either repeat in a rote manner on examinations or comment on and analyze in similar formal examination procedures. The advent of Western schooling did little to alter the rather mechanistic examination procedures, and not until the late 1940s and early 1950s did significant departures occur.

Soviet influence in the 1950s resulted in a more objective evaluation procedure based on a five-point system. While this method clearly revealed precise categories of content for students to master, and thus departed from the previous traditional heritage of subjective evaluation of student essays, it also had the predictable effect of forcing students to study only for the examinations rather than concentrating on the importance of the subject matter. As early as 1956, articles appeared criticizing the evaluation process for the tension it created among students (Chu, 1956). The argument was made that students crammed all the way from elementary school to the university to pass the various entrance examinations and to perform well on similar university examinations:

> . . . a large portion of the students do not consider the acquisition of useful knowledge as the main task, but only worry all day long about how to earn five points. . . . The school and teachers often take the grades alone to measure the academic quality of the students (Chu, 1956).

Special review outlines were published nationally not for the purpose of assisting students in their approach to the subject matter but more for the purpose of directing them to approach the examination successfully. Applicants for the national examination would choose one of three major divisions: (1) engineering and natural science, (2) medicine and agriculture, or (3) arts and history. Successful students were announced publicly and allocated positions in China's select higher educational institutions. Prior to 1966 the basis for such allocation rested on performance on the examinations, although in special cases concessions were granted to students from worker or peasant social class background. As could be expected, elementary and secondary level evaluations were geared to the university requirements. The secondary education curriculum involved more than thirty class periods (fifty minutes) per week and included such subjects as plane, solid, and analytical geometry, trigonometry, geography, and calculus. The two-track educational system began to function as a screening device, as students were required to take entrance examinations prior to admission to the secondary level and were tracked accordingly to either the pre-university academic track or the more vocational educational track (Price, 1970; Tsang, 1968). The outbreak of the GPCR included attacks on the examination system at all levels. Mao Tse-tung himself led the criticism by stating: "The method of examination deals with the students as enemies and launches surprise attacks against them. This is disadvantageous to the development . . . of the young people, morally, intellectually and physically" (Hawkins, 1974). As a result, the entire examinations system was restructured during the period 1966–1978.

The result, especially at the precollegiate level, was a system of diagnostic testing. Often teachers and students would discuss mutually beneficial ways of evaluating not only the student's progress but the teacher's abilities to communicate the subject matter. A mixture of both written and oral examinations resulted, more often than not conducted in an open-book manner with students conferring with one another in order to answer the questions. These examinations were not graded in the conventional sense, but rather served as diagnostic devices to alert teachers to students who were having difficulty with a particular subject. Group examinations were experimented with as well, as were project examinations where students conducted field work (even at the elementary level) in an effort to solve practical problems in the sciences, mathematics, and social sciences (Gamberg, 1977). Yet grading still exists, and even at the height of the GPCR teachers continued to rank students according to a variety of criteria, including social class background and political enthusiasm. Demonstrated ability to work independently and solve practical problems was rewarded, along with intellectual ability as revealed through mastery of subject matter. Students who lagged behind in study and performance were not labeled as underachievers, slow, or problem students. The assumption that most teachers carry with them as a result of teacher education is that all students have enormous potential that needs to be cultivated in different ways. Thus, a student who is "lagging behind" can succeed, but only with group support from both teachers and peers. In theory no student should be labeled a "failure." The Chinese clearly stress that learning problems are primarily the result of poor motivation. Social class, ethnicity, sex, and other variables are not considered the most important; rather the teacher's role in motivating the student and the community environment in support of student efforts are deemed the most essential for student success in school.

Currently Chinese educators are again stressing the need for a more concerted effort to evaluate students objectively according to clear examination criteria at the precollegiate level and according to national examinations at the university level. Chinese students will again sit for national university entrance examinations after a ten-year hiatus. Recent articles have not, however, suggested that the reforms enacted as a result of the GPCR will be totally rescinded. It is likely that a more flexible precollegiate evaluation mechanism will continue to operate, with students taking part in formulating evaluation decisions and the emphasis on motivation continuing to dominate educational evaluation procedures.

## Counseling

Counseling and discipline are directly related in China, for it is unlikely that any form of counseling would take place unless it involved a question of what the Chinese prefer to call self-discipline. The theory behind Chinese counseling and discipline procedures stresses the importance of group relations and group dynamics, and is couched in Marxist-Maoist concepts of contradictions. In this framework each individual and each group has both positive and negative aspects and is in a constant state of change. It is the teacher's responsibility, together with other members of the revolutionary committee administering the school, to counsel individual students or groups of students when a problem arises in their studies or overall school life. The counseling takes the form of group discussions often involving other students, and an effort is made to determine which positive and negative characteristics are present and the social influences responsible for them. For more serious problems, higher level political cadres are in charge of the counseling process; but the emphasis in all cases is on the political characteristics of the individual and the need to redirect the person's energy in more positive directions. If students are achieving at acceptable levels academically, politically, and socially, it is not likely that any formal counseling will take place. If they need advice regarding some aspect of their studies or longer-range career lines, they will either discuss these questions informally with their peers or the teacher, or bring them up more formally with the revolutionary committee administering the school.

In order to understand more specifically Chinese student counseling procedures, it is essential to comprehend the meaning of the "small group" (*xiao-zu*). These are groups of people with between eight and fifteen members; and many social institutions, including education, employ such groups for purposes of counseling, discussion, participation, or as one writer has suggested, to provide a means of "political ritual" (Whyte, 1974). In the field of education, the small group would be the lowest level of organization. Its members, primarily students, would meet together to study, carry out work assignments, and engage in the Chinese equivalent of counseling, termed "criticism and self-criticism" (*pi-ping yu cu-wo pi-ping*). At the primary level students form small groups by rows and organize themselves for various educational activities. At this level the teacher takes the leadership in providing any counseling that might be needed, again through the small group process. At the middle school level, in addition to the small groups, class officers are elected, and they have the responsibility for reporting any counseling problems that might arise out of the small-group discussions.

Part of the reason for what appears to be a rather uncomplicated counseling process in China is the fact that social differentiation is minimal, thus reducing the complexity of choices and decisions for young people. The majority of elementary and secondary school leavers will enter the work force either in the rural sector or in industry in the cities. A select few will proceed to postsecondary training (and they indeed do receive more advice and guidance), and another select group will enter other specialized occupations. Anxiety and frustration regarding career choices, mobility, and achievement are minimal due to the national social guarantees of an occupation, housing, health care, and other social concerns. This brings us back again to the fact that concern for the individual is most aroused when political questions are raised, and this often means some discipline code has been broken.

## Discipline

What kind of discipline problems are present in a Chinese school? At the outset two points should be made clear. First, due to the high level of organization in Chinese society in general and schools in particular, and the very effective peer-group counseling and discipline system (as well as an overall high social regard for education), behavior problems as we may define them (vandalism, truancy, gang, and individual conflict) are virtually absent in Chinese schools. There is an enormously high demand for education, a high value is placed on schooling by parents, and young people are highly motivated to learn and participate in the educational enterprise. For these and a host of additional reasons (the cultural heritage of education as a source of social mobility), school discipline problems do not emerge to any significant degree during periods of relative political stability.

This leads to the second point. The history of the past thirty years in China has been characterized by a series of political struggles that often revolved around critical educational issues. At those times student organizations (even extending to the lower elementary level) have been extremely active in promoting one or another political faction or position. The best-known such movement, of course, was the GPCR, which resulted in the mobilization of literally millions of students, some in support of one faction in the government and others in support of competing factions. Formal education, teachers, administrators, parents, and even military and CCP personnel were indirectly and directly attacked by students. Schools were destroyed, students killed, teachers physically abused, and so on. These actions could clearly fall under the category of "discipline" problems, although in many cases they were officially sanctioned by various government leaders. However, even with such government approval there were times (toward the end of the GPCR, for example) when student violence moved beyond the boundaries of sanctioned behavior, and during those periods strong action has been taken by the government to bring the movements to a halt. So what we see appears to be a dichotomous behavior pattern on the part of Chinese students. On the one hand, under specific conditions, they are highly academically motivated, self-disciplined in the classroom, friendly to teachers and fellow students, diligent in course work, and respectful of property and persons. On the other hand, during political mobilization struggles, they are easily aroused to group mobilization tactics and strategies often resulting in the complete disruption of the schooling process, along with the destruction of facilities and attacks on individuals. It should be stressed, however, that these latter occurrences are almost always related to nationwide disruption and breakdown of discipline rather than actions initiated by the students themselves.

Discipline problems that do not fall into either of these two categories are the relatively minor problems of disruptive classroom behavior, or what Chinese teachers call "mischievous" (*wanpi*) activities. Students who fall into this category engage in disruptive activities such as causing a disturbance in class, failing to complete assignments or not participating in school programs, playing pranks on other children, and occasionally bullying smaller children. In such cases the students will first take it upon themselves to discuss the problems with the guilty party, attempting to find a solution without involving the teacher. If this fails, the teacher and possibly other authorities will be brought in to investigate all factors—home life, past history, teacher behavior toward the child, and so on. Through such discussions and investigations, the child is encouraged to change his behavior to more acceptable norms; and if all else fails, he may be asked to leave the school. School attendance in China is not compulsory, so the logic is, "If you want to study, come to school; if you do not, stay away." Social and peer pressure, however, is very great in support of formal schooling, and every student knows that whatever mobility may be achieved in China is directly related to education. This combination of counseling, group discipline, and self-discipline concepts, and the importance attached by most members of Chinese society to schooling, all serve to produce a fairly stable and harmonious school environment.

## ROLES

One central fact regarding the implementation of Chinese educational policy from traditional times to the present is the mix between official centralization of power in formal offices and the unofficial participation of a variety of other actors at the local level. In traditional China a relatively small imperial administration was nevertheless able for centuries to generate and implement administrative policies effectively in many areas, including education. The Chinese bureaucracy was a complex, sophisticated, and well-developed mechanism. It extended from the imperial capital and the emperor through the famous Six Ministries, to the provinces, circuits (*dao*), prefectures, departments, and counties (*xian*). The officials at each level were signified by their classical training, scholarly background, and administrative acumen. They represented the emperor and made decisions regarding the implementation of Confucian educational policy, including the conduct of examinations and the monitoring of other scholars. While the central level in the capital composed of the various ministries had absolute authority, local leaders and even citizens could at times participate in the implementation of policy (Fairbank, 1967). Against such a background the current Chinese administrative structure and bureaucracy clearly exhibits some similar characteristics. The interplay between central and local actors in educational policy and practice continues to be a hallmark of current Chinese educational roles, specifically those of the administrative structure, teaching faculty, students, and parents. While there exists a cultural legacy, the new Chinese government has instituted several innovative and significant departures.

**Administration**

Any consideration of Chinese administrative policy and practice must take into account the three basic administrative levels: national, provincial, and county (*xian*). The authority allocated to each of these at various times defines the degree of centralization and decentralization present, as well as the degree of popular participation in decision making. This range of options included national emphasis on the ministries to formulate policy from the top down, to periods when the concept of popular management (*min-ban*) and leading groups (*lingdao gugan*) was stressed. In a general sense, the Chinese government has usually relied on a mix between the two. The three levels mentioned are in fact large units covering a very complex infrastructure. At the national level, the National People's Congress has titular authority over the determination of the various ministries (including the Ministry of Education). The Ministry of Education in China has at times contained several subunits, has at other times consisted of more than one ministry (a separate Ministry of Higher Education existed in the 1950s), and during the GPCR ceased to exist at all. The ministers report to the State Council, which has strong powers of authority in the appointment of high officials of education. At the provincial level, the primary organization is the Department of Education, which in turn has subdepartmental units to oversee specific educational issues and problems. Finally, at the *xian* level we find the Bureau of Education which is closely connected to commune, town, and city revolutionary committees. All of these levels represent the state administrative apparatus. It is important to understand that a parallel administrative power is present as well, namely the various units and bureaus of the CCP. Party cadres transmit the prevailing political line to educational administrators and serve on all important committees, including the post-GPCR revolutionary committees. Below the *xian* level, individual schools have had full-time educational administrators (during the pre-GPCR period), and recently have been administered by committee. In all cases, however, the mix between central control and planning, and local control and planning has been a persistent problem. The Ministry of Education in Peking is again reasserting its leadership and criticizing the lack of central control that was present during the GPCR. It is likely that the committee structure and *min-ban* concept will continue to be operational at the local level (commune and city schools), but that more centralized planning in finance, curriculum, and research will characterize the central ministry level (Fraser, 1971; Hawkins, 1974).

## Faculty

A critical teaching shortage faced the Chinese leadership shortly after the establishment of the People's Republic. Teachers were recruited from a variety of sources. Some were retained from pre-Communist days, literate housewives and former students were encouraged to enter the teaching ranks, and educated army personnel and CCP cadres served to bolster the teaching profession until such time as a new corps of socialist-trained teachers emerged. The role of the teacher was ambiguous from the beginning. As early as the Yenan period (1935–1949), teachers or intellectuals (*zhishi fenzi*) formed a class of individuals necessary to achieve social reconstruction efforts but who could not be totally trusted. In terms of Marxist class analysis, they belonged to the broad category of the petty bourgeoisie. The implications of this categorization were several. First, their position in society was considered unstable: ". . . most intellectuals and students are oppressed by imperialism, feudalism, and the big bourgeoisie, and live in fear of unemployment or of having to discontinue their studies" (Mao, 1965a). Second, because of the insecurity in their lives and because of their high level of education, intellectuals and teachers (Mao himself had been a teacher and director of a teacher education institution) were able to grasp radical ideas and play a leadership role in the Chinese revolution. But, in a telling assessment by Mao, teachers and intellectuals were found wanting because

> . . . intellectuals often tend to be subjective and individualistic, impractical in their thinking and irresolute in action until they have thrown themselves heart and soul into mass revolutionary struggles, or made up their minds to serve the interests of the masses and become one with them. . . . Not all of them will remain revolutionaries to the end. . . . The intellectuals can overcome their shortcomings only in mass struggles over a long period (Mao, 1965a).

Following the establishment of the People's Republic in 1949, it was found that teachers and university faculty could be divided into three categories: resolute (completely in support of the revolution), wavering, and antagonistic. Numerous political campaigns were launched designed to re-educate teachers and intellectuals. This constant effort to impress upon teachers their critical and crucial role in educating young people "correctly" has been a source of frustration for many teachers and educators over the years. While the political struggle has involved competing factions in the Chinese leadership (at various times criticizing teachers for not being academic enough, and at other times for being too political), the basic principle for the role of the teacher can be summed up in a statement made by Mao to the effect: "to be a good teacher, one must first be a good pupil" (Mao, 1966a). Because education was singularly important, and because teachers and intellectuals occupied such powerful positions in this respect, the need was recognized to continually attempt to "educate the educators." The role of the teacher, thus, has been a difficult one. They have been an essential ingredient to China's efforts to modernize and develop a literate and articulate citizenry. At the same time, because of their education and training, teachers have been among the most outspoken critics of the Chinese government, offering both positive constructive criticism and at times advocating the outright overthrow of the government. At times they have been a privileged group (during the early 1960s, particularly), and at other times they have been the object of severe criticism and even physical abuse (for example, during and after the GPCR). Recent changes in educational leadership and policy have resulted in an increase in the status and prestige of teachers and the role they play. Teachers are now to be "respected" and are directed to play a more active role in classroom management, instruction, and discipline than they have in the past. Above all, it is now charged that the fundamental role for the classroom teacher is to increase the knowledge of students rather than to play a variety of political and organizational roles. The primary task of the teacher will be to teach, and it is likely that Chinese schools will now experience a period of renewed interest in teacher preparation and performance as measured by the academic achievements of its students (Yuan, 1977).

## Students

While teachers and intellectuals may have been suspect in the eyes of the Chinese leadership, or at the very least, a vacillating group, students have often been viewed as one of the most potentially progressive and important assets of China's future. In an early statement by Mao Tse-tung, the view was expressed that:

> New China must care for her youth and show concern for the growth of the younger generation. Young people have to study and work, but they are at the age of physical growth. Therefore, full attention must be paid both to their work and study, and to their recreation, sports, and rest. The young workers and peasants, the educated youth, and the young people in the armed forces are heroic and energetic and well disciplined. Without them the cause of revolution and construction cannot be successful (Hawkins, 1974).

Whereas it was necessary to utilize the vacillating older intellectuals, the educated youth of China were seen as providing an energetic and active group, many of whom were sympathetic to and had supported the CCP during its struggle in the pre-1949 period. Also in this statement we see the multiple roles that students were expected to play. They were required to engage in productive labor when called upon to do so and to be enthusiastic about work in general. They were also, of course, required to study hard and be disciplined and motivated students. And finally, recreation and play were to be an important aspect of student life. Depending upon the period under consideration, however, one or another of these requirements was given priority. The policy pendulum has swung between an emphasis on work and politics to one on study and discipline.

As we have seen, students have been among the most politically active groups in China. Student mass organizations have played important roles in a number of political campaigns (for example, Great Leap Forward and GPCR). In the classroom, however, particularly during periods of stability and growth, students are exhorted to concentrate on their studies, be disciplined, and strive to achieve to the best of their ability. Individual student achievement has been rewarded differentially, as we have seen, over the past three decades. Generally the Chinese have avoided programs that would accelerate superior individuals ahead of their class. In the past (1949–1977), superior students have been cultivated within their class as tutors and leaders. There have been occasional cases of exceptional students being recruited into special schools (the so-called "little treasure pagodas" of the mid-1960s), and there is some evidence that such a program may be instituted once again; but in general, the tendency has been to "mainstream" exceptional children throughout their school career. A similar situation has been the rule with regard to other special education needs. Students who are identified by teachers and other students as "slow learners" are retained in the same classroom but given special tutoring by the more able students and by teachers. More severe learning disorders, however, are treated medically; but even in cases of mentally retarded children, the attempt is made to allow them to remain in a regular classroom environment. Special schools and classes have been established for the blind and deaf. A Chinese braille system has been developed, as well as a sign language. Again the emphasis is on returning the child to the regular classroom as soon as possible. There are both practical and pedagogical reasons for this approach. Educational facilities are at a premium in China, and special facilities for special educational needs are simply not available. On the other hand, Chinese educators sincerely believe in the value of integrating special educational cases with the mainstream. Thus, even when facilities become more available, it is not likely that the Chinese will depart from this policy to any large degree.

Currently the overall emphasis for students is clearly on academic achievement. Student politics is being discouraged, the enforced work moratorium in the countryside is being decreased, students are being allowed to come back to the cities for postsecondary training, and the value placed on learning and discipline is being promoted in the Chinese press and official statements. Despite these policy variations, including the most recent one, Chinese educators and students have been gradually evolving a role for students that includes the conventional emphasis on academic achievement but also attempts to break away from the traditional role of the student as "striving to become an official." Thus, physical education, political organization, and service to the nation will continue to be positive roles for students to aspire to.

### Parents

The relationship of parents to education and particularly to their children as students in contemporary China can only be understood in the context of traditional parent-child relationships. For more than 2,000 years, the family was the center of loyalty in China, transcending all other social relationships, even to the emperor. One scholar has suggested that ". . . the family was the determining factor in the total pattern of social organization" (Yang, 1959). In the complex of social relationships within the family (differentiated on the basis of age and sex), the most important relationship was that between parent and child (ahead of husband and wife, brother to brother, brother to sister, and so on). Thus, although the Chinese student had certain obligations to his teacher and classmates, in the final analysis it was the family and specifically the parents that formed the basic structural tie for the Chinese child. As other aspects of Chinese society began to change, particularly during the nineteenth and twentieth centuries, the strength of the family was also diminished. Young people began to experience increased contacts outside the family in a host of social, political, and economic associations and organizations. These events were already under way prior to the establishment of the People's Republic but clearly have been accelerated since 1949. Formal and nonformal education specifically have been utilized greatly by the current government as a mechanism for shifting loyalties from the family to the broader society. Students have been encouraged to focus their attention and loyalty on role models other than parents (the party cadre, model army personnel, and teachers).

For their part, parents have also increased their contacts beyond the family. In most families, both parents work and are involved in several mass organizations that increasingly occupy their time and attention. Parents have been gradually acquiring the view that they do not have final authority or responsibility for their children, but that other adults, friends, various officials, and even other young people have a share in the overall process of "parenting." Parents today are exhorted to care for and love their children, and children are instructed to respect their parents, but only in the most general sense. In the end, it is the responsibility of both parents and children to serve national needs rather than narrow family interests, even to the point of reporting family deviant behavior to the proper authorities (as was the case especially in the early 1950s when children denounced their friends for nonsocialist activities).

In education, specifically, parents have been involved in parent-teacher-administrator committees, particularly during and after the GPCR. Parents are often called upon to visit classrooms to serve as teacher aides, instruct students in special skills, or simply to engage in political education by discussing with students their life prior to 1949. It is unclear exactly how much involvement in policy formation is engaged in by parents, but they are clearly represented on local school committees and are very vocal. Parents are consulted when special educational problems arise and are counseled either by teachers or other responsible personnel connected with the school. One obvious reason for the rather smooth relationship between parents, teachers, and students is the lack of incongruity between the norms, role models, and expectations of all three groups. There is little contradiction between what the child learns at school and at home (Gamberg, 1977). There are some differences, however, in child-rearing practices, especially between urban, more educated families and rural, less educated families. In some rural areas more traditional ways persist, and family authority is stronger in some respects. Educational authorities in seven major provinces all responded positively when asked if corporal punishment was still used by parents in the rural sector, even though it is discouraged officially. Similar questions were asked in major cities, and the response was mixed; but most educational officials indicated that urban parents do not use physical punishment as a means of child control, but rather rely on the neighborhood committees and other mass organizations to maintain discipline.[2] Rural parents have also been more likely to oppose sending their children to upper secondary schools and postsecondary training programs. Intensive re-educational efforts have been engaged in by educational officials to change this attitude.

In summary, parents in China have increasingly been shifting their activities and loyalties beyond the nuclear and extended family. Their interest and involvement in education has been one important area of

---

[2]In 1971 the author asked thirty-seven members of provincial-level revolutionary committees in Hopei, Shantung, Honan, Hunan, Anhwei, Kiangsi, and Kuangtung the question, "Is physical punishment still used by parents as a means of maintaining child discipline?" The response was uniformly positive for parents in the rural sector and mixed (twenty-five negative and twelve positive) for parents in cities.

social concern, and this interest has been officially fostered by the government. As has been the case in other areas we have discussed, current changes suggest that parents will possibly have increased responsibility for child rearing, especially in light of the return of large numbers of educated youth who have worked for the past few years in the Chinese countryside. One of the stated reasons for scaling down the "return to the countryside" program has been that children are too far from their parents. The Chinese, it appears, are still searching for a solution to the parent-child-education problem that will satisfy both cultural specific needs and the exigencies of developing a modern nation-state.

## SYSTEM IN ACTION

Although the Chinese educational system has lacked the centralized features of educational systems like the French or the Japanese, and local variation in curriculum, instructional strategy and facilities has been considerable, it is still possible to discuss in general terms how the Chinese educational system operates. The system, as we have seen, consists of a vast network of formal and nonformal educational institutions ranging from preschools through high-level research institutes. In this section we will concentrate primarily on the precollegiate level, as it influences the largest number of students in China and is clearly the base for all other educational activities. We will look briefly, in turn, at preschools, primary, and secondary institutions.

### Preschools

The most prevalent form of preschool education in China consists of facilities attached to a basic productive unit, whether farm or factory, in which the parents work. The Peking Cotton Mill Day-care Center is one such preschool, and serves the needs of parents who work in the mill. On their way to work, parents drop their children off at the preschool located across the street from the mill. A typical day for the children would consist of a mixture of political education, creative play, free play, and physical education (often defined in terms of "productive labor"). The school would be staffed primarily by women, only a few of whom would be specifically trained for early childhood care. While the basic purpose of such schools is to care adequately for the children of working parents, they also perform important educational functions. The child entering a day-care center is not simply "cared for" but is also introduced to basic concepts of politics, computation, and language (up to 500 basic Chinese characters are taught by age five and a half). Political education is transmitted primarily through drama and dance, and children are also introduced to a variety of social roles through the humanities. Part of the day would consist of simple stories on current affairs in China as well as international affairs. Formal instructional activity takes place in a classroom environment where children are introduced to cultural education consisting of Chinese language study, simple mathematics, and science concepts (this primarily for the older children, age three to five). However, roughly 50 percent of the day will be occupied with indoor or outdoor productive activity. Depending upon the school, children will engage in vegetable gardening, building play equipment, and so on.

The preschool is also the site of ongoing contact between the child and China's health care network. Neighborhood or commune health workers visit the schools on a regular basis in order to administer inoculations and generally keep a thorough medical history on each child. The environment throughout the preschool would generally be supporting of the child and very warm and friendly. Teachers, health workers, and parents all interact to care for the educational, emotional, and physical needs of preschool children. Contact with parents would occur during lunch hour and, of course, after work when parents pick up their children to go home. Thus the preschool in China offers a mixture of work and play, serious activity and free time, and clearly serves the needs of China's growing economy by releasing both parents for the labor force.

**Primary Education**

Since 1949 the Chinese have experimented with several forms of primary education, ranging from full-time (seven hours per day, five days per week) programs to half-time and spare-time programs (three to five hours per day, four to six days per week). Since 1968, however, the basic pattern of the school day is from 8:00 A.M to 2:00 P.M. five days per week, with some optional activities on Saturday. A student entering a typical primary school at 8:00 A.M. would find a classroom occupied by an average of forty-seven students and possibly team taught (a trained teacher and a teacher aide).[3] The classroom would be sparsely furnished, desks would be shared by two students, it may or may not be directly lighted, and in the winter months it would be heated by a coal stove in the center of the room. Classes during the day would consist primarily of language study (standard Chinese), mathematics, general science, political education, and physical education. Optional courses in music and drawing may be offered. The basic courses would all be taught by the same teacher, and the student would be in a self-contained classroom.

Although much of the school day would consist of classroom study,

---

[3]Data based on visits to thirteen rural and urban primary schools in 1971.

students also work in groups and engage in large and small group discussions. A portion of the day would be occupied with physical education (organized calisthenics) and, after third grade, some form of productive labor would be required, either at the factory level or with a production team of the local commune. Three times a year the student would have a vacation, normally during spring, summer, and autumn festivals, totaling three months. Although most schools have eliminated the tuition requirement, some schools still charge a nominal fee to the parents to cover office expenditures and administrative fees. Primary financing of the school would be through local sources (commune appropriations or some other form of "self-reliance") and a modest portion from state subsidy (at the provincial level). The average teacher salary would be 50Y per month (about U.S. $25), and teachers would retire with 70 percent of their top salary and all other benefits.

Students would be expected to eat lunch at home (since most attend neighborhood schools), or if this arrangement were not feasible, the school would provide a hot lunch from a nearby restaurant and bill the parents once a month. Examinations would be given twice a year and would include both open- and closed-book exams. Students would be encouraged to help each other during the examination and to ask the teacher for assistance. Until recently the purpose of examinations was to diagnose the student's achievement level and to alert the teacher to any potential problems. At this time (1978) it appears examinations will be offered more often and will be competitive and rigorous in comparison with the fairly relaxed attitude during the past ten years.

This school is, of course, an ideal type—a composite of several that have been studied since the 1940s. And while it provides a picture of primary school life in China, it should be emphasized that the important dimension of interpersonal relations has not been discussed. The physical plant of a Chinese school is rather austere, as are instructional aids and materials. Yet the environment of the school and classroom is warm and supportive of the student. Students work quietly in small groups or individually and receive a lot of attention, especially considering the classroom size. The majority of teacher time is spent in teaching rather than testing and evaluating various aspects of student affective and cognitive behavior. Much use is made of the surrounding environment (partly due to lack of facilities, but also due to a sincere pedagogical belief that school life should not be divorced from "real" life in the community). Students engage in a variety of field work activities, visiting factories, actually working in factories and on farms, visiting public offices and national parks. The community will also interact with the school to a large degree. Parents, community leaders, and "model workers" will visit classrooms to discuss current problems and adult situations with young students. The primary student in China will find little in the way of elaborate school equipment and facilities but will find a motivating and stimulating learning environment.

### Secondary Schools

At age thirteen the Chinese student enters the secondary schooling cycle consisting of three years at the junior middle level and either two or three years at the senior middle level. The average school-leaving age is eighteen. The student would find a large class size, roughly forty students per class; however, two to three teachers would share responsibility for each class. At the junior middle level, seven courses would be taken (Chinese, politics, mathematics, physics, chemistry, geography, physiology), and at the senior middle level, optional courses would be added in the areas of foreign language, history, and the arts. The school year would consist of two terms, roughly five months each. Entrance examinations have been consistently held (with the exception of the GPCR, 1966–1968, period), but the emphasis since 1968 has been on utilizing examinations only for the purpose of developing a profile of the student, not to exclude or track students according to ability. Additional examinations would be held at the end of each term in all courses and, again, would be primarily for the purpose of assessing student progress and teaching effectiveness. Current changes (1978) suggest that examinations will return to pre-GPCR emphasis on evaluating student academic progress in order to differentiate students according to ability and to provide guidelines for entrance into postsecondary training programs. Students have two months of vacation equally divided between productive labor and free time and spread over the school year according to local conditions.

As was the case with the primary schools, secondary school facilities range from rather modern buildings with central lighting and heating, primarily located in urban areas, to abandoned farmhouses and warehouses that have been converted into school facilities in the rural areas. The emphasis is on the transmission of information and knowledge primarily via the teacher, and educational aids and technology are noticeable by their absence. The student finds a classroom environment that places much importance on self-directed learning, small-group discussions, "learning by doing," and interaction with the community. Teachers lecture and present information in a formal manner, but this mode of teacher-student interaction is always seen as only one aspect of the learning process. Despite large classes, the effective use of small groups and out-of-school activities provides a mixture of learning experiences for the Chinese student.

The principle of productive labor is more operational at the secondary level and becomes more so as students move up the educational ladder. A part of each school day would be occupied with student-run enterprises, some of them approaching quite sophisticated methods. Students will often design a project with the assistance of parents who have specific skills and/or with the help of members of the local community. Such projects include electronics assembly operations, the production of circuitry for automobiles, employing corrosion vats for plating projects, and so on. Students acquire a variety of skills and attitudes as a result of this form of productive labor. Of course, basic mechanical skills are an obvious important by-product in view of the fact that most Chinese graduates will enter the technological work force, which is rapidly expanding. Just as important, however, from the Chinese viewpoint, is the acquisition of positive attitudes toward labor, and the juxtaposition of mental labor with manual labor. These two forms of school activities are not considered separate, but rather complementary. The Chinese student, it is believed, will retain more academic information and succeed cognitively only if each school day consists of some form of manual labor. Again, it is the mixture of activities that is stressed.

The secondary school student, then, experiences a variety of activities during the school day in China. At different times the emphasis is on one or another aspect of the curriculum, depending on overall national needs and priorities. Currently (1978) educational policy for the secondary level is shifting to an emphasis on technology and science, and it is likely that the school day in China will also reflect this new direction in the future.

## PROSPECT

Educational prospects in China are very good—this despite more than thirty years of reform, revolution, and struggle on the educational front. Since 1949 serious reforms have been instituted in Chinese education on three occasions. During the first period (1950–1957), the educational system was transformed from the framework of the 1920s and 1930s to one more conducive to the new government. In 1958 the Great Leap Forward included a restructuring of the schools, especially in the area of productive labor. Finally, in 1966 the GPCR resulted in another basic reformulation of the role of schooling. This campaign witnessed the closing down of schools and the elimination of much of the educational bureaucracy. Now the Chinese are in another stage of change, as we have seen, and we can predict that educational change and reform will be a dynamic aspect in the future.

Over these rather hectic years, much progress has been made. The adult literacy rate is over 50 percent, and close to 90 percent for those who have attended schools since 1949. Effective primary school enrollment is 95 percent for the urban sector and over 60 percent for the rural areas. Total enrollment in schools at all levels has averaged over 130 million. There are twice as many institutions of higher learning than there were in 1949 (400), and construction of primary and secondary schools has been a major priority.[4] In the area of science and technology, and especially in research and development, there have been some severe problems. Given the large school-aged population, the Chinese have concentrated their resources on developing primary and secondary education, perhaps at the expense of collegiate and postgraduate training. This problem has now been recognized, and current policy will be adjusted to shift some resources to these areas.

The Chinese have recently developed a twelve-point program for science and education. In summary, it announces that a special commission on science and technology has been established, several universities have been reorganized, special research institutions are being promoted, a series of academic work conferences have been held, a new examination system has been developed for both collegiate and precollegiate levels, a unified set of standard textbooks is being written, foreign technology and techniques will be introduced in greater quantities, and science and technology will be popularized in the society at large through a variety of nonformal educational activities. All these activities are designed to regear Chinese education to fit the needs of a rapidly expanding industrial and agricultural sector better.

Problems still remain, however, primarily in the area of administration. The Chinese admit that administratively there remain many ineffective and inefficient mechanisms for translating policy into practice. The vast population and complexity of the country render educational administration a most difficult task. It is likely that in the future we will see reforms in this area as well. In short, education in China for the past thirty years has been uneven, disrupted by periodic campaigns, and subjected to several reorganizations. Yet, we can say that progress has been impressive. It is clear that the Chinese leadership is thoroughly committed to providing both quality and quantity education. The problems that remain will surely focus on the expanding population, the consequent pressure for universal education, and the needs of industry and agriculture. Given the past experience of the Chinese in all of these matters and the high level of motivation evident in the nation as a whole, the future in education for the Chinese should be encouraging.

---

[4]These figures are estimates only, based on projections made by Chinese educators interviewed in 1971.

REFERENCES

Ayers, W. *Chang Chih-tung and Educational Reform in China*. Cambridge: Harvard University Press, 1971.

Biggerstaff, K. *The Earliest Modern Government Schools in China*. New York: Cornell University Press, 1961.

Chu, W. P. "Why Are University Students Tense?" *People's Education* 11 (1956): 12–23.

deBarry, T., Chan, W. T., and Watson, B. (eds.). *Sources of Chinese Tradition*. New York: Columbia University Press, 1960.

Dow, T. I. "Neo-Confucian Philosophical Systems and Mao's Theory of Multiple Contradictions." Rockhill, S.C.: Association of Asian Studies, 1971.

Fairbank, J. K. "The Nature of Chinese Society," in *Imperial China*, ed. F. Schurmann and O. Schell. New York: Vintage Press, 1967.

Fraser, S. *Education and Communism in China*. London: Pall Mall Press, 1971.

———, and Hawkins, J. "Chinese Education: Revolution and Development," *Phi Delta Kappan* 8 (1972): 487–500.

Gamberg, R. *Red and Expert: Education in the People's Republic of China*. New York: Schocken Books, 1977.

Hawkins, J. "Deschooling Society Chinese Style: Alternative Forms of Nonformal Education," *Educational Studies* 3 (1973): 116.

———. *Mao Tse-tung and Education: His Thoughts and Teachings*. Hamden, Conn.: The Shoe String Press, 1974

———. "Family Planning Education and Health Care Delivery in the People's Republic of China: Implications for Educational Alternatives," *Comparative Education Review* 2 (1976): 151–164.

———. "Minority Education in the People's Republic of China," *Comparative Education Review* 1 (1978): 1–25. (a)

———. "Rural Education and Technique Transformation in the People's Republic of China," *Technological Forecasting and Social Change* 12 (1978): 209–227. (b)

Ho. P. T., and Tang Tsou. *China in Crisis: China's Heritage and the Communist Political Tradition*. Chicago: University of Chicago Press, 1968.

Hu, C. T. *Chinese Communist Education*. New York: Columbia University Press, 1967.

Levenson, J. R. *Modern China and Its Confucian Past*. New York: Doubleday Anchor Books, 1964.

Loewe, M. *Imperial China: The Historical Background to the Modern Age*. New York: Praeger, 1965.

Mao T. T. "The Chinese Revolution and the Chinese Communist Party." *Selected Works of Mao Tse-tung*, vol. 2. Peking: Foreign Languages Press, 1965. (a)

———. "On Contradiction," in *Selected Works of Mao Tse-tung*, vol. 1. Peking: Foreign Languages Press, 1965. (b)

———. *Speech at the Chinese Communist Party's National Conference on Propaganda Work*. Peking: Foreign Languages Press, 1966. (a)

———. "Under the Red Flag of Mao Tse-tung," *Chinese Education* 3, No. 44 (1966). (b)

———. "Resolution of the Ninth Congress of the Fourth Army of the Red Army of the Communist Party of China," Current Background 2 (1969): 888.

———. "A Study of Physical Education," in The Political Thought of Mao Tse-tung, ed. S. R. Schram. New York: Praeger, 1970. (a)

———. "Re-educating Young People," in Mao Papers: Anthology and Bibliography, ed. J. Ch'en. London: Oxford University Press, 1970. (b)

McAleavy, H. The Modern History of China. New York: Praeger, 1967.

Peake, C. Nationalism and Education in Modern China. New York: Columbia University Press, 1932.

Peking Review 2 (1978): 14–17.

People's Daily, August 29, 1977.

Price, R. Education in Communist China. New York: Praeger, 1970.

Scanlon, D. International Education: A Documentary History. New York: Columbia University Press, 1967.

Sieh, M. "The School Teacher—Notes on Professional Tensions in the Education System," in Education and Communism in China, ed. S. Fraser. London: Pall Mall Press, 1971.

Tsang, C. S. Society, Schools and Progress in China. New York: Pergamon Press, 1968.

Walls, P., Walls, L., and Langsley, D. "Psychiatric Training and Practice in the People's Republic of China," American Journal of Psychiatry 2 (1975): 121–128.

Wang, Y. C. Chinese Intellectuals and the West: 1872–1949. Chapel Hill, N.C.: The University of North Carolina Press, 1966.

Whyte, M. K. Small Groups and Political Rituals in China. Berkeley: University of California Press, 1974.

Wilbert, J. Enculturation in Latin America: An Anthology. Los Angeles: UCLA Latin American Center Publications, 1976.

Yang, C. K. Chinese Communist Society: The Family and the Village. Cambridge: The MIT Press, 1959.

Yuan Ting. People's Daily, March 31, 1977.

CHAPTER 4

# English Education

PHILIP H. TAYLOR
ROY LOWE

## DEFINITION

English education comprises primary education, taking children from infancy to age eleven, secondary education (eleven to eighteen), although compulsory education terminates at sixteen, further, higher, and adult education. Further education involves a wide range of both vocational and nonvocational work undertaken outside the university sector. Higher education is taken to mean work of degree level taking place within universities, in polytechnics, and a variety of other colleges. The old distinction between university and nonuniversity work is thus now blurred as many nonuniversity institutions offer work of degree level. Similarly, in practice, there are constant modifications to these general categories: for example, the recent appearance in some areas of middle schools (ages nine to thirteen) threatens the distinction between primary and secondary education.

This system is administered centrally by the Department of Education and Science (D.E.S.), which formulates policy and works through 105 Local Education Authorities (L.E.A.'s). They are responsible for the day-to-day conduct of education in their localities.

This state-provided educational system is matched by an independent sector catering to some 7 percent of the school population. These fee-paying schools are subject to D.E.S. inspection and those considered efficient are given recognized status. The most prestigious secondary schools in this category are members of the Headmasters' Conference and are known as public schools. - Index - See collaty schools

English education is thus characterized by a wide variety of styles at every level, and in this chapter an attempt will be made to elucidate some of these contrasts and differences (1).

## INTRODUCTION

### Objectives of Education

An educational system serves a wide variety of objectives, which may differ from time to time. But while social and economic change may impose stresses upon this system, it is possible to discern a variety of unchanging goals.

Education is the process by which individuals are prepared to play an effective role in the life of their society. At a functional level this involves the transmission of a range of basic skills and abilities without which the individual cannot achieve economic independence and cannot fully participate in the daily life of the society. These basic skills may vary according to the degree of economic development of a particular society or the nature of its technology, although there is some evidence that, of late, in highly developed Western societies, the esteem in which the skills of literacy and computation have been traditionally held may be eroded by the availability of a wide range of technological aids, by the sudden growth of the mass media, and by the coming of general affluence weakening the exclusive position of professions to which access is at least in part dependent on a "literary" education.

A second task of education is the imparting of attitudes and knowledge that will enable the individual to contribute to and participate in the social and political life of the society. Here, too, there will be a wide divergence, in theory at least, between those states with traditions of political deference and those that are participant democracies, although it is significant that all industrialized societies claim some degree of democratic involvement for their citizens, and all are hesitant to condone educational departures that may seem likely to lead to radical political and social change. Education under this head will involve an awareness of political and social forms and structure and will almost certainly involve the transmission of a set of attitudes toward the structure of society. This is often, in practice, done implicitly through the structure and content of the curriculum, rather than explicitly. In this area, educators will also make very significant judgments on their approach to the qualities of discrimination, critical self-awareness, and the ability to make independent decisions. One characteristic of economically developed societies is the emphasis placed upon these educational objectives.

A further goal of any educational system is to enhance individual opportunity for creative self-expression through the arts, literature, and sport. As the amount of available leisure time increases with economic development, this function of education assumes increasing significance.

In all these areas educators are confronted by a sharp choice in determining their objectives. On the one hand there are those who emphasize the role of education in sustaining a learned elite to maintain the cultural and scientific achievements of society. Extreme advocates of this view, such as Eliot (2) and James, (3) have emphasized the need for some selective element within a system providing universal primary and secondary education. Conversely, others such as Jackson (4) have dismissed these justifications as archaic props that have been used to reinforce the position of a governing elite. The alternative view, that a prime objective of education is to stimulate the wide variety of human talents and skills, has led to the rejection, to a greater or lesser degree, of the selective function of education, arguing that social and community adjustments are best fostered in nonselective environments.

## Reasons for This System

At first glance the underlying reasons for the structure of the English system and its practices may appear to be historical, and it is certainly true that some features, such as the widespread retention of school uniforms, seem fully comprehensible only in the light of tradition. But, in reality, almost every aspect of English education represents a response to twentieth-century needs and to contemporary social structures, although the precise form adopted may at times smack of an earlier period.

Evidence for the value of the English system is its durability and its capacity for adaptation to changing circumstances: each sector of the system has undergone significant modifications.

The primary sector, catering to children below the age of twelve, has evolved from the earlier system of elementary schools, and although the 1944 Education Act finally clarified that primary education was to be available for younger children, many characteristics survive from the period when elementary education was intended for the working poor. So, the tradition that the majority of the primary sector teaching force are female, and that they are college-trained rather than graduate entrants to the profession, has been eroded but by no means overthrown. Similarly, the scarcity of funds available to finance elementary schools resulted in a tacit acceptance that less space per child should be available and that class size was larger than in the secondary sector. For this reason the staffing ratio in maintained primary education remains roughly one to twenty-five and that in secondary schools one to seventeen; while only 1 percent of secondary school pupils are taught in classes of over thirty, 45 percent of all primary school pupils are in groups of this size (5). These disparities have a considerable impact upon the power of the teaching staff to modify or vary their teaching methods greatly. Nonetheless, postwar demands for a growing emphasis upon understanding and the importance of experience have led to considerable augmentation of primary curricula, with greater emphasis being placed now than ever before upon affective elements and upon aesthetic experience.

While the wish to promote a fairer and more egalitarian system underlay the introduction of comprehensive secondary education during the postwar period, some protagonists argued that the continued existence of streaming within schools of whatever type presented a further block (5). The past ten years have seen, therefore, not only the widespread implementation of comprehensive education, but within it, a continuing shift toward unstreamed and mixed-ability teaching situations, on the grounds that this allows for freer social mixing and militates against the propagation of social-class-oriented attitudes.

Recent developments in examining have also been geared toward promoting a fairer system. The preexisting General Certificate in Education, administered by several independent but generally recognized examining boards, has been complemented by a newer Certificate in Secondary Education. Although for some years these two were conducted entirely independently, the examining authorities have moved closer together by accepting the highest grade of C.S.E. pass for G.C.E. purposes, and also by conducting a series of experiments toward a sixteen-plus examination applicable across a wider ability range. Beyond this, there has been a shift toward the introduction of continuous assessment at all levels of examining, and some restructuring of syllabuses to accommodate recent academic developments and to encourage the heuristic element in the school curriculum. In this way, what began as a series of scholarship tests for university entry has widened into a national examining system whose credentials are recognized for entry to a wide range of professions and trades. This aspect of the system is justified, therefore, on the grounds that it offers social mobility.

While egalitarian arguments are adduced to justify recent developments in the maintained sector of secondary education, a major justification that is proposed for the continuance of the large private sector is that it offers freedom of choice to parents and a variety of routes through the secondary stage of education. This private sector has grown in recent years, despite its high costs, as some direct-grant schools have claimed independent status rather than conform to comprehensive reorganization schemes. One of the ironies of English education is that governmental attempts to foster a more egalitarian system have resulted in the growth of the private sector.

Within higher education, the justification that a variety of styles is needed to meet the demands of a complex society is frequently adduced. A series of gradual additions to the preexisting university sector had already done much to redefine the concept of a university when Anthony Crosland as secretary of state for education formally committed the government in 1965 to promoting a binary system of higher education. "I feel clear that side by side with an autonomous sector of higher education we must also have a public or social sector" (6). In direct consequence of this policy, there now exist thirty polytechnics, L.E.A.-controlled, awarding degrees validated by the C.N.A.A., alongside the preexisting university system which had already been complicated by the appearance of new and technological universities during the period after World War II.

The "new universities" of the 1950s and 1960s had sought to establish novel curricula, geared particularly to combating that specialism and isolation of studies that were growing features of university life. Similarly, the postwar drive to train a greater number of scientists and technologists initiated by the Percy (7) and Barlow (8) reports was sustained by the promotion of a few colleges of technology, first redesignated colleges of advanced technology and subsequently recognized as technological universities. Further, the growing demand for adult education which existing extramural departments and the Workers' Education Association were finding increasingly difficult to satisfy was met by the establishment in 1969 of an open university, using television broadcasts as one of its major teaching outlets. So fierce has been competition for places that the open university quickly came to belie its name, although it did provide a significant new route for the prospective graduate. Finally, the recognition of work done in teacher training colleges as being of degree standard led to the introduction of B.Ed. degrees awarded either by nearby universities or the C.N.A.A. to students working in colleges of education (9).

This complex and overlapping structure is justified on the grounds that it is responsive to changes in demand and to modifications in government policy, while at the same time offering sufficient variety to enable genuine choice for the entrant to higher education. The appearance of new validating authorities, such as the Council for National Academic Awards, has also enabled an unprecedented degree of curricular innovation. The problem now confronting the universities stems from their success. The 1963 Robbins Report (10) advocated that an appropriate higher education should be available to all capable of benefiting from it. In an age of growing affluence and with universal secondary education recently achieved, developments such as those described here were inevitable if this objective was to be met. Yet this relatively recent system now finds itself confronted by a declining birthrate and a growing hesitancy among the young to commit themselves to degree courses; further restructuring now appears inevitable.

The administration of this system by central and local agencies acting in concert, is justified on the grounds that it ensures responsiveness both to local needs and peculiarities, and to governmental policies. In practice many new initiatives are pioneered locally before becoming incorporated into national policy—middle school education, comprehensive reorganization and, at an earlier date, the introduction of medical and welfare facilities are all examples of this process. The system claims, too, through agencies such as governing bodies of individual schools, to allow scope for local pressure groups and political interests to make themselves felt. The existence of various advisory bodies—of differing degrees of autonomy—is also intended to ensure the responsiveness of the system. The governmental inspectorate, answerable to Whitehall, is matched by L.E.A. advisers and inspectors who concern themselves more closely with the day-to-day running of schools in their areas. The Schools Council, although in receipt of governmental funds, is intended to conduct independent research into aspects of the curriculum and has formulated several external examination schemes designed to foster curricular developments (11).

Supporters would defend this complex system on the ground that it shows capacity for gradual change, for the assimilation of new ideas and concepts whilst preserving many of its central characteristics through time. Critics would see the system as evidence of a heavily class-based society whose structure is reflected in its adherence to a varied educational system in which differing elements are afforded widely different prestige and facilities.

## HISTORY

### Beginnings

During the first Industrial Revolution in England two separate systems of education coexisted and developed largely independently of each other. On the one hand, elementary education was provided by a number of voluntary organizations and catered in the main to the working poor. Secondary education was offered in the endowed grammar schools to members of the middle and upper classes and was oriented from an early date toward the professions. This central fact of English education did much to predetermine the nature of the relationship between elementary and secondary education when the two were eventually fused into a single system (12).

For much of the eighteenth century elementary education was offered by the Society for the Diffusion of Useful Knowledge in Charity Schools, or else in dame schools, which were usually little more than private child-minding ventures. Toward the end of the century the Sunday school movement, heavily influenced by the Evangelicals within the church, proffered the rudiments of learning, as a prerequisite to the salvation of souls, thought to depend in part upon an ability to read the Bible.

Confronted by the sudden growth of population at the end of the century and the consequent appearance of vast urban societies, none of these organizations proved capable of meeting the growing demand for education. This demand arose more from the upper classes, who feared the implications of a refractory, uncivilized urban proletariat, than from the demands of industry. Most of the new textile factories required an unskilled labor force and in fact drew children away from schooling prematurely.

Two voluntary organizations, the British and Foreign Society and the National Society (the latter sponsored by the Anglican church) accepted the eighteenth-century precedent of a relatively restricted curriculum within the elementary school and set about the provision of schooling. But their activities were sharpened by a fierce controversy over the kind of religious teaching to be proffered, nonsectarian or Anglican. This dispute, initiated by Sarah Trimmer in 1808, drew many Anglicans away from involvement in the rival organization, persisted throughout the nineteenth century, and helps to explain the preeminent position of the Anglican church, through the National Society, as a provider of education. The introduction of monitorial teaching methods, using able children to replicate the teaching, was cheap, enabled a quick growth of these schools, and ensured a minimal curriculum, with emphasis upon reading, writing, and arithmetic.

As the "urban crisis" of the nineteenth century developed, parliamentarians became increasingly concerned with the education issue. Through monetary support, commenced in 1833, and from 1841 a system of inspection, central government became increasingly drawn into the working of these voluntary societies. Meanwhile, the appearance from 1846 of pupil teachers provided a subtle transmutation of the monitorial system that was to persist and to influence the work of schools throughout the nineteenth century. Despite Robert Lowe's attempts in the early 1860s to control the teaching of these voluntary societies from without, it became increasingly clear that this indirect government expenditure was failing to provide a sufficiently widespread system. Accordingly in 1870, although the voluntary societies were permitted to continue, W. E. Forster made possible the establishment of local boards, a popular Victorian device, to supervise the provision of the first state elementary schools. This initiated the dual system by which board schools and voluntary schools coexisted. The school boards, with the power to raise funds through local rates (taxes), quickly found themselves in an advantageous position. Their schools were larger and better equipped, their staff better paid, and they were even able, through higher grade schools, to offer a scientific training to older children. So the elementary school system went some way toward meeting the demand for technical training during the 1880s and 1890s, a period of swift growth in the engineering and chemical industries.

Balfour's Conservative administration, largely representative of Anglican interests, made it possible in 1902 for church schools to receive aid from the rates, and also for the first time empowered the new local education authorities (which had replaced the school boards) to provide secondary education. This had two important implications: it allowed the dual system to persist into the twentieth century, with a diminished contrast between the style and workings of state and voluntary schools, and it also removed from the elementary schools the need for a vocational bias. In consequence, while for most of the twentieth-century secondary schools have been tied to the demands of external examinations, elementary (or more recently primary) schools have been freer to develop curricula with the immediate developmental needs of their pupils in view. Their major constraint has been the elementary school regulations, which imposed poor staffing ratios and tight cash restraints.

Not until 1944 was this elementary sector finally transmuted into the primary stage of education and secondary education made universal. So, just as in the late nineteenth century the higher grade schools had provided opportunities for children from within the elementary sector which the grammar schools could or would not, the interwar years saw the appearance of modern schools for older pupils, but run under the elementary school regulations. This attempt to implement the 1926 Hadow proposal for a break at eleven-plus led to the establishment of many schools of low prestige. Their existence was to be of immense significance after 1944 when they were redesignated secondary modern schools in selective systems (13).

Secondary education underwent similar stresses during the period after industrialization and made its own separate responses. The early nineteenth century found many grammar schools in a run-down state, committed to traditional curricula, often oriented around the classical languages as intended by their sixteenth-century founders. The Eldon judgment of 1805 expressly forbade Leeds Grammar School to flout its original statutes by offering a "modern" curriculum and was widely seen as a test case. It was left to the major enquiries of the mid-nineteenth century under Lord Clarendon and Lord Taunton to emphasize how little these schools had responded to the changing demands of industrial society. Taunton's Schools Enquiry Commission laid down a blueprint for the working of these schools, which was to be widely followed. It called for three grades of secondary education, of differing lengths, to meet the needs of the three major social groups likely to send their children to secondary schools. A year later in 1869, the Endowed Schools Act established commissioners with powers to refurbish the statutes of these secondary schools. By the beginning of the twentieth century over a thousand schools had been reorganized. Many had moved to new premises, and in numerous instances attempts were made to establish "classical" or first-grade schools, or "modern" schools, with an emphasis on science and modern languages, to meet the intentions of the Taunton Commissioners (14).

However, the early twentieth century saw something of a reaction against the growing "scientism" of these schools, many of which had been forced during the 1890s into competition with the scientifically oriented higher grade schools. A fear that the professions would be understaffed, together with a reassertion of the values of the "traditional" grammar school curriculum, led Robert Morant, as first permanent secretary of the newly established Board of Education to seek to impose a broad, generalized curriculum on all secondary schools. His 1904 regulations spelled out the amount of time to be spent on each subject in the curriculum in any school qualifying for grant, and although in force for only three years, did much to stereotype the twentieth-century curriculum.

Further pressures worked to intensify this uniformity. New municipal secondary schools sought to confirm their status by initiating more prestigious neighbor schools. The universities, which slowly began to recruit more widely, looked for a broad general education in their entrants. This was confirmed by the introduction in 1917 of the School Certificate, the first generally accepted matriculation examination, which required passes in a wage range of subjects.

The existence of the major public schools was of significance, too. As a state system of secondary schools developed, it took on many of the features of this highly prestigious private sector. So school uniforms, the practice of using senior pupils as "prefects," and the introduction of a "house" system (derived originally from boarding schools but now applied to day schools), as well as an emphasis upon team games, all became important features of secondary school life.

Although the 1944 act, which introduced universal secondary schooling, did not specify an appropriate curriculum for secondary schools, most local authorities responded to it with a bipartite system, which supplemented existing grammar schools with secondary modern schools for less able pupils. This device enabled the more prestigious grammar schools to continue with little if any modification to their curricula, while the secondary moderns, although committed in theory to a more heavily practical bias to cater to less able children, often became pale imitations of the grammar schools. This tendency grew during the 1950s and 1960s as more secondary modern pupils were presented for external examinations. The new G.C.E. examinations were by their nature open to a wider clientele, since entry was for the first time on a subject-by-subject basis.

It was against this background of a highly stratified system of secondary schools that the newly elected Labour administration set in motion in 1965 the process of "comprehensivization." Previously, a few L.E.A.'s had experimented with reorganization schemes; now with the seal of governmental approval, the comprehensive movement gathered pace (15).

Similarly, the university sector has seen a series of accretions over many years to already established institutions. The onset of industrialization found the universities of Cambridge and Oxford quite unprepared to meet the new demands for higher education. These were met initially by dissenting academies, later by mechanics institutes (which appeared in most of the nascent factory towns during the 1820s), and eventually by new foundations. Durham, University College, and Kings in London —the three early nineteenth-century universities, still left a need for the "redbrick" colleges of the 1880s and 1890s which were set up in the major conurbations of the north and were far more closely linked to local industry than any earlier university establishments. The burgeoning demand forced even greater proliferation. With the appearance in 1903 of the Workers Educational Association and the establishment of technical colleges, a varied structure of further and higher education developed, only to be rendered even more complex by the postwar developments already outlined. So, a complex and swiftly changing system of higher education evolved to meet changing needs. Yet throughout this, a peculiarly English concept of a university as a center for both research and teaching, with its own leisured life-style, persisted (16).

This capacity to absorb change without finally eroding its central characteristics has been the hallmark of education in England during the period since the Industrial Revolution.

## Current Status

These historical antecedents have done much to determine the current status of English education. At the primary level the disparities between voluntary and state schools have long since been ironed out, with both now under L.E.A. control. There remain, though, wide differences in buildings, equipment, and staffing between old "inner-ring" schools and those serving new, middle-class housing estates on the fringes of large towns. These contrasts were officially recognized by the 1967 Plowden Report, whose central recommendation, for the establishment of educational priority areas, led to a major initiative (17). Despite governmental attempts to redress these inequalities through a policy of positive discrimination, there remain wide differences in prestige between primary schools in differing areas.

Against this background the primary sector remains, as a whole, less well resourced than the secondary, which itself continues to contain wide disparities. At one extreme the public schools continue to impose high fees and to retain close links with the universities, a disproportionate number of their products gaining entry to Oxford and Cambridge. A few direct-grant day schools in the larger cities rival them in prestige and lay claim to being more genuinely meritocratic by accepting able pupils from poor homes. This claim has been weakened in the past few years as several of these schools have sought independent status in response to governmental attempts to end the direct-grant arrangements by which these schools are financed from central government rather than through the local authorities. In some towns, where comprehensive reorganization has not been rigorously applied, local grammar schools survive, with L.E.A. support. They remain prestigious, and entry to them is keenly sought, but their continued existence is opposed by supporters of comprehensive education. The comprehensive schools vary so widely as to defy neat analysis. Some reorganized selective schools appear to be attempts to impose the "grammar school ethos" upon a comprehensive situation. At the other extreme, some inner-ring comprehensives qualify as E.P.A. schools and inherit the effects of a wide range of social problems. The prestige and effectiveness of a comprehensive school is dependent upon many factors—its location, staffing policy, decisions on streaming, the size of the school, and the nature of its catchment area appear among the most significant (18).

Within higher education, the prestige of the traditional universities remains little eroded despite attempts to modernize and diversify the system through the introduction of polytechnics. Their achievement has been to open up a genuine alternative with curricula that in some disciplines involve novel components. Unfortunately, politically motivated discussions of staffing ratios and cost effectiveness, as well as differing salary structures, have done much during recent years to polarize these two sectors of higher education.

While English education has made a vigorous response to the changing demands of postwar years, it remains highly structured and still exhibits a strong sense of social class. In this way it offers a fair reflection of English society as it approaches the last third of the century.

## THEORY

### Learning

English educators are very practical people. In most respects they eschew theory. Education is something to be practiced, not theorized about. If any theory has informed English education, it is the eclectic theory of the practitioner drawn in part from practical experience and in part from commonsense philosophy. In this situation what learning is, how it takes place, and what it results in is not made explicit.

In English education, learning theory is not used overtly to justify decision and assertions about the system, although it may be implicit. Learning theory does not lead. It follows. A classic instance of learning theory being used to this end is to be found in the Hadow Report of 1926 (19). This report, undertaken on behalf of the government of the day, was empowered:

> to consider and report upon the organisation, objective and curriculum of courses of study suitable for children who will remain in full-time attendance at schools, other than Secondary Schools, up to the age of 15, regard being had on the one hand to the requirements of a good general education and the desirability of providing a reasonable variety of curriculum, so far as is practicable, for children of varying tastes and abilities, and on the other to the probable occupations of the pupils in commerce, industry and agriculture.

This report was widely approved and set the seal on the structure of the system that remains in being in some parts of the country to this day. One of its main conclusions was:

> A humane or liberal education is not one given through books alone, but one which brings children into contact with the larger interests of mankind; and the aims of the schools . . . should be to provide such an education by means of a curriculum containing large opportunities for practical work and related to living interests . . . (p. 84).

The theory of learning implicit in this conclusion is that some students learn better by using their hands rather than their heads; that learning from the abstraction of books is different in kind from learning from the realities of everyday interests. One is seen as bookish abstract and theoretical; the other as direct and concrete. In its extreme form this view led to the Norwood Report (20) on curriculum and examinations which went so far as to identify different types of children. It was on such assumptions about learning that secondary education has until recently been based.

With the development of comprehensive education a more egalitarian idea of learning has developed, which assumes that all students learn both from using their heads *and* their hands, from the concrete and from the abstract; that they do not neatly fall into academic and nonacademic categories, and that if they demonstrate difficulties in learning abstract ideas, the reason may lie more in cultural deprivation, particularly language deficit, than in natural attributes.

However, the idea that students may be categorized in terms of one or another mode of learning still persists and informs many educational decisions, routing secondary school students into academic or vocational courses.

However, English secondary schools remain dominated by the teaching of subjects and by examinations, neither of which is informed by any but the most rudimentary theories of learning. Interest is seen as the main motivator, and a balance of reward and punishment as the means of controlling the setting for learning. Reward is related to work well done, punishment to behavior disruptive of the learning setting.

There have been few studies of learning at the secondary school stage. The most noteworthy have been those pioneered by Peel and his students (21). Peel has attempted to show that each subject contains its own conceptual logic, which has to be understood if the subject is to be learned. Each subject offers a different way of apprehending an aspect of reality and incorporates a particular test of truth. Learning how to apply these tests is part of learning the subject. In many instances the test of truth is a matter of making appropriate judgments. How such judgments are developed in adolescents has been the object of much of Peel's work. He has shown, for example, that judgment in history depends very much on the range of concrete experience of historical instances open to the student. Maturity of historical judgment comes with breadth of exposure to the instances of history. Such a view of learning has considerable appeal to *teachers of subjects* who see what they teach as offering a unique perspective on human experience or on the human condition.

There have been some recent moves to integrate subjects, to cross subject boundaries and, in consequence, new models of learning have been proffered in justification. These models emphasize the role of the student as the active agent of his own learning rather than as the passive recipient of opinions.

However, moves toward integrating subjects have not progressed far nor have new models of learning proliferated, though there are notable exceptions. The Schools Council Integrated Science Project (S.C.I.S.P.) has employed a variation of learning through concept formation as a basis for understanding science (22). The teaching materials are organized around key scientific concepts. Here the work of Gagne and other learning theorists has had an influence (23).

Certainly the work of Bloom and his co-workers on educational objectives and mastery of learning has had an effect on thinking about subjects in the secondary school curriculum (24). But, as Holley has shown, the aims of different subjects are so disparate as, at most, to call for different models of learning to implement them (25).

A large majority of secondary school teachers believe that learning is a naturally occurring process stimulated by interest and dependent for its level on general intelligence. They see virtues in materials that make learning easy and in teaching techniques that reinforce learning. In the last analysis, however, they believe that it is what the student brings to the learning situation that counts. They are also convinced that learning is situation specific, transferable only to a limited degree.

Comprehensive education is forcing them to seek new ways to bring the learning of complex ideas in science, mathematics, and the humanities to students in the lower ability range, with what success is as yet too early to say. Equally on what models of learning teachers are depending is as yet obscure. As was earlier asserted, practice follows theory, here as elsewhere in English education. However, there is some indication that there are two psychological strands toward which teachers are turning for beliefs about the best way to cultivate learning: the psychology of human potential, the self-actualization theories of psychologists such as Maslow, and to the latest manifestations of the behaviorist psychologists, behavior modifications (26, 27). Which will be the most potent source of relevant models is as yet not possible to say.

Learning in the primary school has been influenced by the findings of psychologists to a far greater extent than the secondary school. In recent years the views of child psychologists that *learning is an active process* motivated by *interest* has been especially influential. So has the biopsychology of Piaget in which later learning is seen as depending upon earlier concrete experience which, through the processes of accommodation and assimilation, is incorporated in the individual child's perceptions to provide an increasingly exact schema of reality (28). In this way the child's awareness of the world and understanding of concepts grows and develops. Crucial to this process of learning is the provision of concrete experience that is relevant to each individual child's level of learning.

Taken together these two views of learning have led to the idea that learning in young children is likely to be best fostered by an approach that focuses on the individual child, on his interests and achieved level of learning. Such a theory of learning has lent itself to the development of *open education*.

However, as the work of Bennett suggests, these views of learning are not necessarily widespread in English primary education, though they do inform what some authorities consider to be the best practices. Simpler theories based on the virtues of conditioning and reinforcement are still widespread (29). Drill, the repetition of learning supported by a system of rewards,is still commonly found in primary schools, though not in quite the regimented and rigid form of earlier days.

There are areas of learning in the primary school where theories of learning compete and conflict. A notable one is in the field of reading where look-and-say has competed for some years with a phonic approach, and where the information theory of Smith is making some impact (30). Perceptual psychology has offered some insights, and so has cognitive psychology, but there is no clear model on which teachers of young children may rely. The result is that they depend on a common-sense theory of learning which, because of its inadequate empirical basis may lead to misleading conclusions about how learning to read takes place.

As English primary education remolds itself to accommodate changed child-rearing practices and changing social values, there is a real danger that psychological theories of learning that are being derived more and more from sophisticated mathematical modeling techniques, will be seen by teachers to fit less and less the human bustle of the average primary school classroom and teachers will more and more be forced back to the raw empiricism of direct experience from which to draw their beliefs about how young children learn. Piagetian psychology has been a bulwark against this danger for more than two decades, at least in some of its elements. How long it will remain so is problematic,especially with the powerful social pressure for increased scholastic performance and higher standards.

Learning in higher education, at university and college, is considered to be the responsibility of the student as is motivation. Most university and college teachers assume that students possess sufficient ability to learn for themselves, to work out their own methods of understanding and applying ideas, to seek to remedy deficiencies in their knowledge and to commit to memory essential facts and key principles. This assumption about learning is matched by a comparable assumption about motivation: students are at college and university because they want to be, and this wish entails that they are ready and willing to exert the necessary effort to learn what university and college have to teach.

The assumptions held by the teaching staff about student learning and motivation are reinforced by the beliefs about the nature of the institutions in which learning takes place: free associations or communities of scholars. Students, like staff, in such a community should be free to learn and enquire in whatever way they see fit as self-motivated individuals.

Some rudimentary support for student learning is, however, provided. Many university and college teachers supply notes of guidance to their lectures and guided reading lists. Small-group situations provide a context for the reinforcement of student learning as do essay assignments. Less formal settings in which students gather provide for informal learning. Even so, and even with the advent of self-tuitional systems such as computer-assisted learning, students in English higher education are very self-dependent learners.

However, there is some evidence that the assumptions held for so long about student learning may be undergoing some modification. Many institutions of higher education are showing an interest in improving students' study skills. Booklets or pamphlets on how to study or how to get a degree are made available to students, and sessions on study skills provided. In addition specially constructed learning programs have been and are being developed to provide support in essential areas of student learning. For example, in some science and service subjects, such as computer studies, interface programs using specially constructed materials are being used to ensure that all students possess a minimum of basic knowledge.

One of the major forces in promoting a reassessment of the assumptions about student learning is the work of the Open University. Here student learning is from materials received by post, from radio and television, and occasional meetings with counselors. A great deal of ingenuity has gone into the structure of the materials and into the design of the exercises associated with them. Learning at a distance calls for a view of how learning takes place that depends on rapid feedback from the quick return of assessed student assignments, on strong personal motivation, and on the reinforcement that comes from meetings with a counselor and from one or two residential periods during which the commonly shared travail of undergoing a common and difficult experience gives rise to strengthened resolve to win through. No doubt there is a personality-method interaction element in such a model of learning. Nevertheless, it would appear to work on a sufficiently large and heterogeneous population of students to suggest a certain robust quality. Whether it would work with other than adult students is yet to be explored.

## Teaching

English education is currently undergoing a sharp reappraisal. The *Great Debate* initiated by the prime minister in a speech at Ruskin College, Oxford, in the autumn of 1976 has reached beyond the obvious issues of standards of literacy and computation to those of the social and economic relevance of much that is taught in schools and the participation of parents in the management of education; it has extended to questions of teaching methods, discipline in schools, ability grouping, accountability, and curriculum content (31). Predictably, much of the debate has become polarized, especially over which method of teaching is best, traditional or progressive, formal or informal. Grouping as an issue has received much the same treatment. The battle is joined between those who are convinced that streaming or setting in terms of ability is preferable to mixed-ability grouping.

Not only have issues been raised concerning how schools and teaching should be managed but also issues concerning the system itself, its *raison d'être*. At the extreme are questions of the relationship between the school system and the free enterprise, capitalist society that created and maintains it. Less extreme, though possibly as far-reaching, are the "free" schoolers who challenge the assumptions on which much teaching is based, that without "authority" schools would become anarchic and unmanageable.

It is in the awareness of the continuing debate about English education that we should explore what teaching, including class management, organization, and structure means at each stage in the system, from primary school to college and university.

When one examines teaching in most English primary schools, a clear distinction can be seen between the earlier, or infant stage (five to seven years) and the later, junior stage (eight to eleven years). The distinction is informality. At the infant stage much of the work is individual and informal, with teaching more the process of guiding than telling. There will be some class activities, listening to stories, talking about the day's happenings, or celebrating a birthday. In the main, however, work will be assigned on an individual basis with the teacher carefully recording a child's progress, especially in number and language work.

Much of the work will be geared to the individual child's level of readiness and the atmosphere of the classroom will be one of varied, purposeful activities. It will also be supportive and encouraging with children free to bring both pedagogic and personal problems to the teacher.

In general terms the theory that informs teaching at the infant stage of education is child-centered, rooted in the belief that effective teaching depends on the teacher's ability to recognize when a child is ready for the next step in learning, and grounded in the belief that the child's own interests and curiosity are the only motivating force of any consequence. There is also the acceptance of the need for a supportive, threat-free atmosphere, in which the child may make mistakes without damage to his drive to explore his educational environment and undertake experiments in learning.

Under such a theory of teaching, the role of the teacher is that of the manager of individual learning and the creator of a setting that will be supportive of that learning at an optimal level. Within this generalized role there is much that is founded in common sense and experience. Technical theories of teaching play little part. It is essentially a human and humane enterprise.

Teaching at the junior stage becomes less informal and more didactic, sharply so in some schools. Even so, a degree of freedom to learn remains with the child especially in project work where the children may explore different aspects of a topic or a theme. Life in a medieval manor or trees in nature, prose, and poetry provide opportunities for individual work. However, more teaching will be on a class basis and be formally structured.

With a move away from more informal methods of teaching at the junior stage there is a change in the reward and control structure of the classroom. Teachers require more class work to be completed on time and reward this work less in terms of individual effort and enterprise and more in terms of external criteria of correctness. Discipline is also more in evidence. The classroom is becoming less a personal and more a public place. Even so, learning will still be an active process, and the teacher's role that of managing a stimulating educational environment in a consciously considerate milieu.

In open-plan schools where there are work and teaching areas and no classrooms, and in those schools with classrooms which have developed a variant of open education, the distinction between the styles of teaching at the infant and junior stages no longer applies. The basic assumptions about teaching are informed throughout such schools by a child-centered, child-motivated approach.

Traditionally teaching in English secondary schools has been markedly didactic, the teacher telling, transmitting information, and gearing much learning to the textbook. Class control has been based on the authority of the teacher. Students have been expected to know their place.

Today with the development of the comprehensive secondary school the picture is much less clear. Much traditional teaching remains but is being replaced by new approaches to teaching especially in those schools in which there is mixed-ability grouping and where remedial departments have been established to provide for adolescents with learning difficulties.

Mixed-ability teaching represents an attempt to take the principle of comprehensive education one stage further, especially that aspect of it which is concerned with optimizing equality of educational opportunity, by individualizing instruction. With the mixed-ability group in the comprehensive school, teaching must not only attempt to make subject matter accessible to every student irrespective of ability but also motivate each student to learn.

To these fundamental tasks teaching in an increasing number of comprehensive schools addresses itself. Part of the answer is for the teacher to break down the learning tasks into small units using individualized schemes of work that are to some extent self-instructional and to cater for the interests of the students. Part of the answer is to allow for greater student involvement in learning by increasing the amount of student participation through discussion and group work and by thematic approaches to subject matter. The degree to which teaching becomes focused on student interests and participation varies from subject to subject. It is less so in sequential subjects such as science and mathematics (where certain knowledge or skills must be mastered before the student may proceed to the next stage) than in subjects like English and religious education, where the development of judgments and opinions is wholly or partly the objective of learning.

Mixed-ability grouping has resulted in both the development of new approaches to teaching and the establishment of remedial departments to provide for students with learning difficulties. This is done by withdrawing them from regular classes or teaching them in special groups. In these departments teaching is almost entirely individualized and is based on carefully structured materials; teacher-student relationships tend to be more personal.

There can be little doubt that the development of comprehensive schooling has resulted in a considerable interest in teaching methods. The interest has, however, been in the practice of new methods rather than in developing a new theory. As with much in English education, theory follows rather than leads the development of new practices.

Homework is required of *all* students in the comprehensive school no matter what their level of ability. The requirement is for between one and two hours work to be undertaken at home, though some schools do allow students to do their homework at school after school hours. Written work, exercises, and reading comprise the bulk of homework, and these tasks for some students, especially the more able, will be very demanding. For the less able student such homework is nominal and is set because not to do so would be to risk offending the principle of equality of educational treatment and opportunity on which comprehensive schooling is founded.

Some newly built comprehensive schools are developing resource-based teaching as well as experimenting in team teaching. These schools have a central stock, or resource, of teaching materials—audio tapes, film strips, written materials, diagrams, maps, and the like—which may be drawn on by teachers in constructing learning sequences for pupils. Teaching under such a resource-based regime consists of consulting with students about their progress and prescribing the next set of materials for them to work at. Formal methods of teaching are not precluded. On occasion they are employed to provide students with basic knowledge and understanding. They are, however, not the main form of teaching.

Clearly under a resource-based teaching regime student self-pacing and self-motivation are as crucial as is the quality of the resource materials available.

Other schools such as Countesthorpe College in Leicestershire are developing a much greater level than is customary of student participation in the organization of their schooling. This, too, calls for a different approach to teaching, one in which student and teacher negotiate how the teaching is to be undertaken, at what level, and at what pace.

The recent creation of middle schools catering to children from eight or nine years of age to twelve or thirteen has also called for some reassessment of teaching. In these schools in particular, though not exclusively, is team teaching to be found.

Other structural changes in English secondary education may also lead to new approaches to teaching. In some areas of the country the final stage of secondary education for the sixteen-to-nineteen age-group is taking place in sixth form colleges rather than in the sixth forms of schools. Most of these colleges are open institutions, offering courses for students with a wide ability range. Teaching is on a cafeteria basis. Students attend only their scheduled classes. At other times they are free to spend their time in the students' common room or in the library. They are, however, usually expected to spend a scheduled time in college.

## APPLICATIONS

### Curriculum, Academic

There is a great deal of variety in what is taught in English schools. There is no nationally prescribed curriculum at either the primary or secondary stages. Each school is free to decide what to teach and how to teach it. In any event the differences in what schools teach are less than would be the case if there were no constraints on choice. There are some. Parents, for example, and the public in general, expect primary schools to be concerned with the development of basic intellectual skills, with literacy and computation. The teaching of reading, writing, and basic mathematics thus becomes the core curricular activity. Teachers in the primary school also accept that without the development of these basic skills the future education of their pupils will be hampered.

At the secondary level the examinations taken at sixteen-plus and eighteen-plus are a constraint on much that is taught. The examination syllabus governs much curricular content especially from the fourth year of secondary education, though work in the earlier years will very often be regarded as a preparation for the examination, especially in the linear subjects, mathematics and science.

Despite such constraints, there remains considerable variety in curricular content and materials. Teachers have great freedom in the selection of textbooks and teaching materials and also in the selection of content for the courses of study that they teach. This freedom, though not resulting in marked variations or innovation in curriculum content or structure, is much prized by the teaching profession, and is seen currently as being under threat by proposals to give greater power over the content of school curricula to parents.

This near sovereignty of the teachers over the curriculum is being challenged not only by proposals to grant more power to parents but by a national concern expressed in the great debate about standards of achievement in schools. A proposal is being made that all children should at least have basic knowledge and understanding in a core of subjects, in mathematics, science, and their own language. This core of knowledge and understanding would constitute a common core curriculum in all schools (32).

Supporting this proposal is to be the monitoring of standards of student performance on a national basis using achievement tests. This work will be undertaken by or on behalf of the Assessment of Performance Unit (A.P.U.), a unit set up within the Department of Education and Science working in close collaboration with Her Majesty's Inspectorate, one of whose number has been *seconded* to be its head, and with teachers (32). So far this unit has established specifications for monitoring instruments in mathematics and science and is at work in other curricular areas.

The current national focus of attention on what is taught in schools has not only raised the issue of a core curriculum but also called into question the past decade of curriculum development work, especially that undertaken by the Schools Council, a quasi-official body financed partly from government funds and partly from local authority subvention but controlled very largely by teachers' organizations.

During the 1960s and early 1970s the Schools Council commissioned more than seventy curriculum development projects ranging from

*Science for the Young School Leaver Project* to the *Moral Education, 8-13 Project* and the controversial *Humanities Curriculum Development Project* which, based as it was on the study of such themes as poverty and race through the study of original evidence, called for the teacher to be a neutral chairman (33). This role was to ensure that students understood the evidence. It was not the teacher's function to determine what meaning they should give to it.

This wide-ranging curriculum development work of the Schools Council has had a mixed impact on the curriculum of schools. Some schools have adopted the new curriculum materials and teach to them. Others have adapted them to their particular needs, and others have largely ignored them, preferring to continue to use the traditional materials.

Innovations have been more evident in mathematics and science than in other areas of the curriculum, though at almost all levels of schooling and in most subject areas the work of the council and other curriculum development agencies, including schools themselves, has had some effect on what is taught.

However, the patchiness of the impact of large-scale, centrally initiated curriculum development projects has called into question the model of curriculum change implicit in the process. Preference is currently being given to the support of school-based curriculum development, and to the aftercare of projects as a means of maximizing their impact on schools. Local initiatives are being nurtured and more attention paid to the curricular needs of particular schools.

Both the current educational debate and the initiatives of curriculum development agencies will mean changes in the curriculum of many schools, though certain features of what is taught in schools may remain unaltered for many years to come. It is to these features that we now turn.

Few primary schools would be able to offer a visitor a timetable of the work being undertaken by each class (34). In this respect the curriculum of the primary school is not structured. This does not mean that what is taught lacks organization or pattern. It means that the decision about what to teach and when to teach it is devolved to the level of the class and may be very much in the hands of individual teachers.

In most classrooms one would find very considerable concentration on language and number skills, on reading, writing, listening, talking, and on counting and calculating. In the early stages of primary education the concentration would be on the basic elements of those skills whereas the later stages would emphasize their application in a wide range of contexts. Problem solving in mathematics and reading comprehension are two instances of the kind of academic work undertaken toward the end of primary schooling.

Other areas of academic work in primary education may be science, in which there have been recent interesting developments, and environmental studies. Some history and geography may be studied or incorporated in social studies. In general, however, there tends to be a de-emphasis on teaching bodies of knowledge (35).

Not so in the secondary school where subjects remain largely entrenched though, chameleon-like, changing and adapting to new educational purposes: the timetable of subjects remains the curricular backbone of what is taught.

In the earlier years of the secondary school the timetable will be very similar for all pupils, often still remarkably close to the broad prescription laid down by the Board of Education in 1904. However, a recent survey of the framework of the curriculum has shown differing patterns at third year (thirteen-plus) level (36). Although the majority of third-year pupils will be following a common course outline for most of the time, there are significant areas of the curriculum (craftwork, physical education, minority subjects such as a second modern language) where separate activities are timetabled. In some schools a small number of subject areas each embrace several conventional subjects. For example, "communications" may cover English, French, and English for immigrants. Each child would be expected to follow at least one course in such an area. In some mixed schools a few subjects are restricted to one sex only, although this practice appears increasingly contentious. But a majority of schools appear to hold to a situation in which all third-year pupils take most subjects with a few minority subjects available as options. In a typical school in this category, the survey revealed the following curricular pattern:

| Subject | Number of periods per timetable cycle | |
|---|---|---|
| English | 5 | |
| Mathematics | 5 | |
| Geography | 2 | |
| History | 2 | Taken by all |
| Science | 6 | pupils |
| Art | 2 | |
| Physical education | 3 | |
| | | |
| Needlework | 3 | |
| Home economics | 3 | Taken by Girls |
| | | |
| Combined craft | 6 | |
| French or European studies | 5 | |
| German | 4 | Guided choice |
| Rural science | 2 | |
| Music | 2 | |

This curriculum pattern immediately raises the question of how some pupils make time for minority subjects. No direct question was asked about this, but there are plainly several possibilities. Where there is a straight choice between, for example, French and European studies, it may simply be a question of regrouping pupils for a block of time. But when the minority subjects are extra to the rest of the curriculum, either the pupils must give up another whole subject or spend less time on several subjects.

Beyond the third year the curriculum becomes markedly differentiated for individual students through the working of the options system. This system, it has been argued, is a further adaptation by the schools to the principles of comprehensive education in that it offers to each child equality of educational choice. In theory each child through the options system may select an appropriate curriculum for the fourth, and for most students, final year at secondary school. In practice subjects will be so grouped and the options system so managed by the teaching staff that the less able students will be forced to select vocational or practical courses. In general it is fair to say that the teaching staff through the operation of the options system does its best to ensure that a suitable course of study leading to an appropriate examination is found for most students. In any event all students will continue to study a common core of subjects, usually mathematics and English with science in some form. The examinations that the student will be entered for will be the General Certificate of Education at the "O" or Ordinary Level or the Certificate of Secondary Education.

Beyond the fourth year the secondary school curriculum will become more specialized, especially for those students seeking entry to higher education. In what is known as the sixth form, which may for some students be the fifth and sixth years of secondary education, and for others to be the sixth and seventh years, only three subjects, together with general studies, will constitute the course and tend to be taken on the arts or science side. For example, common combinations of subjects are English, history, and French or physics, chemistry and mathematics. Such highly specialized groups as physics and double mathematics are not precluded. However, there is evidence that more schools are allowing the selection of subjects across the arts-science boundaries than once was the case. Whatever is the case, studying such courses leads to the "A" or Advanced Level Examination.

Other changes in the sixth form are taking place with more and less academically able students wishing to continue in education beyond the fourth year. A wider range of courses is being developed, some vocational courses, such as the pre-nursing course, and others of one-year duration. The shape of the curriculum of what has come to be called the new sixth form is not yet clear, although there can be little doubt that it will be as responsive as possible to the needs of the less academic sixth former (37).

Technical colleges and colleges of further education also offer "A"-level courses, though they concentrate more on vocational and quasi-vocational studies catering to a large extent to students who are released by industry and commerce for one or more days a week to continue their general education.

Universities, polytechnics, colleges of education, and recently created colleges of higher education provide the final stages of academic education with some 15 percent of an age-group taking courses at them.

Universities offer the traditional range of degree courses across the spectrum of the arts, sciences, social sciences, and medicine including courses in business studies and accounting. Polytechnics concentrate more on scientific and technical courses, though they also provide courses in the social sciences and some in philosophy. Colleges of education concentrate on the B.Ed. degree which provides a course for intending teachers and has a strong academic bias especially for students intending to teach in secondary schools.

Colleges of higher education have recently been developed from the retrenchment and reorganization of teacher education and offer general degree courses, mainly in the arts and also the B.Ed. or other teacher education qualifications. How they will evolve in the future and what part they will play in developments in higher education, especially in a period when student numbers are likely to fall dramatically, is problematic.

**Curriculum, Nonacademic**

As will be clear from the previous section, a great many subjects find a place on the secondary school timetable and with the exception of physical education, all may be studied academically and offered for examination. Of course such subjects as home economics and woodwork, for example, may contribute significantly to the development of skills of value in the home and in daily life. Religious education may contribute to the development of a moral sense and art to the growth of aesthetic awareness and creativity. However, each subject is seen primarily as having a content and structure, the mastery of which will *inter alia* call for the development of a range of skills and sensibilities of value not only in themselves but also of application in a wide range of situations, though such application is achieved more by the way of incidental learning than as a consciously worked out purpose.

A few schools have explored through social studies, for instance, education in community care where students will become involved in working with very young children or with the elderly. Others have developed work experience courses where students will spend some time in learning what is entailed in factory work or in a service industry. Such programs are, however, the exception rather than the rule, though there is a current concern for relevance in education.

From time to time courses in citizenship have found a place in school timetables, and currently there is concern about the political education of the young and in teaching politics. Views about this vary considerably, though there can be little doubt that the increased politicization of many activities in contemporary English society is posing problems for educators.

In the primary school much that is taught has both academic and incidental aims in view. Environmental studies, for example, purports not only to introduce concepts such as energy and pollution but also to sensitize the young to their responsibilities in the preservation of the human habitat. It is in fact difficult to distinguish academic and nonacademic, incidental, and personal learning from each other in the warp and weft of education in English schools.

It is true that from time to time specifically nonacademic areas of the curriculum, such as sex or consumer education, will appear in response to publicly expressed concern. It is also true that they will tend to be taken out of the curriculum as public disquiet diminishes. In some schools, both primary and secondary, at all times one will find growing points of a nonacademic curriculum. Equally in all schools one may point to some areas of nonacademic nature concerned to cultivate personal or life skills.

Physical education in some form, as music and movement or games, will be found as part of the nonacademic curriculum of all schools. Its form and purpose have varied from the development of the quasi-martial arts and the pursuit of physical fitness to the discovery of the self through physical activity or the sense of discipline in team games. Its salience as a curricular activity is lower today than for some time. From the pursuit of physical fitness it has turned to the self-discovery of outdoor pursuits —canoeing, rock climbing, mountaineering, and even walking. Even so physical education remains an area of curricular ambiguity.

Neither primary nor secondary schools are deliberately vocational. The direct pursuit of vocational education is to be found in technical colleges and colleges of further education which cater to the sixteen-to-nineteen age-group, both those in full-time education and those released for part-time education by their employers. The range of courses offered is extensive from building education and office management to printing and textile technology.

There are also colleges of art which offer an education in the whole range of arts from painting and drawing to interior design and decoration. The concern in most is with the development of practical talents, though they deal with the history of art and with aesthetics and principles of design.

### Student Evaluation

The formal, written, essay-type examination in one variant or another still dominates student evaluation in English education. The major public examinations—the General Certificate of Education at Ordinary and Advanced Level, and the Certificate of Secondary Education—substantially depend on it as do the examinations that serve the vocational and technical sphere—the Ordinary and Higher National Certificate. Internal school examinations, which are usually set twice a year, also employ the written, essay-type examination.

Some subject areas, science for example, will use in addition to essay-type examination papers, multiple-choice objective tests, and in such subjects as home economics, woodwork, and art, there are practical tests as there are for assessing oral ability in modern languages.

It will, for example, be on the results of performance in "O"- and "A"-level examinations, which are essentially measures of achievement rather than of aptitude, that a secondary school student will be awarded a place in college or university. A report from the school about the candidate's character and the probability of his or her benefiting from higher education will also be taken into account.

Secondary school students take the "O"-level examination usually at sixteen years of age during the last year of compulsory education. They may sit the examination in one or in a range of subjects. Some more able students will sit as many as nine or ten subjects. The examination will be set by one of eight examining boards, which, with the exception of the Associated Examining Board, are associated with universities. Schools are free to select whichever board they wish.

Each examining board sets up subject committees of teachers from schools and universities to design examinations, appoint examiners, and agree on marking schemes. Appeals procedures are also agreed, though the actions of the committees remain confidential.

In addition to the "O"-level examinations for sixteen-year-old students, there is the Certificate of Secondary Education examination (C.S.E), which was designed to cater for the student of around average ability, the "O"-level examinations being designed for the upper 20 percent. This examination is set by one of thirteen regional examining boards awarding not a pass or fail, but a grade from 1 to 5, grade 1 being equivalent to an "O"-level pass.

With the C.S.E., schools may elect for any subject to take one of three modes of examination: an examination set and marked entirely by the board, one partly set by the board and partly by the school and moderated by the board, or an examination set by the school and approved and moderated by the board.

In many respects the C.S.E. has been a marked innovation in examining in English education. Before its introduction a wide range of experimental studies was undertaken, and upon its introduction research was undertaken to monitor the standards of the boards and the relationship of the C.S.E. to the "O"-level of the G.C.E. (38, 39). The C.S.E. Boards, which are governed very largely by teachers, have been more open to alternative forms of examining than have the G.C.E. Boards.

At age eighteen the main secondary school examination is the "A" level of the G.C.E. Students usually take two subjects either on the arts or science side. The "A"-level examination caters in the main to those students intending to continue their education at college or university or to enter a profession.

With an increase in the number of students staying on in full-time education beyond the age of sixteen for whom the "O"- and "A"-level examination is unsuitable, there have been experiments with a new examination, the Certificate of Extended Education (C.E.E) which may be taken with some C.S.E. Boards at seventeen.

With the development of comprehensive education and the concern for a broad rather than a specialized education for the majority of students, the whole examination system has come under critical scrutiny. The result may be to move forward a single system of examining at sixteen and to a form of examining at eighteen that will not force students into specialization at too early a point in their secondary school course.

Achievement examinations, whether external or internal to the school, are not the only means employed of assessing student abilities. There is the school report on student progress usually given twice a year at the end of the winter and summer terms. These reports will distinguish between performance in class work and in examinations, and will indicate either a grade or position in class both subject by subject and overall. They will also report on a student's attitude and behavior (40).

With the less able secondary school students, especially those with learning difficulties, diagnostic tests may well be used especially in language and mathematics. Should a student be referred to a school psychologist, such tests will most certainly be used and their results used as a basis for designing a remedial programme.

At the primary school level formal public examinations such as the eleven-plus selection examination have now been abolished with the exception of one or two local education authorities who are challenging the directives of the Department of Education and Science. Primary schools use a variety of means of assessing the achievement and progress of their students. At the first stages reading tests are commonly used, either tests of word recognition or reading comprehension. They are also used nationally to monitor standards of reading and have been, at intervals, since 1945 (41).

Some primary schools will also use tests of mathematical ability, of general aptitude, and of language skills, though most schools use the work of their students as the basis for assessing ability and educational progress. Teachers keep careful records of progress, and the record cards completed by the teachers are passed on from stage to stage in primary education and may form the basis for allocation to teaching groups on entry to secondary education.

The general issue of assessment, of testing, and of monitoring performance is currently a matter of concern throughout the education system, as has been noted elsewhere. This concern has raised the more difficult problems of aims and objectives and of educational standards. It may be that so far as student evaluation is concerned English education may be on the verge of a new point of departure.

## Counseling

Most local education authorities provide a school psychological service at which students with learning or behavior difficulties are counseled. Parental counseling will most probably be offered in conjunction with student counseling. Officers of the service visit schools as do psychiatric social workers to obtain the views of teachers about students who have been referred and to give advice.

In recent years training courses for educational counseling in colleges and universities have been established. Postgraduate diplomas in counseling are awarded to teachers who successfully pass these courses. Once qualified, the teachers will take up an educational counseling post in a secondary school, probably in charge of pastoral care throughout the school. However, most secondary schools will not have a trained counselor on the staff, and counseling will be part of the responsibility of each form or class teacher, and throughout the school, of a senior teacher; such is the case generally in primary schools.

Vocational guidance is more generally established. All secondary schools will have a careers master or mistress whose role will be to liaise with the Youth Employment Service in giving school leavers guidance about careers and job opportunities. Students will be interviewed in the presence of their parents, with whom there will be a discussion of job opportunities. In some cases interest inventories will be used to provide supplementary information in the vocational guidance process.

During the final year at school not only does the careers master arrange for the Youth Employment Service to interview each leaving student but will also arrange for visiting speakers from local industry to talk to the students, and organize a careers convention or fair open to parents of leaving students and to parents of students in their third year when students choose the subjects they will study in their fourth and final year, the choice of which might well have vocational implications.

Counseling, whether educational or vocational, is like much else in English education, undertaken on a very practical basis. The *how* of the processes is given more prominence than the *why*. However, there has been concern in recent years about the nature and adequacy of educational and vocational guidance and a move away from the oversimplified model based on individual psychology to a more holistic one that attempts to see the individual in his setting and to take into account in the counseling process both subject and situation. In fact the very idea of a service that counsels only the student and *not* his teachers and his school is coming under considerable criticism.

The establishment of special centers to deal with groups of disruptive pupils also represents a move away from counseling based on individual psychology toward a group-based model employing some elements of behavior modification in a social setting. There are clearly trends away from old models of educational and vocational counseling toward new and more sophisticated models that have been called into play with changes in attitudes among students and in society at large. Changes in the attraction of schooling for increasing numbers of young people and in employment prospects for young school leavers pose new problems in counseling. How, if at all, counseling can solve them remains to be seen. At most it may not be possible for counseling to do more than ameliorate their worst effects.

### Discipline

For more than a decade education has been news and, at times, front-page news. The behavior of students in public, the alleged lack of deference to adults, the way they dress, the length of their hair, bullying, truancy, and racism in the playground have each on occasion made the headlines. Not only do these issues arouse concern but so does the vexed question of the punishment of students. Corporal punishment is still legitimately exercised in the schools of some local education authorities. The cane or strap is used to administer it, and each occasion of use must be entered in the punishment book.

Many teachers see corporal punishment as the final deterrent to the disruptive, unruly student—the teacher's ultimate threat. Others are less committed to the concept of a deterrent, preferring to see the control of students based less on a custodial model and more on one rooted in care and considerate, though realistic, understanding.

There are sufficient schools operating differing discipline policies to suggest that what matters is not the nature of the policy so much as the commitment of teachers concerned to seeing that their approach works in practice.

Even with the most enlightened of discipline policies, a school will have some problems with truancy and with children classified as "school phobic." Such problems are most acute in schools in centers of urban decay when family, cultural, and economic problems are compounded.

The general discipline policy of a school will, of course, be reflected in the formulation of its rules and in their enforcement. Schools that set themselves a discipline policy that maximizes the opportunity students have for learning and relating to their peers and to their teachers will see rules not as an end in themselves but as subordinate means to other ends. In fact most English schools exercise this sort of policy. They tend to be caring communities, anxious that students should benefit from the educational opportunities that are offered. Few are overly concerned with rules in themselves, whether they relate to time keeping, deportment about the school, or the use of rooms and facilities. Purges there will be. From time to time a head teacher will tighten up on time keeping, for example. But such is no more than normal institutional behavior.

The school uniform is to be found as a strong feature of some schools, and its absence a strong feature of others. There is still a prevalent belief that the school uniform is a leveler. It makes all students equal. The poor cannot be distinguished from the well-to-do, and the flamboyant cannot distract the more sober from their educational tasks.

Where schools allow a free dress policy, there will be a greater concern to emphasize self-expression and social responsibility as worthwhile aims than where the school uniform is compulsory. The rhetoric of both camps is well developed; and as with most educational issues, and no less so in English education than elsewhere, relates to differing patterns of educational values.

Vandalism, the burning of schools, and the destruction of school property happens, not on a large scale but on a scale sufficient to be disturbing. In no way is school vandalism related to a pattern of positive educational values. It is nihilistic. On occasion, however, the school has failed to recognize a problem in time and must hold itself responsible. Mostly the vandalism is an expression of wider frustrations and to diminish these frustrations schools can do little, at least as they are presently ordered. It may be that alternative forms of schooling would contribute more. Free schools may have had some success in this respect, as may exclusion units. School vandalism may, however, be symptomatic of a wider social malaise, which may be cured only by seeing the educational provision as part of a coordinated social policy. This is currently being attempted as part of the struggle to overcome the urban blight of city centers. Only in future will it be possible to pronounce on its effectiveness.

## ROLES

### Administration

A recent official publication describes the English education system as follows:

> A distinctive feature of the British education service is that it operates on the basis of the distribution of power between central government, the local education authorities and the teaching profession. It is, therefore, correct to speak of it as a "national system locally administered," with the Department of Education and Science a major operational partner rather than its sole controller (42).

This description accurately reflects the basis on which English education is administered. Acts of Parliament define the responsibilities of the two major administrative partners, the Department of Education and Science and the local education authorities. It is the responsibility of the D.E.S. under the 1944 Education Act to promote "the Education of the people of England and Wales" and to concern itself with the development of the education service generally. It is the responsibility of the L.E.A.'s to provide efficient education under the direction of an education committee, which it is required by law to appoint. At least half the members of such a committee will be locally elected to serve on the city or county council and the remainder will be appointed for their expert knowledge of or involvement in the education service.

The D.E.S. will have available the advice of Her Majesty's Inspectors of Schools (H.M.I.'s). From time to time the minister of education is able to convene the Advisory Council for Education in England and Wales which since World War II has conducted enquiries into many aspects of education: into primary education, the less able child in the secondary school, into sixth form education, into the teaching of English and currently into the provision and nature of education for the physically, mentally, and socially handicapped (43). These reports are frequently influential in the formation and development of policy and practice.

The L.E.A.'s also appoint their own inspectors and advisers to be responsible for developments in the schools, men and women of considerable practical experience in teaching, though the main function of the L.E.A.'s is administrative. Matters of curriculum and teaching are largely devolved to the schools, which have considerable freedom to decide what to teach and how to teach it.

Because much decision making in education is devolved to the schools, the head teachers, and teachers, the teaching profession is accounted an important partner in the administration of education. The profession makes its views known through a variety of teachers' organizations, the largest of which is the National Union of Teachers. Representatives of these teachers' organizations find themselves playing a significant role on such D.E.S. committees as those concerned with the training and supply of teachers and in inquiring into stages or aspects of education. They are also to be found on the education committees of L.E.A.'s.

Because of the partnership nature of English education, changes in the structure and organization of education have to be carefully negotiated by all concerned. It has in fact argued that education is controlled not by Parliament but by a subgovernment comprising D.E.S., L.E.A., and teacher organization representatives (44).

A few years ago, in response to growing concern about the accountability of teachers, the Schools Council for the Curriculum and Examinations was established, financed jointly by the D.E.S. and the L.E.A.'s. The role of the Schools Council was to initiate proposals for changes in curriculum and examinations and, as has been noted earlier, during the decade following its creation, the council sponsored a wide range of curriculum projects, research studies, and studies in examining. It also produced more than forty working papers intended to stimulate discussion on educational issues.

The structure of the council gave the representatives of teachers' organizations a majority on all its committees. This domination of the council by the teaching profession has since become a point of criticism, and moves are under way to open the committees of the council to a greater degree of influence by "consumers" of education, industry, commerce, and parents.

However, it remains the case in the administration of English education that the teachers in the schools, especially the head teachers, have the power to make many of the most important educational decisions (45). The main constraints on this power are financial and political. The L.E.A.'s fund the schools through their education committees and its administrative machinery. In turn some 80 percent of their funds are provided by the D.E.S. The balance of 20 percent of monies is raised from local property tax (rates) and means that in matters such as school building, teachers' salaries, and comparable high capital or running costs, the D.E.S. exercises considerable national influence. School governing bodies often have little real power and exist to "rubber stamp" the decisions of the headmaster.

In the political arena the influence of the D.E.S. and the L.E.A.'s* also outmatches that of the teaching profession. Both the D.E.S. and L.E.A.'s can establish the broad parameters of educational policy and possess the means to carry them through. They may also conflict with one another as they have in recent years over the policy of bringing into being a comprehensive system of education and abolishing the selection of children by ability at eleven years of age.

The D.E.S., having exhausted its power of exhortation and persuasion, may turn to Parliament for legislation to compel the L.E.A.'s to comply with a national policy. This happened in 1976 when an act of Parliament required *all* L.E.A.'s to submit plans for making schools under their control comprehensive. L.E.A.'s may challenge the law, especially its interpretation by a minister of education. But for the main part L.E.A.'s respond to exhortation and persuasion in preference to coercion and legal sanction.

In its turn the teaching profession will give its energies to bringing into being the basic realities of an educational policy in the school and the classroom, as they have with comprehensive education. In achieving this the role of the head teacher will be prominent. He or she wields the greatest administrative authority in the school. It has been said that,

> the power exercised by the head in an English school is formidable, and the head can be compared to the sovereign of a state whose powers are limited only by the willingness of his subjects to obey his commands but whose right to give commands is not disputed by his subjects (46).

This may be becoming less true with the development of increased staff participation in decision making in schools, and with the devolution of administrative power in large comprehensive schools to heads of upper and lower schools and to heads of departments. There is also some evidence that heads increasingly see themselves as needing to act democratically in the exercise of their authority.

Even so the head remains responsible for the conduct of the school, although he or she has little or no choice of the students who will attend it, and sometimes, though exceptionally, little say in the appointment of

---

\* Reminder: D.E.S. is Department of Education & Science; L.E.A. is Local Education Authorities.

staff who will be selected by a committee set up by the L.E.A. He has power to suspend students and in very special circumstances to expel them. He cannot of course compel attendance, the responsibility for which lies with the L.E.A.'s, who employ attendance officers to look into cases of failure to attend school and into truancy, which in some urban schools may be 20 percent of the students enrolled.

Heads vary in the ways in which they manage their school. Occasionally, a head teacher will be committed to a particular educational ideology and may pursue the implementation of it despite the opposition of the teaching staff and parents and the advice of local authority inspectors.

The result, unless the head is persuaded to moderate his views, may be administrative action by the responsible L.E.A., as was the case with Risinghill Comprehensive School, whose head was strongly committed to a markedly student-centered philosophy of education, or a public enquiry under an independent chairman, as was the case at William Tindale Junior School (47, 48). In both instances the head was removed from his post.

Thus does the freedom of head teachers, and for that matter of all teachers, find its limits. The checks and balances of a democratic system of education that give none of those involved in its administration and implementation complete power; they work to control any tendency to excess. They may work also to depress the level of innovation of the system.

How, in a heavily bureaucratized administration, to raise the level of innovatory thinking of schools, how to make them more responsive to public need, and how to make them more accountable are urgent questions. The answers may alter the relationships between the central and local authorities, and the teaching profession. The present scenario suggests that the D.E.S. will continue in its present assertive vein with the support of the L.E.A.'s, with the teaching profession under the threat of redundancies brought about by a rapidly falling student population conceding some of its claim to freedom to decide what is taught in schools.

### Faculty

Remarkably free though English teachers are, the freedom that they most cherish is that of deciding how to teach and how to manage their own classrooms. Such practical capabilities are at the heart of the professional self-regard of the English teacher. He sees himself first and foremost as a practitioner and teaching as a practical art. He is not given to theorizing, believing that improvements in teaching come more from practice and experience in the classroom than from any other source, certainly not from developments in theories of learning or child development, though if he is a subject teacher in a secondary school, he will put considerable store in keeping up with advances in his field of scholarship.

Most teachers see their job as being to teach something by way of subject matter and to inculcate ideas of social and moral responsibility. They do not see as central to their role teaching students to be good citizens nor helping them improve their lot in life. They tend to believe that their view of their role and that of parents is at variance, with parents more concerned with social advancement for their children and less with learning subjects than they are. What evidence there is suggests that parents and teachers are in fact remarkably agreed about the teacher's role (49).

In the school the teacher tends to emphasize his personality, the kind of individual he is, as the most important attribute of his role, more important than teaching competence or discipline and control or organization and management. Part of the reason lies in the belief that teachers have in the establishment of good personal relations with their students as the key to professional success and personal satisfaction in teaching. Part is because of the responsibility teachers in England feel they bear for the moral and social attitudes and behavior of their students. There are few counselors in schools. The teacher traditionally incorporates counseling into his role as a general responsibility if he teaches in a primary school or specifically as a form or class teacher in a secondary school.

Teachers, of course, share a whole range of attitudes toward education. Some believe that its purpose is to serve the individual, others to serve society. Their beliefs will affect their role conceptions. Studies suggest that primary school teachers who believe that education is to serve the individual will emphasize the social purpose of education (50).

Other studies suggest that teachers of a subject, science for example, will show differences of emphasis in their role depending upon the degree to which they show a concern with science or with teaching (51).

There are also, as may be expected, variations in roles with the responsibilities that teachers carry within the school. Teachers may be given posts of responsibility, which carry additions to salary, normally based on length of service and qualifications. Such posts are awarded to heads of departments for taking responsibility for curriculum development or pastoral care, in which incidentally there is a large measure of counseling, or for acting as deputy to the head teacher. Each post will tend to carry a somewhat different structure of role expectations from those of the general run of teachers.

Most posts of responsibility are awarded on merit, though seniority also plays a part. Appointment to such posts is generally by the recommendation of the head teacher and is not necessarily based on teaching competence alone. Specialist qualifications such as a master's degree in curriculum development or an advanced diploma in an aspect of special education may be taken into account.

The posts of deputy head, head of upper or lower school, and sometimes such specialist posts as teacher in charge of pastoral care are open to competition. More such posts have been created in recent years partly because of the creation of large comprehensive schools and partly because of the increased professionalization of teaching.

Posts of responsibility do not represent for English teachers the main rewards and incentives in teaching. These are provided by the job itself in terms of the psychological satisfaction derived from working with groups of students. This is not to say that teachers are satisfied with their salaries and terms of employment. They are not and in recent years have become increasingly militant, and more strongly unionized. However, salaries and satisfaction in teaching are only slightly correlated. It is the personal enjoyment to be found in teaching that is the real currency of the profession, building professional self-esteem and providing the motivation to surmount difficulties.

Despite dissatisfaction at times with their salaries and terms of service, English teachers can have little to complain about in the level of provision of in-service programs which range from one-year, full-time, courses at a university or college to evening and weekend courses at a local teachers' center. Not only is there a wide provision of courses, residential and otherwise, outside the schools to which the D.E.S., the L.E.A.'s, and teachers' unions each make a contribution, but there is also currently a developing program of school-based in-service education.

This broad web of in-service provision has grown considerably over the past two decades, accelerating with the establishment of teachers' centers in the mid-1960s. These centers, provided by L.E.A.'s, though jointly managed by teachers and L.E.A. officers, were conceived of as agents for the dissemination of the curriculum developments of the schools council. Each would be under the day-to-day administration of a warden or leader, invariably an experienced teacher, have a library, reprographic facilities, and rooms for meetings, workshops, and exhibitions. Some would have social amenities such as a bar and restaurant, though most would only have facilities for light refreshments. Some centers have become involved in local curriculum development work and others in research into local educational problems. The role of most, however, has turned out to be that of an information center and a place for occasional meetings of teachers. They have not, in general, become educational growing points.

Many larger local authorities have established specialist centers for science, mathematics, and language education. Some have centers for craft education or immigrant education. These centers differ from teachers' centers not only in being concerned with a single subject or area of education but in being part of a local authority's advisory service.

Just how in-service courses will develop in the future is difficult to say. Attendance at them is likely to remain voluntary, though there may well be increased provision of sabbatical leave for teachers. More courses are likely to take on a practical character as workshop or "sandwich" courses in which the practical part of the sandwich will be undertaken in the teacher's own school. Multiplicity of provision is likely to remain, though greater efforts may be made to develop a national policy to ensure the continuing professional education of teachers in line with the recommendations of a recent government report on teacher education (52).

Changes in the structure of teacher education institutions and the pattern of their courses will ensure a steady move toward an all-graduate profession. This may result in demands from teachers for advanced courses at the master's and doctoral levels, as may the increased competition for professional advancement caused by a falling school population. Whatever may turn out to be the case, the readiness of English teachers to be concerned with professional self-renewal will remain strong and the willingness of both the D.E.S. and the L.E.A.'s to provide the necessary financial support will continue possibly at a higher level than at present.

### Students

It has been remarked that in English society, in contrast to American society, most social rewards are reserved to adults who possess the power and the prestige and intend to retain them (53). Undoubtedly there is some truth in this, sufficient to be able to describe student roles as generally deferential to adults in authority. The extent of this deference depends in practice on circumstance and social class. Middle-class students for whom the educational system offers the best prospects of a professional position in society will be readily deferential, working-class students less readily so, though generally receptive to the efforts of the school. Both groups of students will, however, be restless under poor teaching or weak discipline.

There are, of course, always students who are persistent trouble makers, disrupting teaching and challenging the authority of teachers. It is asserted that their numbers have increased in recent years, though this is difficult to verify. Far too many variables are involved to know for sure that this is the case. However, there is evidence that students today more readily voice their criticisms of how they are treated in schools and what they are taught.

The result of student disruption and criticism has been for the system to seek other than the traditional remedies of corporal punishment, now banned in many schools, and exclusion from school. Centers catering to disruptive pupils have been established by some L.E.A.'s in which the re-education of disruptive pupils is undertaken. There is also a great deal more systematic remedial education in schools than once was the case, providing special programs of work for students with learning problems.

Student participation in the classroom varies considerably from primary to secondary stages and from school to school. In general it is not high despite the pioneering work of such educationists as A. S. Neill who at his school, Summerhill, established near complete equality between staff and students (54). There are very few schools in the state system that come anywhere near this level of participation.

Younger primary school teachers tend to encourage a greater degree of student participation in the classroom, being more prepared than older teachers to allow the child to take the center of the educational stage.

At the secondary stage there are teachers who work for active student participation but more to secure a good level of motivation than as an end in itself. For teachers of some subjects, English for example, participation is used as a means of learning. Here the aim is to develop skills of oracy: speaking and listening. In very few secondary schools are students autonomous learners, devising their own learning with the support of their teachers and determining how they will undertake it.

There is frequently student participation in the administration of schools either as members of a school council, as prefects, or as officials of a house. The house system is a means whereby the student body is broken down into houses in order to increase both students' sense of belonging within the school and pride in schoolwork. The success of this or of any other form of student participation is difficult to assess. The impression that one has is that they make little difference to the paternalistic authoritarianism of English secondary schools.

Some effort has been made to politicize the student body. The National Union of School Students was established in the mid-1970s and achieved a fleeting prominence but has failed to secure a following in most schools. However, students have not been averse to making their views known where they feel that their school is being unduly repressive or where they feel that their educational interests are being neglected either by striking or some other form of protest. But students in general, though as ever to a degree resentful of the frustration that schooling may impose on their spontaneous desires, find schools to be concerned and caring communities.

## Parents

For some time English educationists have known that parental interest makes a significant contribution to educational achievement. Nevertheless there continues to be considerable resistance to parental participation in the educational process. This is less evident at the primary stage, where parents may work on a voluntary basis as teachers' helps. Many teachers are afraid that parents may interfere in what they consider to be professional matters, and most schools keep parents at a distance by a variety of administrative devices.

Schools have, however, developed a pattern of relationships with parents that are in the main satisfactory. Parents' evenings, when parents are able to discuss their children's educational progress, are held at regular intervals. Reports on a student's schoolwork are also provided and may be the basis of discussion on parents' evenings, though other matters will be raised by the head teacher in his welcoming address.

In some schools the heads of upper and lower school will have the specific responsibility for liaison with parents. In others the head teacher will see it as part of his role. Whichever is the case, it will always be a senior staff member who deals with parental complaints, though they are not able to deal with a parent's wish to send his child to a particular school. Parental choice of schools is governed by L.E.A. regulations. Each school will serve a specific catchment area, and only children from this neighborhood will be entitled to attend the school except in special circumstances.

This restriction of parental choice has been a cause of much dissatisfaction and, among other reasons, led to the establishment of a national parent body, the Association for the Advancement of State Education. This organization aims to make parents aware of their rights in the educational system and to publicize discrepancies among L.E.A.'s in their treatment of parents and provision of resources for their schools.

Parental pressure of this kind has led to a national committee of enquiry into the government of schools to recommend that parents should be strongly represented on the governing boards of all schools (55). It has also led to the issue of parental choice becoming part of the current national debate on education.

In very many schools parents play a supportive role through their membership in a Parent-Teachers Association (P.T.A.). Such associations tend to confine themselves to raising money for the school and to providing a forum for information about educational matters. In the main they do not exercise much influence on what schools teach and the methods that teachers employ.

Parents do have distinctive views about their roles in relation to the school. Most, however, seem generally satisfied with their children's education, being perhaps least satisfied when the school fails to cultivate instrumental skills and capabilities or to provide access for parents who are concerned with either the educational progress of their children or the way in which they have been reprimanded in school.

Schools recognize that a student's family background is a significant variable in his ability to benefit from schooling and that a broken home and a family in difficulties will jeopardize the student's educational chances. However, it is not seen as the school's function to deal with such families. Official concern at the level of local authority for families in trouble is the responsibility of the social welfare service which will, as need arises, liaise with the school. It is to such a service that parents will turn for help, not to the school, though it may be the school's concern about a student's welfare that alerts the social welfare service to a family in trouble.

Some schools have a role as community colleges, which tends to bring them into closer contact with the adults of the community. Such colleges provide a wide range of both recreational and educational courses and make use of the facilities of the school in the evening and on the weekends. More secondary schools are now being built with such a dual role in view. A noteworthy one is Madeley Court Comprehensive School, Telford New Town, which provides facilities for the community throughout the day. One important consequence of sharing its facilities with the community more fully is the interest that many adults show in contributing to the work of the school, work ranging from clerical help to assisting in the development of learning resources.

Such developments may lead to an easier, more positive role for parents in relation to the work of schools and to a better understanding on the part of both parents and teachers of their mutual interdependence in the success of the educational process.

Child-rearing practices and forms of schooling interact to the benefit or detriment of the educational well-being of a society. As this fact becomes more fully appreciated, the role of parents in English education may become more salient than is the case at present. Clearly moves are being made in this direction. The outcome is, however, far from certain.

## SYSTEM IN ACTION

It is difficult to typify the system in action, since each school has its own "ethos" and style. However, sufficient practices are common enough to enable us to offer this outline of the work of a large suburban comprehensive school for children of both sexes.

Like many comprehensives, the school in question is situated among the "ribbon development" of the 1950s and 1960s on the edge of one of our major cities. It serves a vast council-housing estate and also nearby is a large development of owner-occupied property (detached and semidetached), which also provides a significant part of the intake of the 1,200 pupils of the school. Built in the late 1950s in response to an L.E.A. policy of comprehensivization which anticipated later developments at the governmental level, the school is low-rise and comprises a long classroom block with wings leading from it to house specialist facilities. A visitor to the school sees first a large assembly hall, with a curtained stage and gallery above the auditorium, and an administrative block housing the head teacher, his two deputies, and the administrative staff of the school. These are all reached from a large foyer across which the staff room is also located, so this space serves, in a sense, as the nerve center of the school's activities. Throughout the day there is a constant traffic of children, staff, and visitors in this part of the school.

Children begin to cluster in the large playground, or in inclement weather, indoors, surprisingly early, often half an hour or more before the formal commencement of school at 9:00 A.M. A brief form period of ten minutes, during which their attendance is registered with their form teacher (who is responsible for their day-to-day pastoral care) is followed by an assembly in the hall of the whole school. Here the obligatory act of religious worship (required by the 1944 Education Act) comprises a hymn, a brief talk, dramatization or reading, and a prayer. This assembly is also used by senior staff as an opportunity for announcements of general concern and often for exhortations on behavior and the running of the school. Despite the time and effort involved, many schools continue with this practice of a general daily assembly, so that the first lesson, usually scheduled to commence at about 9:30 A.M., often starts late. Thereafter, the day is divided into teaching periods, seven in the school under review, which is not untypical. In order to minimize disruption between lessons, much teaching is organized in "double periods," although the problems of staffing minority subjects and the nature of some classroom work means that very few schools use double periods exclusively. Consequently at the end of each lesson children can be seen moving around the school in fairly large numbers. In our school a five-minute break between lessons is provided to minimize the problem of children who have had to traverse the whole school between lessons arriving late.

For each pupil the day is subdivided to avoid the boredom of an extended spell at any one subject. The only exception to this is the school's "ROSLA" project introduced two years ago to meet the problems associated with the raising of the school-leaving age. In this program some fifth year "school leavers" spend a half-day at a time on vocationally oriented work. So, for most children, the day will comprise a mixture of single and double periods and a range of subjects, some studied in specialist classrooms, laboratories, or workshops. The school has a swimming pool and two gymnasiums which are in constant use throughout the day. An indoor heated pool is a relative luxury possessed by few schools.

The only group of pupils allowed free periods for private study is the sixth form, who have access to the library (which possesses a few study carrels) and to their own sixth form suite. Typically, a sixth former preparing for three "A"-level subjects will spend seven periods weekly on each of them, have eight further periods devoted to games, liberal studies, and religious education, leaving six periods free for private study.

In the school under review, two morning periods are followed by a twenty-minute break. The younger pupils then have two further lessons before the lunch break which is staggered to meet the difficulties of providing a warm meal for 650 pupils. Older children have three periods of schoolwork before their lunch break. Afternoon school is arranged so that each pupil receives a total of seven lessons daily. All lessons are of forty minutes' duration. The afternoon session is prefaced by another brief form period.

During the lunch break a few school societies meet, some using specialist facilities (the art club, the drama society, the music club). But the bulk of extracurricular work is done during the hour and a half following the end of afternoon school. The school has a full complement of games teams. During the two winter terms, each Saturday, six soccer teams, two rugby fifteens, and two girls' hockey teams are fielded. The school concentrates during the summer term on cricket, tennis, and athletics. The school also enters pupils for occasional competitions in other sports: swimming, badminton, gymnastics. Once a year a school play is produced, with pupils, staff, and parents participating, and a school brass band gives occasional concerts for parents. A school magazine is published twice yearly, and there are parents' evenings once each term when staff are formally available to discuss the progress of children. During the evenings the schools' premises are used for adult evening classes, organized by the local authority. Consequently, the school exudes an air of almost constant activity from early morning until mid-evening, with a lull only at teatime after the departure of the last pupils and before the beginning of evening sessions.

Such a picture is not untypical, although other individual schools vary widely from it. In some community schools there is a far greater air of informality and no school uniforms at all (in our sample school about 95 percent of the pupils are in uniform). At Countesthorpe, for example, students and staff share all facilities and are both represented on college committees. At the other extreme, for example in a public school, not only will all pupils be neatly turned out in uniform but stricter standards of behavior will be enforced within the school. Here pupils will be more deferential to staff and may, in some instances, still be expected to acknowledge formally a member of staff when meeting him both within and outside the school. Although our sample comprehensive school has a prefect system, relationships between prefects and younger pupils will be far more informal than similar relationships in a public school. In a few public schools variants of "fagging," by which junior pupils perform menial chores for older ones, still persist. Although our comprehensive school has shifted far from this degree of formality, pupils are still expected to stand when a teacher or visitor enters a room they are occupying.

Other comprehensive schools vary widely, too, in their practices. Major factors here that influence their working are size of school and decisions on scheduling. Smaller rural schools often convey to a visitor a far greater sense of community than large urban comprehensives. In some towns single large comprehensive schools have been created by amalgamating two or three smaller preexisting schools. In the worst instances pupils are obliged to commute on foot between separate buildings on neighboring streets. The sense of anarchy conveyed by this practice is not conducive to the values of corporate social life. Similarly, scheduling decisions are critical. Some timetables are designed to minimize pupil movement around the school. In other situations the decision is taken to share the use of specialist facilities as widely as possible or to deploy staff across ability bands so as to avoid stereotyping staff as "sixth form teachers" or specialists with the less able. This can lead to far more pupil movement between lessons and thus result in the school appearing, to the casual visitor at least, ill-organized and anarchic.

All these activities vary slightly according to the point in the school year. In most secondary schools there is a keenness during the first (autumn) term to press ahead as effectively as possible with the new syllabus. The second term is frequently in practice punctuated by trial external examinations for older pupils, and the rigors of winter can lead to poor attendance as a result of epidemics or weather conditions. The third (summer) term is always marked in secondary schools by the annual round of external examinations, which can paralyze the school hall or its gymnasiums for up to three weeks. Often, too, staff use this term as an opportunity for a greater emphasis upon field work, museum visits, or expeditions of various kinds.

These overt activities are backed by a range of "behind-the-scenes" work that is not apparent to the casual visitor. Staff are engaged continuously in discussions among themselves with counselors and with parents on individual children. Head teachers and their deputies are in constant touch with L.E.A. officials, pursuing a wide range of day-to-day issues that crop up and may include problems such as the replacement of staff, handling problem children, the provision of a new teaching block, or the repair of a fence. Schools are repeatedly asked to help in the training of teachers, and there will be regular liaison with staff of nearby colleges and university departments, many of whom will visit the school frequently and will be familiar faces in the staff room. At any one time a large comprehensive school may have up to a dozen student teachers on placement. Teachers are also regularly involved in the work of examination panels, and so will be in regular touch with their opposite numbers in nearby schools.

This brief account of secondary school life must be completely reworked at primary level or higher education. Infant and junior schools are generally far smaller than secondary schools and place far greater stress on pastoral care and on each child being supervised largely by a single member of staff. The primary school day is therefore far less structured than that in the secondary school, the teacher far less a specialist, and the administrative backup needed is consequently far less. The inferior staffing ratio of the primary school and the determination to enable the children to work to their own level lead to a situation in which the children are given greater choice of the particular activities they undertake. Against this, the class teacher will ensure that the basic skills of oral communications, literacy, and arithmetic are regularly approached by each child.

Within higher education the situation is far more fluid, with the underlying assumption that students of eighteen and above are mature individuals who can to a large extent organize their own study and examination preparation and who need little pastoral guidance. In this way university and polytechnic teachers justify an emphasis upon academic excellence and a relative disregard for the niceties of teaching method. In summary it should be emphasized that the variety of practice within English education is so wide that any individual school or college may present an entirely different aspect from the particular stresses suggested above.

## PROSPECT

The achievement of the English educational system during the twentieth century has been impressive. English society has undergone major shocks and changes. Its industrial system has been modernized, universal suffrage has been achieved, a major colonial empire has been dismantled, total war has twice been undergone and, in the wake of the United States, affluence has been achieved. Many of these developments would have been unthinkable without the support of an effective educational system: Certainly the fact that many of England's major political and social institutions are little changed in response to these developments must, in part at least, be attributable to the achievements of the educational system.

That system has itself been largely democratized during the twentieth century. In Victorian England, children were born to pursue either an elementary education or a secondary schooling. Now secondary education is universal and the education system itself is an important agency in sponsoring social mobility.

But the commitment of English society to a meritocracy remains partial. Public* schools continue to flourish, and attempts to enforce a more egalitarian educational system do not extend to these schools whose future is, for the moment at least, assured.

It seems, therefore, that several major questions hang over the future of education in England. The major issue appears to be to what extent the English really want an egalitarian and democratized educational system. Will they permit the public schools, which remain popular because of their power to confer advantages of one sort or another, to continue in their present form and thus buttress a relatively unchanging "establishment"? And, even if they do, will they pursue a genuinely egalitarian comprehensive system, or will they as at present, permit some selective schools to coexist with comprehensives? Beyond this the question remains of how far society is prepared to go to stamp out inequalities in status and effectiveness between comprehensives. The evidence of the late 1960s was that vigorous policies of "positive discrimination" were to be deployed toward such egalitarian goals. More recently it appears that society may be prepared to acquiesce in an ongoing situation in which, to borrow a phrase, all schools are comprehensive, but some are more comprehensive than others.

A second major question is raised by recent birthrate figures. It appears that the present population of more than 9 million in receipt of secondary education is to fall to less than 7 million within a decade. The way in which schools respond to these major traumas remains problematic. On the one hand the opportunity clearly exists for a radical improvement in staffing ratios and the use of resources as well as for the establishment of more effective in-service training for teachers. On the other, there is already evidence of a growing competitiveness between neighboring

---

*Note: The British "public school" is equivalent to the American term "private school."
[Editors]

schools for pupils, which may well result in teacher unemployment and school closures.

A further stimulus to change is provided by the increasingly beleaguered situation of British industry during the 1970s. The growing difficulties of some industries close to the center of the British economy may force English schools to a major reconsideration of their curricula during the next few years. It is often commented that the devotion of English secondary schools to a broad, "humane" curriculum throughout the twentieth century is one reason for the inelasticity and poor performance of British industry at the present time. How quickly changing patterns of employment will communicate themselves to the schools remains problematic.

Finally, an educational system devised by Anglo-Saxons for Anglo-Saxons now finds itself serving an ethnically mixed society. Whether the schools will be harnessed to the cause of racial harmony or whether they will be used as instruments by which one social group will seek to sustain its advantages may well be critical in determining the future harmony of English society.

In these ways English education, which we have earlier praised for its flexibility and responsiveness to social change, finds itself confronted by an entirely new set of challenges. We can predict with some confidence that there will be significant responses from educators. To precisely what ends these responses will work is difficult at this time to say.

## REFERENCES

1. Department of Education and Science. *The Educational System of England and Wales.* 1977.
2. Eliot, T. S. *Notes Towards the Definition of Culture.* London: Faber and Faber, 1948.
3. James, E. *An Essay on the Content of Education.* London: Harrap, 1949.
4. Jackson, B. *Streaming, An Education System in Miniature.* London: Routledge, 1964.
5. Department of Education and Science. *Statistics of Education,* vol. 1, *Schools.* London: H.M.S.O., 1976.
6. Brosan, G., et al. *Patterns and Policies in Higher Education.* London: Penguin, 1971.
7. Ministry of Education. *Report of the Special Committee on Higher Technological Education.* London: H.M.S.O., 1945.
8. Barlow Committee. *Scientific Manpower.* London: H.M.S.O.
9. Layard, R., et al. *The Impact of Robbins.* London: Penguin, 1969.
10. Robbins Committee on Higher Education. *Report, Higher Education.* London: H.M.S.O., 1963.
11. Boyle, E., and Crosland, A. *The Politics of Education.* London: Penguin, 1971.

12. Lawson, J., and Silver, H. *A Social History of Education in England.* London: Methuen, 1973.
13. Banks, O. *Parity and Prestige in English Education.* London: Routledge, 1955.
14. Seaborne, M., and Lowe, R. A. *The English School, 1870–1970.* London: Routledge, 1977.
15. Rubinstein, E., and Simon, B. *The Evolution of the Comprehensive School, 1926–1966.* London: Routledge, 1969.
16. Armytage, W. H. G. *Civic Universities.* London: Benn, 1955.
17. Central Advisory Council for Education. *Children and Their Primary Schools.* London: H.M.S.O., 1967.
18. Silver, H. *Equal Opportunity in Education.* London: Methuen, 1973.
19. Board of Education. *Report of the Consultative Committee on the Education of the Adolescent: Hadow Report.* London: H.M.S.O., 1926.
20. Norwood Committee. *Report of the Committee of the Secondary Schools Examination Council on Curriculum and Examinations in Secondary Schools.* London: H.M.S.O., 1943.
21. Peel, E. A. *The Nature of Adolescent Judgement.* London: Staples, 1971.
22. Schools Council Integrated Science Project. *Patterns.* London: Longmans, 1973.
23. Gagne, R. M. *Essentials of Learning for Instruction.* Hinsdale, Ill.: Dryden Press, 1975.
24. Bloom, B. S., et al. *Taxonomy of Educational Objectives: Handbook 1, Cognitive Domain.* London and New York: Longmans, 1956.
25. Holley, B. J. *A-level Syllabus Studies: History and Physics.* London: Macmillan Education for the Schools Council, 1974.
26. Maslow, A. H. *Toward a Psychology of Being.* Princeton, N.J.: Van Nostrand, 1962.
27. Axelrod, S. *Behavior Modification for the Classroom Teacher.* New York: McGraw-Hill, 1977.
28. Piaget, J. *The Origins of Intelligence in the Child.* London: Routledge, 1953.
29. Bennett, S. N., and Jordan, J. "A Typology of Teaching Styles in Primary Schools," *British Journal of Educational Psychology* 45, Part 1 (1975): 20–28.
30. Smith, F. *Understanding Reading.* New York: Holt, Rinehart and Winston, 1971.
31. Callaghan, J., Prime Minister. Speech given at Ruskin College, Oxford, 1976.
32. Department of Education and Science. *Assessment of Performance Unit: An Introduction.* London: D.E.S., 1978.
33. Schools Council. *Project Profiles and Index.* London: Schools Council, 1978.
34. Beauchamp, G. A., and Beauchamp, K. E. *Comparative Analysis of Curriculum Systems.* Wilmette, Ill.: Kagg Press, 1972.
35. Ashton, P., et al. *The Aims of Primary Education: A Study of Teachers'*

*Opinions.* London: Macmillan Education for the Schools Council, 1975.

36. Weston, P. B. *Framework for the Curriculum.* Windsor, England: N.F.E.R. Publishing Company, 1977.
37. Schools Council. *Growth and Response.* Working Paper No. 45, 16–19. London: Evans/Methuen Educational.
38. Schools Council. *Certificate of Secondary Education: Some Suggestions for Teachers.* Examinations Bulletin No. 1. London: H.M.S.O., 1963.
39. Schools Council. *The C.S.E. 1965 Monitoring Experiment Part 1 and Part 2.* Working Paper No. 6. London: H.M.S.O.
40. Green, L. *School Reports and Other Information for Parents.* Billericay, Essex: Home and Schools Council Publications, 1975.
41. Start, K. B., and Wells, B. K. *The Trend of Reading Standards.* Slough, Bucks: National Foundation for Educational Research, 1972.
42. Department of Education and Science. *The Educational System of England and Wales.* London: H.M.S.O., 1977.
43. Kogan, M., and Packwood, T. *Advisory Committees and Councils in Education.* London: Routledge, 1974.
44. Manzer, R. A. *Teachers and Politics.* Manchester: University of Manchester Press, 1970.
45. Taylor, P. H., et al. *Purpose, Power and Constraint in the Primary School Curriculum.* London: Macmillan Education, 1974.
46. Musgrove, F. *Patterns of Power and Authority in English Education.* London: Methuen, 1971.
47. Berg, L. *Risinghill: The Death of a School.* Harmondsworth, Middlesex: Penguin Books, 1968.
48. Auld, R. *William Tyndale Junior and Infant Schools: Public Inquiry.* London: Inner London Education Authority, 1976.
49. Musgrove, F., and Taylor, P. H. *Society and the Teacher's Role.* London: Routledge, 1969.
50. Ashton, P. *The Aims of Primary Education.* London: Macmillan Education for the Schools Council, 1975.
51. Taylor, P. H., et al. "An Exploratory Study of Science Teachers' Perceptions of Effective Teaching," *Educational Review* 23, No. 1 (1970): 19–33.
52. Department of Education and Science. *Teacher Education and Training (James Report).* London: H.M.S.O., 1972.
53. Salter, P. *The Pursuit of Loneliness.* Boston: Beacon Press, 1971.
54. Neill, A. S. *Summerhill.* New York: Hart, 1960.

*Articles*

Luckinsky, J. S. " 'Structure' in Educational Theory," *Educational Philosophy and Theory* 2, No. 2 (1970): 15–32.
Mann, J. S. "A Discipline of Curriculum Theory," *School Review* 76, No. 4 (1968): 359–378.

## Educational Objectives

### Books

Cox, R. C., and Wildemann, C. E. "Taxonomy of Educational Objectives: Cognitive Domain: An Annotated Bibliography." Monograph No. 1. Pittsburgh: Learning Research and Development Center, University of Pittsburgh, 1970.

Popham, J., Eisher, E. W. et al. *Instructional Objectives*. Chicago: Rand McNally & Co. 1969.

Rubin, L. J. *Life Skills in School and Society*. Washington, D.C.: A.S.C.D. 1969.

### Articles

Gribble, J. "Pandora's Box: The Affective Domain of Educational Objectives," *Journal of Curriculum Studies* 2, No. 1 (1970): 11–24.

Smith, M. J. "A Study of the Operational Objectives of Science Teachers," M.Ed. Thesis, University of Birmingham, 1970.

Taylor, P. A., and Maguire, T. O. "Perception of Some Objectives for Science Curriculum," *Science Education* 51 (1967): 489–493.

## Curriculum Evaluation

### Books

Tyler, R. W. *Educational Evaluation: New Roles, New Means*. N.S.S.E. Yearbook 68, Part 2. Chicago: University of Chicago Press, 1969.

Vickers, G. *Value Systems and Social Process*. London: Penguin Books, 1968.

Vickers, V. *The Act of Judgement*. London: Chapman and Hall, 1965.

### Articles

Anderson, G. J., Walberg, H. J., and Welch, W. W. "Curriculum Effects on the Social Climate of Learning," *American Educational Research Journal* 6, No. 3 (1969): 315–328.

Eels, K. "How Effective Is Differential Prediction in Three Types of College Curriculum?" *Educational Psychology Measurement* 21 (1961): 459–471.

Westbury, I. "Curriculum Evaluation," *Revue of Educational Research* 40, No. 2 (1970): 239–260.

## Sociology of Curriculum

Lacey, C. *Hightown Grammar*. Manchester: University of Manchester Press, 1970.

## Curriculum Innovation and Change

Frymier, J. R. *Fostering Educational Change*. Columbus, Ohio: C. E. Merrill & Co., 1969.

CHAPTER 5

# Israeli Education

ELAD PELED

## DEFINITION

Israel's education system is characterized by the following traits:

1. It is a bilingual system: 85 percent of its pupils attend Hebrew-speaking schools; 15 percent attend Arabic-speaking schools.

2. Almost 50 percent of the Jewish pupils in the school system are disadvantaged children. The majority of these are Oriental Jews who originated in North Africa or Arab countries in the Middle East.

3. The state is the exclusive group responsible for educating its children. As stated by the minister who submitted the appropriate legislation in 1953: "Education is a state's domain, within its responsibilities and under its authority. . . . The state is ultimately responsible for the ways through which the development of the young generation will be directed and realised" (Dinur, 1958). This postulate is illustrated by a centralized system which is directed, financed, and controlled by the Ministry of Education and Culture.

4. Ideological orientation is a predominate factor in Israel's educational system since its formative years during the pre-state era (pre-1948). Hence, the schools are a public service, with a social and national mission rather than a commonweal oriented toward the welfare of the individual.

5. Education is almost free but not compulsory between ages three and four; free and compulsory between the ages of five and sixteen; free but not compulsory between seventeen and eighteen.

6. The law grants the parents the right of choice between a state religious education and a state nonreligious education.

7. Israel's educational system may be characterized since its inception by inherent dilemmas and tensions such as: egalitarianism versus elitism;

uniformity versus diversity: centralization versus decentralization; competitiveness and achievement orientation versus noncompetitiveness and social orientation; ideology orientation versus ideology-free orientation; national and social objectives predominance versus child orientation; continuity and tradition versus innovation; predominance of traditional orthodox Jewish orientation versus a "mix" of Jewish orientation and general modern orientation; recognition of the uniqueness and special needs of Arab education versus a uniform approach toward Arab curriculum.

These tensions and dilemmas are consequences of Israel's present social situation and stem both from external constraints and from the historical development of the Jewish educational system in Israel prior to 1948 (Israel's independence).

The Israeli educational system, the psychological-pedagogical concepts, perceptions, and attitudes developed in this system, must be viewed in this framework.

## INTRODUCTION

### Objectives of Education

Two extreme approaches to the study of the role of objectives in education are known in the Western free world and are restated in Israel. The first views education as an instrument to transfer society's past experiences and traditions as well as to train the pupil for his future activities in the society (Eden, 1973). According to this approach, which is a society-oriented approach, educational objectives are based on life philosophy, on the specific characteristics of the society and on its necessities and on the needs of the pupil. The definition of the characteristics and the needs depends, at least partially, on the social norms, values, and "biases" (Eden, 1976).

The second approach (Lam, 1973) denies absolutely any formal and legal setting of educational objectives and claims that a democratic society should not state and formalize its objectives of education. Any legalization of this kind must be viewed as an intervention in private domains, akin to intervention into the domains of those beliefs and opinions.

Furthermore, the political process of educational legislation enhances a vague, unstable, and operationally meaningless statement of educational objectives. Israel, as a pluralistic society, faces many conflicts and struggles reflected in the value systems of its different groups. As a pluralistic society, Israel might have resolved these conflicts in two ways —by avoiding the "issue" as long as possible, hoping for a "peaceful coexistence"; or by according legal rights to maintain separate school systems, each directed by its group values and concepts. Both solutions seem to be unfitted to Israeli society, which strives for a cohesive national unity and social integration. This vital need for unity on the one hand and the political tensions and conflicts on the other hand led the "Founding Fathers" to the compromise found in the somewhat vague legislation of educational objectives, stated by section 2 of the State Education Law, 1953:

> The object of "State Education" is to base elementary education in the state on the values of Jewish culture and the achievements of science, on the love of the homeland and the loyalty to the state and the Jewish people, on practice of agricultural work and handicraft, on pioneer (*haluzic*) training and on striving for a society built on freedom, equality, tolerance, mutual assistance and love of mankind.

This nonoperational statement of objectives has been criticized by people like Lam (1973), who views a political compromise of this kind as one that may lead to the alienation of the young generation from the traditions and inheritance of its ancestors.

It should be noted that democratic societies that legislate their educational objectives view them as a political act, representing a general consensus or a stated will of a majority. As such, legislation of educational objectives helps to mobilize support of parents and others and has a cohesive and an integrative impact on the society (Sheffler, 1960, p. 36). It is clear that this was also one of the purposes of the Israeli legislation regarding educational objectives. The attainment may be questioned.

Traditionally, Jews in the diaspora viewed education as a central issue in their lives. Some of their attitudes toward education, as well as some of the social and cultural values developed and practiced in the diaspora, have been carried out in Israel. The limited space of this article precludes an adequate review of Jewish education outside Israel through almost 2,000 years, but those who are interested in the full picture of the factors at work in the Israeli educational system should look carefully into its conception in the Jewish communities outside Israel.

Israel's present system of education will be discussed in this article, its history in Israel since the return of the Jews to their homeland, the impact of Zionist ideology, and the political and social foundations of its structure.

## Reasons for This System

### History

The Jewish school system in Eretz Israel (Palestine) prior to 1948 (the pre-state era) was a function of various influences: an autonomous and highly centralized system based on a uniform curriculum; a solid and authoritative supervision; and a strong influence exerted by the various political parties, their ideologies and administrations. A further detailed description of this historical development will follow.

### Ideology

The Zionist ideology, with its many variations, has been decisive in the formation of Israel's education, since even before the independence of the state. According to this ideology, the Jewish state (Israel) has a historical vocation and responsibility to develop a "new" type of "Israeli" out of the arriving immigrants; to foster their social qualities, to form a national character, and to reshape their national traditions. It is, therefore, the duty and obligation of the state of Israel to educate its citizens to a complete identification with the country, its future, and its survival. The state educates not only by its laws but by the fact that the "cell" of life is education. It should educate to the realization and the feeling that the state is the home of the individual, and its laws and its regulations provide justice between people and the individual and the community (Dinur, 1958).

### The Social and the Political Foundations

In the Israeli environment, education should be regarded as a subsystem of its society, which is pluralistic from almost any point of view. Nationally, the majority (84 percent) are Jews, while the minorities are Arabs (13.5 percent) and Druze (1.5 percent). Geographically 84 percent of the population is urban while 16 percent is rural. Ethnically (country of origin) the Jewish majority can be grouped into Israeli-born (48 percent), "Orientals" born in Middle Eastern countries and North Africa (25 percent), and "Westerns" born in European countries, America, South Africa and the Far Eastern countries (27 percent). It should be noted that most of the "Oriental" Jews came to Israel after 1948 and were and still are of a lower socioeconomic status in the Israeli society. Religiously, the Jewish majority is divided into religious people who want their children to get a religious education in school, and those who claim the separation of religion and education (an issue that is problematic due to the importance of religion in the Jewish culture) and want their children to get a secular education. Culturally, there is usually a coexistence, but not infrequently conflicts between the "Orientals" and the "Westerns," as well as between the religious and the nonreligious groups do arise.

The special national and linguistic structure of the Israeli population has created separate educational systems for Jews, Arabs, and Druzes. The different attitudes toward religious issues have also developed into two educational subsystems for the Jews: a religious subsystem and a nonreligious subsystem. The constant immigration to Israel has caused and required special attention and focus on the problems of the disadvantaged, and this will be discussed in detail in a following section.

The cultural and ethnic heterogeneity of the Jewish majority has raised a dilemma of its social function: is it a "melting pot" or an instrument to support integration in a pluralistic society; or something that does *not* assimilate its immigrants into the dominant ruling groups but rather encourages the self-identity of the different groups, as well as their social integration?

Eisenstadt (1967) pointed out a change in the role of the education system in Israel: from an important instrument for social change, social innovation and creativity, education turned into an instrument of job selection, a vehicle of cultural transfer and the major means of controlling the "melting pot." Recent pressures of the increasing political power of the Orientals strengthen the trend of the "pluralists" in education. Already in 1969, facing the failure of the "melting pot" concept, a new strategy for immigrants' absorption was proposed: a realization that in Israel there were social and ethnic prejudices that must be rejected; a desire to encourage cultural pluralism in which education should have a central role; a proposal to reform radically all existing traditional institutions of the society, and particularly the school system (Shuval, 1969). The development in the 1970s followed this new strategy.

## HISTORY

Israel's present-day educational system is a continuation of a system that already existed before 1948. In addition to long-standing educational traditions developed in the diaspora that nourished this system, the foundations of Israeli education which were laid down by the Jewish community in the pre-independence era also struggled with the autonomy of its educational system.

Referring to the present situation, it seems that the historical development can be best summarized and understood through four major issues that are and were prominent on its agenda:

1. The sociocultural gap within the Jewish majority between the Orientals and the Westerns.
2. The advancement of the education of the minorities (Arabs and Druze).
3. The role of education in Israel's value system.
4. The adaptation of the organization and the structure of the system to the social and political changes that have been occurring in the Israeli society since the independence of the state.

Israel's education today is a continuation of a prior system, unlike other organizations such as the defense organization, for which the Declaration of Independence was a starting point.

Beginnings

*The Sociocultural Gap*

Studies and surveys investigating the pre-independence era have shown indications of culture deprivation, slow learning, low achievement and high drop-out rates (Brill 1938, 1939, 1941; Dushkin 1938; Baki 1944; Enoch 1950; Osterreicher-Ortar 1948). These phenomena included failure to pass classes as early as the first grade in the elementary school, dropping out in the fourth, fifth, and sixth grades, a substantial decrease in the number of pupils attending the seventh and eighth grades, and only a highly selective minority of pupils attending high school. In Jerusalem, as an illustration, during 1932 and 1937, 50 percent of the pupils dropped out before the sixth grade, and only 20 percent reached the eighth grade (Dushkin, 1938; Brill, 1938). Social workers, nurses, educators, and union activists tried to cope with these problems.

Nevertheless, for Israeli society and its educational and political establishment there was no issue of "disadvantaged children." Perhaps other pressures (the World War II, the struggle against the British government, and economic and political difficulties) attracted the whole energy of the public and its leaders.

*Education of Minorities*

In 1948, when Israel achieved its independence, 16 percent of its population were non-Jews (of whom about 14 percent were Arabs and the rest Druzes and others). In 1972, the non-Jewish population was about 15 percent of the total population.

During British rule in Palestine (which later became Israel and the West Bank of Jordan) there was an administrative separation between two school systems: the Jewish system and the Arab system. The Jewish system was almost autonomous, controlled and financed by the autonomous Jewish community in the country, while the Arab schools were "public schools," owned, financed, and controlled by the government of the British Mandate (Bentwich, 1960).

In 1945, education among the Muslims was not universal (whereas among the Christian Arabs it was almost universal). According to an estimate in 1945, school attendance among the Muslim Arabs in Palestine was: in the cities, 85 percent of the boys and 60 percent of the girls; in the rural areas, 60 percent of the boys and 7 percent of the girls. British officials increased the number of schools, and the number of Arab children who attended these schools grew. On the other hand, their impact on Arab schools became detrimental after the creation of Israel in 1948. The Arab school system, in contrast to the Jewish system, was entirely dependent on the British government in administration and in content (curriculum, methods of teaching, and so on). Most of the top administrators were British officials, and they had superimposed British culture on the schools. The British regarded schools as a vocation and mission of spreading Western civilization. The Arabs accepted this culture ambivalently. Externally, it was accepted, but there was a strong internal nationalistic reaction. Thus, while the Arab schools did not develop their autonomy, they cultivated an external facade of Westernization with a strong nationalistic undercurrent.

Obviously these trends did not help the integration of Jews and Arabs during the pre-independence British Mandate. The War of Independence (1947–1948) and its aftermath transferred to the state of Israel a weak Arab school system, unable to renew itself or innovate from within.

### The Role of Education in Israel's Value System

The pre-independence era may be characterized by three main self-images of Jewish society in Eretz Israel: the national image interpreted by the Zionist ideology and the political organizations of the various Zionist movements; the idea of the major necessary roles and functions in the community, interpreted by the image of the "pioneer" (*halutz*); the ideas designed to shape the internal structure and form of the society, emphasizing ideas of social justice and social equality and interpreted by socialistic ideologies (Eisenstadt, et al., 1972).

A leading educator stated the dilemma of the Jewish education in Eretz Israel in the 1930s by describing the forces that enhance educational ideas and programs. He contrasted social and group solidarity against extreme individualism, postulating that in a static society social solidarity prevailed, whereas in a dynamic society the individual prevailed. In the latter kind of society, individualistic attitudes go together with radicalism and sometimes even with anarchism.

Social and national challenges require a social-solidarity approach, while the individualistic attitude enhances cultural creativity as well as weakens social cohesiveness. The Jewish national challenge of the 1930s was considered to be the creation of a Jewish national homeland in Israel; this consequently required society-oriented education (Rieger, 1940) and made the system heavily loaded with values and ideologies.

### Structure and Organization

Since its inception, there has been no general consensus regarding the structure of the school: an elementary school for eight years and a high school for four years, and the dilemma whether there should be a single and uniform structure for all or a dual structure—eight plus four for the majority and four preparatory years and eight years of high school education leading to higher education for the best and the chosen pupils. In the pre-independence years, the structure was a dual one: most of the schools were eight-year elementary schools (influenced by the European *Volkschule*), where the majority of pupils got their full cycle of studies and only a minority of pupils continued their studies in a four-year high school (Gymnasium). A few schools had four preparatory years and eight years of secondary education leading to higher education.

In the public dispute about the structure of the school, the main supporter of the eight-year elementary school was the Federation of Teachers; on the opposite side were most high school teachers and the university professors.

At the end of the 1930s the director of the British Mandate Department of Education (Farrel) published a memorandum, criticizing the Jewish education system in Palestine, its ideological orientation, and its structure. He proposed a new structure of a lower elementary, infant stage (ages five to seven), a lower elementary, junior stage (eight to eleven), higher elementary, first cycle (twelve to thirteen), and higher elementary second cycle (fourteen to eighteen), much like the British system. The Jewish community regarded this proposition as intervention in its autonomy, and therefore it was rejected, mostly on political grounds. In a letter sent to the British head of the Department of Education in Palestine, the director of the autonomous Jewish Department of Education rejected Farrel's proposition with the following arguments: The structure of the Jewish school is exclusively an internal issue of the Jewish community and there is no place for transplantation of British structures to Palestine; the Jewish national religious education requires eight years. There were additional psychological and pedagogical arguments. The outbreak of World War II and the political and military struggle for independence after the war postponed the dispute and transferred the unresolved issue to the newborn State of Israel in 1948.

### Organization of the System

One of the major features of the Jewish education in the pre-independence era was its division into three almost autonomous "trends" (Kleinberger, 1969), each distinct in its political, ideological, and educational attributes: The *Mizrahi* trend (Zionist-Religious-Orthodox), the Labor trend (Zionist-Socialist) and the General Trend, which comprised all schools that were not affiliated with the first two. Even the General trend was backed and supported by the General-Zionist party (a sort of Liberal-Conservative party). The extreme orthodox Jews were *not* included in the *Mizrahi* trend, due to their anti-Zionist approach.

The beginning of the trends system was made by a political compromise between the *Mizrahi* party (National-Orthodox-Religious party) and the Zionist Executive Committee and its General Conference (1920). The political recognition of the educational autonomy of the *Mizrahi* schools illustrated the existence of the conflict regarding the role of religion in daily life, particularly in education, and its effects on the national and social character of the Jewish community in Palestine (Ormian, 1968) on one hand. On the other hand recognition of *Mizrahi* schools expressed the tendency of a political compromise between the secular parties and the national religious party, which has since then become a part of Israel's internal politics (Abramov, 1976). This tendency was enacted into law in 1953 (State Education Law). After a recognition of the Labor trend in 1923, the Zionist Congress approved the coexistence of three "trends" in education (Harman, 1970).

Each party tried to justify the existence of its specific "trend." The Labor party argued that its political objectives included education of their young potential followers; that the social and educational environment of the school should reflect the values of the Zionist-Socialist ideology and the impact of post-World War I revolutionary ideas from Europe.

The *Mizrahi* trend based its autonomy on three principles: a traditional orthodox religious education combining religious "ideology" with religious way of life; integration of religious orthodox education with modern education; and Zionist education and training.

The General trend argued for separation of education from politics. The school was regarded as a political entity, serving the ideological common denominator of all the Zionist parties, that is, "Zionist" (Ben-Yehuda, 1973). The existence of the trends enhanced competition between them to attract pupils, which ultimately created rivalries and sometimes even hatred and turned into a major public issue.

After the independence of Israel, a fourth trend (of the extreme orthodox Agudat-Israel) was recognized as another autonomous trend. Only after a series of political crises was a law enacted in 1953 that abolished the autonomous trends and recognized two trends within the state administration: a state religious trend and a state nonreligious trend. The extreme orthodox once more got political recognition of their autonomy (as a subsidized "parochial" school) and thus essentially the only trend abolished was the Labor trend.

## Current Status

### The Sociocultural Gap

The massive immigration of Jews to Israel, mostly from the North African and Middle Eastern countries, highlighted the emerging issue of the disadvantaged and culturally deprived children. Problems of slow learning, of large numbers of dropouts, and of insufficient attendance in schools for disadvantaged children have been a permanent trait of education in Israel (even in the pre-state years). Nonetheless, only in the late 1950s did these problems become a public issue, pointed out by practical experience of teachers and supervisors and by scientific research. The fact of a sociocultural gap between "Orientals" and "Westerns" emerged as one of the most crucial social, political, and educational issues.

The different definitions of the "disadvantaged" reflect to a great extent the different approaches and strategies. For a decade (1963–1974), "disadvantaged schools," eligible for extra budgetary allocations and special compensatory programs, have been defined on the basis of the following criteria: the pupil composition of the school (that is, the percentage of "Asian-African" pupils; the mean achievement level of the school according to results of standardized tests at the end of elementary school); and certain characteristics of the teaching staff (lack of teacher certification and residence of teachers in a different locality) (Rokah, 1970). Because extensive changes have occurred over the years in all three of the elements, the need was felt to redefine the problem.

The new definition, formulated in 1974 (Algarrebly, 1975) referred to groups of pupils instead of referring to entire schools and was based on the results of a standard test done in 1972 (the *Seker*). The new definition was a combination of three elements: father's origins (Israel, Europe-America, Asia, Africa), father's education level, and family size. Pupil groups in which 40 percent or fewer attained a score of 70 (the median in the *Seker*) were identified in terms of the three characteristics defined as having poor chances for learning success, and thus as *disadvantaged*. According to this definition, 44 percent of the pupils in the system were defined as "disadvantaged," and 95 percent of the latter were children with parents of Asian-African background.

The issue of the "disadvantaged pupils" has a double meaning, encompassing two different aims:

1. A purely educational aim: prevention or remediation of learning failures in which the aim is to bring slow pupils up to a standard defined by educational criteria, without any connection with the social or cultural group membership of these pupils.
2. A social and political aim: closing the gaps between pupil groups, in which the central aim is to achieve equality between the disadvantaged group and the reference group in terms of learning achievement distribution.

Israeli policy regarding the disadvantaged children has not made clear this distinction. Therefore, a recent critique of the policy argued that therefore, compensatory and rehabilitation activities were not planned in a consistent manner so as to strike a balance between the two aspects of the problem: treatment of serious learning failures and closing the gaps between the two sociocultural groups (Minkovich, Davis, & Bashi, 1977). A recent evaluation of the achievements of pupils in Israeli elementary schools showed a gap of one to two years between low achievers (disadvantaged of "Oriental" origin) and high achievers (of "Western" origin). Nonetheless, there is a slow but steady trend of progress in cognitive achievements of the "disadvantaged" and in their rate of learning in all levels of schooling (Minkovich, Davis, & Bashi, 1977). A study aimed at measuring the closing or the widening of the achievement gap between ethnic groups in the Jewish elementary schools in Israel showed that there is a gap of about six months to two years between "Orientals" and "Westerns" in the elementary school but that this gap is quite stable (Lewy & Chen, 1976).

The human, social, and moral need to narrow the gap between the "Orientals" and the "Westerns" on one hand and the increasing political pressures to do so fast created the dilemma between raising academic standards and solving social tensions. Eisenstadt (1967) claimed that the political compromise of lowering academic requirements was one way of resolving the social tension, the easy way. Furthermore, through this issue another dilemma arose, the choice between the socio-politico-ideological pressure of "free education for all" and the needs of the society and the economy for a diversified and highly skilled work force.

*Minorities*

Fifteen percent of the school population in Israel are minority children (13.5 percent Arabs and 1.5 percent Druzes and others), for whom Arabic is the language. Historical circumstances and the inheritance from the British Mandate era caused a wide gap between the Jewish and the minority education in all aspects. In recent years, a successful effort has been made to narrow this gap. Education for minority students raises some basic problems, such as the definition of the Israeli-Arab identity and its application in the curriculum and the academic achievements of the Arab students. The strategies for aiding the disadvantaged among Jewish children are considered to be inappropriate for the Arab pupils. The Jewish disadvantaged are culturally uprooted from their natural environment and deprived while the Arab low achievers grow in their natural organic environment, which is now going through a process of modernization.

The challenge of Arab education in Israel is to promote the physical development of the schools' infrastructure and to adapt its curriculum to the real national and political environment.

## The Role of Education in Israel's Value System

Israel's present education appears to be getting more and more detached from values and ideologies that characterized the system in the pre-independence era. The educational system that at its inception was loaded and even motivated by the Zionist ideology, by the socialist philosophy, and by the values prevailing in the pioneering society, has turned in the late 1970s into a system that is torn between those values and the norms that have developed in Israel recently. Those norms frequently place the individual and individual rights above the national and social duties and obligations.

### Structure and Organization of the System

Most of the organizational and structural patterns of Israel's education date back to the pre-independence era. Four issues challenge the present system to adjust and adapt the system, its structures, and its organization to the social and political changes that have occurred in Israel's society since its independence: centralization versus decentralization; elimination of the rigid barrier between formal and informal education; reorganization of the supervision of the system; redefinition of the responsibilities of the ministry (national government), local governments, and parents.

The historical development, the ideological orientation and the social needs of the 1950s and the 1960s were the reasons for the high centralization of the system, according the exclusive responsibility for education to the national government.

The minister of education and culture who was responsible for enacting the State Education Law (1953) explained this law by saying (Dinur, 1958): "State education means that education is a domain which is under the authority and responsibility of the State. . . . The State cannot transfer the responsibility for its future to others. . . . It is the duty of the State to educate its citizens to a complete identification of each individual with the State, its future and its survival."

In the 1970s a movement for reform started to call for decentralization of the system and for according a major part of the authority and responsibility for education to local communities and to parents, within the framework of the national objectives of education (Peled, 1976).

The parents' freedom to choose a school for their children (within the framework of compulsory education ages of five to sixteen) is limited to three possibilities: to a state (nonreligious) school, to a state religious school, or to a recognized nonofficial school (mostly extreme orthodox). There is, however, no possibility of choosing a specific school. Registration is bounded by zoning lines, determined by the local governments.

## THEORY

### Learning

In a study done in the 1970s, there is a description of the psychological and pedagogical postulates of Israel's education in the pre-independence era that also prevailed at least during the 1950s, Israel's first decade (Minkovitch & Bashi, 1973). These postulates came from Herbart's psychological theory and have absorbed new ideas from more recent psychological theories, particularly regarding early childhood. The impact of Herbart's theory was the neglect of the developmental approach; thinking processes were considered identical in all ages and in all kinds of learners; the differences were derived from the accumulated knowledge and experience acquired in school. Learning was considered to be a uniform, single process of linking things in an associative and perceptive way. The role of the learner became relatively passive, and the results of learning depended mostly on the method of presentation of the material. In this simplified theory, there is no conceptual distinction between learning and thinking or between "mechanical" learning (associations) and reasoning.

Another psychological postulate on which Israel's educational tradition was established regarded the problem of transfer. There was a pessimistic attitude that doubted the capability of transfer and therefore emphasized the quantity of information that a pupil should memorize and remember.

It seems justifiable to say that the internal conflict between the two approaches—the social and the individualistic—has been reflected in the disputes referring to learning and to the role of the educator in the classroom. Nevertheless, the changes in the theoretical postulates prevailing in the field were not rapid and could be considered only as echoes of problems emphasized by advocates of the different approaches. It is in this context that one can explain why a phaedocentric approach was introduced in Israel only in the 1970s.

This situation may be further clarified by examining what issues spokesmen of the different approaches in the 1970s considered to be of the utmost importance. While Izhar (1974), an eloquent representative of the individualistic approach, called for the exclusive responsibility of the educator to determine what should be done in school, Alon (1973), then minister of education and culture, emphasized the definition of two kinds of goals in education: national-social goals and personal-individual goals. Alon's call for a synthesis between the socially oriented and the individualistic approaches is in line with Eden (1973), who thought that the planning of the curriculum should reflect both the social needs and the individual's needs.

Yet the most symptomatic illustration of the lack of sophistication in that area may be found in a book published by the Ministry of Education and Culture (1977) to celebrate twenty-five years of education in Israel. In this book, most of the aspects of Israel's education are discussed but there is no direct mention of the psychological-pedagogical aspects of the system.

### The Curriculum

In the center of learning in Israeli schools stands the curriculum, the meaning of which has been insistence on scholastic achievement.

As mentioned previously, the curriculum in the early years was uniform. Facing the low achievement of disadvantaged children, a process of diversification of the curriculum was initiated: in the elementary school different curricula for different kinds of children (at the same grade level) and in the secondary school grouping and tracking. Studies have led the educators and educational policy makers to realize that there is no good pedagogical solution to the problem of a heterogeneous class with a uniform curriculum (Adiel, et al., 1970). Social and political pressures and an ideological egalitarian approach enhanced the policy of the heterogeneous class, which was regarded as the basic unit for learning and social activity. But, to cope with the large differences among the pupils in the class, grouping and tracking were introduced in which Hebrew, English, and mathematics were taught according to different standard levels of achievements and knowledge (Adiel, et al., 1970). Apart from these three subjects, the heterogeneous class *is* the unit of teaching and learning. Remedial reading and teaching were introduced to support slow learners.

### The Traditional Curriculum and Teaching Methods

The old, traditional curriculum emphasized the amount of detail that the pupil should acquire in each subject. This acquisition was accomplished by traditional teaching at all ages (excluding the kindergarten) and in all subjects. The curriculum in each subject was mandatory to the teachers and their superiors (the principal and the supervisor). The freedom of the teachers was only in the division of the learning material into study units and its presentation in the classroom. The presentation was "frontal" (a lecture or a questions-answer dialogue, or a combination of the two). The pupils' role was to listen to the teacher and classmates, to supply the right answers to the teacher's questions, to memorize through homework, and to prove knowledge in structured examinations.

In the late 1950s, criticism was aroused, based on more modern psychological and pedagogical theories. The main points of the criticism were:

1. *Age differences.* The learning of meaningful content in any subject includes complex and diversified processes of analysis and synthesis, transformations, coordinations, and generalizations. These processes are active, not passive, that is, they have to occur within the pupil's mind and cannot be given to him by the teacher. The occurrence of the processes and their quality depend, among other things, on the existence of mental constructs, cognitive operations, and basic concepts formed in the pupil's mind during cognitive development. These constructs and operations of the mind are different in the different stages of cognitive development of the individual.

2. *Subject-matter differences.* The old pedagogy neglected another differentiation—differences in the processes of different kinds of learning. There are differences between skills learning and content learning. In a specific subject a young child's learning focused on developing cognitive operations and basic concepts, is different from an older pupil's learning that looks for a meaningful acquisition of knowledge; the older child has already developed logical operations and abstraction. Furthermore, in each stage of development, there should be a distinction between learning of different kinds of subject matter. The learning required in the natural sciences is different from that required in the social sciences, and the learning of both is different from learning humanities, based very much on emotional experiences.

3. *Differences of pupils.* This criticism denies the existence of an "average" or a "normal" pupil. Furthermore, the development of diagnostic tools and methods and test theories in the intelligence level, in personal, and in cultural adjustments have emphasized the need for a clear distinction between different kinds of pupils regarding curriculum and teaching methods (for example, slow learners versus gifted, disadvantaged versus advantaged, and so on).

## The New Curriculum

Behind the new curriculum there is a premise that there is a paradox that deduces a time gap between the training of a teacher, trained in the past to teach in the present and to prepare the pupils for an uncertain future. Even in the humanistic subjects, there is no stability in values and content. On the contrary, there is a gap between the values and content, based on past experience of generations and presented by the teacher, and the new values and content of the pupils who may rebel frequently against this past. These factors call for an inevitable process of change and innovation.

Social, economic, and political developments have imposed a dynamic process of innovation and change on the educational system in Israel. They challenged the system on different fronts: The need for training the pupils for orientation to a changing and developing world caused a search for new ways to form the personality of the pupils and to give them tools and methods for independent thinking, for reasonable value judgment, and for rational decision-making ability. The challenge of raising academic standards in schools has been interpreted to mean increase rational thinking ability; acquiring means and ways for self-studies, replacing condensation of information; emphasizing the ability to gain an overview; offering general education as a broad basis to professional mobility and understanding reality; emphasizing natural sciences and modern technology together with deepening humanistic and Jewish studies, and, finally, looking for ways to compensate for the deprivation of children from distressed environments.

The new curriculum planners were guided in their work by the following factors that serve as sources for considerations and bases for decisions: the individual pupil and his or her needs, society and its needs, the common values system, the psychology of learning and development, and the structure of the disciplines (the subject matter) (Eden, 1971).

### The Needs of the Individual Pupil

For the first time, since an official curriculum was issued in Israel or in the pre-independent Israel, the consideration of the individual needs became important in planning the curriculum. According to Abraham Maslow, the school is seen as an active participant in satisfying the needs of the individual. As the needs rise in their hierarchical scales (biological needs to psychological needs), satisfying these needs is regarded as an obligation of the school and as a leverage for the encouragement of the learning process. The new curriculum, although it is not based entirely on this approach (as an extreme of progressive education), considers the individual's needs as an important element for planning. Its significance is illustrated more in the selection of learning activities than in setting learning goals and objectives.

### The Needs of the Society

The premise is that society has a vital interest in preparing the pupil for participation in social life. Therefore, the characteristics of the specific society and demands from its members have an impact on the goals of education and on the objectives of the specific curriculum. The needs of the society may be interpreted differently, according to one's values and norms.

### Values and Norms

These appear as ideologies, perceptions of life, and education. Different approaches lead to different priorities in the selection of topics, influence the "climate of the school," and guide educational attitudes and teaching methods.

### Psychology of Learning and Development

Among the many items from the psychology of learning that had an impact on planning the curriculum, worth noting are the realization of the boundaries of memory (that have an influence on the importance of information as well as the methods of critical thinking), discovery of the learner's activity encouragement of his motivation, and so on. The learning activities, suggested in the new curriculum depend very much on the extent of interest that is provoked and in the extent of satisfaction to the learner. This satisfaction increases if and when the learner gets encouraging reactions from learning successes. Therefore, important elements in the pupil's motivation are competence and reinforcement. Avoiding a one-sided approach and the use of all the motivating elements increase the probability of success, hence, the insistence on diversification of teaching method is regarded as influencing different pupils differently.

The new curriculum derived some elements also from the findings of developmental psychology, to adjust and fit the curriculum to the different age levels. Different content and skills were sought for acquisition by pupils of different ages. The principle of "preparedness" for learning became a guideline for assigning curriculum material to the different age levels. There was an effort to affect the preparedness beyond biological age. There is still a dispute between the supporters of an accelerated cognitive development and those who argue for consideration of both the cognitive and the affective aspects of the child's development.

Some experiments were done, based on Bruner's theory that every subject can be taught effectively and cognitively, in reasonable fairness to *each* child in *every* stage of development. Piaget's developmental theory and his distinction between egocentric-intuitive thinking and concrete and formal operations have also had a strong impact on contemporary curriculum planning in Israel.

### The Structure of the Discipline (the Subject Matter)

In school and its curriculum the meaning of a discipline is in its content (structure of knowledge) and the attitudes that form its inquiry and research methods.

### The Process of Curriculum Planning

Present-day curriculum planning in Israel was influenced very decisively by B. S. Bloom (1956) of the University of Chicago and his "Taxonomy of Educational Objectives." Following his approach, the process starts with the definition of the aims (the highest level of goals) and develops into operational objectives.

The new curriculum has not been planned in a vacuum. It is the outcome of a historic development which started long before 1948 and of past and current trends in the general world of education.

Curriculum in Israel, as in many other countries, reflects not only the conflict between the past and the future but also the different interpretations that develop according to the needs of society and the role of its individuals. New curriculum generally expresses past changes, as well as laying foundations for new changes and innovations.

In the pre-independence era of Israel, pioneering (*Haluziut*) was the major norm of behavior (Eden, 1976). It meant the preference of social aspirations over personal achievements. The political struggle for national independence gave predominance to a politicization of public and individual life and thus affected the school and its curriculum.

The Religious trend based its curriculum on a blending of religious studies of the old orthodox school and the curriculum of a modern secular school. Time was shared equally between the two. The Labor trend was influenced by strong socialist ideologies and the "new education" movement. The educational ideas that were selected for implementation had to fit the Zionist-Socialist ideology—that is, the idea of manual work, social activities in school, and integration of the Youth Movement with school.

In the didactics there was an influence of the reform movement in Austria; Dewey and Kilpatrick from the United States, and others. On the extreme left schools, there was a strong impact of Freud's psychoanalysis. In the Labor trend schools, there was an emphasis on the social sciences, social activity, manual work, and individual work. The General trend aimed for the middle, between the Religious and the Labor trends.

The common denominator of the three different curricula was the concept that the curriculum's objective was, among other things, to serve social purposes, defined differently by the different political trends; a centralized organization to assure these goals; acceptance of the eight years of elementary education as a full cycle of learning. Hence, there was an emphasis on information. The curricula in each trend were uniform and mandatory.

After passage of the State Law of Education (1953) and the elimination of the autonomous trends, a new curriculum was issued (1954–1955). The law aimed at a national system of education, and the new curriculum attempted to blend the common elements of the previous curriculum for *all* schools. Obviously, there were legitimate differences between the curricula of the religious and the nonreligious schools.

These new uniform curricula and the philosophy behind them were criticized vehemently at the time of publication (Adar, 1956), and their principles were criticized, indirectly, some twenty years later (Lam, 1973).

Lam argued (1973) that objectives defined by formulas of a political compromise are not only noneducative but rather cause an alienation of the young generation toward the generations of ancestors. The other inevitable development of this kind of meaningless legislation is an increasing bureaucratization of the education system. Adar (1956), who criticized the curriculum at the time of its publication, focused on two issues: the uniformity of the curriculum, which he believed would lead to mechanical, routine, and noninnovative teaching, and a strong criticism of the central role of ideology rather than a psycho-pedagogical differentiation, which might lead to a more individualistic and diversified teaching.

Almost twenty years later, ideology is still the major element in Israel's education. But more and more, its role decreases gradually and the individualistic approach gains ground. One of the major reasons for this development is not changes in the dominant philosophy of education but rather the reality of low achievements of disadvantaged children.

## Teaching

Three main approaches to the functions of the teacher, which apply to training, prevail in Israel nowadays:

1. Regarding teachers as implementers of society's demands and, hence, emphasis on their social training and social involvement.
2. Regarding the child as the focus of education.
3. Considering the right of each individual to education and the obligation of the teachers to fulfill this right.

Accordingly, there are three models of teachers' training: (1) focused on social relations and social activity; (2) focused on developing learning abilities, problem solving, creativity, cognitive abilities, and so on; and (3) focused on the individual, on his or her particular personality, and on the affective aspects of development.

In addition to the psycho-pedagogical postulates mentioned previously, there are some additional postulates related specifically to teaching. As already mentioned, one of the commonly accepted assumptions is a pessimistic attitude regarding the capability of transfer among pupils, reflected in the emphasis given to memorizing information and to the amount of information acquired.

Until recent years, the following premises underlay teaching in the elementary school: (1) the need for a "general" teacher, with an educational personality rather than specific professional training; (2) teaching and education as an art rather than a technology. Hence, successful teaching depends more on intuition, a favorable attitude toward the child, and the ability to empathize rather than on the application of general scientific rules and principles. The interest of the teacher should be on the individual child and on the unique and one-time educational situation. Therefore, there should be no emphasis on generalizing psychological and pedagogical theories. (3) In the era of free education for all, it is impossible to have masses of entrepreneuring and initiating teachers, and we should be satisfied with a teacher oriented and trained only to execute directives. Their training should reflect this realistic approach.

In the early 1960s, when the issue of the disadvantaged children was put on the public agenda, many educators criticized the prevailing approach (Frankenstein, 1962). They argued that social and cultural development required a new view of teaching and the teacher. The teacher should be a diagnostician, able to disclose and define the mistakes and failures of the pupils and to find out their psychodynamic and social roots. The teacher should be able to develop didactic methods and educational approaches according to the "changing needs of his pupils," while applying the principles and findings of developmental psychology, social and cultural anthropology, and other fields. This approach was further developed by the view that a modern teacher should fulfill educational functions that cannot be fulfilled anymore by the traditional framework of the family (Kleinberger, 1966). Recent social and political developments, the increase in the role of the state in education, and the decrease in the role of the family create the new pattern of "school without parents." This imposes on the teacher new functions and challenges that cannot be fulfilled by using regular preplanned programs and procedures. Intuition and empathy are not sufficient. The teacher should have a diagnostic and analytical ability and sound knowledge in psychology, sociology, anthropology, pedagogy, and other disciplines.

Lam (1966, 1969) adds to these arguments some additional ones. He argues that teacher training based on acquiring techniques does not encourage the entrepreneur-type, the creative, innovative teacher who initiates changes or who responds to the changing circumstances and needs. Lam thinks that the only way to cope positively with the process of bureaucratization of educational systems (as a part of the bureaucratization process of the welfare state) is by promoting and encouraging the autonomy of teachers.

Simultaneously with the traditional approach, which was reflected in a conservative and rigid teaching, new problems arose and new directions and solutions were sought. One of these new trends has been expressed in a draft of a master plan of education in Israel for the 1980s

(Peled, 1976), postulating new learning situations and pointing to a new direction in teaching and learning. This includes more individualistic and active learning basing a pupil's evaluation on *all* activities rather than only on academic achievements. Once again there is a call for a new type of teacher—innovative, creative, and autonomous.

Autonomy of teachers is set as a target that may raise their self-image and social status; to give them a promotion in "depth" rather than a hierarchical promotion; to reject passive, indifferent teachers, and to encourage innovative and creative teachers.

In the pre-independence era, in the "age of ideology," teaching was a national mission facing national goals, social and national needs, and a view of the pupils as a collective body and not as individuals.

After the independence of the state and passage of the State Education Act, which regarded education as a responsibility of the state, the maximum expected from teaching was its subject-matter context. In the last few years, a new approach has taken place, which defines teaching as a complex of the teacher's activities, aimed at developing in the pupil rational and differential patterns of thinking through knowledge, skills and values that are acquirable, and at developing in the pupils' involvement and responsibility for their thinking and learning. Hence, teaching is the responsibility for the children's development—both their thinking and their personality (Frankenstein, 1974).

## APPLICATIONS

### Curriculum, Academic

#### Basic Academic Skills

Although the Jews are known as the "People of the Book," Israel's education faces the challenge of teaching basic academic skills. In this section only reading will be discussed as an example of these skills.

In an evaluation study of Israeli elementary schools Minkovich, Davis, and Bashi (1977) conclude that "not only has much progress been made in the teaching of reading but also this problem has been almost completely solved" (p. 396). Obviously, this achievement is the result of a deliberate and planned effort to improve tools and methods of teaching reading skills through its curriculum.

The objective of the reading curriculum is to develop the pupil's ability to enjoy and to be impressed by written texts, to understand them, and to act accordingly in a conscious and controlled way. The curriculum aims to enhance the child to be both interested and capable of using the written language for cognitive formation, for the enrichment of personal experiences and the expansion of knowledge, for orientation in the external world (the human and the material), and for recreation.

The selection of the texts reflects the trend to use written texts as tools and means for ethical, aesthetical, social, and human education as well as developing the thinking ability.

There are several premises underlying the reading curriculum:

—The teaching of reading is part of the teaching of language; therefore, there should be an integration between reading and other topics of language teaching.
—A civilized person should read different kinds of texts: literature, practical texts (information, laws and regulations, manuals, and so on), philosophical, and religious texts.
—Different and appropriate methods of reading should be used for the different kinds of texts.
—There is a distinction between a spontaneous and natural responsiveness and a conscious response.
—Reading in general, and reading of literature in particular, has an impact of the formation of the reader's personality.

### Communication Skills

Language is the major tool of communication in the human society. The problem of language teaching is complicated in Israel due to its demographic composition. Whereas among the Arab and Druze minorities the "lingua franca" of the parents and their children is the same, among the Jewish population it is *not*. Israel, as an immigration country, is a multilingual society. More than seventy different languages and dialects are spoken within the so-called Hebrew-speaking population. Thus, for many children Hebrew is *not* their mother's language. They speak different languages: Hebrew at school and some other language at home. Therefore a major effort has been given to Hebrew teaching in schools in Israel both for personal communication and for national formation.

The Evaluation Study of Israeli Elementary Schools (Minkovich, Davis, and Bashi, 1977) concluded that "the achievement level on the language tests was higher than on the other achievement tests."

The premises behind the language curriculum are:

—Elementary school children know their native language directly through their behavior and the behavior of their "social environment" although they are unconscious cognitively of that knowledge.
—It is presumed that language like many other things creates curiosity and inquisitiveness among children.
—The developing cognitive skills of the child enable the child to develop the conscious and learned knowledge of the language.
—The needs for communication and social aesthetic norms require grammatical regularity in all levels of linguistic structures.

—These regularities are *not* acquired naturally and automatically and should be taught in a continuous and deliberate process, which is involved in many problems (educational, psychological, and social).

—Therefore, the requirements for grammatical regularities should be developed slowly and gradually by adapting teaching objectives and methods to the appropriate age and the learning environment avoiding, as far as possible, unnecessary conflicts between the "natural language" and the "regular" one.

Writing (written expression) is a skill whose teaching requires special teaching, appropriate preparedness, and involvement of socialization processes, which develop in the school years.

Communication through writing is based on oral communication but requires special and additional teaching. The relevant curriculum has several stages: in the first stage the emphasis is on developing technical skills; in the second stage, on motivation and practical writing; in the third stage, on the development of the consciousness about the relative alienation between the writer and the reader and consequently the completion and improvement of various means and methods of written expression.

A distinction is made between creative expression and reconstructive expression (which is communication-oriented). An innovation of the new curriculum is the introduction of the teaching of *listening*.

### Creative Expression

Creative expression or educational creativeness in Israel is an innovative, experimental, and frequently radical and nonconformist approach to the educational means, methods, and processes. Creative expression as a method of learning is used differently in several experiments. In this section two of those experimental approaches will illustrate the developing trend of radical educators in Israel.

Creative expression, or activity, is the activity that adds new concerns to the learning and thinking or eases the conception of new relationships; the activity of play or work, embedded in the ideas, the thoughts, and feelings of the individual expressed in a perceivable way; free and spontaneous self-expression articulated in painting, drawing, or other forms of expressive arts that are included in the learning units. This conventional definition of creative expression was extended by some experimenters to fields other than the fine arts.

One group of experiments is an integration of creativity in visual arts and movement (dance). Visual arts include painting, sculpture, and various arts and crafts based on the premises of development of the child's visual perception of the environment; learning the elements of the fine arts; development of personal imagination and expression in artistic creativity; development of aesthetic values. In all of these areas the focus is on the processes as well as on the end products.

Creativity in movement is guided by the following principles and elements: learning the foundations of movement (form, space, time, power); developing body self-awareness and activation in movement; enriching the "movement vocabulary"; developing imagination, self-expression, and personal creativity in movement. The implementation of these premises and principles is based on broad educational principles: the need of activation, personal experience for a genuine and meaningful learning; work in groups enhancing social aspects of education—mutual respect of variety in contrast to a uniform solution. The integration of visual arts with movement also helps the cognitive development of the child by processes of observation, distinction, generalization, and conceptualization.

Another method of creative expression in Israel is through experiments of "creative drama," a creative method of teaching literature, Bible, and history through "active reading." This method was designed to respond to the following needs: to attribute more meaning to the content of studies; to develop positive motivation for learning; to find a way to activate simultaneously children of different cultural levels in a socioeconomically integrated setting; to develop an individual's uniqueness while being sensitive to the environment; to develop tolerance; to discharge personal tensions by forming creative and "constructive" outlets for these tensions; to extend one's ways of expression; to foster initiative, self-responsibility, and autonomous judgment.

These principles are implemented through use of texts with a counselor who helps pupils to find personal and/or social meanings in the texts. The counselor does not impose his views on how to interpret or to "perform" the text. He helps them to find the "appropriate" text. The focus of the method is to help the children to find the meaning of the text within their personal experiences. The aim is to make the children active participants in the "dramatized" text, to make them do, and to make them personally involved in their doing.

Creative expression is growing in the training of teachers for special education.

### Activity Units

Among the experimental innovations in Israel one may distinguish two modern approaches: "open education" in the American and British form and the "active classroom" approach. The second approach, which is growing more rapidly than the first one, adopted the activity, the experience, and the forms of "open education," applying them to the existing frameworks of conventional education. The second approach, the "active classroom teaching," is less extreme and more "moderate" regarding the implementation of the principles of freedom, individuality, and the treatment of the pupil's feelings and emotions. For all practical purposes it is a teaching/learning method following the principles of experience and activity designed to improve the product of the educational system.

A semiofficial publication defines "active classroom teaching" as based on giving the pupil the option to learn through activity and/or personal experience. This kind of teaching is considered to give children an option to learn how to learn and how to be open to many new ideas by independent studies, by small-group learning, and sometimes even by conventional teaching/learning. Active learning enhances the children's interest, initiative, and creativity.

An experiment of combining the active-learning method with socioethnic integration points out four minimal postulates for active learning: activity of the pupil in the learning process; individualization of learning, namely, giving every child a good chance to acquire the required basic skills; spontaneity of the pupil in selecting fields of interest in order to increase motivation for learning and to foster creativity; enrichment through the curriculum and extracurricular activities.

Facing the challenge of educating great numbers of "disadvantaged" and culturally deprived children, more and more educators turn to active learning, replacing the failing conventional learning.

### The Social Sciences*

In the last decade a big effort and great sums of money were invested in new curriculum development. The new curriculum for social sciences may serve to illustrate the demands and constraints of a new program.

The new curriculum of the social sciences was aimed at providing knowledge of the main events and facts, at introducing basic concepts, at developing skills and ways of thinking and learning characteristics of the relevant disciplines, at cultivating understanding and tolerance toward the feelings, traditions, and ways of life of different peoples and nations, and at fostering identification of the students with their people and country.

The methods of learning and teaching used in these courses are varied. An effort is made to bring in the inquiry method to a case studies approach, simulation, the analysis of controversial issues, and to use programmed instruction.

Although some of the topics are value-loaded and controversial, they

---

*This section is based on S. Eden, "Curriculum Development in Israel," in P. H. Taylor and M. Johnson, *Curriculum Development: A Comparative Study* (Windsor, England: NFER Publishing Company, Ltd., 1974).

are not avoided; rather the opposite. The different points of view are presented, and teachers are advised *not* to impose their own ideas, but rather to encourage free and tolerant discussion.

### Special Education

Special education in Israel includes exceptional children, physically and/ or mentally, who cannot use the regular school and need additional treatment in the regular school or special forms. It does not include exceptionally gifted children. In 1976, the population of special education was 9 percent of the population of the elementary schools. Special education pupils are 40 percent mentally retarded and imbeciles, 16 percent mentally disturbed, 38 percent learning disabled, and 6 percent physically handicapped. Special education is an integral part of the regular school system, the goal of which is to rehabilitate exceptional children and to prepare them for productive and positive social life, up to their personal abilities, in the following areas: self-realization, human relations, economic capability, and civic responsibility.

The forms of special education are varied: from special treatment in the regular school, through special education classes in the regular school, and to separate schools for special education.

In its broadest context, special education is defined as a complex of attitudes and educational, psychological, medical, and social services, given to the children who were diagnosed as exceptional (physically and/or mentally).

The appropriate framework for special education (whether within a regular school or in a separate special education school) is based on three basic foundations: trained and motivated teachers, appropriate physical facilities, special and adjustable curriculum (to the specific deficiency of the child). The teachers are trained to handle handicapped children and to treat their specific deficiency.

Whereas the main objective of the curriculum is the educational development of the pupil (cognitive and affective), the aim of the special education curriculum is to enable optimal development of the pupil's skills and personality, oriented toward the rehabilitation of the children by giving them a new orientation on life: self-realization, self-esteem, developing skills that will compensate for deficiencies, developing realistic aspirations, socialization, and so on.

A great emphasis is given to enhancing economic and productive abilities together with civic responsibilities. Children are assigned to special education by a team of teachers, psychologists, social workers, community workers, and school nurses with a close cooperation with the parents.

The grades are divided into four "divisions": preschool to third grade, intermediate grades (four to six), junior high school (seven to nine), senior high school (ten to twelve). The common basic goals of the curriculum of the continuum (one to twelve) are: *personal adjustment*—developing the individual abilities and skills, balancing abilities and deficiencies with the child's and the parents' expectations, helping to establish a positive self-image, self-confidence, and maximum autonomy and independence; *social adjustment*—developing skills and abilities of social communications; *general adjustment*—training for productive life, social discipline, basic skills, and so on; *civic adjustment.*

The aims of the curriculum for the specific "divisions" are: *the first division (kindergarten to grade 3)*—prevention of the deterioration of the child's handicap and preparedness for the coming formal learning. This includes developing skills, senses, and customs and preparing the solid foundations for further education; *the intermediate division (grades 4 to 6*—more emphasis on formal learning of the basic academic skills (the three R's), together with the elaboration of the general objectives; *the junior high school (grades 7 to 9)*—the emphasis moves toward preparing the child for real life; *the senior high school (grades 10 to 12)*—only very few continue to attend school at this level, although more universal attendance is now considered a future goal of the system. Those who attend "school" at this level are employed in a regular business enterprise and receive continuous guidance and counseling by the school. Emphasis is given to vocational training and family and community life.

### Curriculum, Nonacademic

The nonacademic curriculum in Israel is large and diversified, from practical and technical skills to aesthetic, and ethical education. This section will focus on some specific aspects, considered to be typical of this system.

### Attitude Modification

Attitude modification is one of the more complex and complicated tasks of education. It may be done effectively indirectly, through the formal academic curriculum; it may be done very effectively, directly and indirectly, through the nonacademic curriculum and through extracurricular activities. Operationally no one can prove which method is better and more effective.

The targeted attitudes may be in three areas: aesthetic attitudes, social attitudes, and personal behavior attitudes. It is considered that the most effective method to "teach" them is through the formation of an appropriate "climate" in school and by establishing some deliberate and well-defined "ways of life" through which the pupil would not only learn attitudes but also experience them by doing and by participation in activities.

### Aesthetics

Two ways serve aesthetic education: the indirect way of creating an aesthetic environment in the school, hoping that the pupils will acquire aesthetic values through their indirect experience, and a direct way through teaching art in school.

Many reasons have caused art education to become "second" in the "hierarchy" of school subjects. Nonetheless, there is an increasing awareness of its weakness and the need to raise it to a much more important place in school. Art education aims to develop personal creativity and expression, increase visual sensitivity, understand art as a refined cultural expression, and in some cases (special education, culturally deprived children, and the like), serves as a didactic, therapeutic tool.

In grades kindergarten to 6 visual art education is focused mostly on creative expression based on creativity processes and the child's diversified motor activity. A balanced personality formation in young ages will use visual art as means and ends. In grades 7 to 9 more art fields will be included, such as refining the pupil's artistic perception, distinction, understanding, and illustration.

Learning is based on personal experience, on the aesthetic impression of looking at and analyzing classic art, and by the interaction between doing art and experiencing it. The curriculum includes painting, sculpture, history of art, graphics, decorative art, and other forms.

### Enrichment Programs

Enrichment programs are designed primarily for culturally deprived children and aim to complete the deficiency of aesthetic education of those children whose family and social environment lack aesthetic values.

The enrichment programs do not intend to substitute the regular and systematic art education but rather to compensate the lack of artistic-aesthetic stimulus of the child's environment. Therefore, their main objective is to introduce the three aspects of art (visual arts, music, and theater) to the child. The reason for this aim is twofold: to introduce art works to the pupil and thus to enrich his cultural world, and to create in the child a genuine stimulus to absorb art. The stages of this process are from primary sense impressions through personal experience to the ability to evaluate art.

In order to avoid strong alienation between the disadvantaged children (who originate mostly from Islamic Middle Eastern countries) and the

Western art (European and American), an effort is made to present both Western art with the folk art familiar to the children.

### Ethical Instruction

Ethical instruction turned out to be in Israel a major controversial issue under the heading of value education. In the early 1970s some of Israel's prominent educators raised the question "Who needs value education?" whereas others insisted on the predominance of value education, as it has been since the early stages of the Jewish education in Israel, in the pre-independence era.

Ethical instruction as a direct topic in the curriculum almost does not exist. Nonetheless, it is considered to be important and effective only if it is done indirectly, through formal academic subjects (such as literature, Bible, philosophy, and other subjects of humanities and social sciences) and extracurricular, informal subjects and activities.

One may make the distinction between universal ethical values (such as justice, honesty, truth, and so on) and social and national values. Both groups of values are considered to be a necessity in Israel's education.

The educators who are against this approach argue that, first, there is no need for value education as such, because the thin borderline between it and indoctrination is vague and unclear, and second, it is impossible to implement it, and its application is not feasible.

The proponents of ethical education, who are the majority and have control over the system, tend to derive from the curriculum the ability of students to recognize and evaluate moral conflicts and to make moral judgments about moral values that should be meaningful to their personal behavior. Furthermore, being ideology-oriented, social and national values are central in the educational processes. The dilemmas are how to avoid totalitarian indoctrination, while trying to "transmit" values and how to avoid uniformity and conformity in the pluralistic society which is Israel.

### Vocational Education

Vocational education has two distinct levels in Israel: arts and crafts as a subject for all the pupils in the elementary school (grades 1 to 6 or 1 to 8) and in the junior high school grades (7 to 9).

In the late 1970s new curriculum has been developed. The curriculum of arts and crafts in the elementary school is based on the child's needs and on the technological aspects of the modern, technological, Western civilization. It aims to help the child to function in this kind of society, to understand it, and to enjoy it.

Israel's social composition and the great numbers of culturally deprived children require that by teaching arts and crafts not only the arts and crafts will be acquired, but cognitive qualities (such as observation, comparison, distinction, generalization, and inference), manual skills, attitudes (consistency, motivation, innovativeness, perseverance) will be developed and fostered.

By teaching arts and crafts, the school may compensate the disadvantaged child for "natural" deprivation. In the junior high school *all* the pupils are required to acquire general technological knowledge: boys in materials (metals, wood, plastics and so on), electricity and electronics, foundations of automation and technical drawing; girls in textiles, home economics, and office work. Every pupil may choose additional subjects among electives.

Vocational education has been expanded greatly in the last two decades and it includes today about 50 percent of the high school population. A survey of the occupation of vocational education has shown that about 70 percent continue to work in the vocations that they learned at school.

In addition to their vocational education function the vocational schools serve a much more general educational objective as a way to attract and to keep disadvantaged children in school (60 percent of the "Oriental" children in Israel attend vocational schools and 60 percent of these schools' population are of "Oriental" origin).

There are several different forms of vocational education in Israel implemented in different "tracks" in the vocational or comprehensive schools: the technological-academic trend teaches both a full academic curriculum and a full, advanced, and sophisticated technological curriculum; a general vocational track teaches only a part of the academic curriculum and full vocational curriculum; the first two tracks end after the twelfth grade. Another track, a practical vocational track, teaches only a minimal academic curriculum and focuses on less sophisticated vocational training; it lasts between one and four years according to a certain selection. The "lowest" track is a special form of practical vocational education combined with special educational treatment aimed at children who are severely culturally deprived.

Vocational education tries to fulfill two objectives: vocational training to supply trained and skilled workers to the economy, and education, by means of manual work, of populations who cannot adjust to academic secondary education.

### Student Evaluation

Student evaluation has become a favorite fad in Israel's education. In the last two decades the focus of the student's evaluation moved from a subjective evaluation, done by the teacher, to an objective evaluation by means of various tests.

Student evaluation in Israel has several purposes: individual evaluation (of the student), class evaluation, school evaluation, and general evaluations (according to different criteria serving different purposes).

For many years (1955–1972) Israel's school system used a national test, at the end of the eighth grade, as a selection test to assign pupils to the different kinds of secondary schools (academic, vocational, and so on).

Today, objective evaluation is by means of the following kinds of tests: diagnostic tests that help to adjust curriculum and methods to the particular students; intermediate examinations for passage from one group or one grade to another; final and certifying examinations (the most important is the matriculation at the end of the twelfth grade); and different survey tests (to measure abilities and/or achievements).

In the elementary school, student evaluation is spread over the year and along the school grades. The following regular tests serve to evaluate the individual students and the standards of their groups/classes: IQ and personality; preparedness to reading (beginning of first grade); selection tests for grouping; diagnostic examinations (as needed); comparative examinations; reading achievement tests; achievement in different subjects; surveys, studies, and other research.

An important and controversial examination is the academic matriculation examinations (*"Bagrut"*) at the end of the twelfth grade. These examinations are finals for secondary education and are a necessary prerequisite for higher education. There is a strong trend now to make them less rigid and more flexible, and some radical educators demand their cancellation.

In a recent evaluation study of Israeli elementary schools (Minkovich, Davis, and Bashi, 1977) ability tests were administered under the premise that the child's basic learning ability with which he enters school was considered to be the baseline factor. The school was considered to be an important agent in broadening and deepening this basis, but does not constitute the sole contributing factor in this process. Ability tests were used in this study for several reasons, among which was the need to emphasize the differences between verbal and nonverbal abilities. Learning achievement tests were used to assess group (ethnic and socioeconomic) differences and to obtain as clear a picture as possible of the scope and quality of achievements in the school subjects.

Results of verbal and nonverbal tests and questionnaires on motivational patterns and attitudes can be viewed as data concerning the personal traits of the child as well as school outcomes.

In addition to cognitive achievement tests there is a search for appropriate measures of the achievement in the affective aspects of behavior.

Formally there exists a record for every individual pupil in school. This record should be a confidential companion to the child from beginning kindergarten until the child leaves. Recently some legal problems and public debate have arisen concerning the legitimacy of the confidential remarks that may sometimes be a stigma, without the right of the pupil or parents to appeal and to argue against a teacher's subjective remark.

Grade certificates are common in most schools. They summarize by numerical or letter grades the student's achievement. Frequently, additional comments state the student's situation and the requirements for further progress. Grades are given not only for cognitive learning achievements but also for social activity and personal behavior.

Underachievers are expected to get special, additional tutorial work. It is prohibited to hold students in the same grade class for another year.

### Counseling

Whereas the psychologist is employed by the local municipality, the counselor is the key person on the school staff who is trained and employed to deal with the cognitive, emotional, and social development of each student. At times he approaches his task by counseling the individual student who comes on his own volition; at other times the student is referred to the counselor by the teacher, parent, principal, social worker, nurse, or psychologist. The counselor also works with groups of students, whole classes, teachers, and other staff.

To reach an understanding of the manifold roles of the school counselor in Israel, it is best to state the goals:

1. To implement healthy integration of each student into the educational setting both on the social and learning levels.

2. To get to know the student body in order to follow up each student's development so as to help him plan his future.

3. To encourage students to turn to the counselor at times of personal crisis.

4. To cultivate openness, awareness, and flexibility among the school staff.

5. To help create a variety of educational frameworks in the school to satisfy the talents and abilities of all students.

6. To help the student understand himself, his ability, aptitude, and interests. To help him understand the society and adult world in which he will take an active part. To help him reach the best decision vis-à-vis his place in society.

7. To identify, at as early a stage as possible, individual and group problems, collect relevant data, and find the best way to deal with these problems.

8. In the area of special education to assume responsibility for the vocational and social rehabilitation of the student.

Based on these broad concepts of goals, the counselor's duties and responsibilities encompass the whole gamut of student-school-society relationships.

Over 850 counselors serve the schools, most of them in the seventh, eighth, and ninth grades.

The characteristics of the counselor and training are a controversial issue in Israel. One of these controversies concerns the question whether the counselor is a professional, other than a teacher by training and/or experience, or should he be only a specialized teacher. Another deals with the distinctions and the division of responsibility between the school psychologist and the counselor. This controversy extends also to the tools and methods of the counselors: Should they or should they not use individual psychological tests? The common approach is that the counselor stands between the teacher and the school psychologist. Many counselors are experienced teachers who have gotten special training. The counselor has close and direct contact with the pupil and thus is expected to be a better guide.

## Discipline

Discipline has been considered vital and central to education in Israel, and it still is. The system implements this idea by regulations that direct the discipline policy of the schools.

The authority to establish specific regulations at schools lies with the pedagogical council, led by the school principal and comprising the schoolteachers. The ministry's regulations posit guidelines for the specific school regulations: Each school should try to develop a school tradition of its "ways of life," taking into its consideration parents and community expectations, needs, and values. The school discipline and way of life are based on uniformity and consistency, at least within the school. Each teacher is responsible for educating the pupils to observe the regulations through explanation, guidance, counseling, and personal example.

The conventional ways to deal with disturbances and with breaking the regulations are: a personal talk with the pupil by the class head teacher, the counselor, or the school psychologist; a talk with the pupil's parents; a warning; transfer to another classroom in the same school; transfer to another school. Suspension from a single lesson or from the school for a definite period of time and in the very extreme cases, provided an approval of a supervisor, expulsion from the school, are further options. Corporal punishment is strictly forbidden.

Dress codes are flexible. Some schools require a school uniform, and some don't.

ROLES

### Administration

The school principal is responsible for the regularity of the school's educational work, its order and everything that happens within the school. The principal's responsibility extends over general administration, relations with the pupils and their parents, pupils' evaluation, counseling and guiding the teachers as a group and individually, public relations, and school maintenance.

Each principal in the elementary school has to teach, at least minimally, in the classroom. The principal is responsible directly for the school's standards, its budget, the teaching aids, extracurricular activities, and contact with parents. Principals of elementary schools are accountable to the Ministry of Education and Culture through the regional superintendants and their supervisors. Principals of secondary schools are accountable to their employers (the local municipality, or private ownership, or a semipublic organization). There is no direct and meaningful accountability to the parents or to the community.

The supervisors, who are the representatives of the ministry, are responsible for improving the quality of the schools by supervision and guidance. They represent the ministry and its policies to the teachers and principals, and on the other hand they represent the principals and teachers to the ministry.

The functions of the supervisor are two: administrative supervision, and pedagogical counseling and guidance. The supervisors have the direct control over several schools within a geographical area. Subject supervisors are responsible for specific subject matters.

### Admission and Attendance

Admission to schools and attendance are regulated by law and state regulations. The Law of Compulsory Education (1949) makes education free and compulsory between the ages of five and sixteen (kindergarten to grade 10).

Every local municipality, on approval of the ministry's regional superintendant, is mapped into elementary school zones (usually neighborhoods), separately for state religious schools and state nonreligious schools. In each zone there is one elementary school. Registration and admission to these schools are mandatory. The same municipality is mapped into education quarters (separately for religious and nonreligious schools) for junior high schools and in many cases for high schools.

Registration policy is to relate schools to geographical areas. Frequently, one of the major considerations is the social integration in schools. Some schools get official status as interregional schools.

Regular attendance at school between ages five and sixteen is compulsory. Dropping out is a violation of the law. In the last years a big effort has been made to prevent dropping out and to bring the dropouts back to school. Various methods have been tried: detection, as early as possible, of the symptoms of dropping out (usually slow learning and discipline disturbances); close age of the transit stages from elementary school to the junior high school and to the high school; establishing appropriate special programs for the "weak" pupils; strengthening the contacts between the school and the family; requiring strict and regular reporting of irregular attendance and dropouts.

## Curriculum Planning

Since the beginning of the 1970s curriculum planning and development has been under the "continuous assignment" approach in which the principle is a comprehensive, never-ending process of program preparation, piloting, and improvement. Even after the completion of a final version of the specifications that guide textbook authors and even after publishing the tested learning materials, the planners continue to develop additional aspects of the same curriculum. They also observe and review the implementation of the program and follow up any new developments in the subjects, as well as note changes in curricula in other countries.

The planning and development of curriculum is a cooperative enterprise of many groups: subject-matter specialists, experts in curriculum planning, school inspectors, active and experienced teachers, and educational psychologists.

A project group in the Curriculum Center of the Ministry of Education and Culture prepares a curriculum for a specific subject for a particular educational stage (kindergarten, elementary school, junior high school, high school). The project group is organized into a planning committee responsible for planning and supervision of the development of the project, and a working team, which does the "real" work. The sequence of activities is as follows: the writing of the material, the follow-up and evaluation, preparation of material testing, preparation of teaching aids and equipment, and the coordination of the project with instructional television and radio.

There are three stages in curriculum construction: the stage of formation, the stage of tryout (by expert and a small experiment in six classes), and the stage of controlled experiment (in twenty-four to thirty classes).

Only after getting feedback and a final approval by the planning committee is the commercial edition prepared and published.

Faculty

The characteristics and aspirations of the teachers in Israel are a function of a socio-historical development of the teaching profession in Israel.

In the pre-independence era many people who did not have appropriate employment and social outlets (because of the size, economic development, and the colonial regime in Palestine) turned to teaching as their best choice. Consequently the intellectual and social quality of the teachers corps in Eretz Israel was very high (primarily in the Jewish population). Furthermore, being a part of the intellectual elite made many of them active in leadership positions of political, social, and cultural life, which in turn raised, once more, their social status and prestige.

After independence (1948) and the coming of large masses of immigrants, two processes occurred simultaneously: On one hand, independence and the elimination of previous employment restrictions opened many opportunities of employment other than teaching in elementary or secondary schools. Many of the men, of high standards, left teaching and turned to universities (which started a rapid and large expansion), to state jobs, to public services, and to business. On the other hand, the tremendous growth of the population created an unmatched demand for many teachers. Both these processes caused a feminization of the teaching profession (more than 90 percent in elementary schools and about 50 percent in secondary schools) as well as lowering the intellectual quality of the teachers' corps.

About 50 percent of the teachers in Israel do not have regular, conventional training for their job. Many of them have in-service training. We are in a process where teaching is the first stage of upward social mobility for pupils from disadvantaged origin.

Due to the strong political power of the Teachers' Federation and the High School Teachers' Union teachers' salaries are reasonably above the median of public civil servants. Nonetheless the teaching profession is no longer attractive to students of high social and intellectual potential.

Many programs aim to raise the teacher's status and to make teaching more attractive. Fostering the autonomy of the teacher is one such program to raise the teacher's self-image and to attract the innovative type rather than the passive type. Large-scale in-service training is another program. Teachers are encouraged (by financial incentives, promotion incentives, and intellectual need to learn) to attend in-service training programs and courses at the universities, in teachers' training colleges, in special teachers' centers, and elsewhere. Special institutions have been established to give in-service training to school principals and supervisors.

## Students

The role of the students in schools is primarily to learn and to experience Israel's social and cultural values through social activity in schools. The majority of the schools have the conventional approach to the student, emphasizing learning activities and giving only a minor role to social activity. Nevertheless, in most schools the students have an organization like students' council, class committees, and special students' organizations (safety organization, health organization, and so on).

### Handicapped Students

As already pointed out in the preceding discussion on special education, 9 percent of the elementary school population in Israel can be defined as physically or mentally handicapped and thus involved in various forms of special education. Special education, whether in regular schools or in separate special education schools, is always tuned to the requirements and problems of the individual child, and it can be typified as very intensive.

Students who attend special education classes are directed to the acquisition of basic skills and function under very special learning conditions. As the problems of each child are different, the roles that those handicapped children play as students also differ from child to child. By and large one can say that their roles are less competitive, and less achievement-oriented than the role of the ordinary student.

### Parents

Education laws in Israel give the state total responsibility and authority for education and impose on the parents only the obligation to comply with the Law of Compulsory Education and to send their children to school.

According to the law, the parents have the right to demand and to influence 25 percent of the curriculum. This section of the law has not yet been implemented.

Parents' activity is expressed in financial support of the schools, through parents' committees in each school. Only recently have parents started to organize in a meaningful national organization. This organization has become a participant, as an interest group, in the struggle over educational policies and daily issues.

The removal of parents from influential positions has had political and ideological causes (Rosenfeld, 1973), dating back to the Zionist ideology. According to this ideology, parents are the "generation of the wilderness," because they are the carriers of different, divisive cultures and languages. The realization of Zionism requires a melting pot and the creation of a new, integrated Israeli culture. Therefore, parents should not influence the education of their children, because they may perpetuate the traditional differences, rather than blending the different groups and "tribes" into a united nation. Another reason to keep policy and parents apart is the argument that disadvantaged parents cannot understand and consequently are not able to intervene positively in the education of their children.

A new trend is emerging currently in Israel, one to give parents a larger function in their children's education. There are some who claim that this tendency is inevitable (Rosenfeld, 1973). Others see it as an operational proposal (Peled, 1973), assuming that parents' participation will guarantee the pluralism of the Israeli society, will strengthen its democracy, and will encourage the education of their children.

## SYSTEM IN ACTION

At least three issues that are unique to the Israeli situation must be examined in the broad context of this highly dynamic immigrant society inspired by a strong ideology and living under the permanent threat of war.

The following paragraphs that discuss the problems of the education of the disadvantaged, the education of the minorities, and informal education display structures that stem from Israel's complex reality and demonstrate the system's response to acute problems.

It should be noted that structures within the educational system make the system diversified, despite its central administration and control.

The selected three issues also describe, each from another angle, Israel's educational system in action.

### Educating the Disadvantaged

The challenge of advancing disadvantaged children is a major issue of education in Israel. It has long-range implications for Israel's economic and social future and on the morale and values of its society.

Despite being a comprehensive problem referring to different areas—income, housing, employment, and so on—there are strong expectations that education will be the one factor to break the vicious circle of deprivation and retardedness and will enable establishment of a more equal and just society. Without aspiring to be omnipotent, since the end of the 1950s the policy of helping disadvantaged children became first priority in Israel's social policy.

There are many definitions of a disadvantaged child: socioeconomic, ethnic, geographical, and more. Generally there is a high correlation among the socioeconomic variables, the ethnic variables, and the geographic variables. The operational definition in Israel's education is based on an analysis of academic achievements in elementary school, illustrated in comprehensive tests (*Seker*) administered in the high grades of the eight-year elementary school over a period of several years. Following these tests every social group characterized by definite socioeconomic variables was evaluated in terms of "disadvantaged" and therefore eligibility for special allocation of additional resources in order to improve its prospects of success in school.

### The Characteristics of the Disadvantaged Children

Of the elementary school pupils in 1975, 47 percent were disadvantaged. Of this group 95 percent are "Orientals" (originally from Asian-African-Muslim countries). Of this group 90 percent belong to large families, and their father's education is lower than the elementary education level. Elementary schools where their proportion is 70 percent or more have 55 percent of all disadvantaged children.

The "fostering" of the disadvantaged policy in Israel is based on two different concepts: *gap* and *variety*. Gap is the difference (the distance) between the potential achievement of an individual or a group under *appropriate* conditions and their actual or real achievement. Variety indicates differences in character, in individual skills, in traditions, customs and cultural patterns, and behavior of groups.

Educational policy in Israel aims to narrow gaps as well as to encourage variety. The complexity of the Israeli situation in which pluralistic solutions to educational problems are sought is well analyzed by Peres (1976) in his study on ethnic relations in Israel. Peres distinguishes between integrating and disintegrating pressures and claims that social stigmas, frustrated expectations of the disadvantaged, and real deprivations are disintegrating factors while the Zionist ideology, the need to fight together the common enemy, and the striving for the ethnic integration and social mobility are the integrating powers. Peres (1973) and others regard education as the key to social mobility and hence to integration. Nevertheless, statistics show that in the progression toward the higher levels of education, the proportion of the "Orientals" gradually diminishes.

The problem of the gap in the academic achievement between the "Orientals" and the "Westerns" has attracted the attention of researchers as well as policy makers. Is it a result of social and economic factors such as poverty, low level of parents' education, and high birthrate, or is it related to differences in cultural patterns? Is it true that one can argue that "even if there will be equality in family resources, the gap in achievements will not disappear"? (Peres, 1973, p. 121)

Most educators and policy makers agree now that low achievement and restricted intellectual development are mostly phenomena of secondary retardation, which result from the damaging, depriving environment and not from ethnic and genetic factors. Furthermore, in a recent study (Lewy and Chen, 1976), the findings showed that

> the negative influence of the home environment manifests itself when the child of African or Asian parents (Orientals) begins school. However, nothing here signifies that this initial influence continues operating, resulting in a continual accumulation of deficiencies throughout the school experience. All of these explanations do not change the situation. In fact, the gap between the two ethnic groups is quite steady (Lewy and Chen, 1976).

The strategies for coping with the issue of the disadvantaged in Israel have gone since their initiation into different approaches and stages: the voluntary-pioneering stage (pre-1948); formal equality stage (1948–1958); compensatory education stage (1958–1968); structural and organizational reform and social integration (1968–1975) (Smilansky, 1976); community involvement and the massive allocation of resources (1975–present) (Peled, 1977).

The *compensatory education policy* comprised fragmentary strategies lacking a general theory and, therefore, lacked a comprehensive strategy. The fragmentary strategies included: experiments in cognitive development in early childhood and teaching innovations in the elementary school; grouping and streaming within the regular school; promoting and advancing the more talented among the disadvantaged in order to increase their numbers in secondary education; remedial teaching for children who failed in the regular system together with social and psychological services for dropouts; a substantial expansion of vocational education and nonacademic postsecondary education. In order to do all that, the ministry allocated additional resources (money and manpower) for the compensatory activities and extended the school day and the school year for the disadvantaged.

Organizational reform and social integration in schools was the next policy. This new policy included a change of organization of the system, cutting two years from the eight years' elementary school and forming the high school of two divisions; elimination of the formal selection and screening between the elementary school and the junior high school and the junior and senior divisions, replacing it by a system of counseling and guidance; preference for the comprehensive high school and the expansion of vocational education within it; the extension of free and compulsory education to an additional two years (grades 9 and 10).

In order to cope with the challenge of the disadvantaged issue, the new policy was aimed at three goals: to innovate and modernize the high school curriculum; to democratize secondary education (by extending free and compulsory education); and to create within the school a social meeting of children of different social and ethnic groups by imposing, by law, social integration in the junior division of the high school.

In an unpublished report by the director-general of the Ministry of Education and Culture it was argued that the criteria of success of a policy should be examined longitudinally. The question is to what extent the correlation between socioeconomic characteristics and ethnic origin on one hand and academic achievement decreased over time. Examining the official data, he found no significant change in the gap between the average achievements of "Orientals" and "Westerns" (Peled, 1976; see also Lewy and Chen, 1976).

There was progress in basic skills in lower grades and an increase in school attendance in the elementary and secondary schools. There had been an important expansion of vocational education. The gap was still large in academic secondary education and higher education. In 1973, the rate of those who got the *Bagrut* certificate (a sort of a visa to higher education) among the "Orientals" was 7 percent versus 52 percent among "Westerns." In higher education, the "Orientals" were 2.5 percent of the relevant age-group (twenty to twenty-nine) against 14 percent of "Westerns." Dropouts amounted to 8 percent of fourteen- to seventeen-year-olds and were an immediate potential source for delinquency and crime.

Once more, in 1975, there was a change in policy, this time, a gradual change. The prevailing policies have not been abolished, but rather a new policy was initiated experimentally. Social tensions and outbursts with ethnic connotations in the beginning of the 1970s resulted in the formation of a public investigation committee appointed by the prime minister to inquire into the distress of youth and to propose policies. Three years later the published report proposed a long list of strategies. In education these policies focused on *parental participation* and *community involvement* in the education of children.

The new policy that followed assumed that a concentrated *massive allocation* would only make a difference if it involved parents and local communities in forming the particular strategies. This policy is now in the process of being implemented.

It is evident that approaches to the issues of the disadvantaged and the "academic gap" have been continuously changing and developing since 1948. Even now, Israel's educational system is looking for new ways to respond to this persistent challenge. Neither the administrative measures at the beginning nor the compensatory programs (1958–1968) concentrating on the acquisition of the basic skills in the lower grades of the elementary school and on the promotion of the highest quartile of the disadvantaged (particularly through boarding schools) brought about the hoped-for change of bridging the gap.

Since 1968, social integration in schools has been tried, but most recent studies referring to the integrated classroom did not show any meaningful change in the scholastic achievements in these classes when no special teaching methods were employed. In only one specific experimental study in an elementary school in Jerusalem was it shown that the disadvantaged children in an integrated classroom achieved scholastically higher than their peers in homogenous classrooms when special methods were utilized (the active classroom methods). It is worthwhile to note that in this particular study, parents' education and socioeconomic indicators and the school's quality were controlled.

Facing the future, educating the disadvantaged continues to be among the top issues on the national agenda. Some educators are still optimistic and believe that children of African-Asian origin possess the ability to do as well as "Western" children on the same learning tasks provided that the curriculum and the learning speeds are adapted to their needs. Those educators postulate that schools advance all children according to their capabilities, regardless of their ethnic background (Adler, 1976). These educators do not define the causes of the gap as being related to ethnic origin (Lewy and Chen, 1976). Others, like Frankenstein, stress the existence of cultural differences between social and ethnic groups and claim that priority should be given to the rehabilitation of the impaired intelligence and not to administrative social integration.

### Education of Minorities

In 1971, 15 percent of Israel's population (excluding the West Bank and Gaza Strip) were minorities. Arabs (mostly Muslim Arabs) comprised 13 percent; 1.5 percent were Druzes and others. All these groups spoke Arabic as their native language. The differences between Druzes and the Arabs are not linguistic but religious, ethnic, and national. This section will discuss only Arab education.

Arab education in Israel has developed rapidly since Israel's independence: the school population has multiplied over thirteen times while the general Arab population has increased only three times.

The gaps between Arab education and Jewish education in Israel are illustrated by academic achievement, rate of school dropouts, character of secondary education, and quality of teachers, physical facilities, and curriculum.

An indicator of that gap is the rate of *Bagrut* among the Arabs—8 percent compared to 24 percent among Jews in general but 7 percent among "Oriental" Jews. The rate of dropouts is still greater than among the Jews. A possible explanation is the rural character of Arab villages and the Muslim tradition of keeping girls at home.

In the high school, the emphasis is on humanistic rather than natural science studies. Arab students in higher education tend to study humanities and social sciences rather than natural sciences or engineering. One half of the teachers in the Arab section are unqualified (as compared to 16 percent in the Jewish sector).

A difficult problem is setting educational objectives for the Arab education in Israel. The long and durable Jewish-Arab conflict and wars cause a dilemma to Israeli Arabs between their identity as Arabs and their loyalty as citizens of the state of Israel.

Arab society in Israel is in an accelerated process of modernization and urbanization, which accelerates the process of undermining the *traditional* patterns of the Arab society, which was mainly family-centered and rural. These processes have not yet built new, modern patterns for this society. In this process, a change in the status of women is very rapid.

One sociological analysis concluded that "in the case of the Israeli-Arab, the dilemma that follows the modernization processes is more acute than in many societies and the available ideological solutions . . . are insufficient" (Peres, 1976).

Furthermore, this process of modernization and its general "environment" results in a part of the tension and conflict between conservatives and reformers among the Arabs being transferred to the Jewish population and its social and educational policies.

The curriculum of Arab schools has three parts: similar curricula to the Jewish one (natural sciences, foreign languages, and so on), unique Arab curriculum (Arabic, Arab history, Islam), and curricula adjusted to Arab schools (geography, general history, Hebrew).

## Informal Education

Informal education in Israel is based on an educational concept of integrating structural principles, forms of activity, and content to a unified organizational system. This integration has a strong impact on the educational development of the individual.

Informal activity completes, to some extent, formal activity at school and frequently is considered as complementary education. Informal activities in high school were designed mostly to cope with the challenge of teaching social values and on making the contact between the individual and the environment. This activity includes social activity at school and activating the high school pupils outside the school.

The postulates of informal education in Israel are:

1. The need to turn the school to an "educative environment" that offers variety of stimulation and of intellectual, emotional, and social activities; this environment has to be, by its very existence, a model for the expected society.

2. The heterogenic school with a high proportion of disadvantaged children has to offer to each child frameworks of activity, content, and opportunity for success at least in one area. Encouraging personal motivation of each pupil becomes an important educational objective.

3. The social circumstances of Israel create many options for the development of "youth culture" that will look for changing reality and for innovating values and norms that become "established" and old. This process may become positive and constructive if channeled to appropriate forms of activity. It may become a social risk if barred by rigid structures and forms of formal education.

4. For many children and youth, informal education may be an alternative, in different levels of severity, to the formal education that caused their failure.

5. For the "unattached" who do not attend schools at all and do not work at all, sometimes some patterns of informal education are almost the last and the only response and form of "education" that may help them to reenter society.

The characteristics of informal education in Israel are integration of spontaneity and structured activities; vast supply of diversified activities on personal and collective basis equally appreciated by social norms; personal freedom and choice to join forms and frameworks and to leave them; complete absence of compulsory duty as well as direct involvement of the youth in decisions about themselves and their activities; methods of trial and error in different "jobs"; absence of a supreme authority and maximum flexibility in content, methods, and structures.

The particular objectives of informal education in Israel are development of inner attachment and encouragement of personal commitment to the common values, norms, and social ways of life together with development of skills and qualities of the individual that will enable him later to join society.

## PROSPECT

As emphasized in the review of Israel's education, it reflects the social environment and at the same time tries to influence and direct its development. The extent of the responsiveness of an educational system to social and individual needs and demands has an impact on its successes and failures. Israel's education system, like many other national educational systems, lags behind its social environment's development. Nevertheless, in perspective, the system has tried to adjust itself to its environment.

The first long-term master plan for the Israeli educational system in the forthcoming decade was made in 1976 (Peled, 1976). The approach of this master plan was that planning is neither a futurologist forecast nor a rational extrapolation of the past and the present, but rather an attempt to intervene and influence effectively the forthcoming future. This active planning, the meaning of which is active intervention by deliberate policies, rotates between two poles: the present, its problems and challenges, and the goals of the future, determined by a rational analysis and a visionary value-oriented perception.

According to this master plan, ten principles should underlie Israel's educational future:

1. The necessity of having a built-in mechanism for change and innovation based on the concept of continuous process of slow change, rather than a radical revolution.

2. A restatement of the educational objectives is required to synthesize the still prevailing importance of social orientation and value orientation of the system as well as increasing the weight of the individual-orientation strategies.

3. In regard to the process of increasing direct democracy and citizen's participation in policy-making processes, a reciprocal interaction between society and school is needed. Implementation requires a consistent and meaningful decentralization. Transferring many issues to the joint decisions of communities, parents, and teachers will reduce the inevitable bureaucratization of the centralized system.

4. The social composition of Israel's society enhances a reevaluation of the achievement orientation and competitive approach of the schools and their curriculum. More diversification is necessary to adapt educational forms and contents to the different groups of society.

5. In order to eliminate detrimental rigidity of the system, a reorganization of the administration and structure is vital. The reorganized system must be flexible and free of any conservative approaches that hinder innovation.

6. The coexistence of two major socio-educational policies (the "egalitarian" and the "elitist") will be of primary importance. They will accord equal educational opportunities for all children without contradicting the deliberate promotion of high learning standards.

7. Teachers' training, including in-service training and guidance, is fundamental to the future of the system.

8. It is obvious that external constraints limit the freedom of educational policies. But in the long run even external constraints are changeable variables, provided that a deliberately planned intervention is initiated.

9. Even under budgetary cuts and a large proportion of fixed costs, there is still a generous margin of freedom to make the system more effective and more efficient.

10. First priorities in Israel's educational policies are and should be the nurturing of disadvantaged children, raising the standards of the education of minorities, and teachers' training and retraining.

## REFERENCES

Abramov, S. Z. *Perpetual Dilemma: Jewish Religion in the Jewish State.* Associated University Press, 1976.

Adar, Z. "The State Curriculum Criticized," *Megamot* (January 1956) (Hebrew).

Adler, C. "Israel's Educational System as an Instrument in Promoting the Socially Lower Groups." Unpublished paper submitted to the Van Leer Foundation, Jerusalem, 1976 (Hebrew).

―――. "Social Stratification and Education in Israel," *Comparative Education Review* 18, No. 1 (February, 1974).

Algarrebly, M. "Criteria to Characterize the Social Composition of the School and a Method to Allocate Budgets Among Schools to Foster the Disadvantaged," *Megamot* 21, No. 1 (February 1975) (Hebrew).

Alon, Y. "Education in the 1970's, A Policy in Implementation," in *Education in Israel,* ed. C. Ormian. Jerusalem: Ch., Ministry of Education and Culture, 1973 (Hebrew).

Bentwich, J. *Education in Israel.* London: Routledge & Kegan Paul, 1965.

Ben-Yehuda, B. "History of Education in Eretz-Israel in the Pre-Independence Era," in *Education in Israel,* ed. C. Ormian. Jerusalem: Ministry of Education and Culture, 1973 (Hebrew).

Bloom, B. S., ed. *Taxonomy of Educational Objectives.* New York: David McKay Co., Inc., 1956.

Dinur, B. "The State Law of Education," in *Values and Ways,* ed. B. Dinur. Tel Aviv: Urim, 1958.

Eden, S. "Curriculum as an Instrument to Implement Educational Objectives," in *Education in Israel,* ed. C. Ormian. Jerusalem: Ministry of Education in Israel, 1973 (Hebrew).

―――. *Objectives of Education in Israel.* Tel Aviv: Maalot, 1976 (Hebrew).

―――. "The New Curricula—Principles and Processes," in *On the New Curricula,* ed. S. Eden. Tel Aviv: Maalot, 1971 (Hebrew).

―――. "Changes in the Israeli Society and Their Reflection in the New Curricula of the Compulsory Education Ages," in *Theory and Practice in Curriculum Construction,* ed. Ministry of Education and Culture. Jerusalem: 1976 (Hebrew).

Eisenstadt, S. N. *Israeli Society.* London: Widenfeld and Nicleson, 1967.

―――. *The Israeli Society,* 2d ed. Jerusalem: The Hebrew University, 1973.

―――, Adler, C., Bar-Yosef, R., and Kahana, R. *Israel—A Society in the Making.* Jerusalem: The Magness Press, The Hebrew University, 1972 (Hebrew).

Elboim-Dror, R. *Encyclopedia of Education,* Vol. 3, *Organization of Education.* Jerusalem: Ministry of Education and Culture, 1967, 82–114 (Hebrew).

Frankenstein, C. "A School Without Parents," *Megamot* 12, No. 1 (February 1962) (Hebrew).

―――. "Education and the Social Gap." Unpublished paper, Jerusalem, 1973.

―――. *They Think Again.* Jerusalem: 1972.

―――. "The Training Tasks of the School of Education (A Proposal)," unpublished paper, The Hebrew University, Jerusalem, 1974. (Hebrew)

Glikson, M. *Some Aspects of Non-Conventional Methods of Education in Israel.* Research Report No. 137, Publication No. 484. Jerusalem: 1969.

Harman, D. "Developmental Trends in Education in the Jewish Education System of Mandatory Palestine and Israel." Unpublished paper, 1970.

Horowitz, D., and Lissak, M. "The Yishuv as a Political Society," *Megamot* 17 (Hebrew).

Jarus, A., Marcus, J., Oren, J., and Rapaport, C. *Children and Families in Israel.* New York: Gordon and Breach, 1970.

Kleinberger, A. F. "Legislation, Politics, and Guidance in Education," in *Education in Israel,* ed. C. Ormian. Jerusalem: Ministry of Education and Culture, 1973 (Hebrew).

_____. *Society, Schools and Progress in Israel.* New York: Pergamon Press, 1966.

_____. "To the Discussion about the Professional Meaning of Teaching," *Megamot* 14 (1966) (Hebrew).

Lam, Z. "Ideological Tensions—Conflicts About the Objectives of Education," in *Education in Israel,* ed. C. Ormian. Jerusalem: Ministry of Education and Culture, 1973 (Hebrew).

_____. Teaching and Alienation, *Megamot* 14 (1966).

_____. *Teachers' Training in View of the Changes in the Functions of the Teacher.* Hachimuch, 1969 (Hebrew).

Lewy, A. and Chen, M. "Closing or Widening of the Achievement Gap," in *Studies in Administration and Organization,* No. 4 (Fall 1976).

Ministry of Education and Culture. *Education in the Mirror of Figures.* Jerusalem: 1964.

Ministry of Education and Culture. *Statistics of Education* (Appendix to the minister's presentation of budget in the Knesset), 1977 (Hebrew).

Minkovich, A., and Bashi, J. *A Proposal of Reform in the Organization of Supervision and Instruction,* submitted to the Ministry of Education and Culture, Jerusalem, April 1973.

Minkovich, A., Davis, D., Bashi, J., et al. *An Evaluation Study of Israeli Elementary Schools.* Jerusalem: The Hebrew University of Jerusalem, School of Education, 1977.

Ormian, C., ed. *The Educational Encyclopedia.* Jerusalem: Ministry of Education and Culture, 1968 (Hebrew).

Peled, E. (ed.) *Education in Israel in the 1980's.* Jerusalem: 1976 (Hebrew).

_____. "The Hidden Agenda of Educational Policy in Israel." Unpublished proposal for a dissertation, Teachers College, Columbia University, New York, 1977.

Peres, Y. *Ethnic Relations in Israel.* Tel Aviv: Sifriat Hapoalim, 1976 (Hebrew).

Rapaport, C., and Arad, R. *Youth Aliyah,* Research Report No. 136, Publication No. 483, The Henrietta Szold Institute, Jerusalem, 1969.

Rieger, E. *Hebrew Education in Eretz-Israel.* Tel Aviv: Dvir Publishing Co., 1940 (Hebrew).

Riemalt, E., ed. *The Study of the Structure of the Elementary and Secondary Education in Israel.* Parliamentary Report, Knesset, Jerusalem, 1971 (Hebrew).

Rokah, E. "The Students' Population in the Disadvantaged Schools," in *A Decade of Educating the Disadvantaged,* ed. S. Adiel, et al. Jerusalem: The Ministry of Education and Culture, 1970 (Hebrew).

Rosenfeld, Y. "Parents as Active Educational Agents in the Coming Decade," in *Education in Israel,* ed. C. Ormian. Jerusalem: Ministry of Education and Culture, 1973 (Hebrew).

Schachter, H. L. "Educational Institutions and Political Coalitions: The Case of Israel," *Comparative Education Review* 16, No. 3 (October 1972).

Sheffler, I. *The Language of Education,* Springfield, Ill.: Charles C Thomas, 1960.

Shuval, J. *The Integration of Immigrants from Different Countries of Origin in Israel,* in Jerusalem: The Magness Press, The Hebrew University, 1969, pp. 180–184 (Hebrew).

Simon, A. "On the Scholastic Achievements of Immigrant Children in the Lower Elementary Grades in the Negev," *Megamot* 8 No. 4 (October 1957) (Hebrew).

———. "On the Objectives of Secondary Education in Israel," in *Theory and Practice in Secondary Education,* ed. M. Shapiro. Jerusalem: 1962 (Hebrew).

———. "Youth Villages," in *Education in Israel,* ed. C. Ormian. Jerusalem: Ministry of Education and Culture, 1973 (Hebrew).

Smilansky, M. "The Response of Education to the Needs of the Disadvantaged Pupils." Tel Aviv University and the Ministry of Education and Culture, unpublished paper to the 1980s Planning Committee, 1976 (Hebrew).

*Selected Bibliography of Israel Educational Materials.* (Compiled for the Office of Education, United States Department of Health, Education, and Welfare and the National Science Foundation, Washington, D.C.). Jerusalem: Israel Program for Scientific Translations, 1966.

Stanner, R. *The Legal Basis of Education in Israel.* Jerusalem: Ministry of Education and Culture, 1963.

Yizhar, S. "The Shadow of School," *Mibifmim* 33 No. 2 (1973) (Hebrew).

———. *On Education and Education for Values.* Tel Aviv: Am Oved Tarbut Vechinuch, 1974 (Hebrew).

## CHAPTER 6

# Japanese Education

### RONALD S. ANDERSON

## DEFINITION

The structure of Japanese education, at least on the surface, looks remarkably like that of the United States. This is understandable, since during the postwar period (1945–1952) when the United States and the allied powers occupied Japan, the whole educational system was consciously and intentionally modified with the help of American educational advisers on the basis of American practice. Though the model is American, the actual practice is distinctly Japanese.

At age six, all children are required to attend a six-year elementary school, followed by a compulsory three-year junior high school. These two levels are open and free to all. A remarkable 99.9 percent of children of this age-group—six to fifteen—attend. The three-year senior high school is not compulsory. It is articulated with the junior high school, but entrance is not automatic, since most senior high schools require passing a stiff entrance examination.

The single tract system, a postwar reform, is now split into three tracks at the senior high level: (*a*) the academic including (1) a three-year, full-time school, and (2) an equivalent four-year part-time and correspondence school; (*b*) a vocational school; and (*c*) the first three grades of a five-year technical college. Outside the formal educational system there are a variety of special schools, which provide practical, vocational, and cultural instruction.

INTRODUCTION

### Objectives of Education

Education in any society is the process by which society ensures the transmission of the knowledge, skills, and values necessary for survival to the next generation, hence ensuring the continuance of its group life. This is the first and most basic objective of education. Education may also be looked upon as an instrument of social policy, as an important object of economic investment, and as an element of personal advancement.

Education's function is both social and individual—*social* in that it inducts the individual into the society by providing him with the collective experience of the group's past, thus enabling him to make a more effective contribution to the group; and *individual* in that it enables one to develop to the maximum of one's ability, enabling enjoyment of a fuller and more satisfying and successful personal life. In a democractic state, where the value of the individual is cherished, the objective of affording a happier life and developing the person's creativity have become increasingly important. These are known as education for consumption.

Any developing nation's educational system has to answer at least three different kinds of demands: (1) the demand of the state which as part of the national investment requires a pool of the labor force with highly developed skills enabling the state to advance economically and become modernized; (2) the demand of the individual as a consumer of education for the development of personal potential and for preparation for a career, as well as for education as an end in itself, for the individual's own enjoyment—this latter is possible only when the society has become more affluent; and (3) the demand inherent in social change, the extension of equality of opportunity as a way of extending democracy.

A country must decide what priority to give to one or the other of these demands. At an early stage in its development it may feel the prime need for general literacy to provide a base for national unity and to develop an elite group with vocational and management skills to achieve pressing national economic objectives. At a later state it may feel the need to stress formal academic education: first elementary, then as it becomes more stable and affluent, secondary and higher education.

### Reasons for This System

Among the world's more recently modernized societies, the Japanese have been outstandingly successful in using education to build and strengthen their state. They emerged from feudalism in 1868 in what is called the Meiji Restoration and promptly set about modernizing the country through universal public education. They incorporated into the system strong native traditions derived from Shintoism and feudalism, with some aspects of Confucianism and Buddhism, which they had borrowed in ancient times from the then more advanced cultures of China and Korea. The Japanese, unlike the Chinese and Koreans, were noted for their intellectual curiosity and eagerness to borrow from the best of other cultures. Whereas other societies resisted foreign intrusions, the Japanese sought them out and welcomed them, building on them and transforming them to suit their needs. But at the same time they have retained central elements of their tradition. Education in Japan has always been important. Not only has it helped the nation catch up and sometimes even improve on the performance of its mentors, the Chinese, Koreans, and some of the Western industrialized powers, but education has been for the individual the prime means of social mobility.

In the last century, education served to disseminate knowledge about the West and its new sciences. In addition, it taught the technical skills and political and social attitudes required of a modern nation. And the people, with their strong respect for learning derived from Confucianism, welcomed the new ideas and sent their children to school with enthusiasm.

A primary reason for investment in elementary education in modernizing states is the promotion of literacy as well as the creation of an articulate citizenry able to participate intelligently in government or at least obey government orders. At leadership levels the government must also build universities. Most developing countries are so poor that they must make a choice between literacy education and leadership education. Not so the Japanese. Despite poverty and a dearth of resources for modernization, they determined to achieve both goals at the same time. To identify and train the nation's talents, they built a university (later Tokyo University) on the base of the old Confucian college in the capital. At first it was for the samurai elite, but it soon began to consist largely of commoners.

From the beginning of the modern educational system a century ago demand in Japan has always exceeded supply. To succeed in life a youth had to go as far in school as his abilities allowed him, but he had also, if possible, to get into a prestigious university (because he would proudly carry the school label the rest of his life) and do well in his studies. Education became the "escalator" for talent and achievement, and competition for the best schools was keen. Family and community pressure, as well as the desire to qualify for a choice job in government or in a good company, motivated every ambitious youth to aim for the prestige schools at each level, the "first junior high," the "first senior high," and finally Tokyo Imperial University, the apex of the educational hierarchy. The selection process consisted of entrance examinations. Before long the examinations became an end in themselves, dominating and distorting the purposes of all schools. The student's goal was simply to amass enough facts to pass tests. The unrelenting pressures on the individual drove him to cram long hours in school and out. The effect was often devastating on youth, driving them to nervous debility, ulcers (even in the early teens), and occasionally suicide. Teachers were also under pressure to produce successful exam takers, since their reputation and that of the school itself depended on the number of their graduates who entered the better schools. Parents were under pressure to provide tutoring, which was often expensive, in the home or in a cram school, to give the child the best possible chance in the cutthroat competition each faced.

During the last year of each level (that is, the sixth grade of elementary, the ninth grade of junior high, and the twelfth of senior high) the regular curriculum is abandoned for systematic memorization and test taking pointed toward the next entrance exam. At home, the whole family becomes involved in the youth's success or failure. Mothers become assistant teachers working long hours with their children, prodding and cramming and helping with problems. Family life revolves around the exam taker. He is favored with special treats; he may not be disturbed. No single event, except possibly marriage, has greater effect on the direction of a young person's life than the results of these tests.

A recent study shows that the responsibility for providing this forced-feeding type of education, which is felt to be necessary to produce the "high quality" (that is, educated) child, even governs the number of children a family will have. They reduce family size to the number they can afford to educate (Yamamura & Hanley, 1975, p. 117).

Another motivation for the parents' behavior is the strong desire of Japanese couples not to be different. Not doing their best, as others in their group do, not to send their children to a good university, would violate one of the most important Japanese social codes.

## HISTORY

### Beginnings

Japan, an ancient society with a distinctive culture, has survived at least 2,000 years on its island homeland. The primitive Japanese stood in awe of China, their older, more powerful neighbor on the mainland. From about the mid-sixth century the Japanese began a systematic borrowing from great China that produced a cultural revolution and influenced Japanese civilization right up to the present. They adopted the complicated Chinese character system to write their own, quite different language. Schools were founded on the Chinese pattern and taught the highly ethical Confucian classics. By A.D. 700, the Japanese had adopted so many of the institutions of China, government as well as literary, that they became a part of the Chinese cultural realm.

They soon refined and adapted the Chinese culture to meet their own needs. From the ninth to twelfth century they began to develop their own original culture. But parts of certain borrowings remained permanent. One was the political and social philosophy and personal ethical system of Confucianism. In the seventeenth and eighteenth centuries, the feudal Tokugawa Shogunate reinstated the neo-Confucian emphasis on personal loyalty of subject to sovereign as the individual's highest duty. The schools founded in the feudal period taught the Confucian classics. Confucianism became an ethical system that guided the moral and ethical training of youth in the cardinal virtues of loyalty, filial piety, duty, and benevolence. The purposes of this premodern education were to make youth virtuous and shape their character to help them meet the needs of their society.

Youth were indoctrinated with the belief that to study was the absolute duty of every person to pay back his debt to Heaven and to his parents for having been born. It was also a duty to his superior, the lord, so that he could contribute to the clan and thus fulfill his proper function in the feudal society. The solid imbedding of education in the value system helps explain the importance placed on education in Japan today. And the didactic morals training in the feudal school helps us understand the current insistence of modern Japanese parents on systematic morals instruction in schools.

The young leaders who engineered the Meiji Restoration (1868) abandoned feudalism and began to modernize the nation on a Western model. They also embarked on a strongly nationalistic, centralized policy. To train technicians necessary to man the essential jobs of modernization and to unite the loyalty of diverse feudal elements to the emperor-state, the leaders saw the need for a universal public school system. The feudal schools were closed and a national Department of Education was set up in Tokyo to plan and control the nation's schools. In the Fundamental Code of Education in 1872, the nation was divided, after the French school system, into eight academic districts, each of which would have a university, and each academic district was subdivided into thirty-two secondary school districts. Each of these, in turn, was to have 210 elementary schools, for an aggregate of 53,760 elementary schools. By the end of the first year about 40 percent of the boys and 15 percent of the girls were in school, and within three years half the projected number of schools were in operation.

The preamble of the 1872 Fundamental Code of Education departed drastically from the old ways in emphasizing the importance of developing the mind of each individual. It said in part, "there shall be no community with an illiterate family, nor a family with an illiterate person."

Though the structure was centralized after the French model, the Meiji leaders decided that for the curriculum, teaching method, and philosophy, the American solution to the problem of universal education was most appropriate, so they sent the head of the new Department of Education on a fact-finding mission overseas. He and his staff visited American schools, collected reports, and engaged an American college professor, David Murray, of Rutgers University, as adviser to the Department of Education in setting up the national system called for by the Fundamental Code.

For the first decade of the initial modernization, the new system was largely American. Schoolrooms and school plant were built and equipped after plans brought back from Boston. American texts, such as McGuffey's *New Eclectic Primer*, were translated into Japanese, and teachers followed the liberal philosophy and enlightened teaching methods of the Swiss educator, J. H. Pestalozzi, which visiting Japanese students had studied at leading American normal schools. Representative teachers from every prefecture were called to Tokyo to observe the new schools, called "educational museums" and to learn about the new-style programs.

But in the long run the permissiveness of Pestalozzi did not fit the conservative Confucian tradition still underlying Japanese values. Conservatives of the old school, many of them Confucian scholars, condemned Pestalozzi's ideas and methods as being deficient in content and neglectful of the moral teachings the Japanese demanded of their schools. Accordingly, about 1880, Japanese education turned away from American influences. American advisers and professors were sent home, and Japan entered the next phase of its modernization: nationalist indoctrination. The Department of Education officially banned Western ethics texts and returned to Shinto-nationalist and Confucian principles of loyalty, filial piety, and patriotism as the basis for all education. In 1886 the minister of education rewrote the educational ordinances to provide a unified, centralized school system, in which the object of education was no longer the education of the individual, but was henceforth education to serve the state. The new ordinances now stressed morals teaching, military training, and nationalism.

To give nationalist education a semireligious sanction, in 1890 the emperor was persuaded by his advisers, especially his Confucian tutor, to issue the policy doctrine called "The Imperial Rescript on Education." It combined the Shinto ideology of emperor worship with the Confucian ethical principals of loyalty, filial piety, and obedience to superiors. It became a catechism known by all and recited periodically in all schools. It served as a universally enforced philosophy of education until the end of World War II.

The doctrine of the rescript was taught in the core course of morals and permeated the entire curriculum. It choked off the earlier enthusiasm for Westernization and redirected the people's loyalties to native values and the nation. Thus modernization was a liberal transplant grafted on a conservative body. The society was basically a conservative one with one basically liberal aspect, broad access to education.

Although the rescript effectively limited foreign learning to technical matters, new ideas continued to seep in, especially in the so-called liberal 1920s. Democracy and peace, as advocated by President Woodrow Wilson after World War I, attracted the attention of students and intellectuals. There was a revival of interest in democratic education. At this juncture, the premier philosopher of democratic education, John Dewey, was invited to Japan and most normal schools avidly adopted his progressivism. But his influence was limited to urban middle-class intellectuals, and the inexorable march toward nationalism, and eventually ultranationalism, continued. With the rise of the military in the 1930s, the liberal movement in education was suppressed and had to go underground.

The right-wing nationalists and military took over and led the country to war with China and finally to total war in World War II. The educational ministry, now handmaiden of the armed forces, tightened its control on student thought, hoping to marshal the schools behind the war, punishing all dissenters. As war approached the mainland of Japan, nearly all education, except elementary, came to a standstill.

When the war ended in August 1945, Japan was occupied by the allied forces, principally the American army under General Douglas MacArthur. The occupation authorities proceeded promptly to reopen the schools and carry out a program of demilitarization and democracy, based on the democratic principles enunciated in the Potsdam Declaration and succeeding American policy statements. The schools were considered the primary means of reorienting the nation. They were to do this under the surveillance and assistance of the occupation forces. The United States Army now had the unique responsibility of democratizing a people who had been indoctrinated for some sixty years with ultranationalism. But the seeds of the liberal period of the 1920s still survived, and leaders in democratization were often drawn from this group.

The first phase of occupation policy, demilitarization, was completed within one year through the willing compliance of the Japanese, who were thoroughly sick of war. The second phase, democratization, took longer. The visiting United States Education Mission, a group of distinguished American educators, supplied the framework of reform. On the Japanese side, leadership came from the Ministry of Education and the Japanese Educational Reform Council (JERC), who worked with the American mission to determine reform policy. After the mission left, the JERC assumed three major tasks: (1) to develop a new statement of official educational policy to replace the now defunct 1890 Imperial Rescript on Education; (2) to reorganize the school structure into a single track and 6-3-3 ladder; and (3) to decentralize educational administration. Other reforms to equalize educational opportunity and strengthen the new democracy were recommended by the mission, planned by the JERC and the ministry, and implemented by passage in the national Diet. They included the following:

1. Consolidating the five school tracks into a single track.
2. Extending compulsory education to nine years (from six).
3. Developing the comprehensive senior high school.
4. Initiating part-time and extension or correspondence education at high school and university.
5. Introducing coeducation at all levels.
6. Increasing the number of national universities to provide at least one in each prefecture.
7. Establishing junior colleges.
8. Requiring general education in the college curriculum.
9. Offering teacher education in each national university, eliminating normal schools.
10. Increasing vocational education and guidance at all levels through junior college.
11. Making innovative changes in lower school curriculum, for example, social studies to replace morals.

All these involved sweeping institutional changes, but they were carried out and generally survive to the present. Over the years, however, some have been modified. The remarkable thing is that they lasted beyond the occupation, when the Japanese were able to change the laws where they saw fit. Why was this so? To many teachers the occupation afforded a freer teaching environment than they had ever experienced, and they welcomed it. Some of the reforms met long-standing needs; others were in harmony with Japanese cultural values (for example, those providing educational opportunity); and still others were the next step in a process already begun before the war.

Current Status

A continuing issue to the present has been the democratization of education. Since the peace treaty in 1952 there has been a long struggle between radicals and conservatives to define democracy and internalize it as a Japanese value. Ultranationalism was rejected as having led the people into war. But the nation needed to establish its new identity, and in doing so the process of accommodating nationalism and democracy has been difficult, especially in education. The curriculum has been the constant target of political forces, right and left, seeking to use the schools for purposes of indoctrination. The Ministry of Education wants to teach traditional nationalist values, but it is constantly blocked by the leftist Japan Teachers' Union, which in turn is accused of attempting to radicalize the students by teaching communism.

Another issue long under contention is the control of education. Prewar control had been tightly centralized under the Education Ministry. A basic occupation reform had been to give education to local control by means of elected school boards, so as to reflect the will of the people, meet their local needs, and enlist their support. This was, however, not in the Japanese tradition, in which institutions are hierarchically structured, and in which government for most of its history was highly centralized. Accordingly, one of the first steps to reverse the occupation reforms was changing elective school boards to appointive, the local boards by mayors, and the prefectural boards by governors. The motive was clearly political; the conservative party in power hoped to weaken the liberal elements by strengthening its control over the teachers' unions. The process of recentralization of ministry control was further effected when the ministry forced through the Diet, against Japan Teachers' Union violent opposition, several other acts, such as the teachers' efficiency rating system, nationwide achievement tests at the junior high school level, a fixed curriculum and most recently, the institution of a new type of administrative officer, called *shunin* (chief teacher).

Another controversial issue in education was the introduction of a course in morals education, mandatory one hour a week at elementary and secondary levels. It did not repeat the old nationalist indoctrination of the prewar days, but the liberal elements and the union feared that it was a movement backwards. The single track of the occupation days was modified when a new five-year school called the *kosen* (technical school) was instituted at the combined high school–junior college level. It was to train middle-grade technicians for the new industrialization.

Despite these conservative trends, the democratic educational system has gained general acceptance, and its major elements have been integrated into school practice. This does not mean that all segments of society are happy with their schools. In fact, there are complaints from all directions.

For example, Japan, like other nations, was beset with university violence in the 1960s. The government blamed much of it on the postwar democratic reforms, and asked the ministry's main advisory agency, the Central Council for Education, to plan a thoroughgoing reorganization of the entire educational system, its policies, and possibilities for expansion. This became known as the Third Major Educational Reform. The latest projected reform was to examine the occupational reforms and to decide what changes should be made to meet the national needs of the future. The plan, carried out on the initiative of the conservative government, was an attack on many of the surviving democratic reforms and principles. This excited the strong opposition of the Japan Teachers' Union which brought out its own reform plan, translated into English and titled "How to Reform Japan's Education" (Japan Teachers' Union, 1975, pp. 1–210). It argued for further decentralization of power and greater freedom of teachers and for the public to decide the direction of change. The union felt that instead of dismantling the democratic reforms, the government should support them and try to make them work.

At this juncture, in 1973, the oil embargo and economic slump occurred, and the Third Reform was slowed down for want of funds and lack of national acceptance. Debate over the many proposed reforms continues, and the final shape of the more controversial items, especially in higher education, has yet to be determined. But at the end of the first century of modern education, Japan had a viable system, which though beset by hotly contested problems, has been generally effective and successful.

## THEORY

### Learning

The ministry of education, the teacher education establishment, and the professionals in the field of educational psychology are all familiar with the new concepts of learning and teaching that have been developed in the United States in recent years. In 1958 the leading Japanese educational psychologists, headed by Dr. Sawada, attempted to cover the whole field of learning with the publication of a fourteen-volume study entitled *Gendai Kyoiku Shinrigaku Taikei* (*The General System of Contemporary Educational Psychology*). But the concepts therein, which were generally translated from standard American textbooks, are not often applied in actual teaching. Instead, teachers prefer the tested techniques of an elder statesman in the field whose ideas are expressed in terms of formulae and answer the question, "How to do it?" The elder scholar gathers about himself disciples dedicated to promoting his formulae in practice. And it is this body of educational experience, rather than abstract theory, that governs educational practice. Once the teacher-disciples discover a technique that works they cling to it for the rest of their careers and build their reputation on identifying themselves with the statesman and his formulae.

## Transfer of Training

Japanese educators are concerned with transfer of training, since they as well as the public are convinced that, for example, the study of mathematics—their favorite subject—is the best means of strengthening the brain so as to permit the student to learn other academic subjects more readily.

## Learning by Repetition

The Japanese are dedicated to the proposition that students learn best in groups and by repetition. They accept the fact that children have differing abilities, but believe that this does not prevent children from learning at about the same rate. Learning, the Japanese believe, is best done by repetition and drill, continuing until every child in the class masters the subject. So a class may start out with choral reading, after which the teacher may ask questions about the text until she feels they all understand the topic. Then the class all settle down to silent study and memorization of the material, while the teacher moves about the room, checking on progress, helping the slow ones, and answering questions.

This methodology is used for all types of subjects. In some elementary schools a teacher may teach music, art, and physical education in addition to language and arithmetic. She does not shift gears when she moves from subject to subject. The method that works with one subject or child can be used to teach another subject or other children.

The highly successful Suzuki (Consulate General of Japan, 1968, p. 8) method of teaching music to preschoolers is a case in point. Shinichi Suzuki gives five key points as basic to his teaching method:

1. The earlier the learning the better, not only for teaching music, but for all learning.
2. The human being is the product of his environment.
3. Repetition of experiences is important for learning.
4. Teacher and parents must perform at a high level and continue to grow to provide a better learning situation for the child.
5. The system must involve demonstrations for the child based on the teacher's understanding.

## Creativity

It is significant that the topic of creativity has been until recently completely ignored by Japanese educational psychologists. With the publication of the Central Council for Education's *Basic Guidelines for the Reform of Education* (Ministry of Education, 1971), there is recognition of the importance of creativity in school education of the future.

It is important for social progress to foster creativity. In school education this development of creativity now assumes as much importance as does the development of personality. . . . children's progress at school depends as much on creative ability as on their so-called intelligence. The school system has so far, however, done little to encourage creativity, emphasizing instead, learning by rote, technical training, and passing examinations.

An educational system that encourages creativity must build the opportunity to think creatively into its curriculum. It must encourage pupils to search freely for different solutions to problems with which they are presented. Since individual creativity depends more on a balanced personality than on mere intelligence, however, pupils must be encouraged to focus on specific subjects and lines of thought in order to produce something of real value.

In encouraging creativity in school, the class plays an important role, although the teacher's attitude is crucial, too. In general it is felt that teachers over-value the highly intelligent students and under-evaluate those who are highly creative (pp. 166–167).

## Reward

Teachers are careful about handing out rewards to students for excellent performance. Whereas they used to post the list of students by rank order according to excellence, the opposition of the Japan Teachers' Union has made this practice taboo. The teacher may use praise to encourage weak students who have done unusually well, but she does not ordinarily praise the better students. They already know where they stand in the class, and their reward is the grade received at the end of the semester and the later success in the entrance exam. There is no such thing as a national scholastic honor society as in American high schools or the dean's list as at American colleges.

On the playgrounds in competitive sports such as relay races, which are very popular for all ages, all participants are rewarded. In a recent sports festival at an elementary school all participants were rewarded with a pencil and a notebook. The individual winner is deemphasized; rather, the whole class wins. This illustrates the well-known identification with the group in Japan.

*Punishment*

Before the war Japanese teachers freely used physical punishment to discipline their charges, and punishment was taken for granted by teachers, parents, and pupils alike. Slapping was the favored method used by parents, teachers, and officers in the army. In more humane postwar days the law frowns on physical punishment. Article XI of the School Education Law of 1947 says, "Principals and teachers of schools may punish their students, pupils and children, when they recognize it necessary in the light of education, in compliance with the regulations issued by the competent authorities. They shall not, however, inflict corporal punishment" (GHQ, SCAP, 1952, p. 130). But old customs die hard. Even today some parents urge the teachers to slap and otherwise chastise their children when they are mischievous or lazy. And the prohibition against corporal punishment was found to be flexible. So the ministry had to interpret the law. It banned a teacher's "hitting or kicking a youngster, and even denied them other less-violent modes, such as forcing a student to sit erect for a long time, or keeping him after school." Still some teachers circumvent these prohibitions, and continue to slap their students or hit them on the head with closed fists. In one recent case, reported to the author by a parent, a kindly, permissive and popular teacher punished several of his third graders for forgetting to bring their gym caps to school on gym day. He hit them on the head with his clenched fist. His action was known to and approved by the school and the parents. And even the offenders themselves did not resent the punishment, since they felt that the teacher really liked them and was acting in their own best interests. This latter is a frequent excuse for punishment, and it is honored.

Some years ago a student died as a result of a teacher's beating. The public protest was immediate. Both the ministry and the Japan Teachers' Union took action. The ministry fired a notice to the nation's boards of education exhorting them to maintain proper discipline among teachers, and to see to it that they never use corporal punishment again. The notice said further that teachers should guide their pupils with love. The same day the Japan Teachers' Union announced its policy of stamping out violence in the classroom.

In any case of unusual punishment where the student is injured, Japanese custom requires the principal to take responsibility and resign, the teacher involved is fired, and a monetary award is given the family, depending on the severity of the injury.

At high school, misdemeanors calling for punishment include smoking, riding motorcycles, fighting on campus, and tardiness or absenteeism. The offender may be expelled temporarily. A committee of teachers will call on the parents to discuss the problem. And the student is not allowed to return to the school until he and his parents come to the school and apologize.

## Teaching

Teaching at secondary and higher levels usually consists of highly formalized lectures by teachers and meticulous note taking by students. Rote memorization, drill, and constant testing are the most common teaching/learning techniques. The central government of Japan provides free textbooks for each subject and grade level, common to all equivalent schools in the prefecture. Supplementary workbooks for home study often accompany each lesson. The parents are informed by weekly announcements of the pages in the texts and in the workbooks to be covered for the week, and so home teaching is expected to reinforce classroom teaching.

At the elementary level, choral reading is a common method of instruction. Also in the teaching of English (from the seventh grade on) students are asked to stand and read the text aloud. Class discussion, which was introduced in the occupation as a teaching method for all levels, together with class reports, projects, and problem solving, were then used without real understanding of these purposes by teachers and pupils, and are now rarely used. For students busy preparing for entrance exams class discussions were considered a waste of time. The basic concept is to cram into the brain of the Japanese student as much information as possible. We can liken the Japanese concept of teaching as exactly equivalent to storing information in computers for later retrieval.

Pupil-centered teaching has given way to teacher- and textbook-centered teaching, and systematic learning has replaced experience learning. Individualized instruction, a part of the postwar reform, is impossible with classes of forty-five or more, so the teacher generally depends on the single approved textbook and occasionally uses a supplementary text. In the elementary schools teachers generally teach all subjects in a self-contained classroom. In junior and senior high, teaching is largely departmentalized, and the teachers specialize in one or two subjects.

Many of the newer junior and senior high schools, even in remote areas, have well-equipped language laboratories. Most language teachers know how to operate the console, but the ever-threatening bogey of the entrance examination inhibits their using them in teaching language. Students cramming for entrance to a desired junior or senior high school are interested mainly in mastering the grammar and vocabulary of English on which they will be examined rather than the use of the language that the language lab facilitates. As a consequence, Japanese students learn English by reading-translation rather than by oral-aural methods and have difficulty in carrying on a conversation even though they may know grammar well.

University instructional methods are almost entirely lecturing. Few courses require reference reading or term papers or projects. In some of the more commercialized private universities, part-time professors lecture to huge classes over a public address system, a technique called by students, "mass-production teaching." Even at Tokyo University some students complain that the teaching techniques are worn out and ineffective.

## Homework

In Japan even kindergartners must do some homework. And as they move up the academic ladder, they must do more and more. On the grounds that homework keeps the students' minds honed to perfection, they must not only take home tasks every night, but also during summer vacation students are expected to do one or two hours a day of homework. The responsibility for supervising homework falls on the mother. In 1973 the White Paper on Youth put out by the prime minister's office reported that the average junior high school student spent two hours and ten minutes on homework each night. At senior high, when the student is faced with forthcoming entrance examinations, he is expected to study until midnight or after. A popular saying, observed in practice by many students is "Four hours of sleep, pass; five hours of sleep, fail."

Not all students are happy to do homework. The author observed a junior high class in Hiroshima discussing the reasons for homework. They varied from "It is useful for our future" to "It is necessary for the future of Japan." Out of a class of forty, only five boys and one girl said they didn't like homework at all.

## Ability Grouping

Another controversial practice much discussed recently is ability grouping, but neither the majority of the teachers, the union, or the government agree that it is the right policy. When the Central Council for Education included it as one of the suggested reforms for the 1980s and beyond, the Japan Teachers' Union strongly opposed it on the grounds that it would destroy the egalitarian goals of schools. Already in a number of junior high schools a sort of ability grouping is being used in which the college-bound are streamed into a special elite track for such college-preparatory subjects as mathematics and foreign languages. A number of surveys, however, show that on the whole "both the superior and slower pupils make better progress when they are taught in a mixed class, and are only divided into ability groups for [the] few, more intellectual subjects. . . . Pupils will lose their enthusiasm for learning, and teaching will be rendered ineffective if inflexible ability groups are widely used, or if teaching methods suited to individual . . . pupils are not worked out" (Ministry of Education, 1971, pp. 164–165). A further objection, as noted by the Central Council for Education, is that ability grouping is tantamount to classifying students according to their parents' socioeconomic status, and this can have an adverse effect on pupils' adaptation to and outlook on society.

In spite of this, some teachers feel that homogeneous grouping makes teaching easier and may unofficially use grouping, but it is not likely to become a national pattern in Japan's self-consciously egalitarian school system.

## APPLICATIONS

### Curriculum, Academic

The prewar Japanese uniform national curriculum with standard textbooks published by the ministry, was abolished during the occupation and was replaced by a freer, more individualized curriculum at the elementary and junior high level. The course of studies was no longer required, merely suggested. The teacher was responsible to build his own teaching units to meet local needs. But teachers were not used to having such independence. Sometimes they did not understand clearly the content or the methods suggested, and yearned for more direction from above. Furthermore, with an average forty-five students in each class they did not have the time to prepare their own units and study plans. With pressure from both the teachers and the ministry for reverting to standardized curricula, the government was able in 1958 to force through the Diet a revision of the whole public school curricula that toughened it, increased the hours of academic disciplines, set minimum standards for achievement, and laid down time schedules for each subject in elementary and junior high schools. The standards of teaching mathematics and science were raised, on demand of the industrial and business circles that education be made to serve better industrial growth and efficiency. Modern teachers felt the means of raising standards short-sighted, since they meant that experimentation and observation, which had been introduced in postwar years, now gave way to formal teaching of bodies of information that would be tested on in the entrance examinations.

The most drastic change, and one fiercely challenged by the teachers and their union, was the introduction into the curriculum of morals education one hour a week at public school levels. The goal: to give the nation a common ethical base like that of the old rescript.

The new, mandated course of studies was published in the Diet *Gazette* (equivalent to the American *Congressional Record*). Government control over the curriculum was restored, and content shifted from universalism and democracy to particularism and nationalism. The educational policy now has the utilitarian goal of training human resources useful in an industrial society.

In the several revisions since the end of occupation, generally occurring every ten years or so, pressure is placed on students to master ever-increasing amounts of information, introduced earlier and earlier in the school calendar.

The deleterious results of this policy eventually became evident to the government, and the 1970's curriculum council studied the problem and recommended the following remedies to the overcrowded curriculum: (1) a simplification and reduction by some 25 to 30 percent of the amount of the elaborately detailed subject matter to be covered in all three school levels, so that more time could be given to basic skills and so that education could be "humanized"; (2) articulation of the three levels so that there would be a minimum of duplication; and (3) achievement of a more flexible curriculum with more optional courses, especially at the senior high level to meet the diverse needs of the student body. The council noted that "under the existing system, supreme importance is given to the conveyance of knowledge, while the development of the children's personality is neglected. It is necessary to achieve qualitative change in education so that children may acquire the faculties to think and judge for themselves." Courses of studies and texts to implement this plan are being prepared to be effective in the school year 1980 for elementary, 1981 for junior high, and 1982 for senior high.

Let us now turn to the specific content of the curriculum at each level.

*Elementary*

The pattern for the elementary school curriculum, specifying subjects covered and school hours prescribed, is laid out in the "Enforcement Regulations for the School Education Law." The objectives, standard contents, and methods of instruction are outlined in the national "Course of Studies for Elementary Schools" (Ministry of Education, Science and Culture, 1976, p. 1). It says, "Each elementary school is to organize a suitable curriculum in accordance with related regulations and the Course of Study with full considerations given to the actual conditions of the region and the school, to the pupils' state of development and distinctive characteristics."

In 1978 the standard number of class hours (each lasting forty-five minutes) per week varied from twenty-three for the first grade to thirty-one for the fifth and sixth grades, for a thirty-five-week school year. The weekly elementary curriculum consisted of the following subjects:

*Japanese language*—seven to eight class hours per week.
*Arithmetic*—from three hours for first graders to six hours for grades 4 to 6.
*Science*—two hours for grades. 1 and 2 to four hours for grades 5 to 6.
*Social studies*—two hours for grade 1 to four hours for grades 4 to 6.
*Music*—three hours for grade 1 to two hours for grades 2 to 6.
*Arts and crafts*—three hours for grade 1 to two hours for grades 2 to 6.
*Homemaking*—two hours, taught in grades 5 and 6 only.
*Physical education*—three hours a week for all grades.
*Morals education*—one hour a week for all grades (with religious education permitted as an alternative in private or religious schools).

In addition to these courses, there are required "special activities" which include club activities, assemblies, school ceremonies, and excursions for two to three hours per week after school, and homeroom periods daily and for about an hour on Saturday morning. The minimum number of school days per year was 240. Teachers are assigned to a single class of a particular grade and teach all subjects. A few teachers, however, are specialists in fine art, music, physical education, and homemaking.

The junior high curriculum consisted of the following:

*Japanese language*—five hours per week.
*Social studies*—four hours for grades 7 and 8; five hours for grade 9.
*Mathematics*—four hours per week at all grades.
*Science*—four hours per week at all grades.
*Music*—two hours per week for grades 7 to 8; one hour for grade 9.
*Fine arts*—two hours per week for grades 7 to 8; one hour for grade 9.
*Health and physical education*—three and a half hours per week, all grades.
*Industrial arts or homemaking*—three hours per week, all grades.
*Morals education*—one hour per week, all grades.
*Special activities*—one and one-half hours per week, all grades.
*Elective subjects*, including foreign language (most students take English in anticipation of the examinations), vocational subjects, agriculture, industry, commerce, fisheries and so on, and special local subjects—four hours per week, all grades.

Instruction in these courses is here departmentalized, most teaching being by subject-matter specialists in one or two subjects.

The senior high curriculum offers a great variety of subjects, both general (that is, college preparatory) and specialized (vocational and so on), together with "special activities." Subjects are *required* and *elective*; the required are a common basic curriculum taken by all to which may be added certain elective subjects. As with the first nine grades, there is a required one hour of special activities for homeroom, and so on. The basic required curriculum for all senior high students is as follows:

*Japanese language*—two courses, both modern and classic
*Social studies*—four courses, including ethics-civics (morals) and political
science-economics
*Mathematics*—one course, general mathematics or math I
*Science*—two courses, basic science or physics, chemistry, biology, earth
science
*Health and physical education*—two courses
*Fine arts*—one course from music, fine arts, handicrafts, and calligraphy
*Homemaking* for girls

At all three levels, the four subjects receiving major attention are Japanese, social studies, mathematics, and science. More time is devoted to the Japanese language than to any other subject because of the great difficulty students have in mastering the complicated Chinese character system. Social studies is considered next in importance because it is a vehicle for developing good citizens. Mathematics and science are popular for their presumed transfer value in inculcating mental discipline.

Accordingly, the aims of the new 1980s "reformed" curricula are (1) to enrich the humanity of students; (2) to enable them to lead freer, richer school lives; and (3) to emphasize education as basic to becoming a sound citizen, which will be appropriate to the student's personality and ability. To accomplish this, the number of class hours is to be reduced by 10 percent and the content by 25 to 30 percent.

The minimum of school days per year will still be 210, but most schools are open 240 to 250 days per year, in contrast to the average American school year of 180 days. During the nine years of compulsory education this amounts to an extra one and a half full years over American practice. This may explain in part the observation of many outsiders that Japanese youth are well ahead academically of the comparable age-groups in other countries.

### Special Education Programs

A major shortcoming of Japanese education, recognized by the Central Council for Education as well as by the general public, is the area of special education. Traditionally, handicapped children were cared for in the family and hidden from public view as being something to be ashamed of and as being an obstacle to their siblings' marriages. Most mentally and physically handicapped children were excluded from schooling. In recent years the problem of the handicapped has come to public attention, and there is now a drive to correct the situation. In 1973 the ministry of education, recognizing the right of every child to have an education, no matter how severe the handicap, decreed that the compulsory education laws shall cover the handicapped as well, and that all prefectures must provide special schools for them by 1979. Parents and guardians of handicapped are to be responsible for seeing to it that their children attend. Since 1947 prefectures were required under the School Education Law to establish schools for the blind and deaf, but the otherwise handicapped including the physically and mentally handicapped, the physically weak, the partially sighted, and the hearing-impaired were not served in public institutions. Especially in secondary and higher education, such discrimination has been common. The majority of national universities still turn down the handicapped. Private schools are more tolerant.

Today, the handicapped are mostly served by special schools, organized according to the type of handicap, and by special classes within ordinary elementary, junior high, and senior high schools. Special schools are for those with relatively severe handicaps, while special classes are for those who have relatively mild handicaps. Nearly every elementary and junior high school has special classes. In 1976 the author visited a special class in a new junior high in a remote mountain area of northern Japan. A teacher and his aide were handling three mentally retarded children (out of a student body of 267), teaching them to handset type. With considerable help the children were printing the program for the school's sports festival. Special classes are of necessity small, to permit individual attention for each child. While an ordinary class in elementary and junior high school has forty-five students, special classes legally can have only eight, and a class for the multiple-handicapped can have only five students.

The new national policy regarding the handicapped has four major objectives: (1) improved early identification and treatment; (2) diversification of educational programs, including a visiting teacher program for homebound and hospital-bound children; and (3) establishment of national centers for research and training—one to each prefecture; and (4) integration, wherever possible, of handicapped with ordinary children.

Provision for early identification is being made with government support (see Student Evaluation). Since 1973 the ministry has subsidized the visiting teacher program, and in 1974 all prefectures were required to make this program available, but visiting teachers, like special education teachers, are still in short supply.

At the national level a unique institution for the diagnosis, treatment, and education of handicapped children is the National Institute for Special Education at Yokosuka. Its goals are: (1) to carry out practical research into the curriculum and methods for each type of handicap; (2)

to conduct in-service training for teachers of special education; (3) to carry out experiments at the adjacent National Kurihama School for the Handicapped Children in handling the severely and multiple-handicapped; and (4) to advise and train parents on their role in educating and training their handicapped offspring. Parent training is done by a team of caseworkers, researchers, and others who work jointly with parents and patients. Provision is made for dormitory accommodation for parents-in-training for a period of ten days during which they observe the treatment and learn how to reinforce it at home.

The ultimate aim of the new policy is the integration of the handicapped with ordinary youth. Until recently, institutionalizing of the handicapped was the accepted procedure with little flexibility in programming the child. Now the tendency is to consider special education a part of regular education and wherever possible to integrate it with regular education. For the partially sighted, hearing-impaired, speech-disoriented, and the emotionally disturbed, integration is possible in most subjects, supplemented by special classes and "resource rooms" for special subjects, like braille and sign language.

To promote public understanding and acceptance of the handicapped, so difficult when the mother's identity depends on the child's performance in school, the ministry has for the past decade subsidized home education classes set up through local PTA's to study the problem. The ministry also compiles and broadcasts over radio and television excellent programs for the better understanding of the handicapped. NHK, the major educational broadcasting system, subsidized handsomely by required monthly fees from all owners of receivers, beams three twice-weekly broadcasts to the handicapped themselves: "TV School for Deaf," "Speech Correction Class," and "Special TV School." NHK also broadcasts radio and television programs for retarded—one entitled "Merry Classroom." A recent television drama portraying the lives of deaf-mutes aroused great public interest in learning the sign language of the deaf.

These moves show the government's multifaceted attack on the problem of educating the handicapped. Special schools are being built and new special classes set up so that by 1979 all handicapped can be accommodated. Thus the nation is awakening to a need and ensuring that at last the handicapped will enjoy equal educational opportunity with other children as guaranteed by the Fundamental Law of Education.

## Curriculum, Nonacademic

"Special activities" are a feature of the nonacademic curriculum at all levels of public education. This category was devised as a substitute for the "free study" introduced by the occupation but abandoned. The stated aim at the elementary school level is "to promote a harmonized development of mind and body through desirable group activities and, at the same time, to develop practical attitudes toward development of individuality and to [learn to] cooperate with others for better living" (Ministry of Education, Science and Culture, 1976, pp. 205–206).

In effect this is structured training in group activities, requiring all youth in the classes to have experience in planning and leading self-government activities, such as regular assemblies, homeroom meetings, and club activities (the latter from the fourth grade up). Theoretically the students have autonomy, but the teachers must see to it that nothing gets out of hand. They are required to be intimately involved, directing all special activities. Regular school events, part of special activities, consist of ceremonies, cultural events, athletic meetings, school excursions, and safety guidance activities. In each of these, the goals are to "deepen one's feeling of attachment to the group," and to learn discipline (Ibid., p. 208).

The school lunch program and health and safety guidance are considered a part of classroom guidance. One genuinely successful learning experience observed by the author is the school lunch program, from the first grade up. The children are instructed in good manners and in the process of eating together and serving each other, learn desirable habits and good human relations with their classmates. They also learn practical hygiene in food handling as the designated monitors wearing gauze face masks, kerchiefs, and white aprons carry the hot food from the kitchen to the classroom and help the teacher serve it to the children at their desks. The full meal of 700 calories cost the parents less than $10 a month. Poor children get free meals paid for by the local government. About 97 percent of the elementary schools, 86 percent of the junior highs, and 90 percent of the part-time evening students at the senior high schools receive some sort of school lunch. Only remote rural schools in areas of declining population have no school lunch program, but these constitute only 1.3 percent of the total school population.

Spring excursions are also an integral part of the nonacademic curriculum at all three levels. It is the climax of the graduation year; that is, the sixth grade of elementary school; the ninth grade of junior high; and the eleventh or twelfth grade of senior high (before the students have to start intensive cramming for the entrance exam). They go to historic or cultural sites or some spot famous for its natural beauty. Recently some affluent private schools have taken their classes of elementary students to Hawaii for several days of fun in the sun. The students look forward with keen anticipation to the excursion and save regularly toward the cost. Teachers accompany the class and generally plan the event, though about a third of the schools now consider it an appropriate learning experience to have it planned jointly by students and teachers. Millions of children and youth move across country in the annual trek, by bus for the most part, but also by boat, train, and plane.

Most of the trips are on a low budget, but even then some poor children cannot afford to go, and their trip must be subsidized by the local prefectural PTA or government. But generally all go, and it is a gay affair, remembered for a lifetime, and serves to cement class ties.

Some parents doubt the educational value of the experience and oppose it as too dangerous and exhausting. But the majority of citizens see it as a means of building national pride in the country's natural beauty and its history and antiquities. The custom is likely to continue and even to expand despite the increased danger of traffic accidents and exposure of the children to overexhaustion and epidemics.

### Athletics

The physical education program requiring three hours a week at all levels of schooling is highly structured and is a matter of pride. The Course of Study for Elementary Schools prescribes in detail the objectives and contents of each activity to be taught: gymnastics, apparatus, track and field events, swimming, ball games, folk dancing, and other activities. National standards are set, against which the instructor measures the students. Every child is expected to master the sport and do well in it. Health, hygiene, and safety are included in the program for fifth and sixth graders. Swimming is very popular at all levels and compulsory for older children. Teachers must also be able to swim and take their classes on long-distance swims during the summer swimming camp at the nearby seashore. Elementary schools pride themselves on their elaborate swimming pools, often built by the PTA's but with national government subsidy.

A Russian gymnastic instructor visited Japan and was deeply impressed with the complexity of the physical education program he saw. He reported that second graders in the elementary school (seven-year-olds) had to perform forward somersaults, swing hand over hand on a low horizontal bar, jump across a barrier 50 cm high, and perform long jumps and other activities. In a junior high, eighth graders (thirteen-year-olds) were expected to perform cartwheels, handstands, forward rolls from a running start, and jumps over barriers. Not everyone succeeded, but neither did anyone fail. The teacher came to the aid of the poorer performers, and other, more expert, students stood by the apparatus to protect their fellow students from injury. All students, boys and girls, performed with enthusiasm. Every child was involved; none stood idly by (Sabirov, 1974, pp. 108–114).

At the junior and senior highs heavy gymnastics, long-distance running and swimming, ball games such as soccer, rugby, baseball, basketball, volleyball, as well as the traditional martial arts of *sumo, judo,* and *kendo* are popular.

One noteworthy aspect of sports activities in secondary and higher schools is the dependence of the teams on their own training program. High schools and colleges do not normally have coaches for each sport, but students who are interested get together, set up their own training schedule, and do their workouts together. The author observed a track squad at Hiroshima University, made up of about twenty men and four women, working out together, with one of the senior members leading the warmup session, then with both men and women competing against each other. Their dedication to training was obvious; they worked out all afternoon and into the evening as a group.

### Student Evaluation

#### Ability Identification

The Japanese put great faith in the achievement test as a means of student evaluation. From elementary school to university subject-matter tests are utilized for ability grouping, formal and informal. Each university composes its own test as a means of screening out the less able. Further, the fees charged for taking the entrance examination amount to large sums of money, on which the university depends for a source of income. On the advice of the American occupation authorities, subject-matter achievement tests were played down and aptitude tests were introduced. A scientific evaluation program was devised by the Educational Testing Research Institute and established in national institutions. There was much opposition to it from all sides. The union saw it as a government plot to control higher education, the universities didn't want to lose the juicy fees and preferred their own tests, and students found it difficult to cram for a psychologically based aptitude test. Accordingly, in a short time it was abandoned. Not until the late 1970s was a government-subsidized uniform aptitude test devised and introduced side by side with the university's own achievement test. Instead of simplifying the selection procedure, however, it made it more complex. And there is no assurance that it will alleviate the "examination hell."

#### Grades (Scholastic)

In most elementary, junior high, and senior high schools report cards are graded, 5, 4, 3, 2, and 1 (failing), *or* A, B, C, D, E, and F (failing). Universities and junior colleges are free to use any grading system they choose. The most common is letter grades on a four-part scale, with three passing grades, A, B, and C, and one failing grade, F. The F grade is not generally used and hardly ever reported. This is in contrast to the common American university grading system of at least four passing grades, A, B, C, and D, which happens to be the same as the secondary school grading system in Japan.

During the 1960s there was a controversy over the grade distribution "on the curve," with officially fixed quotas for each grade. The vice-minister of education denied that there were such quotas or that the ministry had set certain percentage standards, but one Tokyo principal reported to the press that the quota system was still strongly active. Officially, each elementary school can adopt any method reporting grades that it likes or it can eliminate report cards entirely (*Asahi Evening News*, February 22, 1969). A Hyogo Prefecture elementary school substituted a descriptive narrative on its report cards instead of the number grades (*The Japan Times*, March 25, 1969).

### Identification of the Handicapped

The first of the major objectives of the new national policy on the handicapped, that is, early identification and treatment, is achieved by several institutions starting with the hospital where the child is born. Wherever they are properly staffed, hospitals will do a neurological screening of the newborn, within forty-eight hours of birth and again at the time of the mother's discharge. These examinations plus periodic checkups at the end of the fourth, seventh, tenth, and thirteenth months enable high-risk infants, those suffering from such diseases as cerebral palsy, malformation syndromes, brain damage, and cretinism, to be identified and treatment begun. Cretinism, for example, an important cause of mental retardation, can be prevented by early detection and treatment.

Private as well as prefectural health agencies provide mother and child consultations during infancy, and there is a required examination of three-year-olds. Such examinations are mandated by the Child Health Law of 1965 and are carried out at local health centers. If any handicap is found, early treatment and welfare measures are provided under the law.

On entering school at age six, all children are given a health examination by the local board of education, and this agency must take whatever steps are indicated by the examination if they have not already been taken. If a handicap is discovered, the board must recommend medical treatment, provide health advice, or give the parents or guardians of the child proper guidance regarding exemption from or postponement of school attendance, depending on the nature of the handicap. If necessary, the child must be enrolled in a special school or special class.

Under provision of the Child Welfare Law, each prefecture and the larger municipalities are required to establish a child guidance center, which provides counseling service for all who need it. There are some

139 such centers which diagnose children's handicaps and place them in appropriate institutions. They handle about 300,000 cases annually. Any disabled person or parent or guardian of a disabled child may apply to the governor of his prefecture for a "Disabled Person's Handbook" along with a written diagnosis of his case by a physician designated by the governor. These guarantee medical care, vocational training, and other rehabilitation services on a continuing basis.

Despite the existing laws and centers there are still many handicapped youth who are not discovered early and who are not served in appropriate fashion. Fortunately, the problem is known and action started in this direction.

## Counseling

Guidance counseling as it is known in the West is in its infancy in Japan. It is generally considered an extracurricular assignment for a teacher over and above the regular teaching load. Except for a few progressive systems like that in the city of Yokohama, there are few trained school counselors. Most counseling is academic and vocational rather than personal. So youth who are emotionally upset have few sources of advice. In a poll of high school students it was found that about half kept their anxieties to themselves, while a minority of 7.7 percent turned to their parents, and a mere handful (2.7 percent) consulted with their teachers (Prime Minister's Youth Department, 1967, p. 136).

In a cross-cultural study of Japanese and American college students and their expectation from counseling, the Japanese were unfamiliar with it, since only 7 percent had had experience of counseling, as compared to 80 percent of the Americans. The Japanese students did not, therefore, seek out a counselor, but rather consulted a friend, while the first choice of the Americans was a counselor (Fukuhara, 1973, p. 179).

Personal counseling at secondary and higher education levels is largely a control mechanism to keep students from engaging in political activism. The homeroom teacher does most of the personal counseling, but if he meets a problem too hard to handle, he may send the student to the school counselor if there is one. The most common student problems: (1) deciding what university is most appropriate to try to enter; (2) experiencing boredom with school and desiring to drop out (only 1 to 2 percent do); and (3) disagreeing with parents over career selection (Neumeyer, 1968, p. 602).

The writer visited a lower-class commercial high school in a large city and inquired about the counseling system. He learned that it consisted of the homeroom teachers plus two full-time male teachers appointed by the principal to handle problems of a student body of 1,350 students, 80 percent of whom were girls. (The school had formerly been a girls' high school). When asked if there were problems of boy-girl relations, the counselors denied this, saying that problems of sex were handled in the home, secretly. They did admit to problems of delinquency, lack of motivation, and low morale in the student body because of the school's lack of academic prestige. In a prior year, out of 470 graduates, 20 girls and 110 boys went on to junior college. None went to the national universities, though about ten boys went to private colleges. This school was obviously at the bottom of the high school hierarchy.

This does not mean that counseling is nonexistent in the schools. Since Japan is group-oriented, many counseling problems are handled by the homeroom teacher with the whole class. The approach is traditional, such as the homeroom teacher giving general advice as how to pass the university examinations.

Another type of guidance is given by the morals teachers in their mandated weekly session. The Ministry Course of Studies of lower secondary school directs them

> through systematic and developmental guidance . . . to supplement, deepen and integrate the moral education given in the hours of other subjects and special activities . . . and by so doing the aim should be to have the pupils deepen their understanding about humanity, enhance the ability of moral judgment, and enrich their moral sense, thereby establishing self-control and exalting a positive desire for consistent moral attitudes (Ministry of Education, Science and Culture, 1976, p. 235).

### Discipline

With their built-in respect for learning and the teacher, Japanese students do not present the same severity of discipline problems common in the West. Japanese parents consider discipline of primary importance and try to enforce it at home. In a nationwide poll in 1973 the question was asked: "For a child of primary age schools do you think it is more important to stress the value of freedom or the value of discipline?" Sixty-eight percent favored discipline, while only 22 percent selected freedom (Sakamoto, 1977, p. 18).

From the beginning of schooling, students are exhorted to behave themselves—by the homeroom teacher, the morals teacher, and by frequent homilies by the principal. Traditionally, some of the discipline in the classroom is handled by student-elected class monitors who take personal responsibility for behavior problems of class members, such as breaking a window. Generally, students are well behaved, but recently, because of inordinate academic pressures, some slow learners have been emboldened to become unruly and not pay attention to the teacher.

Particularly, outcaste (*burakumin*—settlement people) youngsters from the traditional outcaste group of butchers, leatherworkers, and so on, who live in ghettos and are still denied the civil rights and freedoms of ordinary Japanese, have exhibited behavior problems reflecting the rising power of this minority group. *Burakumin* youth are not officially segregated in schools, though their residence patterns often result in some segregation. In the regular integrated schools, the children do badly. Lacking family cultural support, they score low on intelligence tests, make poor grades, and have a high rate of truancy and delinquency. Their pressure group, the Settlement Liberation League, insists that schools should expose and counter discrimination through courses called "assimilation education." The courses, like ethnic studies in the United States, are designed to enhance the self-respect of *burakumin* students and at the same time enlighten the non-*burakumin* youth. Histories of the *burakumin* community have recently been written for classroom use. And the national government has provided for each school in *buraku* areas a teacher specifically charged with organizing *buraku*-related activities. A special office in the school board oversees their activities. The budget for *burakumin* education is generous.

These positive activities have reduced discrimination. The once-taboo subject is now examined openly in most schools, especially at the secondary level. More and more *burakumin* youth are enabled through government scholarships to go on to high school, though few reach college. The league has been successful in instilling a new sense of pride in *burakumin* youth. They are less aggressive and less of a behavior problem in school, now that they have been recognized.

Physical punishment is no longer officially sanctioned in schools as it was so commonly in prewar Japan. Nor at home is there much punishment for naughty behavior; rarely is the child scolded or spanked, though occasionally the parents may punish the child with pinching or light hitting.

At school strict rules govern classroom behavior and off-campus activities as well. Students, teachers, and administrators enforce them. Students in a part-time Chiba senior high school were warned on the last day before summer vacation to stay out of trouble and refrain from frequenting coffeehouses, bars, and pachinko (pinball) parlors. If they did get into trouble, they were to hurry back to school and consult their homeroom teacher, who was always on call. Each student was asked to keep a diary of his activities and present it to his homeroom teacher after vacation. Both boys and girls were required to wear their school uniform at all times (for easier identification by the faculty if they were caught off limits). Though there is no uniform national dress code, students at all levels are required by their school to wear their student uniform—blue serge in winter and white duck in summer. Boys wear stiff-collared jackets with visored caps, both adorned with brass buttons bearing the school insignia. Girls wear middy blouses and skirts, and they may not wear makeup or have permanents. When the author queried a high school class in Hokkaido as to their reaction to the uniform requirement, the girls favored it because they said they felt more "disciplined" in it and could study better, since they did not have to waste time competing with other girls in wearing fine clothes. Some of the boys objected to the uniform on the grounds that it inhibited their freedom of movement especially when they wanted to hide their identity. None saw uniform clothing as promoting conformity.

In the past few years, with the rise of the radical student movement, a new phenomenon, violence on the high school and university grounds, in the assembly, and in the classrooms has appeared. At first it was limited to university students, members of the various factions of the *Zengakuren* (All-Japan Federation of Student Self-Government Associations), but in the late 1960s some of the better high schools in the cities were involved. Students struck against school administrations in protest against all sorts of real or imagined injustices. Sometimes they joined forces with the Japan Teachers' Union protesting government restrictions; at other times they protested rising tuition costs, police entering their campus, or even increases in carfare. Occasionally, there was real violence. In one case in 1968, twenty high school students, wielding the traditional bamboo swords and staves, injured nineteen teachers and smashed windows in the teachers' common room. Their complaint was that eight seniors had been kept from graduation on account of their poor grades (*Asahi Evening News*, March 29, 1968). In the mid-1970s the ministry announced that in one year there had been 600 separate cases of violence against teachers. This, however, is miniscule compared to the 5,200 attacks on teachers reported monthly in the United States (*Time*, January 23, 1978, p. 73).

As for violence and radicalism at the university level, Japan led the world in the 1960s—a part of the worldwide phenomenon of student unrest. In the late 1960s one third of Japan's universities, 117 in all, were under student siege and had to close their doors. Buildings were wrecked or burned. Rival factions of the *Zengakuren* fought pitched battles with each other and with the police. The traditional respect for the teacher was abandoned when distinguished presidents and deans were subjected to exhausting "bargaining sessions" and held personally responsible for all the ills of higher education. As many as half the university students were radicalized. They vented their wrath against the establishment, the university, the government, and society as a whole. They were largely responsible for the downfall of the Kishi government in 1960 and contributed to many political crises since then. Besides being a protest against the examination system and the irrelevance of present-day higher education, student activism in Japan, as in many industrialized democracies, probably represented an effort to find identity by opposing the world trend toward human alienation. In the 1970s, however, there was some effort by government to meet the complaints, and the violence waned, until today most campuses have returned to normal.

## ROLES

### Administration

The central educational authority in Japan is the Ministry of Education, Science and Culture, which is responsible for integrating all school education, adult education, and science. Its secretariat prepares budget estimates in these areas, transmits them to the Diet, and drafts all bills relating to education for Diet action. It also conducts frequent nationwide surveys on education, compiles statistics, publishes reports, and on the basis of these sets up curriculum standards. The rationale for this centralized dictation of curriculum is that it enables the government to guarantee equality of educational offerings in all parts of the country, and to maintain high standards.

The ministry is directly responsible for certain national institutions, including the eighty-one national universities, thirty-one junior colleges, fifty-four technical colleges, as well as for twelve youth houses (for the training of youth leaders), and museums (1975 figures). In addition, it supervises, advises, and allocates financial aid to local boards of education as a subsidy to local schools. The ministry has the right to inquire about and order changes in the activities of local educational authorities. Thus the ministry sits at the apex of control, in Tokyo.

At each of the 47 prefectures and in every one of the 3,257 municipalities (1975 figures), there is a board of education. The prefectural board is the highest local education authority. It consists of five members appointed by the governor with the consent of the prefectural assembly. They hold office for four years. They, in turn, appoint the prefectural superintendent of schools, though his appointment must be approved by the minister. At the local level school superintendents of cities, towns, and villages are appointed by the mayor, but must be approved by the prefectural board of education, which in turn is directly under ministry control. The minister thus has express authority to advise, guide, and supervise all local boards of education, and has veto power over their acts. The local boards are accountable up the line to the national ministry, making possible a highly centralized operation. Their function is primarily advisory. They seek support for adequate educational budgets for their communities and in general promote the cause of education. They negotiate with the teachers' union locals over salaries, working hours, and working conditions if the local units request it, but legally they cannot come to an independent collective bargaining agreement.

Prefectural boards also have the following roles:

1. To establish, maintain, and abolish schools under their jurisdiction; and to plan and carry out construction of new schools.
2. To make and revise curriculum according to the ministry's *Course of Studies*, and to administer the counseling and guidance program.
3. To select textbooks and administer distribution of free books to grades 1 through 9.
4. To appoint, transfer, and dismiss teachers and principals, to pay their salaries, and to arrange for their retirement.
5. To purchase instructional materials and to supervise and advise on their use in schools.
6. To conduct in-service training for teachers.
7. To make reports and surveys as directed by the ministry.
8. To supervise and administer entrance, transfer, and suspension of students.
9. To certify all the teachers in the prefecture.
10. To manage school lunch programs.

Since 1956 when the elected boards were abolished and replaced by appointed boards, the latter have lost their independence and much of their original function. Board membership is now generally held by the elite elders of the community, who usually approve the policies of the governor and his party.

Recentralization of ministry power has reduced the power of the local boards to make their own curriculum and to select and screen their own textbooks; so the original purpose of the board, which was to decentralize control to the grass roots, has been foiled. Nevertheless, the democratic principle that the board is accountable to the peoples' representatives still stands.

The central figure in the local educational hierarchy is the prefectural superintendent, since he guides the school board in its decisions and acts in the name of the whole board in administering the system. School superintendents are no longer required to meet certification requirements as they did during the occupation. The job now goes to laymen, retired principals, inspectors, and occasionally ministry bureaucrats sent down from Tokyo to get experience and to forge closer lines of communication between the central government and local entities.

The prefectural school superintendent's role includes:

1. Dealing with school personnel, principals, teachers, and clerks in regard to personnel matters, such as grievances, in-service training, and welfare.
2. Carrying on negotiations with agencies related to school administration such as local government, the teachers' union, and PTA's.
3. Planning the construction of school buildings.
4. Overseeing the internal operation of the school, such as curriculum making and guidance, most of which is delegated to the principals and teacher consultants.

The city and town superintendents are closer to the operating levels, and they must do most of these things themselves without the help of teacher consultants. In larger cities and towns, however, the superintendent has a staff of teacher consultants, just like the prefectural superintendent. Their job is to assist the superintendent in four areas: curriculum, teaching, in-service training, and textbooks.

Most of the prefectural superintendents also have secretariats to take some of the administrative load off their shoulders. They keep the flow of reports and statistics moving up channels, depending on the local teachers and principals to provide the raw data.

The principal, generally an experienced older educator, with an average age of fifty-five and about twenty-five years in the system, has the main duty to provide advice and guidance to the teachers. Since he has not been professionally trained for the job, his advice is of necessity subjective; he is most comfortable giving or transmitting orders. One complaint about principals in general is that their age and experience make them inflexible in handling teacher personnel problems. Their recognition of their own shortcomings is evidenced by the fact that out of 500 principals polled by the Ministry's National Institute for Educational Research (NIER) more than 75 percent stressed the need for professional training in school management, educational administration, and finance. To make up for this shortcoming, most prefectures have held special workshops in these areas for local principals.

In the mid-1970s a new type of administrator was added to the administrative staff of each level of schooling. He is a quasi-administrative official, called a *shunin* (chief teacher) who ranks just below the principal and vice principal. His role is to assume some of the principal's administrative responsibilities, serve as liaison between the principal and teachers, and advise and guide the teachers in his specialty. The stated purpose was to "bring discipline and order into school life" (*The Japan Times*, January 14, 1976).

The teachers' union bitterly opposed the *shunin* system as simply another device by the ministry to check on teachers' activities and weaken the union. Since the new position was to be staffed by experienced teachers, who would receive a special stipend for their services and who would side with the administration, the argument of the union that it would tend to destroy the cooperative relations among teachers and induce them to be sycophant seemed valid. By the spring of 1977 most of the prefectures had complied with the government's order despite union opposition.

## The Teacher-Consultant

Teacher-consultants were the democratic substitute for the old-style, much-feared school inspector who had great power over the teacher. The new officials are subject-matter specialists who supervise and guide teachers at all elementary and secondary levels. At the prefectural level they must be teachers with at least five years' teaching experience and hold a first-class teachers' certificate. Most of them have been promoted from the ranks, and some continue teaching part-time. Many have had specialized training in the numerous in-service courses sponsored by the ministry, and a few have studied in the United States. They may move up to principalships, or principals may interchange jobs with them. Usually, the teacher-consultant is a part of the guidance office of the secretariat of the school board.

As subject-matter specialists, they have to cover their subject at all school levels, traveling several days by train, bus, or boat to reach the more remote schools. Their role includes:

1. In-service training of teachers in their specialty.
2. School visits to help teachers work out courses based on the latest ministry course of study.
3. Demonstration of new teaching methods.
4. Providing feedback to the teachers at the end of the visit, with suggestions for improvement. (The report is not the basis for personnel changes.)
5. Editing a prefectural educational journal in their specialty.
6. Planning annual research conferences.

The TC's are master teachers and teacher-counselors, who, within the limits of their strength, do a superb job of supervision. Unfortunately, they are still in short supply, though the ministry promises to increase their numbers.

### Faculty

In Japan the teacher traditionally holds high status. Teaching was a sacred calling, and the teacher was accorded lifelong respect by his students. The union, however, looks on teachers as educational laborers, affiliated with other labor unions, and refuses to accept the concept of teaching as a sacred calling. Traditionalists, both officials and parents, are offended at this viewpoint and still look on teachers as someone set apart and superior to the rank and file.

Today there are several types of teachers—the self-sacrificing "sacred-calling" type; the aggressive "teachers'-union" type who demands fair treatment in wages, hours, and conditions of labor; and the "urban type," who sees herself as a salaried person just doing her job and no more. Most teachers are a combination of these—high-minded professionals concerned about their students but demanding a decent wage.

The government recognized the necessity for fair compensation in order to attract qualified teachers and twice in the 1970s raised salaries considerably. As compared with the salaries of American public school teachers, the Japanese teacher's salary is higher in terms of purchasing power. In 1973 the government white paper reported that, based on per capita national income as 100, the average annual teacher's salary was 266 in Japan and 223 in the United States (Japanese Institute of International Affairs, 1977, p. 45).

In occupational ranking, teachers stand at about the same position as in the United States: elementary teachers rank eleventh, immediately above section chief in a large company, while university professors rank third, after medical doctors and prefectural governors, who rank respectively first and second (Tsujimura, 1972, pp. 211 and 213).

Women now constitute more than half the teaching force in elementary schools, some 30 percent of all junior high teachers, and 17 percent of all senior high teachers.

As for in-service programs, teachers have the opportunity to attend numerous workshops in subject matter set up by the ministry or the union or, occasionally, by both. Science teachers have especially fine opportunities for in-service training in the well-equipped science education centers set up in each of the forty-seven prefectures. These provide continuous and systematic in-service to both public and private school teachers at all levels, tuition-free. Their purpose is to upgrade science teaching nationally, even extending to the remote parts of the country. Bentley Glass, an American biologist, feels they might well become a model for science education elsewhere (Glass, 1968, p. 47).

The standard workweek for teachers is forty-four hours, and they must remain at school a minimum of eight hours a day. Most stay longer, supervising club activities, sports, student government, classroom cleaning, and school lunch programs. The community also constantly calls on them for out-of-school services, such as running youth clubs. So the teacher has little leisure.

But there are compensations. Teachers receive fairly generous leave benefits, officially authorized annual leave of about a month and sick leave of up to ninety days on full pay. Paid maternity leave of up to twelve weeks is granted by national law. Retirement benefits amount to a minimum of 40 percent of the average salary for the last three years of service if the teacher has served twenty years, plus additional allowances for service beyond twenty years.

*Teacher Evaluation*

In former times, the school inspector, the principal, or the superintendent evaluated the teaching staff. The United States occupation eliminated the school inspector and substituted the teacher-consultant, who is specifically enjoined from evaluating teachers he is working with. His is a service function only.

In 1958 the ministry embarked on a nationwide, compulsory Teachers' Efficiency Rating Plan whereby all principals were required to rate their teachers each year on a detailed scale devised by the ministry. The union charged that the ministry's motive was simply to weed out union members on the teaching staff and strike a blow at the union movement in schools. Accordingly, it threw all its available resources into blocking the government's move. Strikes, walkouts, demonstrations, and even hunger strikes erupted in all but five of the forty-seven prefectures.

The rating scale called for uncommon wisdom and understanding on the part of the principal to assess accurately the teachers' personalities, attitudes, habits, and abilities. Section I called for the principal to judge, among other things, the teachers' zeal in classroom management, ability in psychological and moral guidance, and skill in research and training. Section II called for rating them on love of education and children, sincerity, sense of responsibility, modesty, and dignity. The union and most practicing teachers held that accurate ratings in such areas were impossible and that in fact the whole scheme was designed merely to divide the teachers and weaken the union. Nevertheless, the ministry proceeded to push enforcement of these ratings. As a result the union was weakened financially and lost 25,000 out of about 500,000 members. The struggle over these efficiency ratings lasted a full decade; then the union dropped its protest, finding that it was no longer a threat. School boards, responsible for implementation, had not dared to use the ratings in salary and personnel determinations, for fear of stirring up violence. In many prefectures the completed rating sheets were stored away in safes and never consulted, so after all the fury, neither side clearly won.

After this painful experience the government never again publicly raised the issue of teacher evaluation.

## Students

Students, like teachers, have high social status as a result of the Confucian tradition. They look forward to entering school, and they can be punished by threats of keeping them out of school. Students proudly wear their distinctive school uniforms, with brass buttons bearing the cherished school insignia. Early elementary years are a happy time, highly stimulating to the students. Class friendships are important and often permanent.

Toward the end of the elementary years students begin to experience the "examination hell." In the fourth to sixth grade they begin cramming for the junior high entrance examinations, attending special cram schools after school or having tutors at home if their parents can afford it. They generally forego the pleasures of childhood and are subjected in regular school to an unrelenting regime of rote learning, constant practice tests, and in the afternoons cram schools of more of the same. The freedom and friendship of youth are now sacrificed to competition for grades. The exam hell now produces mutual suspicion and distrust among classmates and militates against the development of firm friendships at an important period of their personal development.

Once in junior high, the target is the entrance examination to the preferred senior high schools, and the exam pressure in senior high is still heavier. At a time when the adolescents should focus on attaining self-awareness and developing successful interpersonal relationships, they are forced to commit thousands of facts to memory and learn the technique of passing examinations. There seems to be little real learning. The ministry's National Institute of Educational Research concludes that this so-called education results in a deficiency of creativity and conceptualization (Nagai, 1977, p. 308).

The family puts heavy pressure on the child, for if he fails academically, all his family are disgraced, especially his mother. This explains why nervous breakdowns and stomach ulcers are found even among teenagers, as reported by Namiki to an international medical conference. He said that this was "dramatic evidence of the unnatural life-style our children are forced into under the pressure of our examination system" (*Honolulu Advertiser*, February 5, 1978). And it helps explain why Japan has the world's highest suicide rate in the fifteen-to-twenty-four age-group.

The violence of the student activists of the 1960s has been explained in part as a backlash against society and the university as a result of the entrance exams. Once the student passes, he loses his single-minded goal of so many years and begins to doubt the purpose of his life. His university fails to come up to his expectation, either in stimulating him intellectually or in showing concern for his individual problems. The result is student alienation, depression, and a groping for something meaningful. Disillusioned, he may easily become radicalized, throw himself into the student movement, and get involved with violence. Japanese university students were recently compared in terms of personality with a group of American students by means of the Edwards Personnel Preference Schedule. The Japanese scored higher in abasement, change, and a capacity for hard work and endurance, and lower in achievement, deference, and dominance. They are less ego-involved with community affairs than Americans and less interested in assuming community leadership and helping others (Berrien, 1971, p. 75).

**Parents**

Feelings of success or failure in school exams are shared by parents and children. Outside the student himself, the most involved person is the mother. She guides his studies and prods him to learn (or does his homework for him). Her status in the community depends on her child's performance. Because of this reflected status, she is often reluctant to enter a retarded child in special classes.

In their relations with the school, parents do not feel it is their prerogative to intrude in school affairs, even though they may be unhappy with the situation. With some pressure from school and community, they will join the PTA and attend meetings regularly. The PTA dues are like an additional school tax, depended on to raise funds for extras, like gymnasiums, swimming pools, band instruments, television sets, and even subsidizing teachers to go to conferences and workshops. The union constantly reminds the government that forced contributions are unconstitutional—a denial of the guarantee of free education during the compulsory years. Some PTA meetings are educational, when they invite a specialist to talk on such subjects as delinquency or child growth and development. Sometimes they serve as political pressure groups. With about 53,000 local units and some 20 million members, the PTA can be an effective force. Though generally sympathetic to teachers, they have frequently opposed the union and can exert conservative influence on teachers. By and large the PTA serves as a liaison with the school, serves to bring the parents into the classroom, and educates the parents on new approaches to teaching. It is thus active in adult education.

Parents have long expressed the great desire for their children to go to the university. In a poll taken of sixth grade mothers in an urban area, 94 percent expected their sons to attend university, and 75 percent expected their daughters to go (Nihon Keizai Shimbun, October 14, 1974).

## Parents' Attitudes

In the poll on changing national values, parents, as well as the general citizenry, were shown to subscribe to change. They were asked, "In bringing up children of primary school age, do you think you should tell them always to be careful never to lose face (a strong traditional value) or do you think you should train them not to be bothered by questions of face or prestige?" Surprisingly, the majority (70 percent) would tell them not to be bothered, a decidedly modern attitude (Hayashi, 1977, p. 44).

Again, when asked, "In bringing up children of primary school age, which do you think is best to teach them: that money is the most important thing in life, or that money is important but there are other more important things in life?" The heavy majority, 87 percent, opted for the latter, while only 9 percent took the materialist position (Ibid., pp. 43–44).

Illustrating the nature of parent-child relations, the question was raised: "If your child has left school and got a job, and is just about to leave home, which do you think is better (to say to him): (a) 'If things go wrong with you in some way, you should always come and consult us first'; or (b) 'From now on, even if things go wrong you shouldn't depend on your parents '?" Here the larger number, 58 percent, voted for the traditional value of amae (dependency, or the right of the child to expect and to depend upon its parents' or its mother's benevolence), while the smaller percentage, 37 percent, opted for nondependency on parents, a modern value.

Lastly, when asked "Do you think filial piety is important [the greatest of all traditional values], the vast majority came out in favor: 'yes, extremely important'—76 percent, 'quite important'—22 percent, for a total favorable opinion of 98 percent, while only 1 percent thought it not very important" (Ibid., pp. 43–47).

In short, the polls show that most of the old restraints on the free enjoyment of family and community life have been reduced in contemporary times. Within the social system people have escaped from the traditional family and gradually moved toward the nuclear family, familiar to the West. They have moved away from excessive concern for money toward more concern for human values, of life, health, and love; from obsessive pursuit of success to greater social concern and warmer family relations. They have modified their value system from one centered on the state, as in prewar times, to one where human life is of more importance (Sakamoto, 1977, pp. 24–25).

*Child Rearing*

Ezra Vogel studied child rearing in a middle-class suburb of Tokyo between 1958 and 1960 (Vogel, 1967, chap. 12. The substance of this section is from this chapter). He found that the typical mother-son relationship was very close, both physically and psychologically, and was marked by mutual dependency (*amae*). The mother sees her child as an extension of herself. Small children sleep with the mother until a second child arrives, when the mother must sleep with the new baby, and the eldest must sleep with the father or grandparent.

Breast-feeding continues for more than a year and may continue until a child enters school. Bathing is another opportunity for close physical contact between mother and child, and it also continues until the child goes to school. Until the child is one or two the mother carries him strapped to her back. Constant physical contact is seen to be a natural expression of affection, important in the proper rearing of the child.

The mother may even encourage her son's fear of the outside world, and shows the child that she will protect him from ghosts, strangers, and unknown dangers. Her attitude causes the child to fear being left alone or making its own decisions. The dual threat of provoking anxiety about the outside world and withdrawing affection keeps the child dependent on the mother from earliest infancy. Whereas an American child will sometimes be left to cry, the Japanese child learns that whatever tensions he exhibits by crying will be relieved by the nearby mother who offers prompt comfort. As a result, when they grow up, few children run away from home. Instead, a child can be punished by locking him out of the house.

In spite of this permissive atmosphere, children learn to be polite in public and are slow to adjust to outsiders, including new school friends and teachers. As they grow up, they tend to transfer their dependency on their family to dependency on school or work groups. As they get older, children grow more independent, but unlike American children, the push toward growing independence seems to come from the mother rather than from the children themselves. In Japan feelings of dependence are accepted as natural, not ridiculed as being childish.

Older children are socialized by giving them responsibility for looking after a younger child. A common sight is to see a four- to five-year-old girl playing children's games with a tiny infant strapped to her back. When older male children reach adolescence, the mother may consult with them about plans for the younger children. The eldest son is expected to take major responsibility for the family, especially since the father spends little time at home.

The youngest child is most pampered, by mother and siblings. Until he is three or four he gets almost anything he wants. When he goes to school he is expected to adjust to others, and then he begins to act more grown-up. The stepchild or the adopted child is generally neglected. In about half the cases of divorce fathers get custody of the children. Until the father remarries, his children must be cared for by his mother or sister. The stepchild is often deprived of the intensive mother-child relationship and suffers thereby as he compares himself with his age-mates.

The father's role in child rearing is nominal. He may play with the children or take them on an excursion on the weekend, but he does not share the responsibility of caring for and training them. He leaves the problem of discipline up to his wife. He rarely chastises or gives orders to the children. He may be fond of them and secretly ply them with gifts, like the divorced father in the United States who overdoes generosity on his visitation days with his children.

But he has potential authority, and though he may never punish them, they often fear him and obey his wishes. This is especially true if the mother, as is often the case, fears or respects the father's authority and transmits this feeling to her children. He does represent and enforce outside and community standards to the children; the children cannot help but see him as an outsider, aloof and frightening. So it is difficult for the father to win the child's friendship, no matter how kind and generous he may be. Even if he is home only a few hours a week, he can still, if he has the support of the mother, act as a role model for his sons. But the intense mother-son relationship is generally sufficient to produce the father's rivalry with the son.

Early childhood is a period of permissiveness by the parents. The child is permitted to run, climb, yell, stay up late, disobey his parents, and strike his mother almost without hindrance. Yet somehow the child learns how to obey, be well behaved in most public situations, be polite to teachers, and considerate of others.

It is true that the mother grows stricter as her son grows older and must represent the family to the outside world. Now the child has a duty to repay the obligation to parents by learning and achieving in an increasingly competitive world.

The mother's success in training without harsh discipline is a result of her teaching the child only when he is in a cooperative mood. She builds upon the close relationship she has with the child to get it to go along automatically with her suggestions. She does not force him to do anything against his will. However, by meeting the child's needs and agreeing with what it says, she in effect limits the child's opportunity to develop a will of its own. By anticipating problems and offering a limited number of ready-made solutions, she encourages the child to accede to her suggestions and in effect to obey her will. She seldom says "no" to his requests, only "later."

She rarely plans how to teach him how to be neat or how to avoid danger, even though the child learns to do these things as early or earlier than the middle-class American child. She neither argues nor reasons with him or explains why. If he gets near a fire, she simply says, "It's dangerous," and jerks him away from it. He soon absorbs her fear of the fire and avoids it. Vogel (1967, p. 247) says, "To offer extended explanations is contrary to the spirit of child-rearing practice. It is inconsistent with the feeling that the child should respond immediately and without question, and that rational explanations are less important than preserving the basic relationship." Later, in school, explanations will be necessary to make him understand the more complex problems he must face.

When the child is three or four, he is taught to inhibit his aggressions. If he hits another child his mother says merely "That won't do," but she never punishes him. Nor does she countenance fighting back even in self-defense.

Certain aspects of child rearing are not automatic, but are the result of conscious teaching. The mother shows the child how to do something, and the child is expected to repeat and practice it until he masters it. With a successful relationship behind them, the mother can expect the child to cooperate with long hours of training. Even before the child goes to school he learns to sit quietly and master tasks of memorization, such as poems, songs, and the Japanese syllabary. Then once he goes to school he is expected to fit into the school regime with the same diligence. But most mothers feel that they cannot teach the child if he is not in the mood to cooperate. If she finds this is the case and there is still homework to be done, she may turn the job over to the father, a sibling, or an outside tutor.

Few sanctions are necessary to get a child to behave—only a vague approval or disapproval. The mother tries always to use positive sanctions, such as praise, and always to stay on the child's side.

The widespread use of fear of ridicule is common to Japanese culture. The mother tells the child he must behave or people will laugh at him. In spite of such a warning, he does not see the mother as an authority-enforcing disciplinarian but as an ally in avoiding the negative sanctions of an outside authority. Even when she invokes outside sanctions, such as father, she carefully avoids putting herself in the role of an authoritarian.

If the child remains uncooperative despite the mother's concern for his doing the right thing, she may make vague threats of abandoning him or throwing him away until he learns to show the proper attitude. The usual response of the child is to try to get back into the mother's good graces. If the relationship leading to automatic compliance is broken, the mother often gets frantic. She has failed. The only way to get the child to obey is to start out all over again in building up the warm, loving relationship.

## SYSTEM IN ACTION

To see how the school system works, let us follow Kenji, son of a typical middle-class family living in the suburbs, through his educational career. During early childhood Kenji established firm ties with his first teacher, his mother, and began the learning process at her feet. He learned automatic compliance with her efforts to get him to master the basic skills, such as reading the phonetic syllabary and a few Chinese characters. With these he can already read simple stories for preschoolers. His parents and siblings enjoy reading, and there are books, magazines, and television available at home. Much of their conversation is about schooling, the family exhibiting a strong faith in the value of education. Thus the family environment is conducive to learning.

Kenji looks forward to going to school, and when the great day comes he proudly dons the new blue school uniform and the knapsack for carrying his books. His mother accompanies him to school the first day. He meets his teacher, Miss Hayashi, and his new classmates, and slowly begins to make new friends among them. Following the policy of enforced integration, he is assigned to a seat next to a girl, with whom he shares a double desk, but he is not especially interested in making her acquaintance.

His first class is homeroom, and the teacher, Miss Hayashi, doubles as informal counselor. Homeroom activities are a part of the required "special activities" designed to give Kenji and his classmates experience in leadership.

After homeroom period, the regular classes take over until noon, with one recess during the morning. The most effectively taught subjects are language, music, arithmetic, and morals. The required morals course is held just one hour a week, and is enriched by school broadcasts over the national ETV network.

At noon the small group responsible for the week collects the school lunch from the kitchen and delivers the trays of hot food to each child at his desk. Miss Hayashi eats with the class. It is a happy time and sometimes noisy, but the children are well behaved; they remain seated and dutifully eat all their lunch. Nothing is wasted. Then the class clears off the desks and the room is ready for the afternoon classes. After the studies are over for the day, the children sweep and mop the room and hallways, since there are no janitors in the school. Every Wednesday after lunch the class is required to help clean the school grounds, weeding and collecting trash.

In the afternoon language class the students read aloud, in chorus or one at a time. When Miss Hayashi calls for volunteers to read, Kenji and his classmates vie with each other for the privilege, waving their hands vociferously and shouting "hai." The emphasis is on speed of response, rather than quality of content. In reciting, each child must stand at his desk and hold the reader at arm's length, a traditional custom.

Kenji's mother is expected to visit his classroom on certain days of the month, to observe his behavior and performance and to get the schedule of assignments for the week so that she may drill him at home on the subjects he is currently studying.

At the beginning of the school year Miss Hayashi hands out the free textbooks supplied by the government and the workbooks of several kinds for the harder subjects such as mathematics. The subject matter of the workbooks is not necessarily covered in class; nevertheless, it is taken for granted that Kenji will study and master it at home and be ready to take a test on the workbooks at the end of the semester. Each day Kenji must submit a notebook to the teacher, indicating what he has studied at home. His mother has to check it each night for accuracy, as a means of adding her pressure on Kenji to get him to do his homework.

When he reaches the third grade Kenji's class is divided into groups of four to six children, and each group in turn takes responsibility for organizing and directing, under the teacher, Mr. Yoshida's, close supervision, the week's self-government activities. The group must also take charge of the homeroom class before and after school to evaluate the day's performance of the class. Sometimes Mr. Yoshida turns over the meeting to the group and leaves the room, though he is briefed on what happened on his return.

Kenji's favorite subject is science, and for this the school is well equipped. Even the third graders have access to the school's special science room, where they may perform simple experiments. For example, Kenji's class observe, measure, and chart the growth of plants during several months, observe and record the shape of the moon every day at 6:00 P.M. for a month, study the mechanics of mirrors and light, of magnets, and of air and water pressure using water guns that they make themselves. In social studies Kenji's class go on a field trip to study their city, its shops and houses, its services (for example, garbage disposal), its sources of footstuffs and their costs, and its geographical features.

In the fourth grade the students study their prefecture in even greater detail than they did the city the previous year.

When Kenji reaches the sixth grade, the last year of elementary school, he has to start preparing for the entrance examination to the Sakura

Junior High School, the famous old private school his father attended. Since Kenji's family wants to insure his success in entering the preferred school, for which there is keen competition, they enroll him in a cram school (*juku*), which he attends every afternoon for two hours and every Saturday afternoon. He studies Japanese and calligraphy, which are his hardest subjects, and since he has had trouble learning to swim, he takes lessons in swimming. Kenji is not happy at first about having to go to cram school, but his mother insists, and Kenji wants to please her. Later, when he discovers that almost all his playmates attend, he decides that just for the sake of companionship and so as not to fall behind them in his studies, he will attend on his own initiative.

The big day for the examination arrives, and Kenji goes with his mother to the school to be examined. The classroom is filled with nervous youngsters and the hallways with even more nervous mothers. Within a week the results are posted, and to his great regret he cannot find his number among the successful entrants. He has failed, but he still has another chance. The public junior high does not require an entrance examination, since it is part of the compulsory system; so, swallowing his pride, Kenji applies for and is accepted in the First Junior High.

The next day his mother buys him a new uniform with the school insignia embossed on the brass buttons. The first day of school begins with a formal ceremonial assembly, with moralistic speeches by the principal and the head of the PTA. The principal lauds the kindness and zeal of the members of his teaching staff. Then a star student, representing the incoming classes, replies in stilted fashion. After that the classes stand, one by one, and each is introduced to its new homeroom teacher, with both teacher and students bowing low. Kenji's homeroom teacher is Mr. Tanaka, fresh from the university and eager to please. Kenji is gratified that almost all his junior high teachers are men.

While Kenji remembers his elementary school days as free and easygoing, he finds junior high life stricter and with more responsibility on his shoulders. For him it is a time of "cultural compression," when the demands on him by his parents and teachers to observe cultural norms are intensified and the range of tolerated behavior becomes narrower (Singleton, 1967, p. 32). Life now becomes deadly serious for Kenji. He must hold high his family's reputation and begin to think of entrance into senior high. Each year during the three years of junior high the pressure for intensive study mounts. During the second year the college-bound begin to take a series of practice tests to get them ready for the ordeal ahead. On the basis of these tests, in the third year, Kenji and some of his old friends are streamed into an academic track, while the rest of his classmates, some less bright or less motivated, or from poorer families, are assigned to a vocational track and are encouraged to go to work after graduation. The academically inclined are the favored ones, and this is naturally resented by the vocational students. An unfortunate incident occurs during his last year in junior high. While Kenji's class is cramming for the examination after regular school hours, the vocational track boys are required to plant trees and prepare the school grounds for the graduation ceremony. The latter are so full of resentment that they waylay the young scholars on their way home and beat them soundly.

Kenji also discovers that the old camaraderie among his schoolmates no longer exists. In the special advanced courses in English and mathematics for the college-bound an intense competition develops among once old friends. They voluntarily take review classes for an hour and a half after school. And just to be on the safe side, Kenji asks permission of his parents to enroll in a cram school which is famous for getting its graduates into the preferred senior high schools. And even for the cram school there is an entrance examination and a waiting list of applicants.

Mr. Tanaka takes a personal interest in Kenji's career—as well as that of his numerous other counselees. He visits them all and discusses with their families how best to prepare for the forthcoming examination. An accurate choice of school is crucial, for this decision may determine a youth's entire career. Fortunately, Kenji's practice test results during the past year are favorable, so all agree that he should try for the elite academic high school, First High.

Kenji's favorite subject is mathematics. When he was a seventh grader (first year of junior high), he participated with other seventh grade classes in the UNESCO study, the *International Study of Achievement in Mathematics: a Comparison of Twelve Countries* (Husen, 1967). Kenji's class was very proud to learn that Japan's seventh graders, including his own class, scored highest of seventh graders of all the countries studied.

Finally, the high school entrance examination is at hand. As in every substantial community in Japan, Kenji's city has several high schools, ranked by seniority and tradition. The oldest, the First High School, occupies the buildings of the prewar middle school and retains some of its tradition and flavor. The other schools range below First High in the hierarchy, down to sixth or seventh—the poorer schools and vocational schools which lack prestige. Students who feel they cannot qualify for the First may grudgingly settle for one of the lesser schools. All ninth graders who want to go on must apply at one of the high schools and must take the same qualifying exam prepared by the prefectural board of education. The exam is given on the same day, and just once. Those who fail must either go to a four-year night school attached to the First High, and which is low-level, or settle for a private high school, which is easier but expensive, or take a year off and cram by themselves or in a cram school until the exam date comes around the next year and affords another chance.

Fortunately as Kenji faces the high school examination, he is well prepared. He is especially good at mathematics and English, two of the subjects stressed in the exam, and he has taken special tutoring in Japanese, in which he was weak. To everyone's relief, Kenji succeeds in the exam for the school of his choice, the First High School.

Now he embarks on three years of vigorous academic training. Most of his classmates are college-bound, but a few are unable economically to go on to higher education, and they are grouped in a separate vocational class and given one of the vocational programs available in the nominally comprehensive high school.

Though he has little time to reflect on what is happening to him in high school, Kenji is vaguely dissatisfied at the constant grind of his daily life. He says that he seems to be constantly judged solely on the basis of examination results and never on his human qualities. He complains to his family that learning places too much emphasis on mere memorization of facts and gives him little time to explore his main interests, such as science. Nevertheless, during the first two years of high school, Kenji finds time to join the science club and English-Speaking Society, volunteer club activities of his school. He does not, however, get involved in the radical activism of some of his classmates who join the Student Self-Government movement (*Zengakuren*) at the nearby university.

During his third year in high school he feels himself forced back into the groove of examination preparation, so he has to drop out of his club activities and concentrate on his studies. Since childhood his dream has been to enter Tokyo University (Todai), the alma mater of his father. But he realizes that this examination is the most difficult of all that he has faced, and that the competition is heavy, with as many as four out of five failing. But he reminds himself that the prestige of being a Tokyo University student will guarantee his future career in a great company. And further, since the tuition is low, he will be less of a burden on his parents, a factor that is important now that his younger brothers and sisters are moving up the academic ladder.

On exam day he almost faints when he sees the questions, many of which are in his weakest subjects, language and literature; for example, "Who were the Seven Sages of the Bamboo Grove? What were the stipends and dispositions of the feudal lords in the Edo Period?" In the field of world history one question is: "When was the Boston Tea Party, and why did it happen?"

Kenji does his best, but he comes away feeling that it is not good enough. When the results are posted, he learns that he has failed. He is heartbroken, especially after he has put six years of constant effort into preparation for it. And the shame that he brings on his family is the hardest to bear. He determines to fight on, however, and try again the next year. He plunges into the life of a *ronin* ("wave-man," or masterless warrior—the name given the thousands of failed students). For a full year with enormous self-discipline he forces himself to sit at his tiny desk until 2 A.M. or later and read on the subjects he is weak in. He memorizes answers to old tests, and toward the end of the year he enrolls again in one of the famous preparatory schools in Tokyo that has a good record of getting its graduates over the exam hurdle. He sits for the Tokyo University exam a second time and this time is successful. The life of a Tokyo University student is his.

Now he can take a respite, for the day-to-day requirements of the courses are nominal. There is little required reading and no reports. He knows that he will not fail and that he is certain to graduate. He begins to suffer from the so-called "May crisis" (May is the month after the new school year begins), a time of alienation and depression. He resents the meaningless asceticism that he has had to undergo in his secondary years. He feels that his high expectations of university life, as a time of intellectual stimulation and concern for him as a person, have not been met. Like many young men of his time, Kenji has sampled the radical movements, but they do not satisfy his yearning for answers. He drifts through his college days, but toward the end there is one more examination to be passed. In his senior year, he takes the qualifying examination of a great corporation, and largely because of his Tokyo University label, he is accepted. He now becomes a salaried man and can marry and start a family.

Kenji's experience would not be duplicated by his sister. Pressure to pass examinations is not as heavy on girls as on boys, though preferred girls' high schools and junior colleges which are most often sought out by girls also require entrance examinations. But the examinations are not as hard, and there is less riding on success in them than there is in the case of boys. Consequently, girls don't worry as much as boys. Most girls' career goals include marriage, and there is still a bias against girls being overeducated for it. In fact, a girl graduate of a good university sometimes has trouble finding a husband. A family is still proud of its daughter's academic achievement, and graduation from a first-rate girls' high school is necessary for her to make a good marriage.

Unless, however, a girl is determined on a professional career, such as teacher, pharmacist, or doctor, which requires her attending a top university, she will not subject herself to the examination hell the boys must face. Accordingly, there is still inequality of educational opportunity for girls, and Japan is still wasting the brains of many of its bright young women.

## PROSPECT

The best indications of future prospects for Japanese education are to be found in the projected plans that the government has already put forward. Not all such plans will materialize, since there is much controversy between the ministry and the Japan Teachers' Union over their implementation, but if we examine the stated goals and compare them with the directions of recent reforms, we can be fairly assured that some plans will in future become reality.

In 1971, the ministry announced a broad-scale plan for reform of the entire system, calling it "The Third Major Reform," projected for the 1980s and beyond. The plan called for the improvement in both quality and quantity of education. With the nation's strong commitment to education as a major value in life, we can be sure that there will, in future, be support for a vast expansion of educational opportunities. There were two major priority items in the "third" reform plan: preschool education and special education. A new school ladder was proposed to function side by side with the present 6-3-3 ladder. It would be a 4-4-6 ladder in which children enter two years earlier than at present; that is, at age four, then move on to a four-year elementary stage, then to a six-year secondary stage. Because the present 6-3-3 ladder with starting age of six is firmly entrenched with its own pressure group (mostly the union, the liberals, and left), it is likely to survive. However, the new type of infant school, providing four years of continuous education from ages four to seven, does conform to the public's demand for earlier and more free public education, so this is likely to be a part of the future public school system, with the present private kindergartens converted to public status or, if not, at least subsidized by municipal funds.

Since most adolescents—more than 90 percent—are now continuing their education through senior high school, there is great likelihood that it too will become a part of the free public school system. The union in particular and the Central Educational Course of Studies Committee have strongly argued that high school education is a right of all young people. There will be little opposition to this from parents, so facilities will have to be expanded and all high school age youth accommodated in public high schools. As a model for the new high schools the union recommends the comprehensive community high, and it may become the model, though tradition is against it. Traditionalists still argue for a diversification of high schools, separating vocational from academic.

The logical next step, in the 1980s and beyond, will be to push free public education up through the junior college years, that is, if the economy permits. Just as the public will welcome free public preschools, so will it welcome free public education at the other end of the school ladder, at the junior college.

The best answer to the problem of vocational education so far has been the introduction of the differentiated, five-year technical college, the *kosen* (grades 10 to 14). The schools have been well supported by the government and industry and are very successful. In future this pattern is likely to be extended to other areas besides industry and technology. And the danger that they might become dead-end institutions is being alleviated by the opening in 1976 of a university of technology and science which will offer *kosen* graduates the opportunity to go on to graduate-level education leading to the master's degree.

The present school week of five and a half days will in future be reduced to a five-day week, as some schools are already doing. Parents and educational authorities will then be concerned with the problem of "the worthy use of leisure time" and will ask the government to provide facilities for this. The rapidly changing society, and the vast information revolution accompanying it, will call for educating people of all ages, occupations, and socioeconomic levels continuously or intermittently in what is called lifelong learning. Expanded school plants or more efficient use of present plants for social education (that is, adult education), together with maximum use of television and radio media for correspondence courses and cultural as well as practical subjects will help meet the demands of lifelong learning. The "University of the Air" which offers working youth and adults higher education courses and a degree program through radio and television broadcasting, combined with a brief on-campus experience at certain universities, is already in the works but had not yet come into fruition by 1978. The facilities of the great quasi-public television network NHK is already the best and most comprehensive educational television system in the world, and it could easily expand its services to include the much larger "lifelong learning" audience that is anticipated in the future.

Public and private school sports facilities, playing fields, gymnasiums, and swimming pools will be opened to the public after school hours and on weekends and holidays. The cost of supervision will be provided by the central government. The ministry has already by a recent "instruction" requested all schools, including universities, to make their facilities available to the public. And the sports-loving Japanese public will certainly take advantage of this opportunity.

The other priority item proposed by the Central Council on Education in its "third reform" is special education. Since approximately one third of handicapped youth are in school and since the government has already committed itself to equal educational opportunity for the handicapped, we can look forward to seeing sufficient facilities and adequate special education staff being made available to all the handicapped youth of the nation, as well as the expansion and improvement of special education programs.

Another significant and essential reform is in the examination system. No longer can it remain the dominant influence on the whole education system, stressing the function of selection over everything else and distorting the whole curriculum. New techniques for selection will be devised. A first step was taken in alleviating the examination hell in the late 1970s when the government subsidized the developing of a unified, consolidated achievement test to screen applicants to the national and public universities. Eventually the examination system will be modified so that it will no longer be just an achievement test sampling ability to memorize a mass of irrelevant facts, but will be a battery of several kinds of tests, aptitude tests utilizing the latest psychological testing techniques, plus oral interviews and the use of high school recommendations and cumulative records from lower schools. The strongest force for reform will be when the supply of education at all levels meets the demand, and there will be enough schools so that young people will not have to be weeded out but will have the opportunity to go as far in education as their ability permits them.

For example, if there are enough high-quality universities to meet all demands, then there can be an easy-entry, open university, with diversified specialties in fields natural to their environment; for example, Kagoshima University may specialize in marine engineering and related subjects, appropriate to its ocean environs.

With such an open university, elitism in education will have been eliminated. The individual student will have a chance to develop his own potentialities and create his own place in society, rather than submitting to the arbitrary selection system of the examinations. Thus the students will not have to adjust to the system, but the educational structure will be adjusted to them.

In the history sequence of this account we saw that in the past education was primarily for the purposes of the state and only incidentally for the development of the individual. As we look to the future we cannot be sure that all the Third Major Reform will be implemented, especially since it still represents the goals of the conservative educational establishment. But given the high valuation Japanese society places on education, the national commitment to democracy in the law, and the existence of highly motivated teachers and eager students, as well as a literate and articulate public, we can be sure that in the future development of the individual *will* be advanced, and though education will continue to serve an enlightened state, it will primarily serve the people, all the people, in lifelong learning.

## REFERENCES

*Asahi Evening News,* February 22, 1969.

Asahi Shimbun Staff. "Teachers, Children and School." *The Japan Interpreter* (1974): 1–14.

Berrien, F. K. "Japanese Values and Democratic Process," in *Selected Readings on Modern Japanese Society,* ed. G. Yamamoto and T. Ishida. Berkeley: McCutchan Publishing Corp., 1971, pp. 73–80.

Consulate General of Japan. "Talent Education Children of Dr. Shinichi Suzuki," *Japan Report* (1968): 8.

Education and Cultural Exchange Division, UNESCO, and International Affairs Department, Science and International Affairs Bureau, Ministry of Education, Science and Culture. *Course of Study for Elementary Schools in Japan.* Tokyo: The Ministry, 1976.

Education and Cultural Exchange Division, UNESCO, and International Affairs Bureau, Ministry of Education, Science and Culture. *Course of Study for Lower Secondary Schools in Japan.* Tokyo: The Ministry, 1976.

Fukuhara, M. "Student Expectation of Counseling—A Cross-Cultural Study," *Japanese Psychological Research,* 15 (1973): 179–193.

General Headquarters, Supreme Commander for the Allied Powers. *Post-War Developments in Japanese Education, II.* Tokyo: GHQ, 1952.

Hayashi, C. "Changes in Japanese Thought During the Past 20 Years," in *Changing Japanese Values,* ed. Institute of Statistical Mathematics. Tokyo: The Institute, 1977.

Husen, T. (ed.) *International Study of Achievement in Mathematics—A Comparison of 12 Countries.* New York: John Wiley and Sons, 1967.

Japan Teachers' Union. *How to Reform Japan's Education.* Tokyo: Japan Teachers' Union, 1975.

Japanese Institute of International Affairs. *White Papers of Japan, 1975–1976.* Tokyo: The Institute, 1977.

Ministry of Education. *Basic Guidelines for the Reform of Education: Report of the Central Council for Education.* Tokyo: The Ministry, 1972.

Nagai, M. "Higher Education in a Free Society, Japan," *Japan Quarterly,* 24 (1977): 306–312.

Neumeyer, C. "High School Counselor in Japan," *Personnel and Guidance Journal,* 46 (1968): 602–604.

*Parade Magazine* in *The Honolulu Advertiser,* February 5, 1978.

Sabirov, I. "Gymnastic Lessons in the German Democratic Republic and Japan," *Soviet Education* 16 (Feb. 1974): 108–114.

Sakamoto, Y. *A Study of Japanese National Character,* part V. Tokyo: Institute of Statistical Mathematics, 1977.

Singleton, J. *Nichu, a Japanese School.* New York: Holt, Rinehart and Winston, 1967.

Suzuki, T. "A Study of the Japanese National Character, Fourth Nation-wide Survey," *Annals of the Institute of Statistical Mathematics*, Suppl. 6 (1970) reprint in English).

*The Japan Times*, March 25, 1969.

*Time*, January 23, 1978, p. 73.

Tsujimura, A. "Gendai Shakai Ron" (Essays on contemporary society), in *Shakai Gaku Koza (Seminar in sociology)*. Tokyo: Tokyo University Press, 1971.

Vogel, E. F. *Japan's New Middle Class*. Berkeley: University of California Press, 1967.

Yamamura, K. and Hanley, S. "Ichi hime, ni Taro: Educational aspiration and decline of fertility in postwar Japan," *The Journal of Japanese Studies* 2 (1975): 83–125.

CHAPTER 7

# Mexican Education

LAWRENCE J. ESTRADA
THOMAS J. LaBELLE

## DEFINITION

The Mexican concept of *educación* carries with it a much broader meaning than the English term "education." *Educación* does stand for learning and teaching within a formal process, but it represents also nonformal aspects of the total learning environment that constitute the formation of human character and personality development. A person's style of dress, demeanor, respect, and the way one conducts oneself in public are all ascribed to whether one does or does not possess *educación*. Within this context, education represents both an individual and an institutional phenomenon.

## INTRODUCTION[1]

### Objectives of Education

Traditionally schools have been designated as those institutions that bear the chief responsibility for transmitting a population's cultural heritage from one generation to the next. Folklore, music, dance, history, and moral lessons have all had major importance within the curricula of past and present educational schemes. That the focus of education in more

---

[1]In this chapter, a number of Spanish and indigenous words are employed. Generally, immediately after the word, the English definition is given. For greater convenience, however, a number of the words are defined at the end of the chapter in a special glossary.

modern times has changed and continues to change in light of industrialization and technical progress can scarcely be denied.

Within recent years there has been a general acceptance of the proposition that economic progress and growth depend equally on the training and development of human potential as on the accumulation of capital resources, equipment, and the cultivation of market outlets. Human resource analysis has become the responsibility of the planner and the focus of study for the scholar. "Manpower development," "manpower resources," and "labor potential" are coined phrases intrinsically linked to both education and the phenomenon called modernization. Research on methodology for determining the strategy for utilizing education for modernization has centered on the building of theoretical models, designing international comparative studies, and above all measuring "returns" to education. Hence, current studies concerned with the development of human resources must take into account the role of the educational process and its impact upon societal and economic change.

There also exists an interest in education for its motivating influences in accomplishing the "modern state." To a large degree, education has become to the social scientist an indicator of cultural attitudes and national priorities. In this regard, there is a natural tendency to assume that education represents little more than a tool of government, reflecting its very thrust and whim. Such an assumption, however, fails to address itself to the critical nature of education and its overall relationship to both the individual and the wider society.

Therefore, although education has been redefined by many nations to meet specific needs, its principal purpose and value lies not only in its ability to increase industrial production or to develop consumption patterns in line with technological development, but also in its ability to bring about individual and collective awareness of latent potential of individuals and the collective society. Within the context of developing nations, the fulfillment of potential through education is often intrinsically linked to national schemes and desires to attain greater self-autonomy within the world community. This is strongly reflected by the many struggles for both individual and group relevance as well as the need to prepare highly skilled manpower for economic autonomy.

In essence, education through schooling encompasses much more than the inculcation of youth with carefully censored and approved ideas or the retraining and mobilization of a labor force. To a large segment of the world, education represents hope for the future. Often, that hope is not only for a thriving economy based on increased consumption and production, but it is also a desire to be self-sufficient and capable of independently fulfilling one's own potential and objectives.

## Reasons for This System

As in many other nations, the educational system of Mexico has been transformed throughout history to meet the needs of a changing and expanding society. In pre-Hispanic times Mexican education was traditional, religious, and warlike. In its purest sense, it was designed to transmit culture from generation to generation. Village education provided for the preservation of religious devotion and the maintenance of the social order controlled by a ruling, noble elite. It was an organic part of the cultural pattern of Indian society.

Following the Spanish conquest of indigenous Mexico, education was dominated by the Catholic church and centered around the conversion of the people to the Christian faith. In line with clerical and colonial dictates, the Spanish language and customs were to supplant all indigenous forms of education.

During the postcolonial period (1821–1917), liberal and democratic philosophies brought about an end to church-dominated education and ensured that education would both become the charge of the state and universal in its application. This trend was to continue throughout the positivist era (1877–1930) brought forth by the "porfiriato" (the ruling period of dictator Porfirio Diaz). A gradual shift toward secular education became a paramount objective.

After the Revolution of 1910 and the establishment of Article 3 of the Federal Constitution of 1917, the decades of the 1920s and 1930s heralded the creation of the common school. Education in the countryside was to be equal to that in the cities. Emphasis was given to rural and technical schools, and higher esteem was given to the role of the teacher. Within this context "socialist education" came into being.

The final stage of Mexico's educational development has been directed to building a comprehensive national ideology. The establishment of national literacy campaigns and regional technical schools in the 1940s underscored Mexico's efforts to bring education to all sectors of the Mexican populace. The presidencies of Avila Camacho, Miguel Aleman, Lopez Mateos, Diaz Ordaz, Luis Echeverria, and presently Jose Lopez Portillo have all emphasized the importance of education and its role within "national development."

In attempting to arrive at a singular notion representative of present trends in Mexican education, the phrase "educar es redemir" (redemption through education) sums up the premium placed upon education by national planners and leaders. Education is seen both as a means for promoting future growth and prosperity as well as a cohesive force for infusing national consciousness. Turner, in describing the Mexican national character and its uniqueness, provides some insight into the Mexican psyche:

> The causes of Mexican uniqueness are multiple, of course, and no single concept elucidates the Mexican panorama. One element pervading each area of distinctiveness, however, is the development of a brand of nationalism that has given the Mexican national community a particular cohesiveness and flexibility (Turner, 1968, p. 4).

## HISTORY

### Beginnings

The historical evolution of Mexican education has transpired over a period of more than 3,000 years. A complete overview of its many diverse forms and its gradual as well as compulsory changes can scarcely be documented in a few pages. For this reason the following historical synopsis will concentrate on only those main institutions and trends that were symbolic of the main focus of Mexican public education during their respective eras. For the sake of chronological comprehension, the history of Mexican public education can be divided into four distinct eras: (1) pre-Cortesian, (2) colonial, (3) postcolonial, and (4) nationalistic.

### Pre-Cortesian

Pre-Cortesian or pre-Hispanic public education in Mesoamerica roughly between the years 500 B.C. and A.D. 1519 was marked by its emphasis and inclusion of the "total being"; religious philosophy, martial skills, social duties, folklore, and history, the dissemination of which was largely the responsibility of public education. Both within the classic (Maya-Toltec) and the postclassic (Aztec-Mixtec) periods of Mesoamerica, public education based on oral tradition was viewed as both an honor and a responsibility, the culmination of which would produce young men and women able to assume their particular moral and communal obligations (Soustelle, 1961; Thompson, 1954).

For numerous centuries preceding the Spanish conquest of 1521, the indigenous peoples of Mesoamerica had built extensive formal public school systems. Best known was the system established by the Aztecs whose rites were largely preserved through the use of codexes. In general, Aztec society was based upon a hierarchical structure consisting of the following classes: warrior nobility, priests, merchants, and a large common class of free peasants. Public education was afforded to all members of the kinship group called the "calpulli." Those outside the kinship group represented the slave and serf population. For this class any type of formal schooling was largely prohibited (Soustelle, 1961; Gill, 1969).

The formal education of male Aztec youth centered upon a duality of religious and philosophical doctrine predicated upon the opposing divinities of Quetzalcoatl and Tezcatlipoca. Each of these divinities was honored by the institutionalization within Aztec society of formal youth schools which represented their character and their teachings. The "calmeac," or Aztec seminary, was based upon the teachings and divine guidance of Quetzalcoatl. It stressed self-sacrifice, penance, intellectual reaching, arts, calendar reading, astronomical calculations, and religion. On the other hand, the "tepochcalli," or school for commoners, was based on the cult of the warlike Tezcatlipoca. It emphasized manual skills, martial arts, dancing, chorale, cooperation, self-defense, and religion. Each of the schools, although drastically different, was felt to be equally important in upholding Aztec society.

From birth, an Aztec child was marked for a predetermined life role. If a girl, a loom was placed in her hands; if a noble's son, an implement of his particular craft. Between the ages of ten and thirteen, the sons of merchants, craftsmen, and commoners were placed in the *tepochcalli* to receive instruction in the art of war, as well as in religion. The sons of nobility attended the seminary-like *calmeac*, where they received instruction that prepared them to be priests, public officials, and military leaders. Teachers for these future leaders were drawn from the priesthood and charged with the task of inducting them into the governance of society (Weinberg, 1977; Soustelle, 1961).

The formal education of the Aztecs resembled that of other Mesoamerican civilizations such as the Zapotecs, Mixtecs, Toltecs, and the Mayas. Mayan youth at the age of seven or eight attended religious schools held in sacred temples and taught by priests. At a later age they were sent to boarding schools called "internados," where they were instructed in martial arts and strategy. Some of the noble class and other high officials attended separate internados. Commoners within Mayan society were restricted from any form of formalized schooling (Thompson, 1964). Benjamin Keen, in his analysis of Aztec life and thought, recounts the words of the nineteenth-century chronicler Francisco Pi y Margall, "Education had made the Aztecs a cultured people; even their plebians were better instructed than the coarse, ignorant Spanish soldiers" (Keen, 1971, p. 456).

*Colonial*

After 1521 and the Spanish conquest of Mexico, all indigenous forms of public education disappeared. Spanish colonial education scarcely resembled the calmeac and tepochcalli, in that its primary function was to initiate the indigenous people of Nueva España (New Spain) into subserviency and acceptance of Spanish Catholicism. From 1519 to 1521, popular education was private, Catholic, and Spanish. Only a minor fraction of the indigenous people of Nueva España benefited. That education was by and large a privilege of the few is indicated by the fact that of the "five million people in Mexico at the end of the colonial period (1821) only 0.5 percent was literate" (Weinberg, 1977, p. 141).

Extensively, the education of colonial Mexico was to be officially entrusted to and carried on by clerical orders. The arrival of the Franciscans in 1521, followed by the Dominicans, Augustinians, and Jesuits, marked the beginning of literacy and vocational training in Nueva España. Teaching a rather limited vocabulary of theological, social, and economic words, the friars in three centuries spread throughout the New World, converting indigenous civilizations to Christianity and "incorporating them into a new socio-economic reality" (McAndrews, 1965, p. 22).

In 1540 the famed Santa Cruz de Tlatelolco Academy, precursor to the University of Mexico, was founded by missionaries in Nueva España. Many of its Indian graduates through the years became instructors in theology, philosophy, and the humanities, taking residency in various monasteries in colonial Mexico. As one writer states, "Some Indians became teachers of their conquerors, who did not feel humiliated to receive training from those who had reached so high a position" (Garrard, 1956, p. 104).

Aside from formalized schooling in urban, colonial Mexico, nonformal education to teach the use of rudimentary agricultural tools and farming skills was to take place on haciendas in the rural sectors of the country for well over 300 years. For the majority of the indigenous population, the haciendas were to be the chief educational institutions in the colonial epoch. For Indians held in social and economic bondage, education on the hacienda represented a mixture of apprenticeship and forced servitude (Ingrams, 1975).

That Spanish colonial education was bent upon eradication of most indigenous forms of culture is probably best reflected in the language policy established by the Spanish crown. The language policies of the colonial period were marked by the decrees and edicts of Spanish sovereigns who dictated that Spanish be the sole medium of communication and instruction in the New World. A 250-year program of "Castillianization," beginning with Queen Isabela in 1493 and culminating in 1793 with the reign of Carlos IV, was intended to supplant and eradicate the use of "infidel" tongues in the New World completely. To no small degree the concept of "Castillianization" represented a completely ethnocentric focus of education manifested in Mexico's colonial period (Estrada & Nava, 1976).

*Postcolonial*

The postcolonial period of Mexican education extended from 1821, shortly after independence from Spain, to the establishment of the Mexican Constitution of 1917. As in the colonial period, the upper echelon of Mexican society, composed of the Spanish and criollo (Mexican-born of Spanish ancestry) classes, continued to dominate the direction and tenor of Mexican education. Formal schooling consisted of a rigid process, beginning with *primeras letras* (early primary grades), through the *colegio* (secondary education), and up to the Universidad Real y Pontifica de México, if one was part of the elite ruling structure. "Schooling became synonymous with governance and leadership and over time, the entire social system became regulated by a clearly defined hierarchy of lawyers and theologians" (Ingrams, 1975, p. 2).

The elitist heritage of Mexican education was not to change appreciably until the inception of the Mexican Constitution of 1857. In the mid-nineteenth century, due in part to church-state conflicts over power and landed wealth, reformist leaders such as Benito Juarez attempted to wrest control of education from the hands of the Catholic church. Under the precepts of the Constitution of 1857, reformist provisions provided for a separation of church and state and established the principle that public education should be compulsory, free, and secular (Gill, 1977).

Although public education for a brief period in the nineteenth century became the province of the nation rather than the church, its impact would not be felt during the "afrancesado" period (or period of French influence) or the "porfiriato" in the latter part of the century. In this era of Mexican history European customs and mores, accompanying foreign political and economic penetration of Mexico, pervaded almost every aspect of the Mexican life-style. The dictatorial regime of Porfirio Díaz (1876–1911) allowed for federal control of education in the federal district and territories, while delegating authority for education in the remainder of the nation to each of the respective state governments. Nevertheless, education, rather than becoming totally state-controlled and egalitarian, remained dominated by the clerical orders and church hierarchy (Gill, 1977).

Until the Mexican Revolution of 1910, the educational philosophy of such reknowned Mexican educators as Justo Sierra and Felix Palavicini reflected the overriding belief among much of the Mexican intelligentsia that education was an essential tool for forging the progress and modernization of the Mexican state. For the most part, Mexican education in the early twentieth century, largely influenced by "científico" (scientific) thinking and French positivism, attempted to accentuate and incorporate European ideals and modes of learning (Sierra, 1948).

In line with the thinking of the científicos, the school system of the porfiriato was designed to enculturate the masses with "desirable" values and to impress the entourage of European investors who supported and profited from the Diaz regime of 1876–1911. In line with this mentality were the words of Justo Sierra in telling the Primer Congreso de Instrucción Primaria (First Convention of Primary Instruction) in 1890 that with a successful primary school program:

> We will have made ourselves worthy of presenting to the eyes of the world a people who work conscientiously to redeem themselves; then we will merit the words of the great French orator Eugene Pelletan, who in speaking of Latin America in the French assembly, before men who belittled us, said, "New generations are arising in Latin America who will transform those societies, because their generations bear the light of hope before them and the thirst for progress in their hearts" (Sierra, 1948, pp. 198–199).

Other educators such as Palavicini tended to disfavor the "European" model of education and instead looked toward North America as an example where education was fitting the needs of a modernizing and rapidly industrializing nation. Where the porfirian elite looked to Europe, Palavicini was indicative of the new middle class, such as the fledgling politician Francisco Madero, which looked to the United States as a model for Mexican development. For Palavicini and others, the United States symbolized "wealth, power and culture" (Palavicini, 1916, p. 81). Largely under his direction, Mexican teachers were sent off to the United States for training and told to observe North American behavior as a model of order and development (Secretaria de Instrucción Pública, 1914).

Another crucial function of education in prerevolutionary Mexico was the engendering of ideals intended to build national cohesion and unification. This was also strongly expressed in the writings of Justo Sierra, "The school should realize the religion of the fatherland in the soul of the child so that it will be a source of pride and delight to him so that as the child is transformed into a man, this holy cult is converted into a resolution to sacrifice for the country" (Sierra, 1948, p. 399).

### Nationalistic

The inception of the Mexican Revolution in 1910 and its culmination in 1917 with the issuance of the 1917 Constitution was to be a hallmark year for Mexican education. In general, the Constitution, which provided for greater federal powers in all sectors of government, was able to provide far-reaching federal guidelines and specific criteria for the administration of Mexican public schooling (Gill, 1977). Much like the reformist Constitution of 1857, the new Constitution attempted to separate clerical influences and public schooling. Under Article 3, it provided for free and secular public education. In this and in Article 27, religious bodies were (and still are) unable to participate in educational activities except as permitted under official supervision. Other articles require the school attendance of children aged six to fourteen (Article 31), the need for some middle- and large-sized commercial and industrial enterprises to sponsor schools for the children of workers (Article 123), and the right of the federal government to establish schools and legislate the basis for their support from federal, state, and municipal sources (Article 73).

The coupling of education, intense nationalism, and industrialization was to be the predominant character of Mexican public education for more than sixty years, from 1917 to 1979. However, rather than seeking to copy European and North American modes of education, Mexican officials and educators began to adopt programs that emphasized Mexican character and gave greater importance to indigenous culture.

With the dawning of the 1920s and the adoption of the Escuela de Acción (the active promotion of education in rural areas) as the official model of Mexican education, the Mexican public school system under the directorship of Jose Vasconcelos became a highly centralized body whose primary objectives were to bring culture to the masses as a means of incorporating them into the public mainstream. As *El Maestro*, the chief publication for the Secretaria de Educación Pública stated, the purposes of the educational program were "not just to cultivate ideas, but to awaken, invigorate, and extend sentiments of love for nationality, the only thing which can save us" (Secretaria de Educación Pública, 1921a, p. 3).

Vasconcelos in his tenure as the head of the Mexican public educational system was to introduce the notion of "misiones culturales" (social action programs) and literacy campaigns directed toward the rural countryside and the indigenous population. These efforts first brought about in the 1920s and 1930s were to lay the groundwork for later literacy and cultural extension programs such as the *campagnas de alfabetización* (literacy campaigns) generated in the 1950s and 1960s during the presidencies of Avila Camacho and Lopez Mateos (Ingrams, 1975).

Throughout the 1930s, 1940s, and 1950s, to meet the emerging industrial needs of the nation, Mexico placed a great emphasis upon technical-vocational education. The creation of IPN (Instituto Politécnico Nacional) in the 1930s and the development of the RTI system (Institutos Tecnológicos Regionales, or Regional Technical Institutes) in the 1940s underscored the Mexican educational efforts to increase the technical-vocational/educational thrust in line with national growth patterns.

The RTIs, in particular because of their regional focus, were promoted to serve the technical needs of the less developed areas of the country. Entrusted with the dissemination of technical skills and expertise to students of various regions, the RTIs were intended to provide the essential technical manpower to develop the Mexican countryside. Between 1949 and 1976 their rate of growth throughout the nation could be considered phenomenal. RTIs presently serve every region and practically every state in the Mexican republic.

A major and growing consideration of Mexican educators in the sixty or so years following the revolution has been and continues to be whether the Mexican public school system will be able in time to incorporate all school-aged Mexicans and to provide the "mechanism needed for integrating all people into one dynamic state" (Ingrams, 1975, p. 4). With shades of the Vasconcelos philosophy of "La Raza Cósmica," Mexican educators continue to be preoccupied with the ability of the state to provide universal education as well as a nationally cohesive program of public schooling.

These concepts were clearly illustrated by the Secretaria de Educación Plan of 1959 headed by Jaime Torres Bodet and given priority by President Lopez Mateos. The plan provided for a comprehensive, national program providing free primary education for all children. The plan was intended to cut the glaring disparity of years of formal schooling between urban and rural youth. To accomplish this, the plan was to span an eleven-year period beginning in 1959 (SEP Plan, 1959). Hence it became known as the "Plan de Once Años," or eleven-year plan, and represented the greatest commitment by the Mexican federal government to provide free universal education to the entire nation. Remarkable both in its scope and success, the "Plan de Once Años" through a vast enlargement of Mexican educational facilities, the contracting of a greater number of teachers, and the number of new pupils brought into formal schooling, ushered the Mexican public school system into the modern era of the Mexican state.

### Current Status

As in the working relationship existing between Jose Vasconcelos and Plutarco Calles and later exemplified by Torres Bodet and Lopez Mateos, much of the history of Mexican education is reflected in the goals and strategies articulated from the office of the president and his appointed secretary of public education. These goals, however, have seldom been met, as the obstacles to their satisfaction often reside in cultural, demographic, and technological constraints beyond the immediate influence of the polity. Hence, the long-term goals of nationalism and the incorporation of the Indian into the nation, the extension of schooling to the rural areas, and the desire to have all citizens literate, continues to be frustrated even though major investments toward their achievement have been made during this century.

The current educational system reflects these continuing themes and frustrations. Its operation and orientation are legally derived from Article 3 of the 1917 Constitution. Although the nation is the only legally authorized body to carry out elementary, secondary, and normal education, others may establish schools if they have the approval of the nation to do so. The professional preparation, morality, and ideology of the individuals in charge are scrutinized, since all educational plans, programs, and teaching methods remain the responsibility of the state. Hence, federal authorization, which may be revoked at any time, must be granted before any private schools can be established. Furthermore, the state may declare invalid courses of study that have been completed in private schools (Chavels, 1968).

In December 1973 a new federal education law was approved by Congress and signed by the president. This law departs from its predecessors by including, first, nonformal or extrascholastic education as a part of the national educational system; second, providing for the school entry or reentry of youths and adults who have been marginal to the system; third, authorizing remediation and accelerated schools; and fourth, permitting promotion by examination at all levels of schooling (Ingrams, 1975). The structure of these programs includes three basic levels: elementary (preschool and primary), secondary (basic and superior), and higher. The program begins with a two-year preschool or kindergarten until age six, followed by six years of primary education, to be completed by age fourteen. Subsequently, a three-year higher secondary cycle can lead in one of the following directions: (*a*) a three-year higher secondary cycle, (*b*) a normal, or teacher training, school, or (*c*) a technical/vocational school. Both the higher secondary cycle and the normal school lead to a *bachillerato*, or secondary school diploma, and are intended to be appropriate preparation for higher education, whereas only some of the technical/vocational programs may lead to the *bachillerato* and some postsecondary institutions (Gill, 1977).

Approximately 75 percent of all children in Mexico are enrolled at the primary level, with more than 90 percent of these children attending federal and state rather than private institutions. Although considerable effort has been made since the late 1950s to bring primary education to all Mexican children, as of 1976, some 1 million children aged six to fourteen were still unserved by the system (CEE, 1977). Furthermore, the internal efficiency of primary schools has not made major strides, as 46 of every 100 entrants in 1969–1970 failed to complete sixth grade (CEE, 1977). There are also great disparities between the rural and urban areas in both school availability and internal efficiency. A report of June 1975 found that primary schooling was available for only 62 percent of eligible students in the rural, as opposed to 83 percent in the urban areas. Rural areas also had many fewer schools that included all six grades than did urban areas (Gill, 1977).

The six-year secondary school (*educación media*) programs are divided into two cycles of three years each, which together are intended to prepare individuals for further education or the occupational marketplace. Through the basic secondary education level, the hope is that eventually all children will complete nine, rather than the current six, years of education. Federal and state schools enroll a majority of the total basic-cycle population, with federal schools predominating (Gill, 1977). At present, a majority of those students who graduate from primary school are enrolling at the secondary level, and the percentage has steadily increased from 1959 to the present. In 1970, for example, 72 of 100 primary graduates entered secondary school, whereas in 1975, 82 out of every 100 entered (Gill, 1977; CEE, 1977). Although the enrollments have expanded from approximately 1,900,000 in 1970 to 2,150,000 in 1976, more than 2,400,000 students were unserved by the system in 1976 (CEE, 1977). Likewise, wastage rates and dropouts from this level continue at relatively high levels (CEE, 1977).

Whereas the basic secondary cycle enrolls almost 13 percent of the total student population in the Mexican school system, the upper or superior cycle enrolls only 4 percent (Gill, 1977). Even though federal and state schools continue to enroll the majority of students at this level, the state schools account for approximately 50 percent of the total enrollment (Gill, 1977). Although enrollments increased substantially between 1970 and 1976 at this level, going from 310,400 to 822,000, the number of individuals leaving the system has also increased (CEE, 1977).

Higher education in Mexico is reflected in a number of different types of institutions under the sponsorship of both private and public agencies. Although university enrollments have grown at a rate of more than 400 percent between 1960 and 1976 to a total of 528,000 (CEE, 1977), postsecondary enrollments in 1975 accounted for only 2.91 percent of all students in the school system (Gill, 1977). Since 1973, all universities have come under the centralized educational system for purposes of coordinating programs and planning. In 1975, there were 124 Mexican higher education institutions, with the 39 located in the federal district accounting for approximately one half of the total national enrollment. Most financial support for public universities comes from federal and state sources, whereas private universities derive their support from tuition or philanthropic donors. Graduate enrollments are small, with the National University in Mexico City accounting for two thirds of 9,165 enrollees nationally in 1974–1975. Gill (1977) reports that new universities are being created to relieve enrollment pressures on existing institutions. Furthermore, new emphases have been placed on, among others, expanding graduate programs and establishing extension mechanisms for granting credit for other than traditional classes.

## THEORY

### Learning

In Mexico, learning theory is related to both a dominant and lesser tradition. In the dominant tradition, knowledge is derived from authoritative or revealed sources. Whereas authoritative knowledge is accepted as true because it originates with respected experts, revealed knowledge is derived from religious teachings and is accepted because of a faith in God. Although such tenets are strongly held in Mexico, both authoritative and revealed knowledge are also complemented by an individual's own reason and experience.

An emphasis on authoritative and revealed knowledge assumes the existence of certain universal truths that all individuals are expected to learn and accept. Formal education has the responsibility of transmitting these universals and typically does so by developing a common core of subject matter to be learned by all children. Such a subject-matter core is expected to acquaint pupils with the basic physical and cultural structures of the universe. Because these structures are the result of divine creation, they are accepted as basically orderly and harmonious. Individuals are expected to learn to adapt to and be tolerant of both the cultural and physical environment. Revealed and authoritative sources, therefore, are the guides to learning to adjust to one's reality.

According to this dominant tradition in Mexico, subject matter is assumed to reflect a logical order and intelligibility. Because order and intelligibility are already built into an objective arrangement of subject matter, however, the learner is expected to acquire logical thinking automatically. Learning is designed, therefore, to give order to a disorganized mind; a coherent subject matter is to provide the vehicle to develop logical thinking (Cummings and Lemke, 1973).

Learners are traditionally viewed as passive recipients of knowledge. Their role is to absorb information dictated by teachers who are accepted as authoritative sources. Further, learners are expected to participate as individuals or as members of a class in recitations and to memorize information for future recall on examinations. Schools in small towns and rural areas, where teachers are among a select number of authoritative sources, are especially characterized by these traits. The teacher in these instances is in complete command of the core subject matter and often delivers it in an encyclopedic manner through a lecture methodology. Students in such situations are expected to take notes and prepare for eventual recitation and recall. Whether such methods are related to a youngster's background and prior experience is of relatively little importance. Even if the subject matter is perceived as abstract and unrelated to the learner's interests and prior experiences, such perceptions do not affect how learning is assumed to occur.

These assumptions differ sharply from a second and much less widely accepted learning theory in Mexico. Associated with individuals like Jose Vasconcelos and Jaime Torres Bodet, this lesser tradition suggests that learning theory must begin with the experiences of learners rather than the authoritative presentation of subject matter. Rather than being viewed as passive and receptive, learners in the view of Bodet and others are active and exploratory, the makers of knowledge rather than merely the receivers of knowledge. Such a viewpoint is especially strong among educators of younger children, where the relevance of what is learned is assumed to be important for a youngster's attempt to grasp the meaning of experience (Kneller, 1951; Romanell, 1971).

These two viewpoints on learning theory, an authoritative and revealed orientation on the contrasting activity orientation, characterize much of the Mexican educational process during this century. The former has emerged as by far the predominant, while the latter has been associated with only a handful of liberal educational leaders. Among these more liberal individuals are Jose Vasconcelos, twice secretary of education (in 1914–1915 for only thirty-eight days and again in 1921–1924 for nearly three years); and Jaime Torres Bodet, secretary of public education between 1943 and 1946 for three years and between 1958 and 1964 for six years.

Vasconcelos stressed the importance of involving the learner in his own education through the use of the school as a workshop and community as well as the community as a resource of teaching and learning. Such an approach during the 1920s represented a dramatic departure from the formalized subject-matter mastery process in evidence earlier. Although this break from tradition left its own mark on the perception of teaching and learning, much as John Dewey's thoughts impacted on similar processes in the United States, the influence of traditional methods combined with problems of overcrowding and efficiency have never permitted any widespread adoption of more applied learning approaches.

Likewise, the influence of Jaime Torres Bodet affected the Mexican approach to education by emphasizing greater learning involvement and activity on the part of students but proved unable to combat more traditional methodologies and long-standing administrative practices. Torres Bodet argued that children learn only when they have had an opportunity to observe, reflect, and experiment. He also believed that education should involve individualized instruction, an adaptation to each child, and an integration of intellectual and psychomotor pursuits. Torres Bodet sought to have learners verify knowledge through experience rather than simply memorize information (Faust, 1971).

As in most countries, it is possible to find in Mexico today a wide range of educational practices based upon different assumptions about the learning process. In the larger cities, some public and many private primary and secondary schools have adopted great flexibility in their curricular and instructional approaches, using methods that involve students in their own knowledge discovery and application. At the secondary and higher education level in Mexico at present, for example, there is said to be renewed hope and emphases on the application of knowledge to the solution of national problems. Such a trend involves greater scientific analysis of social problems in an attempt to raise technical competencies (Rangel Guerra, 1978). Nevertheless, in many primary and basic secondary schools, learning theory is typically associated with abstract content and verbal methods of instruction, and remains linked to the logic of the subject matter rather than to the experiences of either the society or the learner. Although the cognitive development theories of Piaget as well as the theories of other contemporary educators are employed by some Mexican educators and often form part of the curricula of prospective schoolteachers, little transfer of such knowledge is said to be in evidence in school classrooms. Rote memorization, repetition, recitation, and recall continue to demonstrate that revealed and authoritative sources of knowledge are firmly imbedded in the Mexican cultural heritage.

## Teaching

Like the dominant tradition in learning theory in Mexico, teaching theory has its roots in the intellectual influences of Europe and the processes and goals associated with Mexican independence and national development. Often viewed in opposition to one another, this European versus national orientation can be seen in the political history of Mexico, its corresponding chief executives, and the more than forty secretaries of public education who have held office during the last 100 years.

In the late 1800s, teaching was based on the positivist postulate that scientific laws governed the functioning of society and that once such laws had been discovered, the duty of teachers was to reflect those principles in their teaching. Teachers were viewed as scientifically educated, authoritative individuals who would assist in determining and introducing appropriate values and mores. Hence, teachers were not only the creators of truth but were the means for implementing and fostering that truth in others. This authoritative influence of teachers departed radically from not only the classical laissez-faire liberalism and romanticism of the early 1800s, but the goal of national and social integration characteristic of much of the 1900s.

From the time of Benito Juarez and his stress on the lay instruction and social emancipation of the Indian, the emphasis on teaching for national integration was a recurrent theme. Justo Sierra rejected teaching practices like repetition, recitation, and memorization. In the 1920s, Jose Vasconcelos sought to adapt education to reality and to use schools as agents for both forging a new nation and achieving economic prosperity. In the late 1920s teaching followed the activity pedagogy of Vasconcelos, and in the 1930s teachers were called upon to use curricula and instructional practices to serve a socialist doctrine. This latter era was characterized by an emphasis on objective, scientific teaching that was both socially minded and class conscious. Hence, scientific explanations were placed in opposition to the teachings of the Church, and social criticism in teaching was intended to lead to social justice, equitable distribution of material goods, elimination of prejudices, and the enhancement of social responsibility (Thut and Adams, 1964).

In the 1940s, a reaction against these socialist influences led to the more balanced influences of Jaime Torres Bodet, who chose neither traditionalism or progressivism but instead emphasized educational practices that built on cultural traditions and thereby strengthened the national heritage. In the late 1940s, under the administration of Miguel Aleman, industrialization and economic progress became the goals of education, and teaching became more businesslike with emphases on both individual betterment and national economic progress (Kneller, 1951).

National integration, economic progress, and individual advancement and opportunity have remained the guiding principles upon which teaching theory continues to be based. The need to train more children to be effective and productive citizens through job skills has received renewed emphasis. Currently (1979), President Lopez Portillo emphasizes a combination of academic, citizenship, and economic goals. Academically, teaching is to stress intellectual habits permitting an objective analysis of reality and an ability to learn that which is functional for survival. In citizenship, teachers are to emphasize social solidarity, equality of opportunity, and individual fulfillment and liberty. Finally, teachers are to provide students with economic skills to secure productive work in the labor market.

Although teaching theory has been associated with these more general goals, the traditional pedagogy of Mexican teachers has been based on an objective arrangement of subject matter rather than on the relationship between such content and the stages of development of learners. According to the greater tradition, the inner logic of subject matter is not to be disturbed, regardless of the experiences of learners. Learner desires, therefore, are satisfied only if they happen to coincide with the teacher's intention of achieving intellectual goals. The lesser tradition, however, attempts to relate subject matter to the aims, interests, and experiences of students. Learning, according to this latter approach, does not begin until interest is aroused in the learner. The teacher's function is more a responsive than a directive one, with the initiative associated with the child.

These substantive theoretical divisions in teaching pedagogy have seldom been reflected in teacher training institutions, as the bias has been toward the greater, more conservative, rather than the lesser, more liberal, tradition. Teachers in training are typically expected to follow the models supplied by their master instructors through observation and subsequent replication. The methods have usually involved lecture, memorization, and recitation, even though the learning theory studied might have been associated with more liberal educators. Little attention has typically been given to the future teacher in pedagogical methods or techniques before he or she is placed in front of a group of peers or younger children to teach a lesson. Such techniques for prospective teachers are often limited to instructions to speak clearly and organize work logically, as well as to rely upon student notetaking, exercises, recitations, and written examinations.

More recently, teacher training has begun to include attention to methods and techniques that involve children in the application of what they are learning. There is also greater attention to the learner's background, age, and development in designing instructional strategies. Similarly, the rows of desks occupied by docile children being filled with information is, in a few locales, giving way to instructional settings that permit greater movement, inquiry, and exploration. These alternatives to the model of the teacher serving as an authoritative fount of knowledge are becoming more common. For example, some teachers at the elementary and secondary level, depending on the subject matter and the instructional resources available, have been experimenting with less teacher-centered strategies for enhancing children's learning.

APPLICATIONS

Curriculum, Academic

At the pre-primary level, preceding the formal preschool program, there exists a relatively small-scale effort at nursery school and child care for youngsters less than three years of age in a few of the larger urban areas. This kind of program has only recently received centralized coordination at the national level. The preschool or kindergarten program following the nursery school is directed at children four to six years of age. Nationwide, it enrolled 13.6 percent of the total eligible population in 1976. Kindergarten enrollments have grown slowly, and the proportion of children enrolled at this level relative to total school system enrollments (preschool through university), has declined from 3.9 percent in 1970–1971 to 3.3 percent in 1975–1976. These programs are concentrated in urban areas, and most are federally supported. They have not received any budgetary augmentation relative to other levels of the system since 1970 to attend to an ever-increasing number of preschool-age children (CEE, 1977).

The nursery and child-care facilities (*guarderias infantiles*) are designed to reach children and their mothers for purposes of health, educational, and custodial services. Often working mothers leave their children at the centers in the morning and retrieve them in the late afternoon or early evening. Many of these programs are sponsored by various government agencies or by employers for the dependents of employees. The kindergartens (*jardines infantiles*) compose the first rung of the constitutionally defined school system and are intended to provide a wide variety of educational experiences including games, singing, dancing, rhythms, psychomotor and artistic expression, and activities designed to prepare a child for a successful primary education. Also of concern is the emotional, moral, and ethical development of the child, enabling him or her to develop a sense of identity as an individual and as a citizen of Mexico (CEE, 1977; Gill, 1977).

Primary education is a six-year program enrolling children from the ages of six to fourteen. An intensive three-year course of study is available for children ten years of age or older in fundamental education centers (Gill, 1977). The primary curriculum is formulated at the national level and includes mathematics, natural science, social science, arts, physical education, and technical/vocational education. Each of the curricular areas is separated into eight units, paralleling the eight months of the school year. The textbooks used at the primary level in all schools in the country are prepared at the national level and mandated for federal, state, municipal, and private use. The texts are prepared by grade and subject-matter area and distributed free of charge to all children. The textbooks are accompanied by teacher guides, which provide objectives for the instructional program as well as teaching and evaluation suggestions. The guides are quite structured and follow the sequential nature of instruction in the textbooks.

Basic-cycle secondary education is available from general education and technical/vocational schools as well as through nonformal education facilities. The curriculum builds upon a common core of Spanish, mathematics, foreign language, natural and social science, and physical, artistic, and technical content, designed to articulate with both the primary level and subsequent formal schooling and the workplace. The thirty class hours of instruction per week address these content areas and are divided into eight units of work spread throughout the academic year. A curriculum bulletin provides objectives, teaching activities, and a list of supplementary resources for each unit (Gill, 1977). As with reforms in certification at the primary level, any person may take any examination at the secondary level without having attended the corresponding school grade (Ingrams, 1977). This enables individuals to take advantage of nonformal educational programs through textbook self-instruction and television as well as numerous study circles at worksites, social clubs, unions, and the like through the assistance of trained personnel (Gill, 1977).

General, technical/vocational, and normal, or teacher-preparation, institutions exist at superior secondary levels. In the general education institutions, students work toward the completion of the secondary, or *bachillerato* (diploma). These general education institutions are divided into two major types, the traditional *preparatorias* (preparatory schools for higher learning) under the direction of the universities, and the new *Colegios de Bachilleres* (comprehensive secondary schools), subject to the curricular authority of the secretariat of public education. The *preparatorias* have been in operation since the first was established in 1867 under the administration of the National Autonomous University of Mexico (Chavels, 1968), which currently operates on nine campuses throughout the capital. A second type of *preparatoria*, the Colegio de Ciencias y Humanidades (School of Sciences and Humanities), is also associated with the university and operates on five campuses in the Federal District. These two types of preparatory schools have traditionally been the models for other public and private secondary schools under university control throughout the country. The new *Colegios de Bachilleres* were authorized by the Federal Law of 1973 and are intended to provide a curriculum leading both to higher education and to occupational pursuits. It is hoped that these new institutions, totaling only eight as of 1975, will relieve the pressure on the traditional *preparatorias* as well as establish a new curricular pattern in the country. This effort will complement the reforms underway in the *preparatorias* designed to standardize the curriculum, the divisions of the school year into semesters, the curriculum credit hours, as well as combine academic and vocational subject matter (Gill, 1977).

Parallel to the general education schools are other secondary institutions of both a technical/vocational and teacher training type. The technical/vocational institutions are many and varied, combining curricula for the general education, basic cycle of secondary education, as well as preparation for occupational pursuits. As Gill (1977) points out, there has been a dramatic increase in the number of technical/vocational institutions since 1970. This is apparent in agricultural, technological, industrial, fishing, and other types of institutions as Mexico's economy is in great need of middle-level technicians prepared for specific regional and sectoral needs. Completion of a secondary course in a technical/vocational school may lead to the *bachillerato* and higher education or to the title of *técnico* (technician) and entrance into the job market. In addition to technical/vocational schools at the secondary level, there are also professional studies institutions in the arts, allied health, social work, military, pre-primary and primary teaching, and so on. These schools typically require the basic-cycle secondary diploma for admission and may lead directly to work or to higher education studies. There also exists a series of regional technological institutes at both the secondary and higher education levels designed to prepare individuals for a number of technical specialties. There were thirty-two of these regional institutes serving 39,000 students in operation in 1974–1975.

Teacher education represents a third type of upper or superior cycle secondary school in Mexico. All pre-primary, primary, and physical education teachers as well as all industrial arts and agricultural teachers working in basic-cycle secondary schools receive four years of normal school preparation at this level. Teachers for the basic-cycle secondary schools and normal schools are prepared in a four-year superior normal school program that graduates students as licentiates. There also exist two specialized normal schools for preparing teachers of special education. There are no specially designated programs for the preparation of teachers for either the upper cycle secondary schools or for any postsecondary institutions (Gill, 1977).

The normal schools for pre-primary and primary teachers have experienced a dramatic increase in enrollment in this decade and have undergone some curricular revisions since 1975. The curriculum is to have been adapted to the school reform legislation as well as reduced in scope and limited in hours. School officials, teachers, and students were to be involved in planning instructional programs. The new curriculum is intended to focus on three areas: (a) the sciences and humanities; (b) the physical, artistic, and technical; and (c) professional courses including practice teaching. The *bachillerato* diploma is to be granted to graduates of these programs, thereby enabling them to make application to universities and other *preparatoria* institutions (Gill, 1977). Students preparing to become basic-cycle secondary schoolteachers in superior normal schools specialize in one or more of the subjects commonly taught at the secondary level. The reforms of 1975 establish, among others, the licentiate as the minimal degree for teaching in the secondary school, higher admission standards, and provide more mechanisms whereby in-service teachers can earn titles (Gill, 1977).

Study in higher education institutions is intended to prepare individuals for a chosen profession. Professional degree programs at the licentiate level are available in the natural and exact sciences, medical sciences, agricultural and animal husbandry sciences, engineering and technology, social and administrative sciences, and education and humanities. Postgraduate studies have expanded considerably since the early 1970s, involving greater diversity in the fields of study and the initiation of a few programs at both the master's and doctoral level. In 1975–1976 there were 545,182 students registered in licenciate and 18,944 in graduate programs.

At the higher education level, the nature of study is dependent on the institution attended. There exist public autonomous, public state, and private independent universities as well as two hybrid models. These latter two types are public institutions dependent on the government and private institutions recognized by the Secretariat of Public Education, by state governments, or by quasi-governmental organizations (Rangel, 1978). Students at the university level study for a period of four to six years. If they are enrolled in public institutions, they are expected to spend a period following receipt of their degree in a form of social service involving the practice of their profession in the community (Gill, 1977).

The curriculum at a university is usually established within each *facultad* (department) by a committee composed of the dean and representatives of the students and the faculty from that department. In recent years, a trend toward the development of a common core "program," interdisciplinary studies, and a reduction in the number of years required for certain higher degrees has been noted in several institutions (Rangel, 1978). At the same time, the curriculum at the university level has been criticized for its traditional orientation and its lack of response to the needs and problems of the country (CEE, 1977).

One interesting innovation within the Mexican school curriculum has been the initiation of *el sistema abierto* (the open school). *El sistema abierto* features open enrollment in addition to counseling for those involved in adult programs. Great use is made of radio and television programs geared toward an adult audience. Primarily the program has been directed to provide credentials such as the *primaria*, *secundaria*, and *preparatoria* for the working class. However, as recently as 1978, the program received criticism as to the viability of curricula in these programs as well as the follow-through and monitoring of students and their overall plan of study. Its overall effectiveness within the Mexican educational scheme is yet to be assessed.

### Curriculum, Nonacademic

Nonacademic aspects of the school curricula differ in accord with the level, type, and locale of the institution. The extent to which such curricula form an integral part of the educational experience is often decided by school administrators and teachers rather than by representatives of the national secretariat.

In elementary schools, some attention is typically given to physical education and athletics, with calisthenics and marching instruction for both boys and girls accompanying participation in team games like football or soccer for boys and volleyball for both boys and girls. It is also common for elementary schools to pay some attention to music through group singing and perhaps the sponsorship of a select number of students to form a school chorus. Children, especially girls, may also receive instruction in folk dancing. In certain schools, a few children may have an opportunity to participate in special enrichment periods devoted to a form of the arts, including learning to draw or learning to play a musical instrument.

The extent to which an elementary school offers a nonacademic curriculum depends on the resources it has available and whether it is urban or rural. With a very modest facility and limited equipment and supplies, the nonacademic curriculum often represents little more than calisthenics and team sports. If religious or national holiday celebrations are highly valued, practice in calisthenics to make appearances in parades and processions occupies much of the nonacademic school period. During a morning or afternoon recess, as well as during lunch periods, free play may occupy the major portion of the time available for nonacademic pursuits.

At the secondary level, the newer, more affluent neighborhoods may have modern school facilities with classrooms and work areas equipped for cooking, sewing, and typing instruction for girls and carpentry and electricity for boys. Special arts and music instruction may also be available in such schools at a cost above the normal tuition already paid by students and parents for school attendance. Student government activities are quite prevalent, and much time is devoted to student-related activities. In some instances whole days are provided for voting procedures and student demonstrations.

In lower socioeconomic neighborhoods, the nonacademic curricula may include only intramural team sports and a modest program in group singing and folk dancing. Because so many secondary school students are occupied with part-time employment, few after-school activities are planned in most schools. This characteristic also limits the extent to which individuals participate in student clubs or other special interest programs.

At the university level, the dominant organizational unit for students is the major field or *facultad* in which they are studying. Through the *facultad* the students maintain a spirit of cooperation and cohesion, especially for social events and school-related activities. Another important nonacademic unit for students in universities is the political group. The interest of political groups rests largely with national social and economic issues for which the university setting becomes a center for organization and planning. On occasion the university also provides the setting for demonstrations of national and international solidarity of a political nature. A great deal of factionalism and ideological cleavage exist within and between student organizations on the secondary and university levels.

As is evidenced by these examples of student organizations, university students are typically autonomous in their activities, and the university administration assumes little responsibility for engaging them in nonacademic curricula. When the administration does assume some responsibility, the outcomes are likely to include student involvement in university government, athletic competition with intramural or extramural opposition, special interest clubs, or student newspaper publishing. As with the elementary and secondary schools, the extent to which nonacademic curriculum is implemented at the university depends on its administration, clientele, and resources.

### Student Evaluation

Progress through the school system is dependent on students independently achieving a satisfactory end-of-year course or standardized examination grade. Although there is some effort to introduce letter grades, typically teachers record numbers on the basis of a 10-point scale with a 6 or 7 constituting a minimum passing grade. Where letters are used, they are descriptive of a particular level of competency, such as MB (*muy bien*) for very good, B (*bien*) for good, S (*suficiente*) for passing, and NA (*no acreditada*) for not passing (Gill, 1977).

At the elementary level, major examinations occur at the end of each semester. These are standardized examinations prepared by the Secretariat of Education. At the end of the year, a standardized examination is administered over the subject matter covered during that entire year. There is no overall examination at the end of six years of primary school.

Beginning at the secondary level, examinations are no longer standardized; instead teachers prepare their own exams to cover their own particular content field. Students move from teacher to teacher and class to class; hence a single student emerges with separate grades from a series of teachers and courses.

At the advanced secondary, or *preparatoria,* level an examination must be passed to enter the institution. This is a general aptitude and achievement test prepared and administered by universities. The student typically appears at the school where he or she wishes to matriculate and the examination is given at that time. Throughout the advanced secondary school period, course examinations constitute the major source for grades. The examinations occur at the end of each semester and at times in the middle of a semester. Because the advanced secondary school is heavily influenced by the university, there is no examination required to graduate from upper secondary school. One simply applies to the university and, if the grades have been good at the secondary level, acceptance is common. It should be noted that entrance into the university is often incumbent upon the number of student places available. Entrance into parochial and private institutions may be facilitated through political and informal means. Examinations for entrance into the university are generally utilized by departments like medicine, engineering, business administration, and law which are more competitive and tend to have a higher status attached to them.

At the university level, examinations are also by semester. To receive the *licenciatura,* or equivalent to four years of university training, a student in many institutions must also present a thesis and undergo an oral examination. The thesis and examination are used to represent one's competency and ability in a chosen field. A committee of professors typically meets with the student, and the student presents his or her thesis orally. No written examination is required for graduation. Employers sometimes rely on the completion of the thesis and examination as evidence of professional competency.

Because approximately 40 percent of the Mexican population over fifteen years of age has not completed primary education, the new Federal Law on Education now makes it possible to be certified through examination without returning to the primary school classroom. Prior to this new law, an individual would have to return to the last primary grade from which he or she withdrew and complete the remaining primary grades. The new law recognizes that a given individual might well have acquired sufficient knowledge and skills outside of school to permit him to pass an equivalency primary school examination. Such a certificate permits an individual to enter or reenter the formal system at the middle technical/vocational or preprofessional level. This practice makes the prospects for bolstering nonformal education programs, designed to assist youth and adults in learning the skills necessary to pass the primary school examination, quite good (Ingrams, 1975).

## Counseling

It is unusual to find specially designated full- or part-time counselors of either a vocational or personal social-emotional type in the schools at any level of the system. There appear to be two major reasons for this characteristic of Mexican education. The first is a financial one, as the Mexican economy has been unable to support adequate personnel and facilities for education in the country and appears to be falling farther behind in simply providing places for all those interested in entering the system. The second reason is a cultural one in that the extended family and peer group typically act as a collective resource to assist in social and psychological problem areas as well as in career decision making. For these financial and cultural reasons, counselors have not been institutionalized at any level of Mexican education. Although in some public secondary schools a counselor for vocational guidance might be present, apparently few depart from this career focus into other counseling arenas.

At the elementary level in some areas, the teacher may well play an important role in counseling activities. In the rural area, for example, the teacher may be viewed as a community leader, as a knowledgeable source of information about world affairs, and as a fount of information regarding occupational opportunities. As the child enters the early years of secondary school, however, only the exploratory nature of the curriculum provides some exposure to various fields of study. In this sense the curriculum constitutes a form of educational and vocational counseling. As the student goes into advanced secondary education, he or she is likely to hold a job and study only part time. Here the student gets direct exposure to the world of work, and his school studies become secondary. Again, this kind of exposure may be viewed as a form of vocational counseling of a trial-and-error nature.

In higher education, most professors are part time, and counseling is not considered part of their function. Professors are generally poorly paid, must hold down more than one position, and are not, therefore, in sustained residence at a single institution. This takes them away from a potential role as counselor, as they are constantly on the move. The full-time professors are often occupied with administrative problems, and counseling is not viewed as one of their functions. This does not mean that teachers at all levels of the system do not occasionally function as counselors, but that their own perception of their position does not specify counseling as an aspect of their job.

Although the long-term prospects for including specially prepared counselors at all levels of the system are probably present in Mexico as in many other Third World countries, to date educational institutions have not assumed this additional responsibility. Instead, the individual, his or her family and friends, and perhaps other important individuals in the person's life assume the responsibility for vocational and personal guidance. Because students enter the job market at an earlier age in Mexico than in many other countries, they also receive firsthand exposure to the world of work and to potential career opportunities. Cultural and fiscal constraints likely pose the greatest obstacles to altering this noninstitutional yet long-standing approach by youngsters to personal socioemotional and career education.

### Discipline

Discipline in Mexican schools can be characterized as noncorporal in nature with a reliance on psychological and sociological inducements. An infraction of the rules at the elementary level might receive a punishment like standing in a corner of the room for a portion of the day or writing a hundred times that the student will not repeat whatever it was he or she was doing. Likewise, a student may be taken to the principal's office. These types of punishment are typical for classroom infractions of rules concerning talking without permission, not paying attention to the teacher, or some similar behavior.

Social pressure tends to operate effectively for other infractions of school rules. For example, during the 1950s girls were forbidden to wear pants to school. Now they are permitted to wear them during the winter, but such attire is still not completely accepted, and often girls wear a skirt or dress over pants. Such dress codes are generally not a problem at the secondary level, however, as public schools require a uniform for both boys and girls. Boys wear khaki uniforms with a tie, and girls wear a jumper and blouse. The rules of the school combined with general acceptance of appropriate dress codes by the students themselves reinforce the appropriate uniform.

At the elementary and secondary levels of the system, disciplinary infractions might result in the receipt of bad grades, negative reports to parents, or after-school obligations like cleaning up the school grounds. Teachers might call parents and ask them to visit the school to talk about a problem the teacher is having with the youngster. This conference, in turn, may lead to expulsion from the school for a few days, a week, or permanently.

Truancy is monitored by the school system, indirectly through grades, especially at the secondary school level where students can be penalized for missing classes. At the elementary level, attendance is kept, and parents must sign a grade report at the end of each month. Such a policy assists in enhancing school attendance.

At the higher education level, the autonomous nature of universities and the often volatile and politically inclined students may result in the boycott of courses. In many universities there is the practice of "blacklisting" students who participate in disruptive student activities. Action such as expulsion and refusal to grant further enrollment within the school is often leveled against student leaders. It is further assumed that all students will lose in the end, as they will not secure course credits for the periods they did not attend.

Overall, the approach to discipline is characterized by teacher and administrator authority intended to shape appropriate school behavior as well as instill acceptable personal and social values. The peer group is relied on for reinforcing these behaviors and values while the parents and family are ultimately held accountable for the infractions committed by their offspring. The role of the teacher or professor is to rely on his or her legitimacy in establishing and enforcing rules, much as the teacher or professor does in establishing him or herself as the source of valued knowledge.

## ROLES

Despite many recent attempts toward decentralization, the structure and bureaucracy of Mexican education has continued to practice a highly centralized form of authority that has dominated Mexican social and political history. The pre-Cortesian, colonial, postcolonial, and nationalist eras of Mexican education share common roots in that education, and especially the administration of education was always considered to be the province of the church or the republic rather than subject to regional or local discretion. Authority for any innovation, curricular infusion, or pedagogical changes had to always proceed from the capital to the outlying regions and provinces. Complete responsibility and governance of the educational system was always vested in the hands of the clerical or public educational officials who resided and administered in Mexico City.

At present, the educational system of Mexico and its various components continue to reflect the educational organizational patterns of the past. The principal department in charge of Mexican education is the Secretariat of Public Education. Although some specialized forms of education are entrusted to the Secretariats of Defense, Agriculture, and Stockraising, as well as the administration of a few select preparatory schools by the National University, the bulk of federal public education is regulated and governed through the Secretariat of Public Education in Mexico City. Likewise, the various elements of the educational system, especially its administrators, teachers, and students, are governed by the mandates of the secretariat, supplemented by those federal regulations embodied in the Federal Educational Law of 1973. The roles and duties of participants within the Mexican educational process are carefully provided within the parameters of federal regulations emanating from either the secretariat or the Federal Education Law.

### Administration

The overall obligations of the Secretariat of Public Education are vast in scope. It oversees and exercises control over federal schools of all types. Elementary, secondary, and normal schools supported by the states or private sources and all other forms of educational activities intended for farmers or workers as specified under Article 3 of the Federal Constitution are considered to be within the domain of secretariat control (Gill, 1977).

The Secretariat of Public Education is further divided into subsecretariats for elementary and teacher education; middle, technical, and higher education in addition to popular culture, nonformal education, and planning and coordination. The secretariat also appoints a federal director of education to supervise elementary education in each state and territory. Coordinating the work of these officers are the ten chiefs of school inspection zones on the national level (Dunsky, 1972). Working under the federal directors in the states are 500 regional inspectors (Jimenez Coria, 1970).

Under the provisions of Article 25 of the Federal Educational Law of 1973, the actual responsibilities of the federal director of education are specified within ten subarticles. He is expected to be well acquainted with both the urban and rural economies; to coordinate and articulate the educational program with that of the health, agrarian, and other agencies in the rural areas; and, in addition, he is to maintain working relations with the state and municipal educational authorities. In compliance with the education code, the federal director of education supervises the work of the regional inspectors, the school principals, and the teachers of the state. He is further charged with assigning teachers to the schools and transmitting to the central office of the secretariat all recommendations for salary increases and the promotion and/or transfer of personnel. The federal director of education may spend up to ten days per month visiting the schools of the state. Normally, he will make a monthly report to the Secretariat of Public Education regarding: (1) needs assessments of the schools; (2) statistical data regarding pupil populations; (3) decisions he has made pertaining to the schools; (4) recommendations and requests made by the regional inspectors and the principals; and (5) other items of concern to the secretariat (Dunsky, 1972).

Reporting to the federal director of education are the regional inspectors whose main responsibilities are to evaluate and maintain the quality and efficiency of federal educational programs throughout the district. The regional inspector is the immediate superior of the school principals within his district, and it is his job to evaluate their performance. The responsibilities of the regional inspector can be divided into three main tasks. He is charged with all material aspects, including school construction and repair, as well as the preparation and acquisition of teaching materials and the aesthetic and hygienic conditions of school buildings. Secondly, he must attend to technical aspects concerning the compilation and revision of the syllabi in accord with directives received from the federal director of education, which also involve the planning and improvement of teaching methods. His third major area of concern involves social aspects, such as research into the economic and social conditions of the district and coordination of public and private agencies linked with the educational process in his particular district. He is also called upon to develop and to ensure a spirit of patriotism within the schools and the larger community.

The regional inspector normally visits each school in his district three to four times a year. He will collaborate with the principal in decisions regarding the assignment of teachers within the school and the arrangement of the school's daily schedule. The inspector also reports to the federal director on the professional performance of the teachers and makes recommendations for their advancement and approves all requests for teacher transfers (Dunsky, 1972).

In accord with the Federal Educational Code, elementary and secondary school principals are the chief authorities responsible for the proper organization, operation, and administration of the schools. The numerous tasks and obligations of the school principal are enumerated under the regulations for school personnel as established by the Secretariat of Public Education. The chief responsibility of the principal is to foster the daily functions of the school in relation to personnel, maintenance of buildings, student activities, curricula, and discipline. He must faithfully execute all the directives issued by the Secretariat of Public Education, the federal director of education, and the regional inspector. In essence, the principal represents the last link within the administrative structure which extends from the Secretariat of Public Education, housed in Mexico City, to the local school. Each component within the administrative ladder is conscious of its specific role and function within the overall Mexican educational scheme as specified by federal educational regulations and supplemental directives.

## Faculty

In accordance with federal regulations, the teacher is responsible for maintaining school regulations and programs of study, following authorized teaching methods, and imparting the prescribed content of instruction. The role of the teacher becomes increasingly important in those rural schools when he or she actually lives in the school building and is responsible for the care of the property, aiding the parents' association in fund raising, assisting with the annual census, and providing other nonacademic services for the community. In these situations, the teacher's role takes on an added dimension. Not only is the teacher charged with the instruction of young minds for the betterment of the community and the state, but he or she is also looked upon as a community resource and a possible leader by those who are served.

In the selection of teachers, the Secretariat of Public Education lists four desirable characteristics: (*a*) a teacher's vocation, recognized by a desire to teach; (*b*) social and cultural training manifested by the correct use of language, politeness, circumspection, capacity for self-development, and readiness for action; (*c*) the required professional preparation; and (*d*) certain practical skills in such areas as art, sports, and manual work (Ballesteros y Usano, 1970).

The daily activities and duties of the average teacher are specifically enumerated by the Federal Educational Code. They are as follows:

1. To present him/herself as an example of good grooming to the pupils;
2. To be punctual for school work and to remain at his or her post of duty for the time prescribed;
3. To make a lesson plan for each class and to evaluate the progress of each group;
4. To make systematic use of the teaching materials provided for each course;
5. To be responsible for the discipline of the pupils both within and outside of the classroom;
6. To remain with the pupils during special celebrations in which the school participates;
7. To maintain cleanliness in the classrooms and other service buildings attached to the school;

8. To perform weekly surveillance duties;
9. To cooperate fully with the principal in the functions of the school that relate to the local community;
10. To attend all the scheduled meetings and workshops;
11. To deliver to the principal an end-of-the-year statement (*documentación de fin de cursos*) in conformity with the education code (Dunsky, 1972).

In contrast to those teachers on the elementary and secondary levels, the role of the university or higher technical institute professor differs drastically. Unlike his or her counterpart in the lower levels of the educational process, the professor's duties are defined more in consideration of the needs of a particular institution. The main task is the dissemination of particular curricular content relative to a professional specialty. It is also quite common for teachers, other than those within the administration ranks, to have an outside professional job in an area related to a particular teaching assignment. A professor in Mexican higher education, in comparison to elementary and secondary counterparts, is much less affected by time constraints and community obligations. The professor resembles more a paid professional than a public servant (Caballero, 1973).

## Students

The primary role of the Mexican student is to study. Looked upon, especially in the postrevolutionary period, as a national resource and a hope for future national development, students are obligated during their primary and secondary schooling to uphold "standards of excellence" as reflected in the school system and their teachers. For this reason, the role of a student tends to be rather formal. Punctuality and respect are called for within the confines of the classroom. When a teacher enters the room, students must rise and address him or her with an appropriate greeting. In many instances, students are assessed on their manners and general deportment in addition to academic achievement. Within the classroom, students are expected to give undivided attention to their teacher and be ready to respond when called upon in class. All queries or responses in class will not be recognized by the teacher unless preceded by a raised hand or permission to speak. In general, classroom etiquette is constantly observed and enforced with little deviation. From the early years of primary education, a Mexican student quickly learns the rules of appropriate classroom conduct and procedures.

Although students are taught to respect teachers and education at the preschool and primary levels, disrespect for teachers often begins at the secondary level. Possible reasons for this disrespect stem from the absenteeism of teachers, the part-time nature of many instructors, poor teacher preparation, large class enrollments, and the consequent inability of teachers to monitor a student's work individually.

It is expected that each student will strive toward his or her maximum potential while attending school. When failure occurs at any grade level, it is directly attributed to the inability of the student rather than the school or the teacher. The Mexican school system places a great emphasis upon the level of achievement. Often within particular schools, good grades are not only rewarded with commendations, medals, and certificates for outstanding academic performances, but also social privileges and responsibilities. Class officers in primary and secondary schools are often chosen by their teachers and peers, based upon their academic skills. It is common to find that the class president is also the student with the best academic record. Enhancing an individual's status and responsibilities is used as a motivating factor by teachers and the educational system to improve class performance. The Mexican student rapidly equates academic success with success in general.

Although the Mexican educational process is highly competitive, students are also taught to cooperate and to aid one another in their efforts. Often class officers are expected to act as peer counselors and tutors to those students within their class who are having academic difficulties or problems. In some instances, the class president may monitor and review the work of low achievers or students who are not progressing well in particular subjects. It should be noted that throughout the educational system, both on a national and a local basis, cooperation as well as competition is stressed. Government-placed signs such as "educación para desarollo nacional" (education for national development) seen throughout the countryside emphasize the fact that education is viewed as an instrument for the common good, rather than as a vehicle only for individual attainment.

Classroom participation is encouraged both on the primary and the secondary levels. A premium is placed upon reading aloud, recitation, oral interpretation, and critical review of literary and historical works. Much of a student's grade is based upon his or her ability to generate ideas orally within the classroom. Nevertheless, classroom participation is done in a rather orderly fashion and always at the behest and discretion of the teacher. In the later years of secondary training, seminar groups are provided where students can concern themselves with more abstract subjects and theoretical notions in a less confining atmosphere. Here students can freely exchange ideas and are given latitude to interact and discuss with their teacher. This is especially true of the secondary-preparatory cycle.

Students are expected to perform academically and socially in accord with school standards and mandates. They are required to pay close attention to personal hygiene and proper care of their clothing (uniforms are often worn in public as well as private schools). School assemblies are usually held on a weekly basis to inform students of new rules or upcoming events.

In general, student advocacy and activism occur at the university level, rather than the primary or secondary levels. Although secondary school students may voice their political views on issues, they participate at a lesser level in large-scale political or other demonstrations. Within the Mexican educational process, the university has traditionally been the commentator and critic of Mexican national policy and reforms. Since 1968, beginning with the student riots in Mexico City, the university has taken an active role in addressing issues of social and political injustice. Emanating from the National University of Mexico and incorporating other universities like those of Guadalajara, Morelos, and Puebla, within a ten-year span student activist groups composed of both the right and left have actively sought to bring about changes within the national structure (Escudero and Rocca, 1978). Their political tactics have ranged in scope from mass demonstrations, confrontations, strikes, boycotts, and total takeovers of the university.

Between 1968 and 1978, the university movement has given rise to thousands of political activists, radical trade unionists, intellectuals, poets, artists, and leaders. The university movement has conceived political parties, civic groupings, and mass organizations. It has also fostered major democratic movements in the universities, not only in Mexico City, but in Sinaloa, Querétaro, Zacatecas, Nayarit, Monterrey, Guerrero, and Oaxaca (Escudero and Rocca, 1978). The present thrust of student advocacy in Mexico is in keeping with the traditional role and function of the university within Latin American society. The university is viewed as not only a place to study but also an institution where social ideas can be tried and applied within a real context.

**Parents**

It is the major responsibility of all Mexican parents to send their children to school. In general, the concept of *educación* represents not only a formal process of schooling but also a transformation of the self. A person or child who acquires education also acquires the virtues of dignity and respect. Within the Mexican value system, education and its attainment are directly equated with honor and success. For this reason, there are strong motivations for the parents to support and encourage their children to remain within the formal schooling system.

No formal mechanisms exist within the Mexican educational system to cope with parental grievances. Grievances by parents and any informal counseling are usually handled directly between the parent and the teacher. It is generally the responsibility of the individual teacher to contact or call parents in cases of a student-related problem. Generally, once or twice within the academic school year, there are parent-teacher conferences where parents can come to the school and learn about their children's present academic standing. Courses of instruction that deal with family counseling or child rearing are rarely provided for parents. Such activities are generally relegated to the Church and other social agencies outside the educational system.

The major body for organized parental activities within the school structure is provided by the Parents' Association which is required in each school by the Mexican Educational Code (Article 115, 116). The primary purpose of the Parents' Association is to aid the school "materially, socially, economically, and morally." However, it does not concern itself with the technical and administrative aspects of the school. Within the primary school cycle, the Parents' Association is often housed within another administrative body called the Technical Advisory Council. Every elementary school with four or more teachers is required to establish a Technical Advisory Council (*Consejo Técnico Consultivo*) which consists of the following members: (1) the principal and all the instructional staff; (2) a delegation representing the Parents' Association; and (3) a delegation elected from the student body.

The Technical Advisory Council typically meets outside school hours, is presided over by the principal, and treats such matters as the planning of school activities, both curricular and cocurricular, methods of teaching, discipline problems, plans for the improvement of school work, health and hygiene, school cooperatives, finance, the cultural and professional improvement of the teaching staff, and the needs of the community and the involvement of community members in school drives (Dunsky, 1972).

## SYSTEM IN ACTION

Mexico operates a dual educational system, with the federal government and the states each supporting and administering schools, often located near each other. The Secretariat of Public Education has complete charge of all federal elementary schools and also directs those schools that the federal government subsidizes. Originally, Article 3 of Mexico's 1917 Constitution required that: (*a*) instruction would be free, (*b*) instruction in public schools would be secular, (*c*) private elementary schools might be established subject to official federal supervision. Other articles provided for compulsory school attendance of children under fifteen and for school maintenance by agricultural, industrial, and mining enterprises (Gill, 1969, 1977). Ostensibly, the provisions for the establishment of public education have been altered only slightly over the past sixty years.

Mexico is divided into five major school zones: the North Pacific Zone which comprises Baja California de Sur, Baja California Norte, Sonora, Sinaloa, and Nayarit; the South Pacific Zone comprising Colima, Guerrero, Oaxaca, and Chiapas; the Central Zone consisting of Aguascalientes, Hidalgo, Jalisco, Guanajuato, México, Michoacan, Morelos, Puebla, Tlaxcala, Querétaro, and the Distrito Federal; the Gulf Zone comprising Campeche, Quintana Roo, Tabasco, Yucatán, and Veracruz; and the Northern Zone which contains Chihuahua, Coahuila, Durango, Nuevo Leon, Tamaulipas, San Luis Potosí, and Zacatecas (Dunsky, 1972). Although each of the zones adheres to standardized curricula and textbook materials, the educational setting within each differs in accordance with its particular resources and the assessed needs. This regionalism plays a very important part in determining the actual day-to-day experiences and roles that students assume. Urban and rural differences within the educational setting are further accentuated by regional and cultural diversity within the Mexican social milieu. These differences determine many of the curricular and noncurricular aspects of a student's total educational experience.

### Pre-primary and Primary Education

In both pre-primary and primary cycles of Mexican education, there is a strong emphasis on acquiring skills in arts and crafts. The lower grades are especially concerned with the development of such skills as well as encouragement of cultural awareness. Folklore, especially music and dance, receive considerable attention. History and patriotism are subjects that the primary student also encounters at an early stage in formal education. National hymns, patriotic essays, and an emphasis on the rote memorization of historic battles and popular heroes is standard fare in the curriculum of a primary student.

This tendency for an appreciation of the arts and humanities rather than the physical and applied sciences results in a student's day being spent in the acquiring of appreciation for the arts, the reading of literature and historical essays, and a modest proportion of time devoted to mathematics and natural sciences. Within the primary cycle there also tends to be an almost fundamentalist approach to education, emphasizing psychomotor skills at the expense of intellectual and cognitive development. The ability to maintain notebooks, penmanship, deportment, and a conformism to the learning setting at times takes precedence over other aspects of individual growth and development.

Another major factor facing students in the Mexican primary school cycle is the very high student-teacher ratios, in both the urban and rural areas. Crowded classes with little individual student-to-teacher interaction greatly affect the overall schooling process. Lack of student-teacher relationships vital to individual growth and role modeling in addition to nonindividualized instruction are symptomatic of the overcrowding problem in Mexican primary education. This situation, however, is greatly alleviated in private institutions where there are smaller class sizes and where a greater emphasis is placed on individualized instruction and personal development.

An added dimension within the school setting in Mexico, which is symptomatic of other developing nations as well, is the effect that the teaching profession has on the educational process. In both the primary and secondary school cycles is a predominant attitude of a number of teachers that teaching is a means to survival and livelihood rather than a respected profession. Such an attitude is related to low teacher wages and the need for most teachers to hold down more than one job as well as the way in which teacher preparation is viewed in and out of the profession. Nevertheless, it should be noted that the Mexican government has attempted to raise the status of teachers through the use of government-sponsored campaigns to increase trained and skilled teachers throughout the nation. In spite of national efforts to upgrade the teaching profession, Mexican students must still contend with poorly paid and overburdened instructors who have little time to help students individually.

### Secondary

Within the constraints of the educational process, by the time a student reaches the secondary level, he is already likely to have chosen a major field of study. Although the basic secondary cycle offers latitude in the choice of curricula, it attempts to prepare the student for the later entrance into the secondary-technical, normal, and preparatory educational cycles. Between the ages of fifteen and seventeen the students must then select a career. Upon entering the upper secondary level, the student, in accord with the curricular choices given to him within the chosen cycle, often finds that he is virtually locked into his career objective. Courses, in general, are not easily transferred from one cycle to another. An example of this "lockout mechanism" are students who have entered an upper secondary, technical educational cycle who then wish to transfer into the *preparatoria* geared toward university studies. To accomplish the transfer, these students must sacrifice time and accumulated credits. Presently in the upper secondary and higher levels of Mexican education there exist very few avenues for institutional articulation among the various cycles of programming and curricula.

Within the upper secondary levels a student's curriculum, in light of educational decentralization efforts, is often affected by regional differences and needs, especially in upper level technical institutes. A technical institute like the one in the port city of Veracruz would tend to emphasize skills and courses related to canneries, the fishing industry, and oceanography; while a technical institute in the cities of Toluca and Querétaro would emphasize skills related to light industry, mechanics, production, and engineering.

## PROSPECT

Although the Mexican educational system has made great strides in increasing the actual numbers of individuals enrolled and the financial support for schools, many problems and issues continue to characterize the system. For example, a large proportion of the population remains without a basic education, facilities are not available to potential students, and many individuals desert the system before graduation. The quality and preparation of the teachers are often questioned, and the methods and resources they employ as part of their instructional program are said to lead to a less than satisfactory educational experience.

In 1975 the then president of Mexico, Luis Echeverría, highlighted the educational achievements of Mexico for the period 1970–1975. Examples from these highlights include a quadrupling of federal budgetary support to education, more than a doubling of secondary school enrollments, the doubling of the number of technical schools constructed, a fivefold increase in the higher education budget, and a substantial increase in the number of higher education students. The president characterized the 1970–1975 period with these and many other accomplishments in education as without historical precedent in Mexico (Gill, 1977).

As with any national educational system similar in quantitative and qualitative dimensions to that of Mexico, however, educational problems are numerous and complex.

Although such problems might be identified for any country in the world, the fact is that Mexico has yet to provide a basic education for a large proportion of its population and that there is a great disparity between access to schools when viewed by social class and urban or rural residence. Furthermore, because it is important that Mexico become self-sufficient in trained human resources, many of the problems of efficiency, quality, and relationships between education and the work place are major obstacles to further industrialization and national development. Mexico's desire to create a critical, nationalistic, and participatory population is also limited not only by the large numbers who are unserved by existing programs, but by those who are poorly served in institutions of low quality.

As with other countries, many catalysts and solutions to educational issues actually emanate from outside rather than inside schools or other educational programs. In Mexico, the importance of the national political leadership in setting educational plans and priorities, for example, is only partially influenced by members of the education profession. Likewise, the economy of Mexico will in many respects dictate the availability of resources for educational activities. Given a favorable political and economic climate, it is perhaps Mexico's office of the president and his appointed secretary of public education, therefore, more than any other where the prospects for Mexican education rest. Here traditionally the intellectual leadership and the educational futures have been established. Here also the new answers to Mexico's current educational problems will have to emerge. Once the answers are proposed, the availability of resources and the preparedness of members of the education profession will determine their viability.

## GLOSSARY OF SPANISH TERMS

*afrancesado:* Influence of French culture and attitudes, largely brought to Mexico during the reign of Maximilian and the French occupation of Mexico (1861–1866).

*bachillerato:* Technically a bachelor's degree; however, in the American context it is the equivalent of a high school or secondary school diploma. It is awarded after the completion of the *secundaria* or the *preparatoria.*

*calmeac:* An Aztec seminary where the sons of nobility received instruction that prepared them to be priests, public officials, and military leaders.

*calpulli:* Hierarchy of Aztec society encompassing the warrior nobility, priests, merchants, and free peasants.

*científico:* The name given to government officials and civil servants in the era of the profiriato, who adhered to the concepts of scientific thought, foreign investment in Mexico, and French Positivistic philosophy.

*colegio:* That segment of the Mexican educational scheme that comprises the lower and upper secondary levels of education.

*criollo:* That part of the population of Nueva España whose ancestry was completely Spanish but who were born in Mexico.

*escuela de acción:* An educational philosophy in Mexico made popular in the 1920s by Jose Vasconcelos that emphasized the relevancy of education to culture and social action and that actively promoted the proliferation of schools in the rural parts of Mexico.

*hacienda:* Feudal agricultural system (based on the Spanish *encomienda*) which virtually bound most indigenous peoples in Mexico to the land and to the service of a *hacendado*, or landowner.

*La Raza Cósmica:* A term popularized by the philosopher and educator Vasconcelos that represents the homogenization and ascendancy of mestizo culture in Mexico.

*licenciatura:* A degree awarded in postsecondary institutions equivalent to an American college or university B.A. degree. One who possesses the *licenciatura* has the title of *licenciado*.

*missiones culturales:* Teams of individuals assigned to communities in the rural countryside within the "escuelas de acción" period, which emphasized regionalism, social action, and local culture through education.

*Nueva España:* The colonies of Spain encompassing the areas of present-day Mexico and Central America.

*primeras letras:* That segment of the Mexican educational scheme that encompasses the beginning years of primary education.

*porfiriato:* The rule of Porfirio Diaz, president of the republic and virtual dictator of Mexico from 1876 to 1911.

*tepochcalli:* An Aztec school for the sons of merchants, craftsmen, and commoners where the art of war and the basis of religion were taught.

## REFERENCES

Ballesteros Usano, A. *Organización de la Esuela Primaria.* Mexico: Editorial Patna, 1970.

Benveniste, G. *Bureaucracy and National Planning: A Sociological Case Study in Mexico.* New York: Praeger, 1970.

*Boletín de educación* 1, No. 2 (November 1914).

Caballero, F. R. "Consideraciones en Torno al Desarrollo de Nuevas Universidades en Mexico," *Revista de la Educación Superior* 2, No. 4 (1973): 14–22.

*Centro de estudios educativos programa,* 1977.

Cummings, R. L., and Lemke, D. A. (eds.) *Educational Innovations in Latin America.* Metuchen, N.J.: The Scarecrow Press, 1973.

Dunsky, E. S. "Role of the Elementary Principal in Community Developments." Ph.D. dissertation, University of California at Los Angeles, 1972.

*El Gobierno Mexicano.* Publicacion Mensual De La Dirección General de Información y Relaciones Públicas (April 1977).

Escudero, R., and Rocca, S. "Mexico Generation of 68," *NACLA Report on the Americas* 12, No. 5 (Sept.–Oct. 1978).

Estrada, L. J., and Nava, A. "The Long Struggle for Bilingualism and a Consistent Language Policy: Early Chicano Education in California and the Southwest," *UCLA Educator* (1976).

Faust, A. F. "A Cultural History of Mexican Education," in *Mexican Education in Cultural Perspective,* ed. Stanley D. Ivie. College of Education Monograph Series No. 5. Tucson: University of Arizona, 1971.

Garrard, J. L. "A Survey of the Education of the Indian of Mexico as a Factor in Their Incorporation into Modern Mexican Society." Ph.D. dissertation, University of Washington, 1956.

Gill, C. C. *The Educational System of Mexico.* U.S. Dept. of Health, Education and Welfare, Office of Education. Washington, D.C.: U.S. Government Printing Office, 1977.

Ingrams, J. D. "Mexico's Federal Education Law of 1973: Its Implications for Nonformal Education." Paper presented at the Comparative and International Education Society, San Francisco, March 1975.

Jimenez Coria, L. *Organización Escola.* Mexico: Fernandez Editores, 1970.

Keen, B. *The Aztec Image in Western Thought.* New Brunswick, N.J.: Rutgers University Press, 1971.

Kneller, G. F. *The Education of the Mexican Nation.* New York: Columbia University Press, 1951.

McAndrews, J. *Open Air Churches of 16th Century Mexico.* Cambridge, Mass.: Harvard University Press, 1965.

Palavicini, F. *La Patria por la Escuela.* Mexico: Fondo de Cultura y Económica, 1902.

Rangel Guerra, A. *Systems of Higher Education: Mexico.* New York: International Council for Educational Development, 1978.

Romanell, P. "The Challenge of Contemporary Mexican Philosophy to Mexican Education," in *Mexican Education in Cultural Perspective,* ed. Stanley D. Ivie. College of Education Monograph Series No. 5. Tucson: University of Arizona, 1971.

*Secretaria de educación plan* (1959).

Secretaria de Educación Pública *El Maestro* 1, No. 2 (1921a) and 1, No. 4 (1921b).

Secretaria de Instrucción Pública y Bellas Artes. *Congreso Nacional de Educacion Primaria. Antecedentes, Actas, Debates y Resoluciones,* 2 vols. Mexico: Secretaria de Instrucción Pública y Bellas Artes: 1912.

Sierra, J. *La Educación Nacional, Obras Completas,* Vol. 8. Mexico: Universidad Nacional Autónoma de México, 1948.

Soustelle, J. *Daily Life of the Aztecs.* Stanford, Calif.: Stanford University Press, 1961.

Thompson, E. *The Rise and Fall of Mayan Civilization.* Norman, Okla.: University of Oklahoma Press, 1966.

Thut, I. N., and Adams, D. *Educational Patterns in Contemporary Societies.* New York: McGraw-Hill Book Co., 1964.

Turner, F. C. *The Dynamics of Mexican Nationalism.* Chapel Hill, N.C.: The University of North Carolina Press, 1968.

Weinberg, M. *A Chance to Learn: A History of Race and Education in the United States.* Cambridge: Cambridge University Press, 1977.

CHAPTER 8

# Education in the Soviet Union

## BRIAN HOLMES

### DEFINITION[1]

According to the Constitution (Fundamental Law) of the Soviet Union, education is regarded as a human right. Article 45 of the Constitution adopted in 1977 states that

> Citizens of the U.S.S.R. have the right to education. This right is ensured by free provision of all forms of education, by the institution of universal, compulsory, secondary education, and broad development of vocational, specialized secondary, and higher education, in which instruction is oriented toward practical activity and production; by the development of extramural, correspondence and evening courses; by the provision of state scholarships and grants and privileges for students; by the free issue of school textbooks; by the opportunity to attend a school where teaching is in the native language; and by the provision of facilities for self-education.[2]

Terms such as *vospitanie* (upbringing or character education), *obrazovanie* (education), *politekhnicheskoe obrazovanie* (polytechnical education), and *obuchanie* (training) make it possible to differentiate between processes referred to as the upbringing of children, their general, specialized, and polytechnical education, and their training for specific jobs in industry, as athletes, and so on. These somewhat different concepts find expression in the names given to schools which provide a general education (*obshcheo obrazovatelnaya shkoly*), secondary polytechnical education (*srednie politekhnicheskie shkoly*), and vocational training (*professionalno-tekhnicheski uchilishcha*). Such forms of provision are features of a system of schooling intended to ensure that education is available as a human right.

INTRODUCTION

### Objectives of Education

This emphasis on the rights of all Soviet citizens to an education explains the high priority given to equality of provision. In an article[3] by Soviet Minister of Education Mikhail Prokofyev aspects of policy designed to achieve equality of provision are illustrated. Regardless of where a boy or girl lives, whether in a city or a remote village, he or she should have an equal chance of going to a secondary school or institution of higher learning. To make sure children from the many linguistic groups have equal opportunities, lessons are conducted in fifty-seven of the different languages spoken in the country. Provision is made for children who are mentally retarded or physically handicapped, sometimes in special boarding schools. Admission to popular schools, universities, and institutes is based, not on ability to pay, but on a student's qualifications, aptitudes, and interests. Examinations reveal who are the better qualified students, and knowledge is the most important yardstick of success.

Equality of provision is regarded as necessary if all children are to receive an all-round upbringing—intellectual, moral, aesthetic, and physical—in ways that will enable them to contribute to the building of a communist society. N. K. Krupskaya (Lenin's widow to whose views great attention is still paid) wrote that:

> The Soviet system of education aims at developing every child's ability, activity, consciousness, personality, and individuality. . . . We are for the all-round development of our children—we want to make them strong physically and morally, teach them to be collectivists and not individualists. . . . For the collective does not destroy a child's personality, and it improves the quality and content of education.[4]

The promotion of all-round individual growth, through the collective, serves as a major societal objective. The offical view that schools have a common purpose—to train active builders of a communist society—has been frequently reiterated. For example, V. Yelyutin as minister of higher education in the Soviet Union wrote in 1959 that:

> The role of Soviet education is to assist in the building up of a communist society, in shaping the materialist world outlook of the students, equipping them with a good grounding in the different fields of knowledge and preparing them for socially useful work.[5]

State support for education, coeducation, a unified school system, the complete separation of school and other educational and training institutions from the church, and the establishment of broad contacts between school and society represent objectives toward the achievement of which the Soviet authorities have consistently worked. They constitute the basis on which policies have been built since in the early years of the post-Revolutionary period. Lenin, his wife Krupskaya, A. V. Lunacharsky (first commissar of education), M. I. Kalinen, and A. S. Makarenko analyzed the reasons why major changes should be made in the czarist system of education and put forward plans to achieve Communist objectives.

The formulation of policies designed to achieve equality is clearly a major responsibility of members of the Communist party. Article 6 of the 1977 Constitution states that the party is the leading and guiding force in Soviet society. Its members form the nucleus of the political system and all state and public organizations. As recently as 1972, L. I. Brezhnev stressed that any diminution in the role of the party might threaten the gains achieved in a socialist society.[6] The party's program of action, strategy, and tactics is based on the teaching of Karl Marx and V. I. Lenin. Its organization is derived from principles enunciated by the latter. The Communist party is therefore not open to all, but only to carefully selected representatives of the working classes and intellectuals. Its members work in various organizations such as the trade unions, the professions, youth movements, and so on and in their daily work offer centralized leadership. Party discipline is enforced by the majority and by superior bodies in its organization. It is a single all-union party with one program and the same rules. Branches are formed in factories, on farms, in schools, and in institutions of higher education. The Communist party holds a Congress of members not less than once every five years. Its Central Committee of which Brezhnev was elected first secretary in 1964, is elected by Congress. Party Congresses and Central Committees offer political leadership, formulate policy, and organize its implementation. The party's success depends on its ability to educate all Communists to internalize Marxist-Leninist principles.

### Reasons for This System

Any Soviet account of post-Revolution achievements provides reasons why the czarist system of education had to be changed. In a survey by Prokofyev[7] as minister of education, reference is made to the backward state of education in pre-Revolutionary Russia. For example, the 1897 census showed that among people over nine years old, only 28.4 percent could read and write. Among the non-Russian-speaking peoples the proportion of literates was worse, falling to 2 to 3 percent in Central Asia.

In 1911 only 150,000 teachers served a population of 150 million in the immense empire, and only about 8 million children were enrolled in schools. Such neglect made necessary determined attempts to wipe out illiteracy by giving peasants in the countryside, workers in factories, and soldiers in their barracks instruction in Russian or the native language of their choice.

Two or more fundamental reasons for change were made clear by Lenin.[8] The first was that czarist schools had divorced theory from practice and education from life; and secondly, capitalist education had created in all but a few of those who had received instruction a false consciousness that would have to be eliminated if a truly Communist society was to be created.

Lenin's analysis of the situation in a speech to the third All-Russian Congress of the Russian Young Communist League in the 1920's serves to highlight these defects of the czarist system and to explain why he placed on young Communists who had not been educated in czarist schools responsibility for re-educating adults. He urged members of the Russian Young Communist League to learn about communism not only by studying manuals and books about it. Such knowledge would, he claimed, perpetuate traditional mistakes and could well lead to the mere assimilation of Communist slogans. "You can become a Communist" he said, "only when you enrich your mind with a knowledge of all the treasures created by mankind."[9] Thus armed, members of the Young Communist League should help to educate and train their peers in Communist morality, which is based upon class consciousness. Lenin was, of course, speaking about the overthrow of capitalism but was anxious that gains made by the revolution should not be lost. Under the circumstances of the day he advised young Communists to go out into the rural areas to tackle illiteracy and as class-conscious members of society to go out and work among the people. Under present circumstances in the Soviet Union young people who have been selected for their hard work, loyalty, knowledge, and commitment are expected to participate in the education of other youngsters and, indeed, in the education of adults.

Under capitalism a satisfactory all-round development was not possible, but once the Revolution had wrested ownership of the means of production from the capitalists and thus destroyed the economic foundations of capitalism, a form of socialism allowed for the appropriate development and training of individuals. "The victory of the Great October Socialist Revolution and the establishment of the dictatorship of the proletariat signified that the first Programme of the Bolshevik Party had been fulfilled."[10]

With the overthrow of the capitalists, Soviet leaders were in a position to undertake new tasks. Lenin was under no illusions about the difficulties that faced them and the role leading class-conscious members of society as Octoberists, Pioneers, members of the Konsomol and the Communist party would have to play in the transformation of education and the creation of a new Soviet man. The role of party members explains why inevitably educationists eagerly await the major recommendations announced on the occasion of the Communist Party congresses held in Moscow. The evolution of educational policies and the reasons for them can be traced, at least in general outline, by consulting the reports of party congresses. In reviewing the work of the party, its secretary usually refers to directives established at the previous meeting of Congress, reflects on success and failure, and anticipates some general directions of policy. For example, in his report of the Central Committee to the 24th Congress in 1971, Brezhnev reported on rises in living standards, noted that the production and sale of manufactured goods had risen considerably, and made it clear that the party planned in the future to increase the production of and raise the quality of consumer goods and improve the cash incomes of school teachers, doctors, and members of other professions. Significantly, he proposed to raise "the *social consumption funds*" to improve medical services and develop education. The reaction among teachers and educationists when they heard this news was nothing less than joyous.

The success of the party's educational work in creating a new Soviet man with a psychology and morality fundamentally different from those educated in a bourgeois society was pointed out in his report to the 25th Party Congress. Brezhnev said,

> Soviet Man is a man, who having won his freedom, has been able to defend it in the most trying battles. A man who has been building the future unsparing of his energy and making every sacrifice. A man who, having gone through all trials has himself changed beyond recognition, combining ideological conviction and tremendous vital energy, culture, knowledge and the ability to use them. This is the man who, while an ardent patriot, has been and will always remain a consistent internationalist.[11]

The new man is the product of the Soviet school system. The future task of this system is to improve the Communist world outlook of the working people and mold them so that they can actively participate in building communism. The process of molding this new man will, Brezhnev concluded, be undertaken under the leadership of the Communist party, which relies on the foundations of educational method laid down in Marxist-Leninist doctrines, which are fundamentally different from those that informed education in czarist Russia.

## HISTORY

### Beginnings

It would be a mistake to accept uncritically that the present system of education in the Soviet Union has its origin in the Revolution of 1917. Much of what goes on today in Soviet schools resembles practices in Western European schools. Nicholas Hans[12] notes that on the eve of the Revolution the Russian tradition in education included an emphasis on social rather than child-centred aims. It was secular rather than dominated by the Church. Curricula were scientific-utilitarian in character, and humanism influenced the tone of education. Productive work was regarded as part of general education, and the notion of Russian nationalism found a place. Many of these features of a tradition molded by Peter the Great, Catherine II, and Alexander I show the influence of the French encyclopedists and physiocrats of the eighteenth century.

Hans regards Peter the Great as the founder of the Russian educational tradition. On his return from England in 1700 Peter founded a modern school of mathematics and navigation in Moscow along the lines of the mathematical school of Christ's Hospital in England. In taking this as his model for his reform, Peter consciously introduced scientific-utilitarian characteristics and weakened the classical tradition. Later Catherine II, drawing heavily on French ideas, accepted the Austrian school system as a model for the new system she hoped to introduce in Russia. It, too, was scientific-utilitarian, secular, and coeducational.

There can be little doubt that of the Western European influences in the Soviet system of schooling those derived from France and French encyclopedism are the most obvious. The break with classicism made it relatively easier for Russian and Soviet educationists to establish curricula in which more attention was paid to mathematics and the natural sciences than to literary subjects. And among the latter, modern foreign languages rather than "classical" foreign languages receive the most attention. Doubtless the war against Napoleon influenced Russian opinion, and while the reforms of Alexander I (who ascended the throne in 1801) owed much to French ideas, subsequently the movement to resist foreign innovations and emphasize Russian traditions grew stronger. Insofar as education retained a strong Western orientation, it was limited to that received by the upper and middle classes.

Notable among the nineteenth-century molders of the Russian tradition in education, which was inherited by the Bolsheviks, were N. I. Pirogov (1810–1881), K. D. Ushinsky (1824–1870), and L. N. Tolstoy (1828–1910). All these pioneers find some favor with Soviet historians of education in spite of some unacceptable features of their educational proposals. Each had a fairly distinctive role to play in the evolution of a system that when the Soviet government came to power, touched the lives of so few people. Secularism, scientific-utilitarianism, universal humanism, and nationalism were, however, features of czarist schools on which Soviet educationists could build. Today the attention paid to mathematics, the natural sciences, and modern languages in the general curriculum is a prominent feature of education.

Pirogov's central argument was that the main aim of education should be to "develop the inner man." He was an advocate of a general humanitarian education for all, and he wished to draw a distinction between this kind of education and specialized training for various occupations. General education should be provided for some pupils who wanted to go on to higher education and for others who were going into active life. Bifurcation at an appropriate level was to allow for this. Based on a distinction between classical and modern studies, this bifurcation was designed to allow movement between the two branches. His preference was for a humane education based on the classical languages, and he has been criticized for associating one class—those who could afford it—with this kind of education, leaving a modern education for those who could not. Pirogov's child-centred aim also smacked of individualism. Such an aim is of course acceptable to Soviet critics only it if can be reconciled with the kind of society of which they approve.

Ushinsky, whose appreciation of Pirogov doubtless helped Soviet authors to rehabilitate the latter, was born in 1824 and died in 1870. In *K. D. Ushinsky—Selected Works*[13], A. I. Piskunov and E. D. Dneprov describe Ushinsky as "the reformer of the Russian school and founder of scientific education in Russia." They see him as a man of the Enlightenment who applied the idea of general education to conditions in Russia. His scientific study of the nature of man and of the laws of human development made it possible for Ushinsky to show how education was dependent upon social progress.

For example, Ushinsky stressed the importance of education as a social science, and has, rightly, been regarded as pioneering the application of psychology to the study of education. Other related sciences included anatomy, human physiology, logic, philosophy, geography, political economy, statistics, and the history of education. Through these sciences, he maintained, knowledge of the nature of man as the subject of education can be revealed.

His practical concern, the urgent need to reorganize Russian schools, was intimately linked with his theoretical position. For Ushinsky, the laws of human development had to find practical expression in Russia. As a pioneer of comparative education he analyzed the common historical foundations of European education, took a deep interest in the major controversies among his contemporaries in Europe, and wrote about and compared features of public education in Germany, England, France, and North America. He came to the conclusion that to borrow foreign experiences and ideas senselessly and to transfer a school system mechanically from one country to another were doomed to failure. Along with other comparative educationists he concluded that "the educational ideas of every nation are permeated with national character more than anything else, permeated to such an extent that it is impossible to even think of transferring them to an alien soil." His reform proposals were based on the need to make Russian schools Russian.

This involved teaching children their native language, giving priority to the study of the history and geography of their native land, and developing their national self-consciousness. He criticized the "tyranny of classicism in the Russian schools" and proposed that the content of education should conform to the logic of the subject and be presented in such a way as to make it accessible to the age-group for which it was intended. The stress Ushinsky placed on general education, on its national character, and on the need to provide it through the mother tongue of pupils is acceptable to present-day Soviet educationists.

Leo Tolstoy (1828–1910) is regarded by Soviet authors as a special case among the idealists of the nineteenth century. As a literary figure he is seen as representing the growth of national consciousness and the mounting protest among the Russian peasants against the existing regime. As a young man he taught the children of peasants. Some years later in 1859 he started his own school in Yasnaya Polyana. Here he tested his educational ideas and at the same time castigated existing schools everywhere. As an acknowledged leader of the progressive education movement he may well have been influenced by Rousseau's views. Interested in the education of the masses, he too rejected the notion that German, English, or French institutions would work in Russia. With many of his European contemporaries he drew a distinction between education and training. Education develops human beings, gives them a wide ideology and new knowledge. Teachers have special roles to perform. They should influence pupils by the love they have for their own subjects. They should not interfere in the formation of a child's character or in its training, which is the job of the family. Freedom for the children should, according to Tolstoy, affect the organization of schools. As time went on, his ideas changed somewhat, so that eventually the moral and religious aims of education become more important to him than pure knowledge, and he criticized materialistic interpretations of life. He also conceded that education in a general sense must, after all, include training. The contradictions in his analysis and his failure to understand the causes of a social crisis that could only be resolved by revolution were among Lenin's criticisms of Tolstoy. Lenin[14] was proud of him as a creative writer, and subsequent Soviet opinion recognizes Tolstoy as a defender of the personal rights of children.

Soviet writers, understandably, pay attention to nineteenth-century figures who received favorable mention from Marx or Engels. N. G. Chernyshevsky (1828–1889) and N. A. Dobrolyubov (1836–1861) were two such figures. Chernyshevsky was a consistent critic of capitalism and brought to the Russian intelligentsia some knowledge of revolutionary movements abroad, played an active role in the revolutionary movement at home, and was banished to Siberia for some years. Dobrolyubov was also an active revolutionary who contributed to the development of Russian social thought. Both are regarded as materialists. Both were responsible for advances in psychological theory. Chernyshevsky placed great importance on the influence of external conditions on psychic phenomena. Dobrolyubov may be regarded as an early physiological psychologist in that he pointed out how exceptionally important the brain was. These trends were in line with Marxist educational thought, which had already begun to develop in Russia in the nineteenth century. G. V. Plekhanov (1856–1918),[15] for example, popularized the basic tenets of Marxism and applied them to economic conditions in Russia, literary criticism, and education. By the turn of the century Lenin (1870–1924) and N. K. Krupskaya (1869–1939) were writing about education. The former stressed the idea that education had to be linked with productive work. Krupskaya's post-Revolutionary contribution to educational theory is of great importance.[16]

Krupskaya, Makarenko (1888–1939), and Lunacharsky (1875–1933), S. T. Shatsky (1878–1943), P. P. Blonsky (1884–1941), and L. S. Vgotsky (1896–1934) are among the personalities which in the evolution of Soviet educational theory bridge the pre- and post-Revolution periods. Not all of them have consistently found favor with Soviet authors. Krupskaya's work on the upbringing of children and Makarenko's analysis of the educative value of the collective have, however, given direction to Soviet thinking on education throughout.

It should not be assumed that debate has been absent in educational circles. The influence of John Dewey was apparent in the 1920s. Pedology had a vogue. It represented in Soviet terms a theory of child development taking into account the physical and psychological growth of children. Perhaps during this period Soviet educational theory came nearer to American theory than at any other time. Psychological and intelligence tests were accepted, and the project method and the Dalton Plan of teaching were admired. During the 1930s a reaction against pedology set in. One of its most famous proponents, Paul Blonsky, was disgraced, and in July 1936 a decree issued by the Central Committee of the Communist party condemned pedology as anti-Marxist and unscientific. Many observers of Soviet affairs note that the succession of resolutions passed by the party during the early 1930s was intended to strengthen school discipline, to reduce the influence of progressive educational ideas, and to build up as quickly as possible cadres of specialists. These were regarded as vital to the defense of the country against the growing threat from Hitler's Germany. Whatever the reasons, there seems to have been a sharp reversal of policy and practice during the 1930s.

During World War II commitment to Communist orthodoxy in education was suspended rather than abandoned. In the interests of waging a war during which an estimated 20 million men, women, and children lost their lives, the schools were geared to helping the war effort. In speeches[17] to members of the Young Communist League Kalinin (1875–1946) praised them and cautioned them, praised them for the work their colleagues had done as propagandists, agricultural and industrial workers, partisans and soldiers, and stressed the importance of their leadership role. He warned them of the dangers of overexaggeration in stimulating support and in general presented a realistic picture of wartime conditions and the threat to the country.

Policies also reflect this all-out commitment. Fees were reintroduced, technical and vocational schools were opened, and courses provided for twelve- to thirteen-year-old pupils to train them to work in vital industries. Coeducation was abandoned so that boys and girls could be trained for specific roles. Boys were prepared for the armed services. An emphasis on their role as wives and mothers was given to the education of girls. In these ways two central principles were held in suspense, namely that free general education should be offered to all throughout the period of compulsory schooling, and second, absolute equality of provision.

The context within which Soviet educationists place their discussion of aims and achievements is, of course, the Revolution. In October 1917 the Bolsheviks planned and carried out an armed insurrection; the provisional government was overthrown; the first Soviet government was set up in Petrograd, and Soviet power was established in Moscow and other centers. The previous failure of czarist governments to establish an adequate school system and to combat illiteracy and the subsequent achievements of the Soviet government place the Great October Socialist Revolution in its usual perspective. It transferred power from the bourgeoisie to the workers and allowed new aims and objectives to guide the establishment and development of a Soviet system of schools. In the field of public education, the basis of Communist party policy was adopted at the 8th Congress in 1919. It was to change the schools "... from having been a weapon of the class superiority of the bourgeoisie into a weapon for the complete abolition of the division of society into classes, and for the Communist rebirth of society." Quite evidently the new leaders recognized the importance of education as an agent of social reconstruction, and they saw the overthrow of capitalism and the establishment of Communism as the goals. Any explanation of events in the Soviet Union is provided within this frame of reference.

The Revolution is taken as the start of a new era. Its purpose was first to remove the inequalities of a previous regime and thus establish a foundation on which the achievements of culture, science, and art could be made accessible to all men and women whether they were manual workers or professional people. Czarist policies had created great inequalities. The situation inherited by the Soviet government was particularly bad in the hinterlands where national minorities were not allowed to have their children taught in their native language. Among the 100 nationalities the Russians constitute more than half the total population of the Soviet Union. The Ukrainians come next. In czarist days forty-eight nationalities had no written language of their own. Workers of non-Russian origin were almost totally illiterate. Soviet policy[18] was designed to equalize provision by creating written languages (over forty nationalities have done so).

Faced with this situation, the Communists set out after the Revolution to destroy the ideology of bourgeois schools and to build a Communist society with the help of the schools. These were to help mold the character of individuals to create a generation of new Soviet men and women. High levels of general and specialized training were to develop the spititual potential, the political maturity, the ideological-moral, and general culture of all young people. In addition schools were to train them to work in productive industry. Thus explicit in the aims of Soviet education from the start was the notion of all-round development and all-round training of individuals.[19]

Lenin was aware that all-round education of the new Soviet man was possible only in a socialist society. The overthrow of capitalism and the creation of a new social environment were prerequisites if social aims of Communist education were to be realized. He gave cultivation of political consciousness among workers high priority. The schools should do more than teach the principles of communism; they should also teach future workers how to organize their affairs in a Communist society. These political aims are repeated in the literature frequently on the authority of Lenin.

As for the development of the economy, educational establishments were given two functions to perform. First, they should ensure that the levels of general and professional training were appropriate to the needs of industrial development. Vocational, technical, and scientific education thus has an important part to play. Perhaps more important than technical skills is knowledge about the organization of industry under communism. Most important of all are the attitudes toward work and toward fellow workers. Thus the economic objectives of schooling require for their achievement far more than skill training. The new Soviet man was to participate in the economic life of society with a new awareness of its needs.

Lenin's criticism of czarist schools was that they provided only book knowledge and crammed pupils by using the methods of the old drill sergeant. They based ethical teaching on the commandments of God or idealist phrases. Czarist vocational schools turned out servants needed by capitalists. While rejecting these features of education, Lenin stressed the importance of learning and knowledge in the education of young people in a Communist society.

Lenin was convinced that in a new system of education students should acquire knowledge of fundamental facts, that what they learn they should learn thoroughly. These beliefs stemmed from the opinion that to "learn communism," students should, like Marx, make a profound study of capitalist society and the laws governing the development of human societies. This development is the result of the struggle of workers to free themselves from the constraints of the old society. Out of this struggle Communist morality and ethics are born.

Thus new objectives were created for schools in the immediate post-Revolution period. At first great attention was paid to the destruction of an old morality and to the creation of a new morality.[20] Political and economic aims tend to dominate the literature, but culture and the arts are not neglected. These societal aims cannot be achieved unless attention is paid to the all-round development and training of individuals.

The conditions created by the Revolution, the war, and their aftermath help to explain some important features of Soviet educational theory and practice. Mention has been made of the high rate of illiteracy. A major campaign to combat illiteracy was made on the assumption that only a literate population could ensure political and economic development. There were, however, other pressing problems, one of the most important of which concerned the care and education of the thousands of waifs who had lost their parents and were roaming the countryside. Makarenko[21] made his reputation on his educative work with these children in the Gorky Labor Colony and the Dzerzhinsky Commune. The former was for juvenile delinquents; the latter was an educational community operated in accordance with Makarenko's confidence in the educative role of the "collective" or group. He is perhaps best known for his elaboration of this principle, which remains central to Soviet pedagogy.

The need to create a new man follows logically, and inevitably, from a Marxian analysis of workers under capitalism. They were exploited.

Conditions of work in factories had made it impossible for them to maintain the kind of relationship a craftsman had with the products of his labor. Such workers participated in all aspects of making, let us say a chair and could be proud of their product. Under capitalism the specialization of labor alienated workers from the things they helped to make and from their fellow workers. Exploited workers are hardly likely, therefore, to possess the outlook and attitudes that make for harmonious relationships in the industrial life of a Communist society. If the false consciousness of such workers and alienation are to be eliminated, education has to be transformed.

### Current Status

The current status of the Soviet education system can be judged only by reference to the history of its development and the role it has consistently been asked to perform in creating a new kind of man and a more truly Communist society. Initially the class consciousness of workers is important in the class struggle. In a new socialist society, in which ownership of land, factories, and equipment is no longer in the hands of individuals, class consciousness takes on a new meaning. Workers and farmers should have a profound understanding of their place and roles in a classless society—that is, a society in which all men and women are equal. The class consciousness of the new Soviet man has a positive role to perform. It ensures that individuals will not behave in terms of what they conceive to be their own self-interest but in accordance with the needs of fellow workers; that is, the collective. Communist ethics and morality are subordinated to the interests of the working class. In this sense, therefore, the criterion against which moral behavior is judged is related to the welfare of the group (or collective) rather than to the welfare of the individual. Compared with the stress laid on individualism in other philosophies, Soviet aims are less child-centered than those in many countries.

Given this fundamental shift in the organization of society, child-centered educational aims were reviewed. Krupskaya, Lenin's widow, was a major figure in the development of these aims and the principles of child-centered education. Her works along with articles and books by Ushinsky and Makarenko remain important in the present climate of educational thinking in the Soviet Union. She was the author of many articles on the theory and practice of preschool education, the Pioneer movement, the education of communities of children, and on the kind of education needed to develop appropriate industrial attitudes. General themes running through her writing are the all-round development and upbringing of children.

According to Marx and Lenin in a "classless" society of workers, farmers, and members of the intelligentsia, basic class conflicts in capitalist societies disappear and the all-round—intellectual, moral, physical, and cultural—education of individuals can proceed. Today Soviet spokesmen continue to emphasize that the creation of favorable socioeconomic conditions determines what can be achieved in schools. The tasks facing Lenin and his colleagues were necessarily different from those facing educationists in the 1970s. Today's conditions in the Soviet Union satisfy many of the requirements of a truly Communist society.[22] Workers are organized into what may be described as a "workers' democracy." Theoretically they have no domestic enemies and group solidarity, class consciousness, collectivism, and nationalism present, under these conditions, no threat to the satisfactory all-round development of individuals. The enemies outside the country are the capitalists and imperialists. Internationalism, which is a strong feature of Soviet education, has to be seen in relation to the slogan "Workers of the world unite." In this context working-class solidarity, Soviet style, and internationalism as an educational aim are not inconsistent. Soviet educationists look toward a world of workers. National unity and international friendship are two faces of the same desired "classless" world. Basically both worlds ought to provide socioeconomic conditions in which the workers have been released from the most important constraints on freedom, namely, conditions of work under capitalism.

Equality and brotherhood rather than liberty dominate the aims of educational provision. Consequently in practice Soviet educationists make every attempt to create a unified system of schooling throughout the whole country. This means for them a unified curriculum, the same syllabus and textbooks for each subject, the same methods of teaching, and the same examinations. It also means that salary schedules and per capita expenditures should be the same throughout the country. Uniformity is an objective; equality the aim. They justify a measure of centralized control that would be unacceptable in countries where liberty is stressed at the expense of equality.

Belief in a unified system of schooling is not simply a matter of political philosophy. In the Soviet Union it receives psychological and epistemological justification. According to Soviet educationists the use of IQ tests is suspect. They are neither objective nor scientific and should be administered only to diagnose brain damage and other defects. The physiological basis of Soviet educational psychology is derived from the work of I. P. Pavlov. Insofar as it is behavioristic, it provides support for the environmentalists. Given the same conditions, the argument might run, individuals will reach the same level of achievement. Serious failure is due to physiological causes. Given this kind of commitment, it is not surprising that Soviet educational psychologists can dismiss the value of Freudian and Piagetian[23] theories while looking with more favor on the theories of B. F. Skinner and R. G. Crowder. It also explains some of the conclusions reached when proposals were made to reduce primary schooling from four to three years. These conclusions were that far more children than had been previously thought possible are capable of learning abstract principles and deducing from them a wide range of detailed information. Uniformity of provision can be justified on psychological grounds.

It is also possible to do so by reference to a theory of knowledge that asserts that using the methods of scientific inquiry, absolute and entirely objective knowledge can be acquired. In this theoretical framework what is taught and how it is taught are not and should not be matters of subjective opinion but the outcome of scientific investigation. Subjectivism has no place in the preparation of syllabuses, textbooks, and manuals about teaching methods. When describing their research, Soviet educationists seem to call more heavily on documentary material than on empirical evidence.

Knowledge, scientifically acquired, is the cement that holds together child- and society-centered aims in the Soviet Union. We have noted how Lenin urged young Communists to learn all about capitalism and the accumulated knowledge of mankind in order to understand Communism fully. Today it is held that scientific knowledge should inform policy and that it is essential to Communist morality. It even informs matters of taste so that art can be judged as bourgeois or true art. This faith in the certainty of knowledge and its historically determined structure helps to explain why Soviet curricula and syllabuses are unified. The history of a subject determines its content. The physics syllabus[24] includes material drawn up from Archimedes to Einstein and beyond. Statics, dynamics, heat, light, sound, magnetism and electricity, and modern nuclear physics are well-known subsections in a comprehensive program. Educationists, faced with an explosion of knowledge, are reluctant to select bits from the mass of accumulated knowledge for teaching purposes. The syllabus of each subject follows its historical development, and methods of teaching are based on objective research.

It is relatively easy to conclude that the all-round development and socialization of individuals in the interests of a truly Communist society are dependent on the acquisition of knowledge. From outside the system it is easy to conclude that uniformity is a political aim and that the power of the Communist party and the educational bureaucracy is directed toward the establishment of uniformity for political reasons. These two explanations are compatible because the strength of the Communist party is derived from the ideological commitment of its members and the fact that its activities are based on objective laws of social development.

This commitment to scientific knowledge and to ways of acquiring it sharply differentiates the status of Soviet education from that enjoyed by education in North America. Less well-defined theories of knowledge, to be sure, inform some Western European systems of education, but it should be recognized that Soviet theories had their origin in and remain very much a part of the heritage of Western Europe, itself rich in assumptions about knowledge and the extent to which its acquisition legitimizes the aims and objectives of education.

Soviet psychology and political science, of course, also justify the view that an individual's behavior is conditioned by the environment. Soviet educationists do not accept that individuals are innately unequal and that intelligence is distributed unevenly throughout any population as a result of birth. Inequalities in attainment are seen as due to environmental conditions. Serious underachievement may be the result of brain damage. Consequently the elitism of conservative psychologies is largely absent from the theories accepted in the Soviet Union. The "new man" is an equal among equals in a "classless" society. His class consciousness, sense of unity, and harmonious all-round development are only possible in a socialist society. Under these conditions education can play its part in preparing a generation of comprehensively developed people.

A second major difference between Soviet theorists and many educationists in Western Europe and North America turns on concepts of the good society. The former look forward to the overthrow of capitalism and the creation of a classless *industrial* society. Many laissez-faire liberal educationists frequently yearn for a return to a modified agrarian society and to the attitudes and behavior patterns of the eighteenth and early nineteenth centuries. Soviet educationists accept industrialization; indeed, Lenin proposed to measure economic development in terms of the growth in electrical power, but they reject capitalist ways of running industry. Their aims are consistently directed toward the improvement of life in this kind of economic world, and thus there is less ambivalence on the part of educationists.

A major objective of education, therefore, in a socialist industrial society is the realization of "polytechnical" education. Such an education has as its central aim the all-round development and all-round training of young people for productive life. It emphasizes the need to develop appropriate attitudes toward the collective ownership of the means of production and toward relationships between people in industry, in commerce, and on the farm. Since these relationships are, according to Marxist-Leninism, determined by the modes of production employed, the task of educating the new man is to make him aware of socialist modes of production and to mold his character, attitudes, and behavior patterns in accordance with them.

Krupskaya in an article entitled "The Difference Between Professional and Polytechnical Education" wrote that in a rapidly industrializing country even apprentices require some knowledge of the entire production cycle and any technical innovations. Such a person would be in a position to adapt himself to technological change and indeed to the changes he may be called upon to make. Polytechnical education should do more than teach young people a particular industrial skill. It will teach him a lot of what he must know if he is to work in a factory. He must also know the role played by his factory and the industry in which he works in the economy of the Soviet Union and the world. He will learn where raw materials come from, how machines are built, how methods of production are organized and products distributed. Krupskaya concluded:

> The school will stimulate pupils' interest in production and their desire to raise production to the highest possible level. On the other hand, the factory training school will acquaint the pupil with labour organisation in factories and plants and, for that matter, everywhere else, individual and collective. It will teach him to create the necessary hygienic working conditions, acquaint him with the fundamental of labour protection and industrial safety at any enterprise, particularly in a textile mill [Krupskaya was drawing all her examples from the textile industry]. Lastly, the factory training school will teach him the history of the labour and trade-union movement at home and abroad, and acquaint him with the struggle waged by the workers, particularly textile workers the world over.
>
> All that will give the pupil not a narrow profession that may prove unnecessary on the morrow but broad polytechnical education and working habits possessing which he will come to the factory not as an inexperienced worker who is more of a hindrance than help, but as a mature and skilful worker who requires only a short-term specialisation course.[25]

The status of education, then, according to Marxist-Leninist theory, is determined by the economic structure of society. Reforms in Soviet education have consequently been directed toward the adjustments needed when after the Revolution, capitalism having been destroyed, perfecting a socialist and then a Communist society was the major aim of policy.

## THEORY

### Learning

Central to Soviet educational theory is this notion of polytechnical education. Without some knowledge of the assumptions on which it is based it is not easy to understand learning and teaching theories advanced and debated by Soviet philosophers, pedagogues, and psychologists. The theory suggests that the all-round development of individuals should take place in the context of productive life in an industrialized, or industrializing, society. All-round development includes the inculcation of appropriate attitudes toward work and work mates. Attitudes can, however, only be inculcated successfully if the socioeconomic framework is satisfactory and the base of knowledge is adequate and is presented in an appropriate manner. Polytechnical education is firmly rooted in socialism and a particular epistemology that suggests that true knowledge is acquired only when a synthesis is made of knowing and doing, or of theory and practice, or when the social and industrial implications and applications of knowledge are made explicit.

During the post-World War II period emphasis on the theory of polytechnical education has ebbed and flowed. Krupskaya's initiatives have been referred to, and they have provided Soviet theorists with a legitimate source on which to develop their views. Interest in the theory peaked in 1958 when the law bringing education nearer to life was passed. It remained high for some years when educationists worked hard to realize the principles of polytechnical education in practice. These endeavors included attempts to introduce a period of work experience for young people leaving school who wished to go on to higher education. Reform involved sending pupils out into firms and factories and on to farms during the school year and bringing industrial machinery into schools. It also implied changes in emphasis in methods of teaching and the inclusion of illustrative material from industrial life. The theory was comprehensively presented in S. G. Shapovalenko (ed.), *Polytechnical Education in the USSR* (1963), and the practical proposals were spelled out in the law *On the strengthening of the ties of the school with life and on the further development of the public education systems in the USSR*.

The basic assumption that learning only takes place when theory is related to practice is found in the work of Marx, who was impressed by R. Owen's New Lanark schools. Marx wrote in *Capital*,

> As Robert Owen has shown us in detail, the germ of the education of the future is present in the factory system; this education will in the case of every child over a given age, combine productive labour with instruction and gymnastics, not only as one of the methods of adding to the efficiency of production, but as the only method of producing fully developed human beings.[26]

From this point of departure it is evident that, if it is to be approved in the Soviet Union, learning theory has to stem from or be compatible with a materialistic philosophy. N. V. Lomonosov (1711–1765) is praised, for example, as a founder of the materialistic tradition in Russia because he rejected the theory that ideas could be innate, defended the view that knowledge was derived from experience, and developed views on the nature of the material world and how, using the methods of the natural sciences, knowledge of the world would be acquired. Among the Revolutionary Democrats, A. I. Hertsen (1812–1870), V. G. Belinsky (1811–1848), Chernyshevsky, and Dobrobyubov are regarded as classical Russian materialists who helped to create a psychological tradition on which Soviet psychologists could build. I. M. Sechenov (1829–1905) and Pavlov (1849–1936) are esteemed as the Russian founders of Soviet physiology. The former had made a bold attempt to discover the physiological principles needed to explain psychic processes and put forward the theory that psychological phenomena were integral parts of brain reflexes. By the beginning of the Soviet period Pavlov had made major contributions to physiology. He had examined processes in the functioning of the cardiovascular system, created a physiology of digestion, and was working on theories associated with higher nervous activities. Thus the Russian origins of psychology lie in materialism and physiology. Since 1917 the line between psychology and physiology has from time to time been redrawn. After 1930 the label physiological-psychological became less and less appropriate as the gulf between Soviet psychology and Soviet physiology widened. Commentators suggest that the divorce was never absolute but there is a good deal of evidence to show that not until 1950, shortly after the 100th anniversary of Pavlov's birthday, were scholars encouraged to return to his principles. Theoretically the recognition by linguists that Pavlov's "second signal system"—that is, people's use of words—helped to explain the growth of consciousness in individuals adequately explains the rehabilitation of physiological-psychology in the Soviet Union.

The origins of pedagogical theory in materialist philosophy are similar but by no means the same. As mentioned, the views of Hertsen, Chernyshevsky, and Dobrolyubov are regarded as important precursors of Soviet pedagogy. Ushinsky's contribution to this science has also been mentioned. His basic assumptions were that progress in education depended upon understanding the development of logical thinking and the acquisition of practically useful knowledge. While Ushinsky attached particular importance to physiology and psychology and recognized the importance of socioeconomic conditions in the process of learning, he nevertheless pioneered the view that an independent science of education should be built up as an independent branch of scientific knowledge.

Makarenko doubtless gave support to the view that useful though the social sciences including psychology were, they were not the same as, nor could they replace, educational theory as such. His own educational theories undoubtedly bridge the periods of development in the Soviet Union. He was, for example, a stern critic of pedology. He rejected the emphasis given to biological factors and the acceptance of heredity and an unchanging environment as the determinants of a child's personality and achievements. He also rejected the apparatus of psychometric testing associated with pedology. This included intelligence and attitude tests which he regarded as artificial and defective methods of studying children.

Makarenko's theory was, he claimed, based on observing children in his colony and on the teachings of Marx, Engels, Lenin, and Stalin. As an autonomous theory, pedagogy should take its logic from the educational goals established by society. These, according to Makarenko, change as society changes; hence, in the 1930s he was very interested in the development of character traits appropriate to the needs of an emerging classless (that is, socialist) society under the dictatorship of the proletariat. Consequently he would have nothing to do with educational theories based on the subject-centered psychology of Herbart or on faculty psychology. He maintained that educational theory divorced from "real life" was useless. In his own theory he combined great stress on discipline as a way of building character and respect for individuality. This combination would best be achieved by an education in, through, and for the collective. Groups of children or adults only become "collectives" when they become aware of their common tasks, mutual interests, and purposes and work for the common good. They are societies in miniature and can therefore educate and train their members. Makarenko in fact was committed to the view that education and training were essential if the potential of individuals was to be realized in a society in the process of development. His reputation is firmly based on his success in the Gorky Colony (1920–1938) and the Dzerzhinsky Commune (1928–1935), where, in practice, he combined book learning and productive labor and according to observers, brought to a high degree of perfection the unification of mental, physical, aesthetic, and polytechnical instruction. It is, nevertheless, necessary to look briefly at theories that, while not deviating from Makarenko's central position, add to an understanding of present-day theory in the Soviet Union.

Post-1950 learning theory includes physiological and psychological components. A major key to their reconciliation, as mentioned, is in Pavlov's theory of a "second signal system." This feature of his theory was a later and not prominently developed addition to his work on classical conditioning. Pavlov maintained that the nervous system controls all physiological activity. It can inhibit some responses, thus protecting itself, delay responses, or trigger them off. Thus, according to this theory the nervous system is adaptive, capable of analyzing, selecting, and synthesizing stimuli, and allows the organism to anticipate events that are signaled by preceding events. Consequently the organism can respond in advance of an event or stimulus with an appropriate reaction. This version of behaviorism is suitably materialistic. The cerebral cortex is the material on which stimuli work. It pays no attention to any external world of ideas and leaves out of account both consciousness and introspection. In America it attracted psychologists such as J. B. Watson (1913) who were interested in the environmental control of behavior under laboratory conditions. As developed by B. F. Skinner, American behaviorism stresses that behavior can be controlled through the systematic manipulation of the consequences of previous behavior. Thus, rewards are made contingent on the pupil's own behavior. Correct behavior is rewarded and reinforced; incorrect behavior is discouraged by coupling an unpleasant consequence with it. The central idea is reinforcement, and the theory suggests that knowledge of the operant reinforcer is a necessary and sufficient condition if behavior is to be predicted. Control over the reward or unpleasant consequence makes it possible to control behavior.

Classical conditioning is now regarded as a special case of operant conditioning. Learned emotional and cognitive reactions may be analyzed as conditioned reflexes. Voluntary behavior may well require the reinforcement of a reward and hence cannot be analyzed simply as an example of classical conditioning; moreover, is not susceptible to the procedures appropriate to this special class. Classical conditioning represents a deterministic theory of learning, dependent upon stimuli from an unchanging environment. While it may adequately explain the behavior of nonhuman organisms, it does not take account of the socio-historical experience of humans. This kind of experience makes people unique among the animals. Along with animals, human behavior is conditioned by the mechanisms of heredity and stimuli provided by the environment. In short, all animals behave according to biological inherited instinct—a form of unconditioned reflex activity centered in the nervous system— and individual experiences provided by the environment. People alone have developed higher characteristics of mind as a result of their history. It was this accumulation of experience, transmitted from one generation to the next, that Lenin regarded as the foundation of true knowledge. To be sure, social circumstances may distort learning and teaching so that book knowledge acquired by rote learning may well bear little or no relation to practical life. Lenin nevertheless maintained that only through the critical assimilation of the total sum of human knowledge was it possible to establish the intellectual foundations of communism.

Any theory of physiological conditioning that ignored this view of Lenin is bound to be suspect in the Soviet Union. It is not surprising, therefore, to find Soviet psychologists criticizing and rejecting earlier forms of American behaviorism because they did not take account of the socio-historical determinants of learning and behavior. Frequent mention is made in the literature to American behaviorism and those Soviet psychologists of the 1920s who acknowledged its influence on their thinking were held to be among those responsible for the perversions of pedology when they were exposed in the 1930s. So long as physiological theory found no place for the historical dimension of knowledge, it could not, in the Soviet Union, dominate educational psychology or replace pedagogical theory.

Language is, of course, the transmitter of human socio-historical experience. Once Soviet linguistics recognized the relevance of Pavlov's "second signal system" to their analysis, the stage was set for the development of a more comprehensive learning theory based on Pavlovian principles and the reunification of physiology and psychology. As part of the nervous system the second signal system[27] mediated by language reflects the social aspects of the human environment. It becomes important in any analysis of learning by conditioned reflexes because the external stimuli, which imprint themselves on the cerebral cortex, arise under the influence of teaching and education. This aspect of Pavlovian theory makes language, and human use of words, a central feature of school education. It also confirms the decisive role of schooling in the learning process. The teacher becomes a central figure in the child's environment because he or she supplies the latter with stimuli from the socio-historical experiences of humans.

This relatively neglected aspect of Pavlov's theory offers a materialistic explanation of consciousness. Behaviorism does not include such unacceptable notions as "free will," introspection, Freud's unconscious, and other subjective elements; and idealist conceptions of consciousness fail to explain the development in people of their true "consciousness." Pavlov's theory of conditioned reflexes accounts for human temperament. Environmental stimuli build up organs in the cerebral cortex essential to the specific functions performed by the nervous system. If as scientific materalism would assert, the mental processes are localized in specific morphologically reinforced structures of the brain, then the development in human beings of specifically human mental processes depends upon the possibility that cerebral organs are formed that are used to perform specific acts. The second signal system permits cerebral organs of true consciousness to be developed. Education, with the help of speech, guides this development as the child interacts with the natural and social environment. In appropriating socio-historical experience, functioning cerebral systems are formed that, in the event, control human behavior.

This kind of consciousness should, according to Soviet theorists, be the effective agent in the direction of human behavior in the real world.

Conscious goals should play an essential part in voluntary action. Consciousness tied to action should free people from the constraints of the immediate situation and direct their behavior to more distant goals. Thus, provided capitalism and remnants of it can be eradicated from the social environment, conditions of learning will enable the growth of people's true consciousness so that the New Soviet Man can become a conscious, purposive builder of socialism. Once socialism has been achieved, it is no longer necessary to consider making fundamental changes in society to improve human nature. But the New Soviet Man has consciously to build in socialism so that a truly communist society can be created. This New Soviet Man, the product of biological inheritance, the result of a definite level of socialist production and living conditions, and the influence of socio-historical experiences transmitted through education, is master of his own fate and free, in the sense that he has been liberated from error. For Soviet writers, freedom is found in the recognition of necessity.

This physiological-psychological theory may be difficult both to understand and to accept. It is placed in perspective when criticisms of Western European and American psychology are examined. These criticisms are that theories of development advanced by idealist psychologists mistakenly claim that a child's development is inevitably predetermined by biological age and the stimuli to which he or she is subjected during the process of education. Soviet critics claim that these factors assign an entirely passive role to the child and condemn the biological theories of inherited intelligence as "idealist" and, as mentioned, behaviorist theories are too narrowly deterministic.

## Teaching

Of interest is the debate about the interrelatedness of learning development and teaching. Vygotsky (1896–1934)[28] analyzed the relationship shortly before his death in the light of several theories of child development. According to Vygotsky, Piaget's theory suggests that learning follows the stages of a child's cognitive development. It is a child-centered theory of individual growth and development that pays scant attention to the influence of various environmental conditions. A second set of theories declares that learning is development. The two processes are accomplished at the same time. Indeed, according to some theories, it is difficult to differentiate at all between them. Other theories suggest that there is interaction between these two basic processes. The process of maturation prepares for and makes possible learning, while, in turn, the latter stimulates and advances the process of maturation. Finally, a third set of theories suggest that learning precedes development. Herbart ascribed to different subjects a particular significance in the mental development of children. Vygotsky took the view that the influence of learning was never specific. The only good teaching goes ahead of a child's development because the process of learning does not coincide with the process of development but precedes it. Learning thus creates a zone of potential development. Even before going to school, a child begins to learn from the people around him, but the process differs from school learning. Adults create a zone of potential development by answering his questions during a specific stage of learning.

The significance of Vygotsky's theory for school education is considerable. It, too, points to the danger of assuming that development and learning are determined by a process of maturation of the organism. It throws light on the role of testing as a way of finding out the actual development of the child. What is important to know, however, is something about the child's potential development. Testing may discover actual development but fails to measure potential. And finally the theory asserts that teaching is vital to the realization of potential and hence future development.

In 1975 an account and evaluation of a long-term, mass-scale curriculum development project directed by L. V. Zankov (1901–1977) was published. Zankov was head of the Laboratory for Problems of Teaching and Development of School Pupils of the Institute of General Pedagogy of the Soviet Academy of Pedagogical Sciences. Apart from working on this twenty-year research he had contributed to Soviet literature in educational psychology since the 1930s. As a leading scholar his investigation has received great attention and probably influenced the decision to concentrate into the first three years of schooling what had previously been offered in the first four years.

Zankov takes as his point of departure the analysis by Vygotsky in the 1920s and 1930s. The substance of distinction he made between learning and development and the relations between them is repeated in his report on *Teaching and Development (an Experimental Pedagogical Study)*[29] which repeats Vygotsky's assertion that teaching should be forward-looking and should precede the next stage of development of children. After describing the methods and organization of the research, which included observation techniques in a network of experimental schools, Zankov and his collaborators present the results of their study of observation activity, mental activity, and the practical activity of children during the course of their development. In the section of the report dealing with the learning of mastery of spelling, the formation of the concept of a "problem" in the pupil's learning process and on learning and life after the elementary grades is described. The teaching of the major subjects in the elementary school was thus the object of experimental research.

The basic aim of the teaching in experimental schools was effectively to promote the general development of school pupils. One way of assessing general development was to draw distinctions between giftedness and special abilities and to improve general and special development. Further distinctions were made between general and mental development and between the latter and physical development. These distinctions, however, were made with the clear intention of studying the all-round development of children rather than their special abilities. This all-round development included the development of powers of observation, reasoning, and practical activity.

Apart from Vygotsky, authors of a previous period to whom reference is made include Ushinsky, Lenin, and S. L. Rubinshtein. Among foreign scholars Jean Piaget, Karl Bühler, William Stern, and Kurt Koffka receive critical but professional attention. A. N. Leontiev, M. A. Danilov, B. P. Espiov, M. V. Zvereva, B. G. Ananiev, G. S. Kostiuk, F. F. Korolev, S. V. Ivanov, M. N. Skatkin, N. A. Menchinskaya, P. Ia. Galperin, E. I. Petrovsky, D. B., Elikonin, V. Z. Smirmov, and M. A. Prokofyev are among the many distinguished Soviet psychologists and educationists whose work had some bearing on a report that will influence the practice of teaching young children for many years to come.

In his summary Zankov points out that some colleagues wished to approach the problem from the stage-by-stage formation of mental activity by processes of assimilation. Zankov cannot accept this position, claiming the support of Lenin who explicitly identified the historical study of the mental development of the child as something on which theory should be based. He goes on to accept Vygotsky's views that affective and intellectual processes are unified in the stages of development, and the way in which a pupil is taught determines the development of pupils. Zankov points to the influence of other external and internal factors.

As part of the research, comparisons were made between pupils who had studied the new curricula in experimental and conventional schools. In the areas of the development of observation, reasoning, and practical activity, pupils from the experimental schools were more able to relate speech and action and were more likely to bring the components of mental activity into a coherent unity. They were also more strongly motivated and more readily able to master grammatical and other concepts. In short, the project seemed to confirm the general theories on which experimental teaching was based and justify the new curricula and the reorganization of elementary schooling.

This theory bears closely on the aim of all-round development of children. In summary, it rejects the view that this development can be regarded as a process of biological motivation or that it is simply determined by forces in the environment. The child does not develop on the basis of an age-norm schedule. Nor is his or her development to be seen in behavioristic terms. A third component contributing to the comprehensive all-round development of children is their social history. This is the link that unites child- and social-centered aims in Soviet education and is included in theory on the insistence of Lenin. Mediated by language, human socio-historical experience helps to form individuals and to develop their consciousness. Under satisfactory social conditions, individuals can acquire the kind of consciousness that will free them and give them the power to influence events through rational, purposeful action. Theory is thus unified with practice and individuals are consciously able to participate in the improvement of society.

Against these Soviet theories of all-round individual and societal development, the analysis made by Communist party leaders can be judged. Since 1917 conditions of life have changed. During the first post-Revolutionary stage, education was constrained by many remnants of capitalism. During the period of socialism new opportunities to educate a New Soviet Man were opened up. Now, according to party leaders, the stage is set for new initiatives in education. The theoretical bases have been laid as a consequence of research on teaching and development, on secondary school curricula, and on the realization in practice of the principle of polytechnical education.

To do justice to theoretical debate during the three stages of development, namely between pre-1917, between 1917 and 1936 or 1950, and from 1936 or 1950 (however the victory of socialism is dated) would require considerably more detailed knowledge of Russian and Soviet physiology and psychology than I possess, and indeed more familiarity with the details of Western European and American debates among psychologists than can be expected of someone who is not a psychologist. Consequently, I have based my presentation not on the differences in theory that have been debated in the Soviet Union but on some rather major points of disagreement and convergence between Soviet psychologists and their Western contemporaries. In doing this the nuances of debate in the Soviet Union have not received the attention they deserve.[30]

## APPLICATIONS

### Curriculum, Academic

There is little doubt that curriculum policy has been the subject of much research in the last twenty years. The commitment, sustained by Lenin and encyclopedism, to crowd as much of the accumulated knowledge of mankind into the content of school education has created problems. One solution was to crowd into the first three years of schooling what had previously been taught in four years. A major revision of secondary school syllabi in the 1960s was designed to bring in new information and scientific principles. It is difficult to assess the effectiveness of these policies because in spite of the pressures created by the explosion of knowledge, education remains highly prized, alternatives to study remain few, and the rewards of hard work and success are so obvious.

In general, curricula are the same throughout the country and are encyclopedic at all three levels or stages—primary, secondary, and tertiary. In the first three grades emphasis is placed on the native tongue and mathematics but a range of other subjects is prescribed. They include history, geography, and the natural sciences. For selected pupils, a modern foreign language is introduced in the second grade. The most popular foreign language is English, but French and German can be studied.

At the next stage, from the fourth through the eighth grade, curricula in the schools of the fifteen autonomous republics are by intention the same, although each republic has the power to adapt the content of schooling to meet its own needs. This finds most obvious expression in the medium of instruction. In Latvia, for example, Latvian is the medium of instruction for those children whose parents choose to send them to these rather than to Russian-language schools. A similar choice is open to parents living in other non-Russian-speaking republics.

It should be noted that while a majority of Soviet citizens (about 60 percent) speak Russian as their native tongue, more than 100 languages and dialects are spoken throughout the vast nation of 250 million inhabitants. These languages differ, of course. Some are major languages spoken by many people, are written, and have a considerable literature. Others do not satisfy these criteria. The languages spoken by nomadic tribes in the far north of the Soviet Union are in the process of being written and have no literature. The freedom given to pupils to learn through the medium of their own native tongue introduces considerable variety into the system as a whole.

Nevertheless, in schools throughout the Soviet Union all pupils must study the same subjects. Their own language, if not Russian, a modern foreign language from the fifth grade on, mathematics, physics, chemistry, biology, history, and geography constitute the core of a common nationwide curriculum. Additional subjects vary somewhat in the different grades, but in general the balance is in favor of mathematics and the physical and biological sciences. In the early 1960s major studies were carried out by members of the Academy of Pedagogical Sciences[31] with the intention of improving the curriculum. In scope, however, it remains much as before, but a considerable amount of new knowledge and concepts have been included in the syllabi of the subjects.

Textbooks, whether in Russian or other languages, are the same everywhere, and interpretations of content in the exact sciences are the same. Language teachers within a prescribed framework may introduce illustrative material of their own choice. In history, textbooks and teachers consistently offer a materialistic interpretation. Similar, authorized interpretations of biological phenomena are commonly taught. All such interpretations are regarded as "scientific" and therefore not open to serious reconsideration.

The accumulation of "scientific" knowledge in recent decades has made it difficult to include everything in a curriculum offered to and followed by all pupils. In the seventh grade "options" were recently introduced so that some pupils at least could add to their basic knowledge of some subjects by taking courses based on up-to-date information and new concepts. The number of such optional courses in the seventh and eighth grades is strictly limited, for these two grades complete the period of compulsory schooling.

The ninth and tenth grades (and in non-Russian-speaking republics the eleventh grade as well) constitute what is called "complete secondary education." In these grades options are offered, and pupils can specialize to some extent before going on to tertiary education. These options are designed to provide potential scientists, linguists, or social scientists with up-to-date knowledge relevant to the major courses they propose to study later.

Other pupils at this stage may be offered additional courses in the "basic" subjects, for example Russian and mathematics. These options are intended not so much for potential university and institute students but for pupils who are not expected to do more than complete a secondary school course successfully. This kind of differentiation in terms of the curriculum implies that some pupils are not as capable as others of covering a common range of subjects in the same time and of reaching the same level of achievement. It also suggests that high achievers can benefit from specialized additional knowledge before they go on to a university or institute.

Such differentiation of content is not representative.[32] For the most part, all ninth and tenth grade pupils take the same subjects, and these as before include mathematics, language, the natural sciences, and the social sciences. In addition, pupils are introduced to dialectical materialism as a basic philosophical component, which is also included in the content of courses in institutions of higher education.

If curricula at each stage of education are basically designed to transmit to all children the socio-historical experiences of mankind—suitably interpreted—extracurricula activities play a major role in the ideological and political upbringing of children and young adults. This involves the development of high moral standards and good manners and a Communist outlook based on class consciousness and loyalty to the ideas of Marxism-Leninism.

Within weeks of entering school for the first time, just before the October Revolution is celebrated, young children become members of the Little Octobrists' Organization. They are given a small badge in the form of a red star and as members of a close-knit collective are expected to carry out certain assignments. These include looking after books, games, do-it-yourself materials for use in class, potted plants, and any pets kept in the school. These simple tasks give them a sense of responsibility and help to socialize them. They learn about the Young Pioneer Organization and pledge themselves to be loyal to their country and to the revolutionary struggle. They learn to honor the memory of patriots and workers.

When they are ten, they are admitted with much ceremony to the Young Pioneer Organization, put on the distinctive red kerchiefs, and learn about the contribution made in the past by Pioneers who helped with the harvests in the 1930s and collected funds and scrap metal as well as helping the soldiers during World War II. They are encouraged in peacetime to carry on this kind of community work by planting gardens and organizing leisure activities. In school they participate in organizing exhibits in rooms set aside to display notable aspects of Marxist and Soviet history. The lives of famous people from home and abroad are illustrated. A bust of Lenin and his famous slogans may provide foci of interest in such rooms. From among those who actively participate in these collective activities future leaders begin to emerge.

At the age of fourteen Young Pioneers may join the Young Communist League (*Komsomol*), which helps to supervize groups of pupils in the senior forms of secondary schools and in higher education through committees elected by pupils and students. They assist in the running of education institutions and are quite clearly expected to offer leadership. One of their chief duties is to teach each other and younger children how to be purposeful, how to show initiative, and how to study hard. Outside the school members of the Young Communist League have a history of service to the community and state. Early on they helped to teach illiterates. Then they participated in instruction work in the drive to electrify the country. As mentioned previously, Young Communists actively helped in the war against the German armies and air force. Their heroism is described in detail as an example of patriotism to the country and solidarity to the international fraternity of workers.

Today the Young Communist League has more than 23 million young people in schools, institutions of higher education, on farms, in factories, in offices, and in research organizations. They continue to help in construction work, particularly during the vacations, helping to build schools, houses for teachers, and sports grounds. They also organize sports camps, leisure and work camps, and over weekends throughout the year run hobby groups and take part in a range of aesthetic activities. Meeting a group of such youngsters in Leningrad, I could not be other than impressed by the mastery some members showed of English, the seriousness of purpose they displayed, and the charm and skill with which questions asked by foreign students were answered. In many schools I have visited, similar qualities have been displayed against a background of unshakable ideological commitment.

A vast network of Young Pioneer Palaces and Houses—there are nearly 4,000 of them throughout the country—provides leisure-time facilities. The houses tend to serve rural districts and city neighborhoods. The palaces, often in handsome pre-Revolution buildings as in Leningrad, are bigger and offer a wider range of activities designed to develop the interests and talents of young people. The Pioneer Palace in Moscow is very modern and with its many workshops, halls, and studios can accommodate more than 5,000 children all at one time. The palace in Riga is indeed a former castle or palace, and its rooms and halls offer a pleasing setting for a range of activities.

A Young Pioneer House is often organized into departments. Each of these has hobby circles and studios run by experienced specialists. Some classification of the activities provided will indicate the range of interests shown by youngsters and teachers. There are circles in which model aircraft, boats, and motorcars are built. Then there are natural science clubs in physics, chemistry, and biology for young people who want to develop their own interests in these subjects. Well-equipped laboratories provide them with this opportunity. Other circles meet the interests of children who enjoy folk dancing, ballet, music, the film, and theater. Inevitably there is a chess club. All prominent Soviet chess players, it is claimed, learned how to and began to play in Young Pioneer Houses. Over and above these cultural, intellectual, and practical pursuits the ideological and political education of young people is the central aim of the organizations associated with the Young Pioneers.

Books, magazines, feature films, and documentaries aimed at school children, Young Technicians' Centers, Young Naturalists' Centers, Children's Excursion and Tourist Centers and libraries supplement the education given in schools and Pioneer Houses and Palaces. Together they contribute to the learning society and to the all-round development of children in a socialist society.

Curriculum, Nonacademic

The Soviet Union is, of course, famous for its specialized technical and vocational schools.[33] These are in many respects similar to the technical schools of Germany. Pupils enter them after completing eight years of compulsory education. Technical school courses last two, three, or four years depending upon the occupation for which they prepare pupils. Training is indeed very specific and specialized. The skills appropriate to every industry and sections of it are taught in factory schools. Some schools train fitters, molders, and turners for heavy industry. Other schools train future railway workers for specialist tasks. Young girls learn how to design, cut out, and sew dresses. Future printers learn their trade in special schools. Electrical engineers are trained in appropriate schools.

In many cases pupils prepare products for sale. Girls accept orders to make dresses. Printing schools prepare posters and pamphlets. Young carpenters make furniture for sale. These are only some examples of the range of schools and the type of skill training provided. Often these technical schools have a boarding establishment so that young people from smaller towns and villages have an opportunity to learn a trade. Stipends are given to ensure that the expense of keeping a son or daughter in school does not deter parents. The popularity of technical schools is understandable. When pupils complete their course, they can expect employment in the occupation for which they have been trained. Salary scales tend to reflect the number of years of schooling a young worker has completed. The incentive to train for highly skilled jobs is high, and many technical schools have more candidates than they can accept.

The emphasis in courses in technical schools is changing somewhat. Previously they included a small general educational component. In the first year it constituted a substantial proportion of the timetable but was progressively reduced until in the last year of the course practically all the work was specifically vocational. More recently technical-vocational schools have provided a complete secondary education for an increasing proportion of fifteen- to nineteen-year-olds. With a complete secondary schooling, pupils are qualified to compete for admission to an institution of higher education. While pupils in a general secondary school complete their secondary education in ten years, those attending technical schools are likely to take longer. Nevertheless, this move has made it possible recently to increase rapidly the percentage of young people completing secondary education.

Student Evaluation[34]

The work of pupils is continuously assessed. For each answer, whether oral or written, a pupil is given one to five marks. A mark of 5 is excellent,

3 is satisfactory, 2 and 1 are not. Over the year a dossier of marks is compiled for each pupil. Some Soviet experts consider that too much time is spent in schools examining pupils. They claim that examination takes place at the expense of teaching. In 1976 a report was published on research carried out to establish the optimum period between testing a pupil's knowledge of the same item. The conclusion seemed to be that an interval of about seven days was most appropriate. Pupils are not promoted automatically from one class or grade to the next and almost 8 percent of them repeat a class in the course of their school career. This is not regarded as satisfactory, but if poor marks have serious consequences, high marks ensure success. With a school record of marks of 5 a pupil may almost certainly be able to enter an institution of higher learning of his or her own choice. National Olympiads and entrance examinations are used to select from among the many who apply those who are admitted to a university, polytechnic, or pedagogical institute.

Of the relatively few universities Moscow and Leningrad enjoy the highest prestige and select from a large number of applicants the few who can be accepted. These universities, like other similar institutions, have their own entrance examinations. In the case of Leningrad University special boarding schools help children from rural areas, where the quality of teaching may be lower than in the cities, to prepare for the university's entrance examinations. During the five-year university course leading to a diploma students tend, within a faculty system, to concentrate attention on a limited number of subjects but some general subjects are compulsory in laid-down curricula. As part of their specialist studies students are instructed in methods of teaching. In lecture seminars, for example, at the University of Moscow, students of English study aspects of the language as well as ways of teaching them. A feature of the system ensures than young people who are not able to gain admission to full-time courses can complete higher education part-time. Institutes of higher education, universities, polytechnics, and pedagogical institutes provide part-time evening courses for working people.[35] Frequently full-time *Komsomol* students help run these courses, which lead to comparable awards to those obtained by full-time students. Correspondence courses also make it possible for working people outside the major cities to return to a sequence of studies that may have been interrupted. Faculty members in city institutes participate in these correspondence courses by visiting centers in provincial capitals and other parts of the country. Correspondence students are encouraged to visit the major institutions in order to follow short courses regularly.

Examinations dominate the system, and it is therefore important to see what influence they may have on teaching and learning. Two features characterize the system. The first is that many tests of attainment are oral.

Russian and mathematics examinations are exceptions to this rule. Consistency between schools and regions is a function of the belief in the absolute nature of knowledge. To most, if not all questions, about mathematics, physics, history, or language there is an unequivocal answer so that oral tests are seen as reliable and valid. At the final leaving examination, pupils are offered a large number of questions on "tickets" from which they select a few. The element of chance makes the system something of a lottery. It compels pupils to cover all the material in the syllabus and emphasizes the fact that encyclopedic knowledge is highly prized. Written examinations are reserved for core and specialist subjects.

Greater freedom of choice is introduced in language examinations, but the whole system has been criticized as too demanding. Nevertheless, examination success is important. Success means promotion, not only in the education system but subsequently outside. It is a factor in the election of older students to membership of the Young Communist League (*Komsomol*)—itself an organization from which many members of the Communist party are subsequently drawn. Length of schooling and examination success are still very important to the future of young people in the Soviet Union.

## Counseling

The scope for counseling within the school is limited. All pupils follow the same courses. A proportion of each class is made to repeat it, but the majority of pupils proceed each year from one class to the next. The transition between the third and fourth grade is not traumatic. In the first three grades, pupils get used to the same class teacher; in and after the fourth grade they have to get used to specialist teachers; and in and after the seventh grade they may be advised to choose and follow an option. In a nonselective system in which curricula are common, competition and motivation based on the social, economic, and political benefits that flow from educational success doubtless influence pupil choices and teacher advice. It seems likely that pupil ambitions are fostered throughout the school and by parents so that as the time approaches when pupils are to leave school, they know where they want to go and what they want to do. No structured system of guidance and counseling exists, but nevertheless pupils heed the advice of teachers.

Equality of provision means that the same demanding curriculum is offered to all children—in cities and villages—unless they have special handicaps. (Even then sustained efforts are made to keep them in the normal school system.) Consequently, counseling does not constitute a major problem. It would be unusual however to find that all pupils enjoy the same subjects and that all of them are equally able to master them.

Preferences become clear as young people approach the age when they can leave. Many will go on to a technical-vocational school of their choice after the eight-year school. A large proportion will stay on to complete the secondary school curriculum.

Young people in these pre-higher education classes speak freely about their ambitions. Some express the hope that they will be able to follow in the footsteps of mother or father. Others aspire to enter a famous university, polytechnic, or pedagogical institute. Some young people modestly suggest that they may not be clever enough to gain admission to a prestige institution. The obvious need to work very hard in competition with their peers discourages some young people whose order of priorities is different.

Choice of subject is also discussed. The pure sciences come high in the list of desirable subjects. It would be a mistake to think that pupils who attend schools where a foreign language is introduced in the second grade are all potential linguists. More often than not they hope to study mathematics or physics at Moscow or Leningrad University. Engineering is popular. Medical studies seem to be less often mentioned. Teaching does not appear to rank very high as a possible profession. It is clear, however, that intellectual occupations are held in high esteem, and membership of the intelligentsia a worthy goal.

The preferences of boys and girls differ. Evidently a far higher proportion of young women train as engineers in the Soviet Union than in most countries. The proportion of women in the medical profession is also high—much higher than in Western European or North American countries. As elsewhere a large proportion of teachers, particularly in the lower grades, are women. The balance is different in universities and other institutions of higher education except in the language departments, which attract a disproportionate number of women students and faculty members. Intourist guides are usually women in spite of the demands the job places on them as wives and mothers.

Choice within the common school curriculum is therefore a matter of personal preference to some extent. Before entering higher education, students pick out their favorite subjects, for a variety of reasons, and work diligently in what is, despite disclaimers, a competitive system. The widespread and well-publicized provision of evening courses and correspondence courses for students who either do not want to remain in full-time education or cannot do so perhaps eases tension. Nevertheless, the atmosphere of school and college is permeated by seriousness of academic purpose. There are indeed few signs of real discontent among school children in the Soviet schools I have visited.

The explosion of knowledge has made educationists ask whether school programs are too heavy. There is a division of opinion. Some teachers think that pupils are expected to spend too much time at their desks and doing homework and do not get enough fresh air and exercise. They think that the timetable should be reduced and that there should be no school on Saturdays. Opponents of these views claim that school life should be demanding in order to build character and to induce a sense of loyalty in pupils. They argue that habits of hard work and study can only be learned at school, and without them a person's life will be so much less rewarding. Makarenko's insistence that great demands should be made of individuals and Vygotsky's theory that teaching should precede development reinforce what seems to be a majority view among educationists.

But how can all children cover the same demanding curriculum? The Soviet answer stems from recent research including that undertaken by Zankov and his colleagues. Methods of teaching should seek not to overload the pupil's memory with facts but should face him with difficult tasks to develop abilities of abstract thinking and powers of logical reasoning. Thus armed, the pupil will be able to extend his range of knowledge by deducing details from general principles. Polytechnical instruction will enable him, moreover, to recognize the social implications and practical applications of these principles. All pupils should therefore in theory be able to complete the same program of studies.

### Discipline

Discipline in schools rarely seems to present problems. In accordance with Makarenko's principle it is strict, but pupils seem at ease and strive to please their teacher, who is very demanding. Physical punishment is forbidden by law, and a teacher who breaks this law may be dismissed. Punishment is restricted to a reproof from the teacher recorded in the mark book. Or the principal may reprimand a pupil for misdemeanor. Other members of the class have, however, an important role to play. Their collective criticism is salutory and encouraged. Competition, however, as a way of promoting good behavior and stimulating achievement is not encouraged because of its negative consequences.

Expectations regarding conduct are high, and positive incentives receive attention. Good conduct, hard work, and academic achievement seem inextricably interrelated. Under present circumstances there is no reason to question the effectiveness of the methods adopted to socialize young people into a clearly stated secular role of ethical behavior.

ROLES

## Administration

Since 1966 there has been an all-Union Ministry of Education, responsible for preschool, primary, and general secondary schools. The all-Union Ministry of Higher and Specialized Secondary Education has a longer history. It is responsible for universities, polytechnics, pedagogical institutes, and technical schools. The Ministry of Health, however, looks after medical institutions. The Ministry of Agriculture and the Ministry of Communications are responsible for educational facilities in their respective spheres. The Ministry of Culture has under its general supervision conservatories, art schools, theatrical and cinema institutes, and so on. The State Committee for Vocational Training is in charge of training skilled workers in a network of vocational schools. Responsibility for education and training is thus shared by a number of all-union ministries.

There are fifteen union republics each with its own constitution and a ministry of education, which is subordinate to the Ministry of Education of the Soviet Union. Autonomous republics are constituent parts of the union republics and have their own ministries of education. In addition, regions, territories, areas, cities, and districts complete a complex pattern of administrative control. The principle of democratic centralism, however, ensures that each executive body is responsible to a local Soviet (committee) of Working People's Deputies. These committees and bodies are linked in a hierarchy that ensures that educational problems are tackled on a national level and local needs are met. The authorities take pride in the fact that the Ministry of Education of the Soviet Union is responsible for ensuring equality of provision throughout the country.

Major principles of policy were laid down in the Fundamental Legislation of the Soviet Union and the Union Republics on Public Education adopted in 1973. Apart from the provisions made in the Constitution, the legislation[36] is designed to ensure that there is a unified system of schooling through which all pupils can pass smoothly from the lower to the higher stages. To guarantee this curricula, syllabuses, and textbooks (even in the different languages) are the same. Education is secular and schools are coeducational. The role of the Communist party in the formulation of policy is crucial.

The program adopted by the Communist party in 1919, for example, revealed the scope of the task of linking education with life. The analysis was sharpened in Lenin's speech to the third Congress of the Young Communist League in 1920. Shortly after Lenin's death in 1924 at the 13th

Russian Communist Party Congress, a call was made to improve the educational work among young party members. At this time, of course, attention focused on the need to maintain party unity against the threat of counterrevolutionists and of Trotsky and his followers.

The People's Commissariat for Education of the Russian Republic had been set up immediately after the October Revolution. With Anatoly Lunacharsky in charge, its task was to eliminate illiteracy[37] and educate the population politically. Alongside the program issued at the 8th Congress in 1919, which stressed the free, general, and polytechnical education of all children, were adult literacy activities. In 1918 a decree signed by Lenin was designed to mobilize all literate adults to work with illiterates. Some 800 delegates attended the First All-Russian Congress on Adult Education in May 1919. In December of that year all those who could not read or write were required to learn as best they could. Working people were allowed time off; party leaders, women's organizations, trade unions, and newspapers participated in the work, and "Down with Illiteracy" became the slogan and the title of a popular primer for illiterates. Lack of resolution was condemned at the 11th Congress in 1922 and a special committee was established to maintain momentum. The elimination of illiteracy for the eighteen-to-twenty-five age group was set for 1927. By 1926 the country's industry had been restored to its pre–World War I level, but the percentage (55 percent) of illiterates remained high in spite of considerable successes, a 2.6 percent annual increase in literates.

In this campaign, under difficult conditions, Krupskaya, D. Elkina, N. Bugoslowskaya, and A. Kurskaya, members of the Young Communist League, and students played important roles. In spite of their efforts, in 1927 among levels of literacy in Europe the Soviet Union ranked nineteenth. Concentration on heavy industry, the inability of cities to help the countryside, the lack of schools, shortages of reading rooms and libraries, and lapsed literacy are reasons given for slow progress. The importance of the campaign was repeatedly stressed, and the successes of the Sarovites publicized. The drive gained momentum, and no congress or conference called by government or the party failed to report progress. Day-to-day propaganda through press, radio, lectures, and in factories, clubs, gardens, and cinemas was part of the anti-illiteracy drive. At the 17th Party Congress in 1934, a resolution to end illiteracy during the Second Five-Year Plan was adopted, and the concluding phase of the campaign was introduced. By 1936 the "Down with Illiteracy Society" had virtually fulfilled its task and was disbanded. Meanwhile, for pupils with limited schooling, schools for semiliterates were opened in big factories or in district schools where the factories were too small to have their own. Evening schools, correspondence courses, and study circles helped to achieve this major objective of Soviet policy; namely, the elimination of illiteracy.

The 16th Party Congress in 1930 was a landmark in that members recognized that the Soviet Union had entered a period of Socialist development. By 1934 the basis of the country's economy was considered industrial rather than agricultural, and at the 17th Congress it was decided to intensify the party's ideological and political work. During this period the Central Committee, while appreciating some success, condemned some of the methods employed in schools and aspects of their organization and the content of the courses provided. Decrees between 1931 and 1936 criticized primary and secondary schools for not preparing pupils for higher education and for the distortions introduced under the People's Commissariat of Education (*Narkompros*). They were to correct these errors by reintroducing textbooks as the major teaching aid, strengthening school discipline, revising the teaching of history and geography, and restoring the system of grading (5 to 1) that had been used in czarist schools.

When nationwide literacy had been achieved, the next task of the Communist party was to universalize general secondary and polytechnical education. So, for example, at the 19th Party Congress in 1952 directives were issued for the development of polytechnical instruction in general education schools. Syllabuses in physics, chemistry, and biology included information about the main branches of production. And at the 20th Congress in 1956 note was taken of the divorce of education from real life and of the inadequate training for work of school leavers. N. S. Khrushchev's report of the Central Committee to Congress placed the need for polytechnical education in perspective. The schools were training young people for higher education, but the majority of them were being absorbed immediately into the work force when they finished school. The solution, polytechnical instruction, was tried out in a few experimental schools, then in another 580 schools during 1956–1957 before being extended to the whole country. Then in 1958 Khrushchev submitted plans to the executive body of the Central Committee of the Communist party, and after nationwide discussion they were adopted by the Supreme Soviet of the Soviet Union in December and by union republics the following year.

The law of 1958 bringing education nearer to life was the outcome of many years of discussion and experiment. In 1919–1920 the People's Commissariat had set up adult education centers to combine instruction with productive work. Experiments were also carried out in pilot schools for school children. Communes sprang up where the basic educational principle was to link school with work in plants, in factories, and on farms. Schools for rural youth and seven-year factory schools paid great attention to the polytechnical principle. Mistakes were admittedly made, and in many schools polytechnical education had taken on a formal character. Between 1931 and 1933 model schools were set up in every district to show what could be done. Lack of properly trained teachers and poor technical equipment contributed to the lack of success of labor instruction, and it was taken out of the curriculum in 1937. In rural and urban schools during the war, millions of Soviet school children did some kind of socially useful work. After the war school children no longer worked in industry, and the schools reverted to preparing them for specialized secondary and higher education.

In practice the major intention of the 1958 reform was not immediately realized.[38] There were, in fact, too few teachers who fully realized that polytechnicism was not a separate subject but was a principle that should inform the teaching of every subject. The faults of a traditional system of education, so clearly recognized by Lenin, lingered on. The intellectuals knew little about production. The workers had too little scientific knowledge to relate practice to theory. The notion that working life in industry should be the source of a sound general education is nevertheless extremely important, and the efforts of Soviet educationists to translate the theory of polytechnical education into practice were extremely instructive.

Central though polytechnical theory as a societal aim has been since 1945, other prewar preoccupations have given shape to developments during this period. Theories of teaching and learning have been reconsidered with the idea of individualizing both. Sight has not been lost of Makarenko's insistence that teaching and learning should be in and through the collective or group. The explosion of knowledge has been recognized and taken into account in discussions of organizational and curriculum reform.

Policies have been influenced by research. In the sphere of education it is organized by the Academy of Pedagogical Sciences; formerly (from 1946) an institution of the Russian Soviet Federative Socialist Republic[39], since 1966 it has had all-union responsibilities. An elected presidium is responsible under its presidents and vice-presidents for the conduct of the affairs of the academy. Membership is restricted to outstanding educationists. New members are elected by existing academicians who numbered in 1970 some forty-eight full members and seventy-eight corresponding members.

Research is conducted in twelve institutes, each divided into departments responsible for special aspects of educational research.[40] The institutes and departments have laboratories and/or libraries relevant to the research carried out. In experimental, boarding, specialized boarding and other schools research is conducted under field conditions. On any criteria some of the research is noteworthy. At the Institute of Defectology, for example, children with brain damage and congenital handicaps are studied in very favorable conditions with a view to helping individuals and developing general therapeutic techniques. Language, child development, aesthetic education, and physical education are thoroughly researched in other institutes of the academy. Preschool, general, and vocational school curricula and methods of teaching are subjects of research in some of the other institutes. An important center devoted to the study of foreign systems of education is located in the Institute of General and Polytechnical Education. The academy publishes a number of scientific journals and reprints classics in the field of education. In departments of education and psychology in over 200 universities and pedagogical institutes research is carried out.

### Faculty

Young teachers have some opportunity to choose their first job. Many of them wish to stay in the city, and some of them are assigned to more remote schools. Their salaries are negotiated nationally, and every teacher is required every five years to attend a refresher course. Considerable pressure, however, is brought to bear by colleagues and inspectors on teachers to keep up-to-date and improve their competence. It is evident that motivation is high and is stimulated by the collective. Promotion prospects and higher salaries are incentives. So too is the prospect of returning to the city.

Nevertheless, it is not unusual to find young people who have trained to be teachers but for one reason or another—frequently discipline problems—have left teaching for some other job. On the other hand, the career prospects for those who stay in teaching are quite attractive. Retirement ages are relatively early, and pensions are generous. Outstanding teachers receive national recognition by the award of one of several categories of "honored" teacher. The reward system is similar to that found in most countries, and the evaluation of the teachers, as elsewhere, is based on formal and informal procedures in which inspectors and colleagues have roles to play. Teachers, as in continental European schools generally, have fewer pastoral duties to perform than is the case in England or North America.

Teachers generally take pride in the success of their pupils. There is no doubt that the teacher's success is judged in terms of student learning. This success is monitored by school inspectors and by the principal of the school. The collective is important, and in every school the Communist party has its committee and the trade union its representatives. In secondary schools, teachers receive a full salary for teaching eighteen lessons a week. In the elementary grades teachers have twenty-five lessons. They have some freedom to arrange these lessons to suit their convenience, and for the most part pastoral care is not highly developed.

Principals are appointed from among experienced teachers. They usually apply for these posts and are appointed by the local authority. Their salary is higher than that of the classroom teacher, and they are regarded principally as administrators rather than teachers. Their role in the school is clearly to manage the institution rather than to offer academic leadership. Frequently, in schools in which children take English from the second grade on the principal does not speak English. Classroom management within the constraints placed on them by a prescribed curriculum, approved syllabuses and textbooks, and acceptable methods of teaching is the responsibility of the classroom teacher. As a matter of judgment it seems that teachers of the same subject in a school know each other well and know teachers of the same subject in the system quite well. They also know nationally famous masters of method and are familiar with the research carried out in their subject at universities, pedagogical institutes, and research institutes. Organizations inside a school that cut across subject boundaries are the Communist party, the trade union committee, and to some extent extracurricular activities organized for and by the Pioneers and members of the Young Communist League. In short, specialization of function informs roles and relationships in Soviet schools.

### Students

Until recently there was little evidence to suggest that pupils were other than extremely happy to be at school and anxious to succeed. There is no doubt that the ability of the authorities to control many aspects of the economy made it possible for them to relate wages, salaries, and levels of accommodation to the period of time spent in school. It is equally clear in a country yet to experience the full range of distractions created by a consumer economy that traditions of learning and scholarship inform the attitudes and behavior of large sections of the young population. A few personal observations may serve to illustrate the sense of commitment shown by pupils and students.

Visitors to kindergartens are impressed by the control shown by very young children who invariably put on a short concert for their guests. Without embarrassment they sing and dance to the noisy accompaniment of a piano. They play with toys but are trained to look after them well and return them neatly to the places where they are stored. Some are clearly anxious to learn how to read and write and are helped to do so. Having observed these young children in many kindergartens over a period of twenty years, I can only conclude that they are happy to be there and are extremely well cared for by qualified nurses, doctors, and teachers. Relationships seem warm and loving.

The atmosphere of the general incomplete and complete secondary schools depends, apparently, on the personality and organizing ability of the school principal and his or her staff. Members of the Pioneers with their red scarves are immediately obvious. Their role in helping to run the school is apparent as is the contribution of the older pupils who are members of the Young Communist League. Loyalty to their school and the achievements of Communist heroes at home and abroad and a desire to succeed in their own work and for the school are expressed in a variety of ways. Foreign visitors can converse in their own language with many of the senior pupils. The Pioneer and *Komsomol* rooms set aside for the display of information about aspects of communism exemplify the extent to which schools socialize young people.

Equally important in this process are the Pioneer Palaces. The aesthetic and physical development of pupils receives considerable attention. It is not easy to reach a firm conclusion about the proportion of youngsters who take advantage of these facilities. They do, of course, offer for young people whose parents work a place where they can spend the afternoon and evening hours profitably. Doubtless enthusiasm for organized activities ebbs and flows, but the enjoyment of those who attend the Pioneer Palaces is evident.

As for university, polytechnic, and pedagogical institute students it would be unwise on the evidence available to make assertions about them with any confidence. Since 1960 sartorial styles have changed. So too has the kind of music favored by the younger generation. There has always been evidence of the extent to which students of English read as widely as possible outside prescribed course books. For many years the works of John Galsworthy constituted a basis on which English style was studied. Students at the Maurice Thorez Pedagogical Institute for Foreign Languages show a remarkable commitment to the study of languages and are well able to describe in the foreign language of their choice not only their interests but the work they do with adults in evening and correspondence courses.

Student unrest is not much in evidence. Concern is expressed about the incidence of hooliganism among the groups known as *Stilyagi* and *Guligany*, but many observers agree, and research seems to confirm, that students in the educational system are well-behaved, highly motivated, and for the most part achieve the objectives set for them by their teachers.

### Parents

Great efforts are now made to strengthen the links between home and school. As in most European countries the concept of the teacher with esoteric knowledge and skills has helped to place him or her in a somewhat isolated position. A leader in a village community, the teacher in a big city may become anonymous. The need to draw parents more actively into the school has been recognized in the Soviet Union, so that it is no longer simply that parents are expected to support teachers and help to motivate their children.

Encouragement is now given to parents and teachers to discuss together the academic and personal problems pupils might face. With so many young mothers engaged in industry or commerce, it is usually the grandmother who comes to collect the child at the end of the school day around noon. Parents' meetings are arranged so that teachers can report on the progress of children and discuss their future. On the basis of visits made over a period of nearly twenty years my impression is that traditionally the distance between parents and teachers was considerable, that their roles were regarded as distinctly different, and insofar as parents had a role to perform, it was to support the teachers by acknowledging their special knowledge and skills and by supporting the schools in efforts to inculcate appropriate attitudes and forms of behavior.

In conversation, parents and grandparents show the same concern as elsewhere for children at school. How they like it, how they are getting on, and what they hope to be after leaving schools are natural topics for discussion. The importance of schooling is rarely, if ever, questioned and respect for teachers is high.

The complementary and traditional role of the family in the Soviet Union has been much discussed. Until recently something like an extended family system still made it possible for grandmothers living with their married son or daughter to look after grandchildren after school. The rapid erection of new apartment blocks around the cities of, for example, Moscow, Leningrad, and Riga, has doubtless provided many young parents with separate accommodation. Growth in the number of nuclear families seems likely to place new responsibilities on kindergartens, schools, and Pioneer Palaces.

## SYSTEM IN ACTION

In general schools serve a particular neighborhood. Preschool institutions are organized by the department of public education, factories and other industrial enterprises, local government bodies, and collective farms. Kindergartens are frequently situated so as to serve families living in adjacent apartment blocks. Great attention is paid to the physical well-being and early socialization of the young children. Many of them learn to read and write, however, and are frequently more advanced socially and educationally when they enter the first grade than children who are starting school for the first time.

Almost 11 million children attend nursery schools and kindergartens.[41] Since 1920 when 250,000 children were in crèches or attending kindergartens and playgrounds, numbers have risen enormously, and particularly since 1961 when 3 million children were enrolled. This growth reflects the high proportion—about 50 percent of the work force—of women who work in industry, commerce, and the professions, and the speed with which young couples are being rehoused so that grandmama is no longer with them and able to look after the children while their parents are at work.

Nursery schools and kindergartens are usually fairly small, often taking care of less than 300 children from the immediate neighborhood. They are often surrounded by a square of apartment blocks. This arrangement frequently means that the parents of most of the pupils work at the same local factory which may, in fact, help to support the school by buying extras for it. Parents pay a small amount per month but it is not intended to meet more than a tiny proportion (about one fifth of the total cost of caring for and feeding their children while they are at work.

To meet the needs of parents, nursery schools and kindergartens may open at 7 o'clock in the morning. Staff may be on duty until 8 o'clock at night. In some cases, two groups of teachers work in two six-hour shifts with children split into groups of twenty in the nursery class up to three years of age and into classes of twenty-five for children between the ages of four and seven. Some children may live at a kindergarten for five days of the week, returning home at week-ends. Most are picked up between 5 and 6 o'clock by one of their parents after work.

Daily routines are designed to prepare a child for school. They include short lessons in reading, writing and speech, counting, music, craftwork, poetry, and physical education. The number of lessons per week increases as the children grow older. Each day, however, they are given substantial and well-balanced meals. They walk and play when possible in the open air and sleep in dormitories after their mid-day meal. They are trained to look after themselves and to mix with other children. Medical doctors visit regularly, and trained nurses are in permanent attendance. Children are checked for complaints like tuberculosis. Great attention is given to the health of these young children, and their diet, sequence of injections, and general progress are recorded. Delicate and otherwise handicapped children may be sent to special kindergartens. There special facilities are available, but the aim is to prepare children to take their place eventually in a regular school.

In the case of speech defects, therapists check on all five-year-old children in kindergartens. If a defect is diagnosed, the child is referred to a special education/medical commission to be examined by a psychiatrist, psychoneurologist, and neuropathologist. The child may then be sent to one of the previously mentioned special kindergartens where he or she will be assigned to a small group on the basis of the disability. If there is no improvement in the child's speech by the age of seven, he or she may be transferred to a special school. In cases of extreme disability further diagnostic and remedial work are undertaken in the hope that transfer to the first grade of a regular school will be possible at the age of nine.

Members of the teaching staff are trained in special faculties of the pedagogical institutes. The course consists of general educational theory and practice, social subjects, Russian literature, and physical education. Policy has been directed in recent years toward ensuring that all kindergarten teachers receive an education in an institution of higher learning of the same length as that offered to teachers in other schools.

There is no doubt, on the basis of many visits to kindergartens, that the aims expressed by principals and teachers inform practice. Quite evidently the physical well-being and health of children receive great attention. They are in the process of being socialized into acceptable forms of good behavior. They learn what is good and what is bad. They are taught to love nature and appreciate music. They also learn how to read and write. This all-round upbringing of young children and the methods of teaching them have been the subject of much research by the Soviet Academy of Pedagogical Sciences and the Academy of Medical Sciences.[42]

Surveys have shown, and indeed the assessment of first grade teachers confirm, that nursery school children are on average better developed mentally and physically than those who have been kept at home—some justification of the Zankov theory. They are more sociable and more easily able to concentrate on schoolwork. Among nursery school children entering first grade, a higher proportion than among those who have not attended preschool institutions had had defects of speech, hearing, and physical movement corrected. Intellectually they are able to apply their knowledge to new situations more quickly than the others.

All children, unless they are very seriously handicapped, must attend school when they reach the age of seven. The majority go to regular neighborhood schools and remain there for at least eight years of compulsory schooling or for ten years, enabling them to complete secondary education. This period is extended to eleven years in the non-Russian-speaking union republics. Primary schooling now lasts for three years instead of, as before, for four years. During this period children stay with the same teacher who is also responsible for all their lessons. After the third grade pupils are taught by specialist subject teachers and move from one classroom to another.

September 1 is a very special day.[43] It is the day on which the school year begins. Nearly 50 million Soviet children return to school after the holidays. Among them are the seven-year-olds who are starting regular school. In the Baltic republics they start at the age of six. Everywhere, however, great efforts are made to make them feel that the first day at school is a happy and important occasion. Boys in white shirts and girls in starched white pinafores carry bunches of flowers as they make their way to school. Older pupils and teachers welcome and look after the beginners. It must be said that this early enthusiasm is sustained throughout their school life. To assume that Lenin's admonition to Young Communists to "study, study, study," explains the obvious enthusiasm for learning is too simple. The rewards for doing well at school are evident in Soviet life. Even so, teachers sometimes complain, as elsewhere, that young people do not work as hard as they used to and are less interested in studying.

Parents usually enroll their children in the nearest school. Schools range in size from between 400 and 600 pupils in a district center to around 1,000 in a big city. Larger schools of 1,500 to 2,000 are not favored. Hence most schools serve a neighborhood, and housing allocations help to determine the family background of children in a particular school. Nevertheless, there are no rules stating that a child must attend the local school. Parents have some choice, and so it seems have principals as far as admitting children whose parents ask that they be enrolled.

Admission to special ballet and music schools is on the basis of ability. On the other hand whether a handicapped child should be admitted to a regular school or sent to a special school to be cared for as uneducable by the medical authorities is decided during the first year of schooling after prolonged medical and psychological investigation.

Normal children arrive at half past eight every morning. The little ones are brought and taken home again later by mothers or grandmothers. They hurry to their classrooms after taking off their coats and hats in the inevitable school cloakroom. Lessons last about forty-five minutes, and between each of them there is a ten- or twenty-minute break. A recess is a fairly noisy affair. Older children are moving along wide corridors from one specialist room to another. Younger ones may be romping about in a rather healthy manner. No one stays in the classroom, so that during bad weather the corridors serve as playgrounds.

As soon as the bell rings order is restored, frequently by a Young Pioneer with his badge of office. Pupils enter the classroom to await a second bell and the arrival of the teacher. All the children stand up when he or she enters the room, and indeed do so whenever a visitor enters. The atmosphere in a classroom is very dependent on the teacher and the taught. Usually it appears to be fairly relaxed. Children sit at desks usually in columns and rows and face a blackboard. Overhead projectors, televisions, record players along with more traditional aids are found in most rooms. Specially equipped rooms are provided for language, natural science, and mathematics teaching. In spite of these aids many lessons follow a similar pattern. Pupils are questioned, the correctness of their answer praised or if wrong, corrected. A mark is awarded for each answer. Then for a period pupils will be given written assignments before the teacher winds up the lesson by reviewing its content and assigning homework. Naturally this pattern is varied by individual teachers and particularly in language classes children are expected to participate orally in the foreign language in a most impressive manner. Frequently no word of Russian is spoken in such a lesson.

In the first four grades pupils have twenty-four lessons per week.[44] In the fifth and sixth grades the number is thirty. In addition, two extracurricular lessons with a choice of subjects are taken in the seventh grade. This number rises to four in the eighth grade and to six in the ninth and tenth grades. The total number of lessons in any subject is calculated on a yearly basis. Over the ten years of schooling mathematics tops the list followed closely by Russian grammar, Russian literature, history, physics, and a modern foreign language come next but occupy less than a third of the time devoted to either mathematics or Russian grammar. Two lessons each week are given over both to physical training and to shop. Some selection of subjects is now possible in and after the seventh grade.

Pupils attend school six days a week. They have five or six lessons a day (a maximum of thirty-six per week) depending on their age and up to three-hours homework a night. Many students remain in school after formal lessons are over in what are termed "prolonged day" school.[45] In 1975 almost one sixth of the total number of schoolchildren were in such groups. Most of them were from one of the first three classes. The growth in these schools has helped to meet the needs of children whose parents work. Lunch is served to these and other pupils during one of the twenty-minute recesses. The three-course hot meal costs parents a very small amount of money. After lunch, children may play in the school yard or a neighboring park and do their lessons or attend hobby circles under the guidance of teachers. They return home at five or six o'clock.

Considerable publicity has been given to boarding schools in the Soviet Union. Soviet spokesmen are at pains to make clear that they are not institutes for a privileged few. Rather they offer opportunities for several categories of pupils who for one reason or another might not be able to take full advantage of day schools. At boarding school children are provided with meals, clothing, shoes, textbooks, and so on at government expense. Parents contribute something according to their means toward the keep of their children, who stay at these schools all the time except for holidays and occasional days off. Some pupils go home at week-ends.

Orphans constitute an important category of children who attend boarding schools and are fully maintained by the state. After both world wars, large numbers of children were without parents. The memory of these trying times lives on, and orphans and children from broken homes or whose parents travel extensively inside the Soviet Union and abroad are regarded as being in special need. Indeed until 1956 boarding schools were only for children and teenagers up to eighteen in this category.

Now boarding schools have been set up for physically handicapped children—blind, partially sighted, deaf, dumb, and hard of hearing, and the mentally retarded.

Carefully selected sites in the country ensure that children live in beautiful surroundings but are usually near enough to a town to make possible visits to cinemas, museums, and other places of cultural interest. Forest schools, in particular, meet the needs of those who are rather delicate.

The timetable varies depending on the age of the pupils. Senior pupils are given considerable time for independent study in libraries or well-equipped laboratories. Younger children have a carefully regulated daily routine. These always include outdoor exercises and an afternoon nap for the seven- or eight-year-olds. Indeed special attention is given to the physical well-being of all pupils. Every school has its own workshops, vegetable garden, and rooms for extracurricular activities. Teachers give the lessons, and specially trained tutors look after the work and leisure to ensure the all-round upbringing of the pupils under their care.

Around 1958 policy was to make the boarding school the basic type of secondary school for all children. Teachers underwent special training and in some cities a number of boarding schools were opened. The belief was that an all-round polytechnical education could best be provided in institutions fully under the control of trained teachers. The cost of maintaining such schools may have influenced the decision to develop prolonged day provision rather than full boarding schools.

Nevertheless, in rural areas the network of boarding schools is expanding to meet the needs of children who may have to attend rather poorly equipped local schools run by teachers who do not possess up-to-date qualifications. Leningrad University, for example, has links with a number of boarding schools for rural children. The intention is to give the latter the same opportunities as their city cousins to enter the university. Rural boarding schools are often small, enrolling between thirty and fifty children. They are open to pupils who live too far away from a school to get to school and return home every day.

Some boarding schools seem to have among their pupils a high proportion whose parents hold important positions in the armed forces or professions and who move about considerably. They give an impression of privilege because classes are very small and the teachers are obviously enthusiastic and well trained. Such schools, often located in a residential area, are not representative. More usually a boarding school is attended by children from one of the categories mentioned. This policy is in line with the major aims of making sure that regardless of their position pupils receive the same quality of education.

The school year lasts until May 20 or June 1. Midwinter and spring breaks are short, but the summer holidays last for three months. Every summer about 15 million school children go off to Young Pioneer, school, health, or tourist camps. The Young Pioneer Camps accept any child. In their early days they were rather simple affairs. Now a Young Pioneer Camp has all the amenities of a small town, including stadiums, buildings for clubs and hobby circles, and so on as well as dormitories and dining rooms which may accommodate up to 600 persons. Factories and trade unions contribute generously to provide good camps for the children of workers. Children who remain in the towns and cities may attend special camps and may participate in excursions, sports, and organized walks.

Life at a university or pedagogical institute in the Soviet Union is similar in many respects to student life anywhere else. The number of lecture-seminars per week is heavy and prescribed. Classes are usually small, and methods of teaching take into account the maturity and motivation of students. A required course is dialectical materialism. Other required courses ensure that in spite of considerable specialization in a faculty or department the content of higher education is fairly broad. In all institutions and departments great attention is paid to a scientific knowledge of the subject. Rigorous criteria of scholarship are laid down, and students are expected to meet these criteria. In language classes textual analysis is frequently combined with oral practice and references to methods of teaching the material. In physics classes, students work in laboratories performing basic experiments from instructions on worksheets. Teaching is reminiscent of what goes on in universities in England. Students take examinations at the end of each academic year and prepare a dissertation for their diploma, which they receive usually after five years of study. Subsequently some may proceed by thesis to a *kandidat* degree—somewhat comparable to a Ph.D. in England and North America. Without a higher doctorate, an academic cannot become a full professor. Promotion within the academic world is consequently dependent upon scholarship as measured by research and publication.

Students training to be schoolteachers devote a great deal of time acquiring mastery of the subject they are going to teach in middle and complete secondary schools. Less time than some teachers would wish is spent on psychological and foundation studies but during their training, students spend some time in schools on supervised teaching practice. Specially appointed members of the faculty are concerned with methods of teaching and teaching practice. A majority are highly qualified in their subject. This is perhaps less so among faculty members in departments of primary education in which students intending to teach in kindergartens or the first three grades of school are trained. More attention is paid in these departments to psychology and child development, and, of course, the class teacher is responsible for all the subjects taught to children between seven and ten and hence is less of a subject specialist than the secondary school teacher.

Universities are run along traditional lines. The rector as administrative head is elected for a limited period of time from among the professors. He is assisted by deputy rectors with specific responsibilities. The universities' relationships with the All-Union Ministry of Higher Education are laid down in regulations and in practice are conducted in the light of tradition and convention. The fact that a great deal of applied research is carried out in special institutes associated with the university and financed by government industrial contracts makes it possible to draw a distinction between university- and government-sponsored research.

Within the university faculties are organized in departments. The concept of the chair persists. Its holder has associated with him teachers and research workers. As in other European universities the chair is specific to a field of enquiry, and it is the responsibility of the chair to develop his subject as he thinks fit. As mentioned, no professor can occupy a chair without a doctorate. Such academics, of course, dominate the work of a university and enjoy considerable freedom to pursue their research in accordance with their own interests. Some areas of enquiry are obviously more sensitive than others as the Lysenko controversy some twenty years ago demonstrated. Evidently developments in the social sciences and in education are more susceptible to ideological political pressures than is work in the pure and applied natural sciences.

## PROSPECT[46]

According to Marxist-Leninist theory the future of education in the Soviet Union will depend on the rate and success of moves to create a truly Communist society. From a Soviet point of view it is necessary to place the achievements made since 1917 in the longer perspective of the historical development of societies.

Thus, the author of "The Communist Party of the Soviet Union" in *Soviet Union*[47] states that the October Revolution and the establishment of Soviet power signified that the first program of the Bolshevik party had been fulfilled, and the second program of the party had been fulfilled when, after the Great Patriotic War (World War II) the economy of the country had been rehabilitated and the victory of socialism assured. In educational terms the achievement of nationwide literacy represented the completion of a major program. The next task of the Communist party was to universalize general secondary and polytechnical education.

The history of this endeavor is frequently told in statistics.[48] The period of compulsory schooling was gradually increased—first in towns and cities, then in the rural areas. Universal eight-year schooling was introduced in 1958. Between 1939 and 1959 the number of people with a secondary education increased 3.7 times. By 1975 the ten-year secondary education was available virtually to everyone. In 1976–1977 there were 159,000 schools including 52,000 ten-year schools attended by 46.5 million pupils. Nearly 5.25 million pupils completed eight years of compulsory schooling in 1976, and of these 97 percent went on in general secondary schools or in other establishments providing secondary education. Plans for 1976–1980 included the provision of general education for some 7 million pupils of whom 4.5 million were known to be in rural areas.

In 1977 the system of vocational training enrolled 3.5 million boys and girls in 6,100 schools. More than 1,000 specialist courses were on offer. Increasingly young people attending these technical vocational schools can complete a general education that will give them access to an institution of higher education. Early in 1977 some 40 percent of those enrolled in day vocational schools were in this position. Urban schools train young people for industry, construction work, and transport, trade and municipal services. Rural schools train tractor drivers and machine operators who will work on the farms. Practical training occupies up to 60 or 70 percent of the total time and is given first in factory or farm schools and then in industrial plants or on farms.

Specialized secondary schools admit young people who have completed either eight years of compulsory schooling or ten years in a general education school. One group of specialized secondary schools train people for industry, commerce, and agriculture. A second group trains paraprofessional workers such as elementary school teachers, medical staff, musicians, art workers, seamen, and so on. For pupils who have only eight years of schooling, the general education and theoretical and practical training as a specialist lasts three or four years. For pupils who have completed the ten-year school, a course in a specialized secondary school lasts two or three years. These years are largely devoted to practical instruction. Altogether in 1976–1977, there were 4,303 specialized secondary schools enrolling 4.6 million students of whom more than a million were studying by correspondence and another half million were attending evening courses.

Higher education has expanded greatly. In 1976–1977 there were some 859 institutions of higher learning of which 65 were universities. Some 5 million students were enrolled, more than half in day-time courses, 1½ million were studying by correspondence, and the rest were attending evening courses.

On these crude statistics, comparisons can and have been made with Western European systems and with the United States. American observers in the late 1950s were particularly impressed by Soviet schools. Nicholas DeWitt's[49] careful estimates of the number of scientists and technologists trained in the Soviet Union and the United States were used by congressmen to gain acceptance in 1958 of the National Defense and Education Act, which granted from federal sources monies to improve mathematics, science, and modern language teaching in American schools. On such criteria the Soviet system of education bears comparison with those of other developed nations, and Soviets can look forward to a further expansion of provision which will ensure that all children complete ten years of compulsory schooling. But a foreign observer may be forgiven for pointing to some problems that might be faced by educationists as they move toward this goal.

There are within the educational system itself, regardless of politics, problems that as yet do not seem to have received due attention. The first of these is curriculum development. The studies undertaken in the 1960s did not lead to the abandonment of an encyclopedic theory or to syllabuses that include all the data accumulated in the course of a subject's development. The hope that all knowledge can be successfully taught to all children is probably mistaken. Appreciation of this is doubtless a reason for the introduction of options into otherwise common curricula. The universalization of secondary and the growth of higher education is bound to create problems. Even if appropriate methods of teaching can ensure that all individuals can be taught and can learn abstract principles in a way that will enable them to deduce details from them, there is the question of motivation. How many young people will be prepared to study difficult subjects in the hope that in several years time as adults they will be suitably rewarded? The way academic school subjects are taught in the Soviet Union may be a disincentive. Certainly, reversals of policy in the 1960s suggest that successful ways of polytechnicalizing subject matter and linking school with life have yet to be devised.

One safeguard against disenchantment is in the shift of emphasis from the general complete secondary school to technical schools. Young people learning a trade may be prepared to complete their general education more willingly. What proportion of the population will be prepared simply to work for a place in a university, polytechnic, or pedagogical institute is a question of some importance. The answer to it will influence the future pattern of higher education in the Soviet Union. If more and more young people demand higher education as their right, the difficulties of linking it closely to manpower needs will increase. At the moment it is the government's control over the economy and the rewards it allocates to workers that make possible a reasonable match between schooling and manpower. Even so there is evidence to suggest that the two are less well matched than before when the economy demanded production workers and technologists in large numbers.

A match between schooling and industry depends not so much on the knowledge and skills acquired in schools but on attitudes toward work. The need to develop appropriate industrial attitudes has long been recognized in the Soviet Union. These attitudes are to be contrasted with those proposed by Dewey who wished to see the virtues of the American frontier perpetuated in industrial America. These were the virtues of laissez-faire agrarian republicanism and small-town life. Soviet educationists in their proposals to polytechnicalize education have seen the need for attitudes appropriate to large-scale modern industry and have rejected the values of capitalism. As far as the changes brought about by the application of technology are concerned, their analysis is sound. Rejection of capitalism is obviously a matter of political and ideological commitment. Whether education has yet been fully transformed is doubtful. Scholasticism is deeply ingrained in the outlook of teachers. Even in the physical sciences, teachers do not habitually exemplify the social and industrial applications of the principles they teach. One reason, perhaps, is that economic development has only just reached the stage when the products of modern industry are becoming available to individual consumers.

In two respects therefore, curriculum development appears to pose problems. How to manage the explosion of knowledge under conditions of universal and equal provision? And how to relate aspects of the curriculum to industrial life in a Communist society? Unless these problems are solved, dissatisfactions may create tensions in the system. These may not be politically motivated but are likely to have political consequences. At the moment students have shown few signs of protest. They have an honored place in society, are amply rewarded for their efforts, and through party organizations are drawn into the political system. As the economy develops, it seems likely that some of the problems faced in Western Europe and North America will become more difficult to deal with. Whether the school system has been reformed sufficiently to meet them effectively is a question of some importance.

For example, the benefits derived from a common compulsory curricula, authorized textbooks, national systems of teacher training, and national salary scales are obvious, and provision has been equalized to a considerable extent. As skilled people crowd into the cities, it may not be possible to maintain equality of provision between the city and country. Moreover, whether the same education should be offered to everyone is a question that cannot be answered unequivocally. In a mass system of schooling, demands to meet individual needs and aspirations cannot easily be reconciled with considerations such as manpower requirements. Incentives that have worked thus far may not work so well in the future, and more attention will undoubtedly have to be paid to ways to modify methods of teaching with the intention of individualizing instruction.

As for the socioeconomic context in which education will develop, Brezhnev may have strong grounds for asserting that the final phase in the evolution of Soviet society is in sight. This claim should be seen in the light of earlier assessments of economic change. On one interpretation of events the assertion was made that socialism had been established in the Soviet Union in December 1936 when a new Constitution was adopted. It reflected the fact that public ownership of the means of production had been achieved, a system of "socialist" relationships in all branches of the economy had been established, and the second program of the Communist party had been successfully completed. Evidence from Soviet sources places this final victory of socialism somewhat later, that is, after the Great Patriotic War and the period of economic rehabilitation that followed. According to this kind of theory the successful development of education is dependent on the successful evolution of a society moving from socialism to communism.

From a different perspective, the very success of the Soviet authorities in building up the economy of the country, in surviving a frightful war when millions of lives were lost, and in placing the Soviet Union as a superpower among the nations of the world may bring its own problems. In this vast country, minority groups, identifiable on the basis of language, religion, and nationality, have spokesmen who seek to preserve the identity of the groups they represent and wish to use the schools to do so. Language policy, which ensures that parents can choose the language of instruction for their children, promotes diversity. Within the schools, agencies promote loyalty to the party and its principles. Nationalism and internationalism permeate the work of the schools. Wider international contacts have influenced attitudes and transformed aspirations. It is within this kind of context that the future prospects of Soviet education should be assessed. They are, perhaps, less certain than might be supposed.

## REFERENCES

1. The international framework within which definitions of education are at present debated was provided by the United Nations Universal Declaration of Human Rights adopted by the General Assembly in 1948. Article 29 stated The Declaration was adopted unanimously, but the Soviet Union and some other member states abstained. See, *Human Rights: a compilation of International Instruments of the UN*. New York: United Nations, 1973, pp. 1–3.

2. *Constitution (Fundamental Law) of the Union of Soviet Socialist Republics* (Moscow: Novosti, 1977); see also *New Steps in Soviet Education, Materials of the Sixth Session of the USSR Supreme Soviet, July 17–19, 1973* (Moscow: Novosti, 1973) for the fundamentals of legislation of the USSR and union republics on public education.

3. Mikhail Prokofyev, "The Right to Education," in *The Rights and Freedoms of Soviet Citizens* (Moscow: Novosti Press, 1977), pp. 34–40.

4. N. K. Krupskaya, *On Education*. (Moscow: Foreign Languages Publishing House, 1957), pp. 119–120.

5. V. Yelyutin, *Higher Education in the USSR*, Soviet Booklet 51 (London, 1959), p. 41.

6. L. I. Brezhnev, *Following Lenin's Course* (Moscow, 1972), pp. 284–285; also *The 24th Congress of the CPSU and its contribution to Marxism-Leninism* (Moscow: Novosti Press, 1972); also M. Souslov, *Le PCUS, Parti du Marxisme createur* (Moscow: Novosti, 1972); and for the number of party members who are in the Ministry of Education see *Biographic data from the Institute for the Study of the USSR*; Munich, and its *Biographic Directory of the USSR* (New York: Scarecrow Press, 1958): and from the USA see J. Pennar, "Party Control over Soviet Schools," in *The Politics of Soviet Education*, ed. G. Z. F. Bereday and J. Pennar Atlantic Books, Stevens and Sons, 1960).

7. Prokofyev, "The Right to Education."

8. V. I. Lenin, "The Tasks of the Youth League," in *Lenin, Marx, Engels, Marxism*, Scientific Socialism Series (Moscow: Progress, 1970), pp. 116–132.

9. *Ibid.*

10. *Soviet Union* (Moscow: Progress, 1977), p. 177.

11. *Ibid.* p. 459; and XXVe Congrès du PCUS, *Rapport d'activité du Comité central du PCUS et taches immédiates du parti en politique intérieure et extérieure* (Moscow: Novosti, 1976).

12. Nicholas Hans, *The Russian Tradition in Education* (London: Routledge and Kegan Paul, 1963); see also by the same author "Recent Trends in Soviet Education," in *The Annals: The Soviet Union since World War II*, American Academy of Political and Social Science, May 1949; also *The Principles of Educational Policy*, 2nd ed. (London: King and Son, 1933).

13. A. I. Piskunov and E. D. Dneprov (ed.), *K. D. Ushinsky—Selected Works* (Moscow: Progress, 1975).

14. See V. I. Lenin, *Articles on Tolstoi* (Moscow: 1953); and for a brief account of Tolstoi's career, S. A. Tostaya (ed.), *Tolstoi's Moscow Home* (Moscow: Foreign Languages Publishing House, 1957), which gives the main dates in Tolstoi's life.

15. G. V. Plekhanov, *Fundamental Problems of Marxism* (Moscow: Foreign Languages Publishing House, n.d.).

16. For a comprehensive survey in English of the Soviet Union based on Soviet sources see Robert Maxwell (ed.), *Information USSR* (New York: The Macmillan Company, 1962). This book lists Russian and Soviet scholars who have participated in various aspects of life.

17. M. I. Kalinin, *On Communist Education*, Foreign Languages Publishing House, Moscow, 1950.

18. For an analysis of the language situation in the Soviet Union, see M. I. Isayev, *National Languages in the USSR: Problems and Solutions* (Moscow: Progress, 1977). Language has occupied a central place in Soviet Educational policy see for example D. P. Korzh "Public Education in the Far North of the USSR"; A. Rudakov, "Public Education in Komi Autonomous Soviet Socialist Republic"; and S. J. Savvin, "Education in the Yakut Autonomous Soviet Socialist Republic" all in *The Year Book of Education 1954*, ed. R. K. Hall, N. Hans, J. A. Lauwerys (London: Evans, 1954).

19. Medinsky, *Public Education in the USSR:* "The all-round development of the individual, the training of the fully educated, active and conscious builders of a communist society, their education in the spirit of Communist morality—such is the aim pursued by the Soviet school." p. 13; and A. P. Pinkevitch, *The New Education in the Soviet Republic*, trans. Nucia Perlmutter, ed. George Counts (New York: John Day, 1929), pp. 26–28.

20. B. P. Yesipov and N. K. Goncharov, "For Bolshevik Character: The Principles of Moral Education" and "For the Common Good: Education in Collectivism," in *I Want To Be Like Stalin*, trans. G. S. Counts and N. P. Lodge (London: Victor Gollancz, 1948).

21. See Y. N. Medinsky in *Anton Makarenko, His Life and Work* (Moscow: Foreign Languages Publishing House, n.d.); also Frederic Lilge, *Anton Semyonovitch Makarenko: An Analysis of His Ideas in the Context of Soviet Society* (Berkeley: University of California, 1958).

22. Constant reference is made in the literature to the stage in the evolution of society reached according to the laws of social development by the USSR. Communist party programs are geared to an assessment of progress along the road to Communism.

23. See A. V. Petrovosky, "Basic Directions in the Development and Current States of Educational Psychology," *Soviet Education*, 15, No. 5–6 (March-April 1973). The whole volume is devoted to Soviet educational psychology and on p. 109 it is stated that Soviet psychologists "refute psycho-analytical theories and theory of inborn quality and came to the conclusion: the mental development of the child, the formation of his cognitive processes, psychological traits, and personality features are determined by education and upbringing, i.e. by the way in which the adult

person directs and organises his assimilation of social experiences." See also S. Vygotsky, *Thought and Language*, trans. and ed. Eugenie Hanfmann and Gertrude Vakar (Cambridge MIT Press, and New York: Wiley, 1962) in which the author discusses Piaget's work and rejects one important point made by him, pp. 116–117.

24. See Brian Holmes, "Science Education: Cultural Borrowing and Comparative Research," in *Studies in Science Education* 4 (1977) Centre for Studies in Science Education, pp. 83–110.

25. Krupskaya, *On Education, p. 190; also Pinkevitch, The New Education in the Soviet Republic;* and Karl Marx, *Capital*, Vol. I (Moscow: Progresss Publishers, n.d.) "From the factory system budded . . . the germ of education of the future. An education, that will, in the case of every child over a given age, combine productive labour with instruction and gymnastics, not only as one of the methods of adding to the efficiency of production, but as the only method of producing fully developed human beings". pp. 453–454.

26. Karl Marx, *Capital*, Vol. 3 (London: Lawrence and Wishart, n.d.) p. 614.

27. Asratyan, *I. P. Pavlov*, makes reference on pages 100–102 to the second signal system which became important in the revival of Pavlovian theory.

28. Vygotsky's use and criticism of Piaget is important. Piaget modified his views later. See L. S. Vygotsky, "Learning and Mental Development at School Age," in *Educational Psychology in the USSR*, ed. Brian and Joan Simon (London: Routledge and Kegan Paul, 1963); also Vygotsky, *Thought and Language*.

29. For the influence of Vygotsky on recent research see also L. V. Zankov and others, "Teaching and Development: a Soviet Investigation," *Soviet Education* 19, Nos. 4, 5, 6 (February, March, April 1977).

30. See Brian and Joan Simon (eds.), *Education Psychology in the USSR;* see also John McLevush, *Soviet Psychology: History, Theory, Content* (London: Methuen, 1975), and particularly Chapter 8 "Half a Decade of Pavlovian Psychology"; and B. G. Annaniev, "The Psychophysiology of the Student-Age Population and the Assimilation of Knowledge," *Soviet Education* 15 (March-April 1973) in particular. "The role of environment, upbringing and education actively shapes abilities, and is not merely a prerequisite to the manifestation of some a priori genetic feature. The role of genetic make-up only indirectly influences the development of abilities; and while solely determining innate disposition, cannot decisively influence the development of abilities," pp. 143–144. See also Michael Cole (ed.), *Soviet Developmental Psychology, An Anthology* (White Plains, N.Y.: M. E. Sharpe).

31. See A. Markushevich, "The Problems of the Content of School Education in the USSR," in *Curriculum Development at the Second Level of Education*, Ed. Brian Holmes and Raymond Ryba. Proceedings of the Comparative Education Society in Europe, 4th General Meeting (London, 1969).

32. *Public Education in the USSR: in 1975–1976* (Moscow, 1977) makes the intentions for introducing optional courses clear. "One should see the introduction of optional courses in the senior grades. Over 8.5 million students attend such classes at present. More than 80 optional courses have been devised for classes in the Russian (or the respective native) language, and literature, history, social science, mathematics, physics, biology, chemistry, nature protection, labour training, pedagogics, psychology, ethics, aesthetics, and other subjects. Most of these courses envisage broader and deeper study of individual aspects or of key problems of the subject in question," p. 58.

33. Vassili Severtsev, *L'enseignement secondaire specialisé en URSS* (Moscow: Novosti, 1972); also Alexei Kalinin, *The Soviet System of Public Education, Its Organisation and Functioning* (Moscow: Novosti, 1973).

34. See V. Strezikozin, "The Soviet Union," in *Examinations, World Year Book of Education*, ed. J. A. Lauwerys, and D. Scanlon (London: Evans, 1969), pp. 152–169; also University of London Institute of Education, *Education in the USSR*, 1976, 1977. For some discussion of factors motivating children see L. I. Bozhovich, "The Personality of School Children and Problems of Education," in *A Handbook of Contemporary Soviet Psychology*, ed. M. Cole and I. Haltzman (New York: Basic, 1969), pp. 224–225.

35. "Decree of the USSR, Council of Ministers, on Part-time Education, April 1964," in *Izvestia, 23 April 1964*.

36. *Fundamentals of Legislation of the USSR and the Union Republics on Public Education* (Moscow: Novosti, 1975).

37. See M. Zinovyev and A. Pleshakova, *How Illiteracy Was Wiped Out in the USSR* (Moscow: Foreign Languages Publishing House, n.d.).

38. For a more recent discussion of polytechnical education see V. G. Zubov, "Polytechnical Education Under Present Conditions," *Soviet Education* 18 No.2 (December 1975), devoted to labor and education in the Soviet Union.

39. The Academy of Pedagogical Sciences of the Russian Federation was organized in 1944. Compare with the Academy of Sciences, which was established in 1724.

40. See S. G. Shapovalenko (ed.), *Polytechnical Education in the USSR* (Paris: Unesco, 1963), for example: "Each Union Republic has a pedagogical research institute coming under the Ministry of Education; whilst the RSFSR has an Academy of Pedagogical Science comprising 10 research institutes and attached to the RSFSR Ministry of Education," p. 90. For more detailed and up-to-date information see *Education in the USSR*, Reports of the University of London Institute of Education tours to the USSR, annual 1960–1979.

41. See University of London Institute of Education, *Education in the USSR*, (Annual reports of Comparative Education tours to the USSR, 1960–1979) for detailed impressions of nursery schools and kindergartens; also Ludwig Liegle, *The Family Role in Soviet Education*, trans. Susan Hecker (New York: Springer, 1975), in which it is reported that 80 percent of

working women have preschool age children (p. 57); statistics show (1970) that of the 2.6 million children in nursery schools and kindergartens more than half were two years and under.

42. See Urie Bronfenbrenner, *Two Worlds of Childhood, USA and USSR* (London: George Allen and Unwin, 1971) for comparisons that have received favorable mention in Soviet articles.

43. For much of the information in this section (confirmed by personal visits to Soviet schools) see S. Soloveichik, *Soviet Children at School* (Moscow: Novosti, 1976); see also Spartak Gazaryan, *Children in the USSR* (Moscow: Novosti, 1973); and *USSR Education* (Moscow: Novosti, 1976).

44. For details of curricula and lessons per week see *USSR 77*, and *Public Education in the USSR: in 1975–76* (Moscow, 1977), p. 47.

45. See Liegle, *The Family Role in Soviet Education*, p. 90, for an assessment of plans announced at the 23rd Congress of the party in 1966 to double enrollments in prolonged day schools and his view that the boarding school no longer occupies a prominent position in party policy.

46. See *Soviet Union* for an account, based upon reports presented to the 25th Congress of the Communist party, of future developments in the Soviet Union.

47. Apart from the reports presented at the 24th and 25th Congresses of the Communist party some general lines of development may be gained from M. Prokofyev, *Public Education, USSR, Yesterday, Today, Tomorrow* (Moscow: Novosti, n.d.), and A. M. Arsenyev, *The Soviet School of the Present and Future* (Moscow: Pedagogica, 1971); and from the reports sent to the International Bureau of Education for the biennial conferences held in Geneva attended by delegates from ministries of education of member states. See also the whole volume of *Soviet Education* 19 (November 1976), for a review of policies up to 1980.

48. Seymour M. Rosen, *Education in the USSR—Recent Legislation and Statistics*, U.S. Department of Health, Education and Welfare, Washington, 1975; also *Education and Modernization in the USSR* (Reading, Mass.: Addison Wesley, 1971). See also N. DeWitt, *Soviet Professional Manpower: Its Education, Training and Supply* (Washington: National Science Foundation, 1955).

49. DeWitt, *Soviet Professional Manpower*; also National Science Foundation, *Education and Professional Employment in the USSR* (Washington: Government Printing Office, 1961). Contributed in *Soviet Union*, p. 177.

CHAPTER 9

# West German Education

## HANS SCHIESER

### DEFINITION

The German educational system has influenced many other systems throughout the world and has remained more or less unchanged in its structure until recently, generally retaining the principles that made it so highly successful through such catastrophic events as the demise of the monarchy following World War I, the totalitarian dictatorship of the National Socialists, and the disasters of World War II, with the vast destruction of cities and virtually all major industries during the 1940s.

Most schools in Germany are public, but there are many "free" schools controlled by churches or private agencies, but these too are generally supported by state money. Practically all schools are tuition-free in Germany, even the universities.

In West Germany all children attend a four-year elementary school, then about 50 percent of them branch off to the *Realschule** or the *Gymnasia*. The other 50 percent continue through the ninth year of elementary school and then enter vocational training, and most of them go through a three-and-one-half-year apprenticeship.

---

*Definitions of the many German terms in this chapter will be found in a glossary at the end of the chapter.

INTRODUCTION

Objectives of Education

Throughout the history of formal education, various objectives have been proposed and emphasized: salvation, function in a given social setting, and knowledge. But no consensus has been achieved as to the importance of the one over the other.

All three objectives must be present in the process of *educere* (or *educare*, meaning to lead out). Depending on the developmental stage of the individual and on the existing environment in which he or she is educated, one or the other of the three objectives will be emphasized.

For the young child, "functioning" in the family and in the classroom is an important goal; later on, when he is to live in a complex or even totalitarian society, this functioning may be crucial. To make a living, one certainly has to know many things. In our times, with a fast-changing economy, the constant upgrading of knowledge is also a matter of survival on the job market. Finally, the goal of "salvation," however diverse its interpretation may be in its religious or secular connotations, is always present, even subconsciously, with educators who want to help the young generation "make it"—into heaven or on society's socioeconomic ladder.

Contemporary trends in society such as socialism, massive manipulation of public opinion, and economic crises challenge educators much more than at any time before, to "lead out" people from the power fields of pied pipers and "hidden persuaders" and make them "propaganda proof." The English historian Arnold Toynbee saw this as the foremost task of education today. The emerging threat of bioengineering that promises to "breed" perfect human beings without the unpredictable (and so far unsuccessful) efforts of shaping man through schooling will challenge educators to clarify their objectives even more.

What is ultimately at stake with any education, be it geared to salvation, function, or knowledge, is the freedom of a person to decide about one's salvation, the role to function in a society, and obtaining the knowledge that seems worthwhile to the individual. Whenever attempts were made to take away these decisions from the person and have them predefined by an "authority" (be it the Church or a state, parents or teachers), negative reactions increased with the maturity and critical awareness of the respective individual. Regarded as an *a priori* element in human existence, this desire to be free has been manifest throughout the history of mankind. Maybe our century is characterized more than any preceding century by the struggle for freedom. "Emancipation" is a common slogan in German education today. It has been picked up by others recently, but always with the connotations that Karl Marx attributed to the term: *the revolutionary change of man's situation in a corrupted society and economy.* Looking closer, we see the "emancipators" at work alienating youth from their existential ties with the family and their environment and leading them to a "critical," that is, negative, attitude toward everything in their lives. The insights of Johann Pestalozzi almost two hundred years ago have been confirmed everywhere:

> Man's domestic relationships are the first and foremost ones of Nature. Man toils in his vocation and bears the burden of communal duties in order to enjoy his home in harmony and peace. To this peaceful enjoyment man's education for his vocation and for his social rank must be subordinated! (Pestalozzi, 1780).

It does not look as if contemporary education helped the majority of our young generation to achieve this goal: to enjoy a home in harmony and peace. We do not see a positive relationship to nature, to fellow man, to society. We do see increase of crime, running down the environment, and increasing mental health problems. While we claim to have achieved unprecedented insights into the workings of the human mind and body, we still seem to lack the ability to apply them to our benefit.

Education must primarily lead the young generation to a positive relationship with itself and to the existing environment. Only on the basis of such a relationship will attitudes arise that make possible changes that will improve conditions. Concretely, this means that the elementary curriculum is to be geared to a love of nature and of man. This is what we see as a fundamental principle in European education and the outcomes are visible: people love their homes and the environment, they keep both in shape, and they get along with each other as long as they are left alone. Only through agitators like a Napoleon, a Hitler—who want to impose their ideas upon the people—do conflicts and wars arise.

Similarly, the goals of secondary and higher education are to be geared to a positive role of individuals in society. The development of an elite in society does not *per se* lead to a polarization but only when knowledge detaches itself from service to mankind. Both the worker and the academician have an obligation to work for the well-being of all; with emphasis on freedom of choice; whatever one chooses to learn and to do finds its meaning in the application for improvement of the self and of others. This is not a contradiction to the classical ideal of *artes liberales*, of the pursuit of knowledge for its own sake, but is the very basis of this ideal. The community can function only when knowledgeable citizens exist who have a positive attitude toward their fellow citizens and respond to their needs.

Education must lead to the "peaceful enjoyment of home and life" without the interference of an almighty state or of a party.

## Reasons for This System

The present system, which prepared several generations for a successful life, in spite of many interfering powers at work in Germany during the last 150 years, approaches formal education's first phase—with an elementary curriculum that integrates the cognitive and affective domains. The three R's and a love for people, animals, and the *Heimat* (home world) are the basis for an educational continuation on the secondary and tertiary levels. There, the basis for a *Beruf* (vocation) is laid through either technical or academic education.

The recent politicizing of German education through socialistic ideological reforms and the establishment of some experimental schools with a curriculum that abandoned established fundamental principles have drawn heavy criticism and reactions from many people. Many private schools still successfully keep the standards of the *Bildungsideal*.

The constitutional basis for funding all schools, including private ones, through general taxes provides for a wide variety of educational opportunities. Schools are not necessarily equal, as the aspirations and the potentials of individuals never are equal, but they offer access to virtually all roles that a person can possibly assume in a complex society like Germany's. The limited amount of control that state authorities have over the schools allows also for a coordination of offerings and allocations with a highly diversified economy tied in with worldwide structures of production, trade, and monetary conventions. It allows also for the free establishment of supplementary educational institutions, which have developed at the highest rate recently: academies and other continuing education programs that offer opportunities to upgrade education and to change occupations.

## HISTORY

### Beginnings

Formal education started in Germany under the auspices of the Church. Throughout the Middle Ages, monasteries and cathedrals in cities were crystallization points of education. Not only those who intended to join the religious orders but also the Laity were educated through a comprehensive program that included the classic *artes liberales* and Christian life-style. This provided the fertile grounds for a *universitas*, the widest possible basis of education institutionalized under the charter of the Church.

The developments of the Renaissance and the emergence of science moved education into the hands of worldly sovereigns and created a split that would run through the schools up to our times: the separation of *theoria* (which we must understand in the wider, original sense that will be discussed later) and *praxis*. In concrete terms, this meant the evolution of the two fundamental principles that determine the German education system: *Bildung* (*Bild* meaning image, idea, ideal), or education along the lines of the classic liberal arts leading to a *Weltanschauung* (world view) on one side, and *Ausbildung* (training) on the other. Many of the German states established public schools as a vehicle for cohesiveness. The first ones were in Gotha (1642) and in Prussia (1716) held that schools should not remain vehicles for rulers to prepare their populace to be "good subjects" only. His famous *Reden an die Deutsche Nation* (1808) was influenced by the Swiss educator Johann Heinrich Pestalozzi (1746–1827) who also had demanded the development of man's potential as the basis of a humane society. Many educators in Europe were inspired to work toward the ideal of a humanistic world. The key figure that gave direction to the German and the world's secondary education systems was Wilhelm von Humboldt (1767–1835), the Prussian minister of culture and education. His view that the major objective of education, "the utmost development of the human potential," can happen only when the student is free to learn (*Lernfreiheit*) and the teacher free to teach (*Lehrfreiheit*), promoted a thoroughgoing reform of secondary and higher education.

With the Industrial Revolution gaining momentum during the nineteenth century, industry with its growing need for trained people wanted education as a vehicle for its own purposes.

Around the turn of the twentieth century, the superintendent of schools in Munich, Georg Kerschensteiner (1854–1932) gave a new stimulus to elementary and vocational schools with his idea of the *Arbeitsschule* (inadequately translated as "industrial school"). He pointed to the future need of more reliable and responsible workers when technology makes skills less important with the development of automated machinery. The development of "virtues" along with skills, or the mature personality through meaningful work, became the major objective of vocational education. This training, he maintained, should start as early as the first grades of primary school. The teacher is to insist on accurate and punctual work: writing neatly and keeping exercise books in order.

The fruits of the *Arbeitsschule* were soon visible: the label *Made in Germany* became a mark of quality on the world market. Modern German vocational education still adheres largely to the principles formulated by Kerschensteiner.

In the 1930s Hitler's powerful hordes swept all reforms away in the "equalization" of all schools. For the first time, Germany was truly "unified," and the schools in the hands of a central authority. But this came about only with brutal force. Many teachers were arrested and sent either to the front with the army or to concentration camps. The students and professors of the universities were dismissed if they refused to join the National Socialists. Even Martin Heidegger (then at Heidelberg) bent to the pressures and became a Nazi. Hitler realized that the process of educating a "new generation" went too slowly with the schools. He reshaped the strong Youth Movement (*Wandervogel*) that had existed since the turn of the century into the compulsory *Hitlerjugend* (Hitler youths). Boys had to "serve" from age twelve to about eighteen in this pre-military and ideological program, girls in a corresponding branch that cultivated domestic skills. The program had a strong appeal to younger boys and girls, as it was practical (hiking, camping, physical fitness, and activities like model making, automotive, navigational, and aeronautical training, cultural activities and homemaking, baby care, and the like), and avoided the academic; also it was conducted by young people, not by older teachers. It also kept "the kids off the streets" and solved the problem of youth delinquency completely. But the price for this was too high.

For the elite who were meant to run *Grossdeutschland* (Great Germany) as the leading nation of the world, several *Hitler-Akademien* were built. Blond, blue-eyed, and above-average intelligent boys were recruited (often against the will of their parents) for tough training and ideological education for several years. The students had to disavow all religious affiliation and could not spend much time with their families. The idea was to train absolutely reliable functionaries with 100 percent loyalty to the ideals of National Socialism. The SS man was the typical product of these "academies."

## Current Status

The present situation of the German education system is characterized by tension between *Bildung* (ideals) and *Ausbildung* (training), i.e., a purpose-free, ideal-oriented education of the whole person and the development of the human potential, on one side, and a practical, vocationally oriented training of competent and reliable individuals, on the other side. The system works toward this dual goal based on vertical movement. Only successful passage through one level will allow entry into the next higher one. Attempts to change this to a "horizontal" structure, like the integrated form of a secondary school that would comprise all three types—*Hauptschule*, *Realschule*, and *Gymnasium*—have met with fierce opposition from educators, administrators, parents, and political authorities.

By law, children start to attend school at age six or seven. There is no compulsory preschool program, but many children attend a Kindergarten with some kind of pre-academic program. Parents have a choice of sending their children to public or private schools, both funded by tax money.

The minimum school attendance nationally is nine years, leaving an option to those states that wish to add a tenth year to elementary school. After this, partial school attendance is mandatory in conjunction with vocational training. This means concretely that an elementary school graduate must attend either a trade school, coupled with an apprenticeship program (once a week), or a similar program if he or she does not enter an apprenticeship. Thus, some kind of school attendance is compulsory until a youngster is eighteen years old.

For those who branch off to secondary education after the fourth grade of elementary school, access to *Realschule* (roughly an equivalent to the American high school) or to *Gymnasium* is contingent on passing an entrance exam or, at least, on above-average grades at fourth grade. Recommendations by the homeroom teacher have decisive weight. This early transition to secondary education has often been criticized as too unrealistic, since the decision has lifelong implications. Later changes in interest involve costly and time-consuming adjustment programs. The proposed solution, simply doing away with the differentiated secondary tracks in a *Gesamtschule* (General School), was rejected mainly on the grounds of taking away opportunities from those who do benefit from such early specialization.

All schools are structured in classes, that is, the students are grouped by age. Alternatives such as "courses" that would meet individual differences or "cooperative learning" to foster solidarity have never found much following. Most parents and teachers agree on the advantages of a classroom that supports the young child's personality through his or her peers. Youngsters in secondary schools prefer also the class with its "spirit" and a teacher who remains with the group for a few years. While most schools were separated by sexes (except in rural areas) until the 1950s, virtually all are coeducational now.

The *Hauptschule* (grades five to nine) has a vocationally oriented curriculum: concrete application of the three R's, science, *Arbeitslehre* (nature and structure of industrial and commercial work), a foreign language (usually English), and civics make up most of the subjects. Some of these, like *Arbeitslehre* and English, were formerly part of the secondary curriculum. It seems that many of the students in the upper grades of elementary (that have lost the good achievers to secondary schools) are simply overburdened with such studies. A growing number of youngsters do indeed fail to achieve in the reformed *Hauptschule* and flunk out at the end. Others are transferred to special education, though they do not really belong in programs geared for learning-disabled youngsters. The call for the "traditional" elementary school that seemed to do a better job is heard again.

On the secondary level, the former *Mittelschule* served as the "lower level" of secondary education, in contrast to the higher form, the *Gymnasium*. With the reorganization of the elementary school, particularly with the ninth and tenth year added, the distinction between *Hauptschule* (upper elementary) and *Realschule* (as the *Mittelschule* is now called) became blurred. The curriculum can be compared to the American high school's. Recently, it began to serve for many as an intermediate vehicle to achieve access to the *Gymnasium* at a later age, and even to college-level education in a restricted field. Such *Aufbaugymnasien* bring students to a level of competence that allows for admission to college within a specified field only.

The *Gymnasium* has remained the higher form of secondary schooling with the primary goal of college preparation. The graduation examination (*Abitur*, or "maturity exam") entitles one to study at the university. It has, however, undergone significant changes in the last twenty years: the classical distinction between the "humanistic" form with its emphasis on ancient languages (Latin, Greek), history, and literature, and the "realistic" form with science and modern languages (English, French), has almost entirely disappeared. Many of the once-compulsory major subjects were made optional and new, "more relevant" courses, mostly in the social sciences area, were introduced. This devalued the *Abitur* that was once recognized throughout Europe as a guarantee of high-caliber study skills and a firm foundation of knowledge and personal culture ("maturity"). Now students "make it" with an accumulation of "points" which can be earned through good grades in the preferred "easy" courses without any fundamental knowledge in the basic subject areas. Neighboring Switzerland was the first to deny acceptance of the new *Abitur* as no longer consistent with the standards of an education that could serve as a basis for higher studies. The German universities encountered the same problem: they reject to make up for the deficits the majority of the *Abiturienten* have in their basic knowledge. They are demanding that the *Gymnasium* do a more consistent job as in the past. Many students seek admission to private *Gymnasien* that still adhere to high academic standards.

With the lowering of standards for the *Abitur* and its devaluation, an explosive rush to the institutions of higher learning occurred. While there were about 300,000 students enrolled at West German *Hochschulen* (universities, technical universities, teacher education academies) in 1960–1961, the number jumped to 600,000 in 1971 and was close to a million in 1976. New universities and *Gesamthochschulen* (comprehensive institutions of higher learning that combine many different types of higher education) were established to meet the rush. But it still could not handle the crowds. So a quota system was invented. A newly created agency, the *Zentralstelle für die Vergabe von Studienplätzen* (Central Bureau for the Allocation of Study Placement) has tried to meet the demands of students who have a constitutional right of access to higher education and of the universities' need to reduce admissions drastically. The formula applied now demands a grade average that had been achieved by fewer than 40 percent of the *Abiturienten*. Even the digit behind the decimal point can now determine acceptance or rejection. In 1980, a new formula has been developed which should allow for more realistic and just quotas as it considers not only the grade average of the applicants, but also the availability of places at the universities. There will nevertheless be many who either have to wait for years or never make it into college.

The assessment of the German education system cannot exclude institutions that go parallel to the regular schools on three levels: special education, vocational training, and continuing education. All three have a long history and have been regarded as essential supplements to the regular schools. Thus they are all funded or at least subsidized by the government. There are numerous institutions for handicapped and disabled children. While all cities have a school for learning disabled children, smaller towns have special programs or send these children to the larger city. Specialized schools for the blind or for physically handicapped are mostly boarding schools. They are generally operated by the Catholic church but funded by the state. The tendency is toward more comprehensive help for these children and youngsters in so-called *Rehabilitationszentren* that comprise kindergarten through vocational education.

The majority of the population, however, goes through the other two tracks that offer a most diversified program of education: vocational education and training, and adult education.

More than 60 percent of an age group go through an apprenticeship program after graduating from elementary or secondary school. The curriculum, duration, and quality of this training is controlled by industry (organizations of the respective trade, similar to the guilds of the Middle Ages) and the state (Ministry of Labor in the state and federal governments).

The Germans have undoubtedly been highly successful in providing educational opportunities, though not necessarily equal ones, to all. The participation of both industry and society, government and churches, and the openness to ideas from abroad (American influence has been strong since the end of World War II) have resulted in high standards. Critical reactions from all these partners, including of course parents and students, will guarantee the continuation along these lines.

The formation of a National Committee for Education (*Deutscher Ausschuss für das Erziehungsund Bildungswesen*) by the Conference of the German Ministers of Culture in 1963 was meant to provide an official forum for the best ideas to "reconstruct the world of education in Germany" (Theodor Heuss). It did not quite meet the expectations but led to the Council of Education (*Deutscher Bildungsrat*) in 1965 and a committee where both the states and the federal authorities will cooperate and coordinate educational matters. The planned reforms of the German education system that are evolving from this *Bund-Länder Kommission für Bildungsplanung* may well become one of the most comprehensive national projects in education that ever were undertaken in a free country.

## THEORY

### Learning

#### *Anschauung*

The most general principle that stands out in German educational theory is *Anschauung*. Though not always explicitly stated, it serves both as starting point and objective for education. The term, derived from the verb *anschauen* (to look at), does not have a corresponding English concept, because it connotes a special way of looking at something or someone. Pestalozzi, for example, held *Anschauung* to be the child's natural endowment: the ability to look at the world with a "loving eye." The first (normal) view in a child's life is seeing mother. Naturally, it is a positively charged view. Throughout life, a person more or less retains or develops this ability, unless experiences turn him or her away, toward the negative. In concrete terms, this can be seen when a child sees a toy. The first encounter is joyful. A child simply expects the object to be "likable." If it does not "correspond" (answer on the same wavelength), the child will turn away and lose interest. If, on the other hand, the object lends itself to a joyful experience, the encounter will be carried on to a deeper involvement. This "Law of Anschauung" applies at any developmental level, at any age. It is the most fundamental principle in most European, particularly German education. On the elementary as well as secondary level, the teacher tries to *veranschaulichen* whatever he teaches; that is, to present subject matter in a way that the students can "see and enjoy" (*anschauen*). Each school has a collection of *Anschauungsmaterial* for virtually every subject taught. Often, teachers make their own models or pictures which are not primarily seen as "instructional aids," helps for teaching, but rather as stimulators of *Anschauung*, challenging the student to get involved on both the cognitive and affective levels. The ultimate goal that evolves is a *Weltanschauung*, a view of the world characterized by positive emotional involvement.

Modern education theorists who usually speak of the cognitive domain only and try to explain learning as a "conditioning process" or even as a "mechanism" operate on a much narrower basis. Their goal is thus naturally just as narrow: the conditioning of the individual through "objective" or emotionally neutral activities. The emphasis is, for the behaviorist, to learn "whether you like it or not"; with *Anschauung*, the educator's primary concern is to lead a student to enjoy it. The writer would not insist that all German school children like all subjects, but the fact is that students have a more positive attitude toward their schools and toward learning than the average American child. Love of nature and of people is a *leitmotiv* in German education. When such setbacks into barbarism as Nazism happen, they can be traced back to an education that betrayed or ignored these principles. The contemporary problems of terrorism and youth delinquency come also from a shift in education from the whole-child approach, with *Anschauung* as the principle, to the behavioristic, merely cognitive and conditioning approach. The modern principle of *Gesellschaftskritik* (social criticism) is the very opposite of *Anschauung* with its negative and ultimately destructive tendencies. When, for example, schoolbooks in Hessen and Nordrhein-Westfalen try to make first graders (!) become "aware that they are exploited by their parents, and the parents are exploited by capitalists . . ." and when there are more themes of abuse and dictatorial authority in the elementary readers than "nice" stories, then further steps will, no doubt, be negative too.

### Heimat

While teaching and learning are based on the ability of a person to "know and enjoy," the corresponding object of this knowledge and enjoyment is the environment in which a person is brought up. The first environment is naturally the home, with the parents, brothers, and sisters being the first persons to whom a child relates. The range of experience widens as the child learns to walk, to talk, when one goes to school, and eventually is on his or her own. Pestalozzi describes this process in terms of concentric circles that widen throughout life:

> The sphere of knowledge from which man in his individual station can receive happiness is limited; its sphere begins closely around him, around

his own self and his nearest relationships, from there his knowledge will expand, and while expanding it must regulate itself according to this firm centre of all the powers of truth. . . . (Pestalozzi, 1780).

European education has recognized the validity of Pestalozzi's points. Elementary curricula have been geared consistently to the *Heimat* (home world) of the students: by emphasizing the positive relationship that all children normally have with their homes and families, with their familiar environment with its natural and cultural phenomena, and the religious world that permeates both the home and the land. In German elementary schools, *Heimatkunde* (social basics) or *Gesamtunterricht* (comprehensive instruction) is the major subject. It comprises social studies, sciences, as well as the three R's and is intended to make the children aware of the scientific, cultural, religious, and political dimensions of their environment. The major objective is to achieve an "integrated and comprehensive view of the student's *Heimat*." The primary focus is on deeper understanding and positive appreciation of all the natural and cultural givens in the environment in which children grow up. In this view, it is more important for a ten-year-old to know how to handle, feed, and take care of a cat with her kittens than to study the dinosaurs that might have lived in the area thousands of years ago. It is also much more beneficial for the growth of a healthy personality when a lesson on the local city government emphasizes the functions and services for people rather than discussing corruption and political intrigues.

The negative approach of a *Gesellschaftskritik*, which has been proposed recently, and implemented in some schools by "reformers," abandons the principles of *Anschauung* and *Heimat* and lays more emphasis on the "scientific method" and on artificial structures, as opposed to natural ones. This is exactly what the National Socialists did when they put into the foreground of education "national pride" and the "love of a fatherland" while people identified much more with a local town, and their love was rather for the hills and rivers of their own region.

Social psychology now confirms what Pestalozzi intuitively recognized: that without this "firm centre, according to which all human powers regulate themselves. . ." the individual will inevitably end up in alienation and turn against the environment. Discipline problems in school and in society, violence and vandalism among youth and adults are only symptoms of "homelessness." To state it in more positive terms: An individual with positive attitudes toward others and the environment is motivated to engage in meaningful relationships and activities. If learning is connected with such positive attitudes and aims at developing them further, all such problems as serious discipline disorders, frustration, and aggression must disappear.

## Motivation

The *a priori* assumption that man is a *homo sapiens*, that is, able and willing to know, is the basis of all education. To preserve the curiosity of a child which, later on, shrinks to a minimal interest span in so many cases, has been the concern of educators throughout the centuries. Educators have held that this loss of interest in the pursuit of knowledge stems largely from formal education, that is, from the educators themselves.

While psychologists have tried to develop various techniques of motivation, the classic four principles of education are still valid. They are the basis of German teacher education and of the remarkable effectiveness of their schools. They are: *Didactic*, the art of presenting knowledge in an orderly and understandable way; *rhetoric*, the art of persuasion; *poetic* (in the original sense), the art of presenting truths and facts with such "aids" as dramatization, audiovisual and "*Anschauungsmaterial;*" and finally, *dialectic* or the exchange of views and opinions in personal communication.

What this means concretely has been confirmed by modern learning theory with its emphasis on presenting the learning materials in a way that the learner can assimilate (Piaget), preparing subject matter carefully, and applying methods that are "convincing," with the help of materials that allow the student to apply all, or as many senses as possible. German teachers often make their own models and learning aids. But schools have also good collections of instructional aids. Dialectic is visible in the teacher's attempt to involve the students as much as possible in a dialogue, to challenge their opinion and exchange of ideas about the subject matter of a class.

## Teaching

### Gestaltung

The concept of *Gestalt* has been used in English in various contexts. In German education, the process of "giving shape," with the specific connotation of a skilled and planned activity that is both creative and functional, is called *Gestaltung*. It spans from the child's ability to make something out of a lump of clay, in a playful act, to the teacher's efforts to structure his experience before sharing it with the students, and ultimately, the goal of "giving direction" to one's life (*Lebensgestaltung*) in the process of self-realization. Teachers and parents must be aware of the pattern that underlies all personal development toward a mature existence: first, the parents *gestalten* (give shape and direction) the child's life, together with the environment (culture, society, nature). Then the school merges with the parents' efforts. Once the school counteracts the influence of the home, a parallelogram of forces arises that disrupts the continuum of growth. Normally, the roots in the *Heimat* (family, ethnic, cultural, religious factors) prove to be stronger, but often the formal structures (school, state) prevail for a time and create tensions in the individual that become, sooner or later, problematic. When the school cooperates with the parents, the individual finds it easier to develop identity and mature to the point where he or she becomes free to *gestalten* (shape) his or her own life.

The ambiguity of *Gestaltung* has always been alive among German educators: How much do environment and heredity influence the individual's *Lebensgestaltung* (life-style), and how "deep" does the school reach in its attempt to lead a person beyond these existential ties? The fact that much of our teaching effort affects a student not only on the conscious, but at least as much (if not more) on the subconscious level, makes it not only difficult to resolve these questions but also throws light on the serious responsibility that a teacher has in guiding students toward a positive *Lebensgestaltung* (life-style). The personal relationship that Socrates had formulated as the very basis of education and that so many German (and German-speaking) philosophers and educators interpreted in their pedagogic writings (Pestalozzi, Froebel, Buber, Scheler, and others) is the principle of all *Gestaltung*. It found its realization in the ideal of a teacher who is a respected professional with a genuine interest and concern for his pupils. The majority of the German teachers meet this expectation.

*Arbeit*

The perennial dispute over whether the primary goal of education should be knowledge for its own sake or useful knowledge cannot be settled by an "either-or" proposition. All knowledge is somehow useful, and schools cannot reject the obligation to help people to "make a living." On the other hand, if we should orient our educational efforts entirely to the development of practical skills, will there be a "side effect" in the affective domain? German schools before Kerschensteiner emphasized the double value of "school work": any work well done has a moral value. With the ideas of Kerschensteiner in the earlier twentieth century, schools applied this insight much more consistently, however. Each child has a *gestaltende Kraft* (form-giving, creative power) that needs to be developed toward a balance of given structures (*Gestalt* or prescribed shape)—as for example, in writing cursive letters, the child has to write exactly between given lines, to make the e and l distinguishable or a worker has to follow the specifications of the blue print accurately—and the creative, joyful activity (like writing a story or making something in the workshop). Accuracy, neatness, completeness, and mastery are fundamental components. When a student finishes his task, and when the product meets the expected standards, the teacher or master will praise it. But a child and a worker can enjoy the achievement even without such a praise.

Arts and crafts are compulsory subjects from kindergarten through secondary school. Beginning with simple operations that increasingly demand dexterity and allow for creativity, the students are challenged to develop *Arbeitsfreude* (enjoyment of work), the strongest motivator going from school throughout life. The philosophical basis for this attitude has undergone some changes: In the traditional school, the emphasis was on the individual's fulfillment that arises naturally from good work. The balance between *sachgerechte Arbeit* (proper use of tools, correct operations) and creativity was the major objective. In recent theories, originating mostly from collectivism, the goal is the "emancipated" person who escapes "exploitation" by doing "relevant work." What this means concretely has never been shown. Most of these ideas have been proposed by theoreticians without any practical experience. With all the discussions of "allocation" and "qualification processing," with the demands for a "reorientation and democratization" of vocational education, wherever these "reforms" were implemented, the results were the very opposite of an "emancipation": increasing joblessness among youth because of a shortage of apprenticeship places for the graduates of the schools, and the lower motivation of youngsters to go through such a three-year training. The lack of *Arbeitsfreude* is the fruit of a one-sided approach that emphasizes only function (*Leistung*). Johann Herbart had already warned of this, as early as 1810:

> [We are against] . . . the State's goal to make the schools an agency of allocation of vocational and social opportunities and the erection of political compulsory structures . . . ! The public schools must give up their claim of a pedagogic monopoly!

His insights were confirmed again, at this time, where functionaries of the state with bureaucratic power but not necessarily practical experience and genuine concern for the well-being of the individuals ruled on curricular directions. The reaction to this trend is the stepped-up efforts of other agents of education (private schools, supplementary education) to offer both training and education with professional staff and realistically sound programs. Here, practitioners, students, theorists, and industry work together with the authorities of church and state in order to meet the changing demands of a working society and the unchanged need for fulfillment of the lives of men.

The concept of *Arbeit* as used by Kerschensteiner goes beyond the activity of man necessitated by the need for making a living. It is rather similar to Karl Marx's view of a "complete human act" that would be the opposite of dehumanized industrial work. We see three steps in this "complete act," which can be described in these terms: At the beginning, man conceives the goal of work and "sees" the finished product ("opus") in his mind. Then, material is to be found that lends itself to the transformation leading to the goal. The structure and form of this material are then changed with effort (labor). Finally, the finished product or opus arises from man's hands. Marx saw the problem of industrial work in its reduction to mere labor. Hence, alienation and frustration arise. But there is no return to the times of the artisan who still did the "whole work," from designing to finished product. Kerschensteiner was more realistic than Marx. He foresaw the shifting emphasis from skills to attitudes in the future and the need for meaningful activities that compensate for fragmentation of work. Machines and the assembly line made it easier to acquire a skill and require minimal skills. But at the same time, the workers have to be more careful with these machines. Accuracy, punctuality, and responsibility (which Kerschensteiner called "virtues") become primary objectives in vocational education.

Progressive theorists of recent times ignore both the fundamental "Law of Self-activity," which had been scuccessfully applied since the times of Froebel and Pestalozzi, and the nature of work in its human quality. Their definition in terms of exploitation and societal needs is inadequate and not fruitful for pedagogic efforts to lead youth to this "pursuit of happiness" which cannot be done without the basis of making a living.

### Religion

In our western culture, religious institutions were the originators of formal education, Up to this day, German schools on the elementary and secondary level count religious instruction as a "basic" compulsory subject, unless parents sign a formal "release" for their children. The principle of religion is, however, not exclusively defined in terms of established church form, though classes are taught by ministers or teachers certified by the respective churches. The two major denominations in West Germany are Catholic (45 percent) and Lutheran (49 percent) whose influences reach deep into everyday life.The attempts of the National Socialists to replace this influence by a new *Weltanschauung* were not successful. Nor have recent trends of a resurgent anti-religious sentiment succeeded in "secularizing" the schools entirely, though many of them have alienated some German youth from their religious and cultural roots. An anti-religious tendency has been with the European intelligentsia since the French Revolution and the Enlightenment.

The old accusations that the churches "brainwash and indoctrinate" the people are reemerging though experience with totalitarianism should have taught that religion as a personal commitment to values that transcend the givens of a society was the only guarantee of freedom, and that churches were the backbone of resistance against the tyrants of the Third Reich.

Until the 1960s most German teacher education institutions (*Pädagogische Hochschulen*) were either "Catholic" or "Protestant", and so the majority of the students and the curriculum were oriented toward the religious perspective. After the mid-1960s this religious orientation was changed simply by decree and by an increased emphasis on the "scientific" nature of the teaching profession. Many of the younger teachers were thus alienated from their churches, only to fall victim to the leftist ideologies. Those who adhere to the values and personal commitment to religion choose largely private schools that are increasingly established throughout the country. The constitutional basis for tax support of such schools make such alternatives possible. It also realizes the clear statement of religious freedom and the value of religion in society that is found in both the federal and state constitutions of West Germany: no society can function without this freedom and many of the institutions that serve people (the schools are only some of them) are best because of their religious commitment.

*Progressivism and Gesellschaftskritik*

In 1967, Saul B. Robinsohn, an American who became director of the Pedagogical Research Institute of the Max-Planck Gesellschaft (Berlin), published a book on a throughgoing reform of the school curriculum. Robinsohn insisted that the contents and organization of formal education badly needed an adjustment to contemporary demands. Each step in the process of education, he said, should be defined and carefully evaluated to achieve optimal efficiency. The "prescientific" orientation of didactic and contents according to human and cultural values was to give way to a "scientific, value-free, and theoretical view of education on the basis of controllable and analytic categories" (Boventer, 1975). A comprehensive plan for the entire education system (*Bildungsgesamtplan*, 1973) was adopted by the federal and state governments, while some states (especially Hessen and Nordrhein-Westfalen with their socialistic governments) simply decreed school reforms that instituted behavioristic principles and central controls. The promise of an equal opportunity for all, and a "differentiation of achievement and of theoretical knowledge" (which is the very opposite of equal opportunities) which would eventually lead to "the emancipated and critical individual" did not convince many educators.

The positive emotional perspective (*Anschauung*) gave way to the "objective *Gesellschaftskritik*" (critique of society). Andreas Flitner, a leading German educator, stated in his critical assessment of the German *Bildungspolitik* (1977) that too many "experts" had developed models without having done sufficient research and without proper practical experience. Reforms were mandated without prior consultation and communication with teachers and administrators, let alone parents. The major input came, in fact, from the social "scientists" at the Max-Planck Institute of Berlin.

The impacts of the new ideas were felt most clearly at the *Pädagogische Hochschulen* (teacher education for elementary schools (PH) ); classic "foundations of education" were de-emphasized if not altogether abolished as required subjects. Some of the programs were merged with the university (Nordrhein-Westfalen will close down all of its PHs as of 1979 and integrate them into the university). Instead of methodological studies, ideological dogma are furnished to serve as a "basis for a progressive professional education." The new texts in use in some states are meant to make children "aware of a deeply corrupted society that needs to be reconstructed." Such "antiquated forms of social life as the family and religious institutions . . ." which are based on the "exploitative structure of capitalism" are to be abolished in order to achieve a humanistic society. (Excerpts from elementary texts.)

The universities realized immediately what the results would be of such a reform where the "basics" had given way to "relevant" subjects: many of the students would lack the foundations for higher studies. The secondary schools had largely done away with the traditional classroom and the heavy demands of fundamental knowledge. Instead, the students could take courses that were more "relevant." Most of these courses were chosen for their "easiness" which brought good grades within reach. A mass of graduates from *Gymnasien* rushed to the universities, which could not handle the crowds and would not undertake the task of making up for deficits in fundamental subjects.

Vocational education encountered the same problems with more and more youngsters applying for an apprenticeship (if they even decided to go through such an "exploitation") with a lack of both fundamental skills and attitudes toward work. How could a youngster, all of a sudden, follow directions and learn from a master craftsman if all he had learned so far was to "criticize" and reject any authority? Many masters simply refused to put up with such attitudes. The resulting upsurge in unemployed youth is now to be met by keeping them in school longer (tenth-year elementary).

While there cannot be any doubt about the need for changes and constant reform in the education systems of any society that undergoes so many transformations, schools can meet new challenges only with carefully tested and expertly guided measures. The theories of the "progressive" camp are either unproved and coming from social scientists who see the objectives of education in "reforming society" along the lines of dogma and ideologies, or they have been adopted uncritically from other cultural or societal settings. In the case of the German "curriculum movement," the adoption of some American practices that even in America are of questionable value (and for which we had to pay a high price already), and the repetition of some of the same mistakes which were made by the Nazis not so long ago led to many undesirable, though not unexpected, outcomes such as the hitherto unknown symptoms of a malfunctioning school: dropouts, failure, polarization of students and teachers, and an increase in serious discipline problems.

The criticism of the "curriculum movement" comes mainly from scientists, not only from the "conservatives." They point to the narrow and contradictory basis on which such "theory" stands. Johann Herbart, whose educational thought already had elements of a "curriculum theory," held that the learning process cannot be defined entirely in scientific and measurable terms. Modern science has also rejected deterministic certainty and proved the impossibility of any objective description of a process (*Ablauf*) because of the unpredictable variables on one hand and the subjectivity of the observer on the other.

## APPLICATIONS

Some hints at the application of the diverse principles of West German education were already given in the Theory Section. Now more detailed illustrations of how German education implements these principles will be given. This can only be fragmentary, since further detailed descriptions, with illustrations, would be necessary to render a more adequate view of so complex a phenomenon as an education system.

### Anschauung

All methods and learning materials in German elementary and secondary schools more or less reflect the contention that the intellect is only one dimension of the human mind. Particularly the lower elementary grades use materials that are mostly interdisciplinary ("whole-child" approach). The teacher tries to involve as many senses in the instructional process as possible: letting the children see and touch, smell and manipulate whenever the material lends itself to do so. Most of the teacher's task is to prepare lessons and provide adequate *Anschauungsmaterial*. So-called audiovisual aids are not regarded as good helps. Preferred are models (stuffed animals, technical replicas, and so on, of which each school has a good collection), a sandbox in the classroom that allows for creating whole landscapes or city models, pictorial charts, and whenever possible, the real thing or a field trip to see it in the natural environment.

Items and experiences in the child's immediate environment (family, school, village, or neighborhood) are topics also used in arithmetic, reading, and religion. The students are encouraged to bring things to school that they have found in nature or to tell what they observed on the way to school. The teacher uses this mostly as an opportunity to introduce some new subject matter. Her goal is, however, to lead to a view that contains both understanding and liking. This goal of an eventual positive *Weltanschauung* (world view) is, of course, a high ideal in a time where so many "hidden persuaders" make one "see" what they want us to see. But the consistent application of this principle of education has helped many to remain critical: to see for yourself and judge for yourself, then compare what others have seen and said. Only then one should act. Or, as Pestalozzi formulated the basic rule for instruction: Present the real thing first, let the children see, touch, and manipulate it, then ask them what they think and how they like (or dislike) it, and do not hesitate to express your own opinion, too. Finally, let them use it, try out, and apply. The priority of the concrete over the abstract is a safeguard against manipulation.

### Heimat

The proverbial "efficiency" of the Germans has its counterbalance in *Gemütlichkeit* (the warmth, coziness of a home). It is visible in each classroom of a German school. The students and their teachers make it into something like a *Schulstube* (living room in the school) with pictures and collectibles, plants, and products of their arts and crafts classes. The teacher takes care that the "homeroom" deserves this name. But already the buildings and the furnishings are set up in a way conducive to this attempt to make pupils feel "at home" in a school. There is a tendency now toward the large and impersonal school with special rooms for almost each subject. But the elementary school (first four years) has remained untouched, and the other grade levels have retained a homeroom with a minimal but still visible component of this *Heimat*. The content of all subject matter, way into the secondary grade levels, is based on the home environment of the students. Mathematics, reading, writing, and the sciences take their examples from the child's or youngster's immediate experience and emphasize the positive values.

The comprehensive approach (*Heimatkunde* or *Gesamtunterricht*) leads beyond the classroom and the academic to the understanding and appreciation of the cultural, political, and natural environment. Field trips and visits to religious, cultural, political, and industrial institutions or monuments are as important as the regular (prescribed monthly) hikes through nature. Every two or three years, a class spends two to three weeks at a *Schullandheim* (school in the country) with their teacher. Specifically prepared hostels in the countryside—usually in the Alps, on the seaside, or in other scenic areas—accommodate classes for this *Schullandaufenthalt* (staying in the country with the school) that has regular classes and many open-air activities. There are more than 200 of these "homes." State funds are specifically allocated for this purpose, so that every child can participate. These experiences provide the opportunities for a more personal relationship between teachers and their students, toward a positive attitude to nature and fellow students, and they work as a major motivating experience.

The twenty-four hour approach to education that takes children out of their limited environment and often narrow range of experience is a necessity for those children who do not have a good home. While West Germany can boast to have virtually no poor people due to a well-functioning system of social services many people still live in substandard conditions. Others who are unable to keep up family standards find help through the social agencies that can, in extreme cases, authorize the transfer of children to Boys Towns or other full-time youth homes. There are many such homes originally inspired by the American priest Father Flanagan or by the Italian priest Don Bosco. After the war, the SOS-Children's Villages of Hermann Gmeiner (Austria) provided homes for many war orphans, and they still exist for those who do not have this normal start in life. They all base their educational efforts on the insight that "the home is the basis of all education, the home is the school of morality and of the state . . ." (Pestalozzi, 1780).

*Motivation*

Visitors to German schools are always surprised by the motivation of the students to learn. Part of this is due to the strong belief that characterizes all Germans: "it pays to have a good education" and "What you have learned will never be devaluated or stolen from you." The experience of many changes, even the destruction of most of their acquisitions through inflation and wars, have developed this belief. But schools also try to keep a child motivated. This starts with the careful screening of children entering schools through *Schulreifetests* (school-readiness tests) at age six, when they enter first grade, and also before transfer to secondary and vocational education programs. No child will be admitted when success is doubtful. Parents are unhesitatingly advised to wait for another year in such cases. Retention is mandatory when a student does not "make it" at the end of a school year.

Teachers are well trained methodologically and usually conduct their classes in an interesting and appealing way. Class periods are forty to fifty minutes (graduated by age level of the students) with a five-minute break after each period (twenty to thirty minutes after the first two hours) when all children have to leave the classroom and move around. Classes are held normally only during the morning hours, with only one or two afternoons, during the week when exceptional circumstances make it necessary. But then only nonacademic subjects will be scheduled: arts and crafts, home economics, physical education, music, and so on. The shorter school day gives youngsters more free time to play and to engage in youth activities programs offered through Boy Scouts, sports clubs, church youth groups, and the like. Most youngsters participate in such organizations. Of course, some time in the afternoons is taken by regularly assigned homework. The balance between school and free time, or of commanded and free activities, prevents the erosion of motivating forces in the student. This is easily proved by the *Ganztagsschulen* (full-day schools) established in some German cities during the last years: truancy and failure immediately occurred once the school day was extended.

The content of instruction, taken from the students' experience and their immediate environment, is much more motivating than remote and merely "academic" subject matter. Likewise, a "whole-child" approach that addresses both the cognitive and affective domains of the student is challenging, demanding an active involvement of the student.

## Gestaltung

This principle is closely connected to motivation and work in its application: the didactic aspects of education are essentially connected by a personal relationship between the teacher and the student. Only through a personal interest on the side of the teacher, concerned with both the student and the subject matter, and the student who likes his/her teacher and who develops an interest in the subject he or she teaches, will motivation be sustained. This is why German schools have emphasized the personal element in teaching and, whenever possible, let a teacher keep a class of students for several years. The same is true with vocational education where the same master craftsman trainer accompanies an apprentice through the three or more years of training. On the basis of such a length of time, the teacher can build up a repertoire of experiences with students that involve more than academic knowledge. The teacher becomes a model, particularly in the phase of puberty and adolescence when the youngster detaches himself from his parents. As we will see later (see Roles), most teachers are aware of their responsibility and make up an important factor in the youngster's *Lebensgestaltung* (life-style).

The average lesson in a German school is well prepared and structured according to the students' developmental level. Teachers have a strong background in methodology, particularly on the elementary level (secondary teachers get fewer methods courses at the university but through continuing education, they pick up very fast) and on the vocational sector. Also, the students take an active part in this *Unterrichtsgestaltung* (giving direction, structure to instruction) by planned and spontaneous activities. The activities that most youngsters engage in after school, in youth organizations or—later on, as adults—in continuing education programs, which are all conducted by professionals, provide various challenges to develop one's own life-style and high standards of competence. The diversity is an important factor that had been ignored by the totalitarian system of *Hitlerjugend* (though it still offered many options) and the contemporary "progressivists" with their trend toward "total schooling," imposing structures and life-styles upon youth.

### Arbeit

The other side of the principle of *Gestaltung* lies on the vocational sector. From the first grade of elementary school, the child's abilities to be creative (*gestaltende Kraft*) are challenged and systematically developed. Simple crafts, beginning with paper (folding and cutting) and leading to wood and metal or fabric, are part of the regular curriculum through secondary school. Emphasis is on the *sachgerechte Behandlung* (working with tools and the materials in a proper way). The fact that creativity without mastery of the material (and tools) is impossible makes teachers spend much effort to teach the proper use of tools and thus lead faster to success than letting children experiment or dabble. A good example might be a comparison between an American "science fair" where most of the exhibits are dilettantic and sloppily made, and the exhibition of products of the arts and crafts classes of any German school at the end of the school year. The difference lies in the high standards that come from a consistent work on *all* domains, the cognitive, affective, and practical. The same applies to vocational training that builds upon the work school has done in the preceding years: the apprentice has had already the experience of making something from scratch and its fulfilling achievement ("look what I made!"). He knows of *Arbeitsfreude* (enjoyment of working) because most of it was merely guided, not commanded (arts and crafts classes leave as much freedom to the student as is possible), and failure has been largely absent (proper use of tools and materials inevitably lead to success).

We may look at the exercise books of an elementary student, which have to be kept neatly and which often contain illustrations drawn by the student, or a work diary of an apprentice who has to enter a daily report with technical drawings of his work. In both cases, neatness, completeness, and organization are demanded (and graded). The recently introduced workbooks of the American style, where only blanks are to be filled, lead away from the "whole job" and correspond to assembly-line work in a factory: only a fragmentary job is to be done that requires minimal effort and no thinking.

The German teacher demands a "whole job" during the lesson and in the homework: a composition may be complemented by an illustration; in mathematics, the answer has to be written out in a complete sentence; with projects that might involve a whole class for several days, the emphasis is not on time ("this has to be done by that time . . .") but on completion and on quality, corresponding to the child's ability ("do as well as you can"). This has resulted in a high degree of efficiency and critical awareness of quality. Being constantly criticized by the teacher makes you critical too, even to the point where it becomes negative. In fact, Germans are often "critical and intolerant" and fast with their (negative) judgment. But it has also led to high quality and standards in both industry and everyday life. The same can be said, of course, about the Swiss and other European nations with education that works toward a positive attitude to work and with high demands in this respect. The "average" European worker is capable of working independently, and the percentage of rejects in industrial production is much lower than in America (Switzerland, 15 percent; West Germany, 25 percent; USA, over 50 percent).

Another aspect of this principle's effects on education is the high percentage of handicapped people who become employable through special education. The various *Rehabilitationszentren* (rehabilitation centers), often school complexes that comprise kindergarten through vocational training in an articulated structure, for children with physical handicaps, have a long history of success. Though their achievements will remain within a limited range, even severely handicapped youngsters, such as the so-called Thalidomide children who were often born without limbs and only rudimentary hands, can reach high levels of competence and leave these institutions as employable and reliable workers. The application of Kerschensteiner's principles has mostly resulted in a fine balance of competence and creativity. Of course, not all teachers achieve this balance, and many may lean toward the emphasis on obedience and function. But the common attitude with parents leans more often in this direction too: "No one was ever fired because of being accurate and conscientious."

Recent developments in some states have taken out of the school curriculum these prevocational and practical subjects. The new models emphasize the cognitive competencies, leaving the practical training to vocational education systems. Other agencies, like the Kolping Society, have stepped up their efforts to provide compensatory programs which so far have already helped many of the foreign "guest workers" who came to West Germany to find work and a living without much of a background in vocational terms.

### Religion

The German Constitution (*Grundgesetz*) spells out a "separation of Church and State," but it does not mean the same as in America. The two churches (Catholic and Lutheran) cooperate with the state in providing services essential to society: education, health care, and others. The state cannot control the activities of the church except in those areas where tasks overlap; even there, the church is not subject to the state's authority. Specific treaties (*Konkordate*) between the two partners spell out competencies. So, religion as a subject in the school curriculum is the responsibility of the church, even in public schools that cannot exclude it from their programs. Individuals, though, can be excused after a formal request (to be signed by the parents). All schools usually have one hour of religious instruction on their schedules in addition to a religious service once a week (usually scheduled during the first period of Wednesday or Thursday morning), in a nearby church.

Attendance of the liturgical service is optional, but the lessons are compulsory (with the above-cited exception). Either a minister of the respective creed or a licensed teacher conducts these classes, separately for Catholics and Lutherans. The content is mostly catechetical-biblical and emphasizes a personal commitment to faith. The religious feasts (Christmas, Easter) and the sacraments (first communion or confirmation) are major items in the curriculum, but also incidents in everyday life in society, and politics are discussed and examined in the light of religious beliefs. Outside of these religion lessons the *Heimatkunde*, or *Gesamtunterricht* of the elementary, or history, literature, and civics, on the secondary and vocational (trade school) levels, deal with religious feasts of the year, traditions, and cultural events. The texts contain many stories and facts directly relating to religion in everyday life or the past.

During the last ten years, increased requests for release from religious instructions have been filed. But the majority of the students still participate and feel that religion is important in their lives. The fruits of the National Socialist era, when religious instruction was eliminated entirely from the schools, are felt now. But there, too, the underground activities of the church youth organizations (for example, *Neudeutschland* to which the two young Scholls belonged when they were executed for their anti-Hitler activities) supplemented the school's task. When they resurfaced after World War II, these organizations continued their activities, which now combine cultural, recreational, and religious programs. Many youngsters engage in social work or volunteer in jails, hospitals, mental institutions, and so on or even serve their alternative to the military draft in a *Sozialdienst* ("social service year"). The religious organizations that cooperate with churches and schools still attract many young people through such programs, but the majority of the young generation seems to have become more alienated from the established forms of religion. Among the non-Christian religious groups only the Jews are significant in numbers with small communities (Köln). They attend the regular German schools with some religious activities offered by their communities.

Anti-Semitism now is virtually nonexistent just as the traditional tensions between Catholics and Protestants are absent among youth.

### Progressivism and Gesellschaftskritik

Though highly propagated and widely discussed in some of the states (primarily the Socialist-run Hessen, Niedersachsen, Nordrhein-Westfalen, and the city-states of Bremen and Hamburg), the progressive trend in education with the "curriculum theory" of the behaviorists has not brought thoroughgoing changes in all German schools. However, the increasing influence of the federal authorities implemented some of the plans of the ideologues that want the schools to lead

> the student . . . to the ability and readiness to critically examine (*kritisch hinterfragen*) the established political and social structures and, if deemed necessary, to reject and change them, and, at the same time, act in solidarity (Derbolav, 1977, compare also Stokes, 1980).

What this means becomes obvious when we examine some of the readers (elementary and secondary level texts) published and approved by the school authorities in Nordrhein-Westfalen. The youngster learns that "parents belong to the passing generation; that you should not accept anything unexamined from them. . . ." In spite of heavy protests from parents and professional educators, such texts were introduced. Courses in sex education were mandated with a Sex Atlas as a text. The opposition was not so much to the subject matter but the methods and systematic negative influence against the home and parents, encouraging young children to disobey parents and ignore all moral standards.

The fruits of such a "pedagogy" ripened fast in Germany: a wave of radicalism, especially in secondary and higher education, swept through the big cities of these states. Even children participated in rallies against the city governments, for abortion laws, for amnesty for terrorists, and other issues. The wave of radicalism has ebbed off in the meantime, but the threat of terrorism and a rising youth delinquency remain. Mostly young people, these "radicals" are avowed "critics and emancipators of a corrupt society." Instead of the much promised "enlightening of the young generation about the socio-political and collective implications of life, and the maturing of intelligent action," did the schools (and political ideologues who used them) only manipulate and radicalize youth (Bartsch, 1978).

The flight into private schools with a "conservative" philosophy is phenomenal. Many parents send their sons and daughters to private schools and abroad (even as far as to the United States) to get a "decent" higher education.

In the elementary schools, the "progressive movement" had its first inroads with the implementation of the *Ganzwortmethode* (whole word method) during the 1950s: learning to read the "whole word" instead of attacking it phonetically (German is a consistently phonetic language) was borrowed from American education. It was later abandoned because of an upsurge of *Legasthenie* (dyslexia). Then, the "scientification" (*Versachlichung*) did away with *Anschauung* and *Heimat* as educational principles. Though parallels with the Nazi time were carefully avoided, the same principles were applied: the priority of the social over the individual values, the breaking of traditional ties (family influence, village schools, religious teacher education, and so on), and the "streamlining" (equalization) and "modernizing" (collectivization) of the schools was meant to exclude all counteracting influences to the leftist ideologies.

The shifting emphasis from the affective to the cognitive domain brought both the demand for earlier schooling of children (compulsory preschool programs were proposed but did not meet enthusiasm) and the diversification and extension of the primary and secondary school, mostly at the cost of the "basics." Now you can pass the *Abitur* with a failing grade in German (in some states). This was impossible before, when literature and history were *Hauptfächer* (major compulsory subjects).

Most teachers and parents remain unconvinced that the "traditional and conservative" schools were so bad, after they had provided a generation that survived a totalitarian system, rebuilt the country, and brought a totally destroyed economy back to first rank in the world.

Fortunately, many alternatives exist in those states where the reforms did most damage: private schools and a well-functioning system of continuing education offer programs in virtually all possible subjects. Many young and older students are found in the courses of the *Volkshochschulen* or *Volksbildungswerke* of the cities and their branches that reach even the smaller villages. There, the pressures that have increasingly been introduced into the schools with their testing procedures after each step and the increased requirements of high grade averages at the universities are absent. Without compromising quality (most of the instructors at these academies are university professors who prefer to work there), true academic freedom is made possible.

Almost all these institutions are carried by the churches or the local communities. Thus they are independent from the central authorities. But they are still funded partly or fully from tax monies, and many of the participants in their programs receive subsidies from their employers and/or from the State.

The same applies for the youth organizations that offer a multitude of programs: from the religious orientation of the Catholic or Lutheran Parish Youth, the Young Christian Workers, or the Boy Scouts, to the leftist *Gewerkschaftsjugend* (Labor Union Youth) and the "Falcons" of the Socialist party. They all receive subsidies, sometimes even have their meeting places furnished free by city governments that have a budget item for "youth activities," but they are completely free in their program offerings. Mostly they offer a more or less structured program which, once or twice weekly, attracts youngsters to sports, education, or religious, cultural, political, or vocational activities. During week-ends, or in the summer, most groups go out for hikes or campouts. The federal railroads offer reduced rates for such group travel, and youth hostels have reserved space for any registered youth organization. In 1976, about 28 percent of the fourteen- to twenty-four-year-olds in West Germany were members of at least one such youth organization. The impact of this type of education upon the young generation cannot be accurately assessed. But as the original Youth Movement (*Jugendbewegung, Wandervogel*) was a reaction to the "establishment" and had the imprint of *Gesellschaftskritik* and progressivism and had a decisive influence upon the young generations in Germany, the postwar and contemporary youth movement's role will not become clearly visible before another generation grows out of it. Recent surveys suggest that in spite of this loosely institutionalized form of education, with its influence upon youth in the decisive years of adolescence, the firmly structured influence of the family, the schools, and vocational education still prevails. On the other side, most of the leadership in church, politics, and sports have grown out of the respective youth organizations. And most teachers had their first "teaching experience" as leaders of such groups. Almost everybody in Germany agrees that they found valuable experiences during their years with the youth movement. Many found a way to learning that had been blocked by low achievement in the school, through participation in a group where grades did not count.

It seems thus that some of the reforms that are so strongly pushed have long ago taken place, outside the schools, and had far better results than the theorists ever can show with their model schools.

## ROLES

### Administration

Most of the states of the Federal Republic of Germany have a three-tiered system of educational administration: The lower level is the local *Staatliches Schulamt* (State School Office), headed by a *Schulamtsdirektor* (formerly *Schulrat*) who cooperates with the municipal authorities responsible for school affairs, particularly the buildings, operations, and so on (*Städtisches Schulamt*). The middle level is the regional district (*Schulbezirk*). Usually, there are several such districts in one state. The *Oberschulamt* of the respective district regulates regional affairs and coordinates local matters. It is also responsible for placement of teachers. Finally, the higher level of administration is the *Kultusministerium* in the respective state capital. There are specific offices in charge of the various levels of schools, of finances (teachers are state officials), and planning, supervision, and development. The *Kultusminister* and his officers cooperate also with the churches and other private carriers of educational institutions. General tax money is allocated in each state for education, including private institutions. Though the state does not have complete control over private education, it establishes mandatory guidelines that guarantee professional standards (requirements of teacher education, graduation standards and so on). The Constitution (*Grundgesetz:* Article 7, § 1) and the Concordate with the church regulate the range of responsibilities of church and state.

The decentralized structure does not allow for much involvement of the federal government, but via the *Kultusministerkonferenz* and the federal minister of science and education increasing influence has been possible. Attempts to establish a comprehensive plan for all education (*Bildungsgesamtplan*) in 1970 that would standardize the whole system came mostly from the Socialists who had achieved a majority with the Liberal Democrats several years before. They pushed for a standardized curriculum that would provide "equal opportunity," for a more efficient utilization of hardware and software, and systematic planning that would make it easier to control and evaluate the system. The ideas came mostly from socialistic theories, particularly from the field of *Bildungsökonomie* (economics of education), which has been developed in Marxist countries on the basis of their ideologies, and from bureaucratic circles who were often unrealistic about the implementation of their plans. So most of the middle and lower level administrators have remained highly skeptical. Although the *Gesamtplan* was abandoned to a large degree due to untenable assumptions and impossible implementation, more and more rules and directives come from "above." Principals complain about the overburden of paperwork and their loss of authority.

Teacher placement (hiring and transfers) is in the hands of the regional administration (*Oberschulamt*) in accordance with the local office and, if possible, with consideration of the requests of the candidates. A young teacher is usually supervised by his (her) principal who has to see and evaluate his (her) weekly journal and (occasionally) classroom performance. A regional supervisor comes regularly to observe the teacher in his (her) classroom, inspects the students' exercise books, and evaluates the teacher's diary. Monthly workshops and seminars on the regional level are compulsory for all teachers until they passed the "Second State Exam" (tenure). These continuing education programs are held by experts and usually provide valuable experience and help for the teacher's work. Travel costs to these events are reimbursed.

Independent (private) schools are controlled by their "carriers" (church, or other organization), mostly on the local level. They cooperate with the state authorities; no significant conflicts have occurred as the relation is regarded as "partnership." Often, retired teachers and administrators of the public school system continue a few more years working with private schools.

Higher education is structured differently: according to a new law (*Hochschulrahmengesetz*) of 1976, institutions of higher learning are "corporations" and at the same time state institutions. This unique dual position is meant to guarantee independence of the academic sector (the university is thus responsible for faculty affairs, discipline, curriculum, and so on) and efficient functioning on the administrative side (the state is in charge of providing the buildings, hiring and paying personnel, organization of operations, and the like). Each state has different ways of resolving the sometimes complicated overlap of tasks. The *Hochschulrahmengesetz* mandates a coordination of these diverse administrative structures by 1979.

During the last fifteen years, many private institutions of higher learning have been established or expanded. Most of them are carried by the Catholic church. These comprehensive or specialized colleges attract many students because of their smaller size and a more personal atmosphere. These private institutions are fully recognized by the state and receive tax money, as their faculty are employees of the state with the same pay and fringe benefits.

### Faculty

In contrast to America, in Germany teachers have long been acknowledged as professionals. Until recent times, female teachers were rare. But since World War II, and particularly during the last few years, more women have entered the teaching profession. Elementary and special education teachers study at the *Pädagogische Hochschule* (now integrated or at least on an equal rank with the university), while secondary teachers get their degrees from the university. Beginning salaries are relatively high (rank of state official; presently about 2500 Deutsche Marks with two-year automatic increments and additions for married persons and for each child) and include many fringe benefits (50 to 60 percent reimbursement for any medical expenses in addition to insurance coverage, pension plans, and so on ). Secondary teachers start at higher salaries than elementary teachers and faculty at institutions of higher learning receive the highest pay. They also rank among the highest in terms of social status.

Generally, all teachers are respected as professionals and state officials who take their *Beamteneid* seriously. (All state officials have to render an oath at their induction, which does not so much mention "loyalty" to the state but emphasizes the incorruptibility and ethical responsibility that is the basis of a professional: ". . . not to be partial to poor and rich, and to be concerned with the wellbeing of the entrusted children . . .") Their relationships with parents and students are normally good. Conflicts arise naturally when children are involved, but the teacher's authority is still respected in most cases. Only recently have some of the left-oriented and activist teachers caused negative attitudes toward teachers in some regions, particularly in some of the big cities. They should not be taken as typical, however. Faculty at the universities usually do not have the same relationship that we observe at our American colleges. Their classes are straight lecture with no discussions. Only seminars and *colloquia* held in smaller settings allow for interaction. At smaller institutions, such as the private *Hochschulen*, the traditional gathering at a *Studentenkneipe* (restaurant) or a hike with the professor on a day off is still occasionally observed. But the trend has been leading away from the personal relationship toward mass education. On the other side, the old structures of the universities with the *Ordinarius* and *Privatdozent* positions have been largely abandoned. Now, opportunities for younger faculty are more open, as a position is no longer held by one individual for life. But it also brought problems. The principle of "parity in control" at the German universities brought in many unqualified faculty members, by decision of the students (mostly leftist student organizations that were active) and bureaucrats.

Unions do not play a significant role in the teaching profession, due to the official status of the teachers. The *Gewerkschaft Erziehung und Wissenschaft* (Union of Educators and Scientists) has some influence, but such organizations have not attracted the majority of the teachers. No teachers' strikes have occurred so far. Unions cooperate in planning and developing programs but do not run any schools. The majority of the teachers prefer membership in professional associations of which the

Lutheran teachers and a Catholic Female Teachers Association seem to be the largest.

Advancement in the school system goes automatically with years of service. Tariffs and rank scales are standardized more or less throughout the country. For example, an elementary teacher enters as *Hauptlehrer* (or *Referendar*, in some states) and becomes *Oberlehrer* after passing the Second Exam, receiving tenure, and serving satisfactorily for several years. The position of a school principal is open to any experienced teacher. Openings are publicized in the circulars of the district. Applicants must be recommended by the local and regional *Schulamt* and get appointed through the *Kultusministerium*. A secondary teacher starts also as *Referendar* or *Assessor* and advances to *Studienrat, Oberstudienrat*, and, when he assumes the position of a principal at a Gymnasium, *Oberstudiendirektor*.

Continuing education programs for all teachers provide a constant up-dating and opportunities of exchanging experience. After the Second Exam (tenure), attendance is no longer compulsory but the *Akademietagungen* (academic conferences) of the various state academies are well attended. There are workshops and seminars (days, week-ends, weeks) on virtually any subject on any school level. A catalogue of the State Academy of Calw (Baden-Württemberg) lists more than 170 courses for 1978. Some of these courses are run in conjunction with private agencies, but they are all funded by the state, and participants get most or all of their expenses refunded.

### Students

Except for some of the big cities, where a high concentration of youngsters in big schools has led to conditions similar to the American metropolitan schools, though not so acute, German educators do not complain about serious problems with their students. Discipline is, of course, always a problem, where youth and adults come together, but well-trained teachers and adequate facilities alleviate the problem before it develops beyond control.

The previously discussed principles and their consistent application have been successful in creating a generally positive attitude of students toward their school. Attendance problems and vandalism, which we must see primarily as symptoms of a negative attitude, are very rare. Classes normally contain twenty-five to thirty-five pupils. There is a "class spirit" that we observed everywhere: a solidarity among the students of one classroom which shows in the collective competition (in Germany, it is classroom against classroom, not the best in class against the others), in the relationship with the teacher, and in lifelong friendships that develop. Annual class reunions are held for up to fifty years after graduation. This "togetherness" of the Germans in their classrooms brought up "democratic" decision making mechanisms long before the institution of the so-called *Schülermitverwaltung* (student co-determination in the administration of the school). A "class speaker" who represents the class in the teachers council and vis-à-vis the teachers has been a long-standing tradition. The deterioration of the respective structure on the college level (ASTA-*Allgemeiner Studentenausschuss,* or General Executive Committee of Students) during the late 1960s, when leftist students' organizations at some universities had seized control of the student representation, never affected the secondary and elementary level. The short school day (mornings only) does not allow for much involvement in school matters, anyway. Extracurricular activities are not run by the school but by the various youth organizations. There, each member is *au par* with others in the absence of grades and promotion procedures.

Advancement within the schools is based on achieving the goals of each respective grade. A student has to reach a minimum grade average in major subjects to be transferred into next grade at the elementary and the secondary levels. The high demands of the upper grades of Gymnasium filter out many students who made it through the first five years. But the opportunity to switch over to lower level *Realschule* or to a vocational program eliminates the drop-out problem and the stigma of "not having made it." Though the *Abitur* (graduate examination of the Gymnasium; an equivalent to the American B.A. and the entitlement to study at the university) is a reputable achievement, it is not necessarily regarded as "higher" than a vocational degree as the *Facharbeiter,* particularly now with the *numerus clausus* and other conditions at the university and on the job market.

The college student usually lives in the city where the university is located or finds a room in a nearby village. Housing is the biggest problem in crowded cities with overcrowded universities, not only finding accommodation but also to paying the usual high rents. There is, on the other hand, no tuition charged by the university. Only a nominal administrative fee and insurance have to be paid by the student. Almost everyone receives a *Stipendium,* a state grant which has to be partially paid back after graduation. This is true for all universities and all fields also for teacher education. Certain grade levels are to be achieved to keep the grant going, but virtually everyone qualifies.

The German university does not have an undergraduate program but starts right at the graduate level. There are only minimum study length requirements prescribed for the respective fields, at the end of which a candidate may report for the comprehensive examination. Normally, no semester examinations are taken, and the sequence of courses is at the student's option. The trend is toward more planning and compulsory structure to get the students "through" as fast as possible to leave the space for others. This has deep-going implications for the traditional academic freedom (*Lernfreiheit*) of the students and their roles and rights. The "free life of a student" of the Old Heidelberg romanticism and the tradition of studying at as many different places with the professors of one's choice, is largely a dream of the past.

Apprentices in vocational training programs have specific duties and rights spelled out in contracts with the training master or the company that offers the program. New laws have overemphasized the rights, often to a ridiculous extent. A baker can no longer require that his apprentices get up at 4 o'clock in the morning. So many regulations coerced shutting down apprenticeship programs and deprived thousands of youngsters of an opportunity to learn a trade. The majority of the boys and girls in the fifteen- to eighteen-year age bracket still choose a trade and go through a three- (or three-and-a-half) year program of apprenticeship. There are no significant barriers for girls to enter any trade they want. Most choose training in retail business, office work, services, and home economics (there are regular apprenticeships for all of these occupations available; even the sales girl at the grocery store normally has a diploma!).

In general, the role of youth in German society is not characterized by "age segregation" as in America. Young people are much more integrated and meet the older generation in everyday life, at work, and in the various educational and recreational institutions. Only recently have such terms as "generation gap" and disrespect for the aged come up, through the "anti-authoritarian" and *gesellschaftskritische* education of some circles. They are not typical patterns in a society that does everything for the aged and encourages the services of the young to the senior generation. Mutual respect for the different roles and positive expectations from both, students and teachers, young and old, are still the rule.

### Parents

The experiences of two wars, of totalitarianism, and of economic disasters have created a strong belief in education among the Germans: "What you have learned can never be devaluated or destroyed!" So parents are generally on the side of the school and support the demands of the teachers when children complain. They respect the teachers as professionals and expect them to exercise authority. Of course, conflicts arise occasionally. There have been some lawsuits against teachers, pursued by angry parents, but they are rare and usually the judgment is in favor of the teacher.

The establishment of Parent Councils (*Elternbeirat*) after the war institutionalized parent codetermination. But most parents do not want to get involved in the decision-making process of the school. Only in metropolitan areas have parent groups become more active. For the most, their role is on the receiving end: to get information about school matters and to react to new regulations. Teachers and administrators encourage a more active involvement, but the recent practices of the socialist governments in some states did the very opposite when they decreed reforms without consultation with parents. Only in one case where the state of Nordrhein-Westfalen established a new school form against the fierce opposition of parents did their initiative prevail against the school authorities of the state (Referendum against the "Coop school," 1978). The Constitution (Art. 6, §2 and 7. §5) provides the basis for the parents' role in the school system and their rights to establish private schools. This has been exercised most often in the recent decade, particularly in those states that had implemented some of the above-described reforms and which did not meet the parents' approval. But there are no fund-raising activities and the like involved, because of the constitutional support of these private schools by the state. Only a few small experimental not publicly recognized schools run by parents and not by professional staff exist in West Germany.

Generally speaking, the roles of various groups in German society are fairly well defined and established through traditional patterns. The disastrous end of World War II and the influx of millions of refugees into Western Germany have brought changes in these patterns. But the majority of the Germans still adhere to the traditional life-styles and social patterns that make up the social and economic stability of this country. Deviations from these patterns, during youth and early adulthood, merge back after a while, much to the disappointment of many "progressive" social scientists who complain about the recurrent *bourgeoisie* of the young generation. This is similar to the developments in American society from the "rebellious generation" of the Vietnam era to a more "conservative" trend. It seems that societal and cultural roles cannot be changed so easily, as some education theorists would have liked to believe.

## SYSTEM IN ACTION

To show an education system in action would require a several weeks' study tour and observation of some schools over a series of consecutive days. Here, we can only outline briefly what a school day looks like and stimulate the reader to go and look for him(her)self.

### Elementary School

A typical elementary school in West Germany is housed in a modern building. Most schools in the cities were destroyed during the war; they had to be rebuilt. The old remaining buildings, all over the country, were modernized during the 1950s. The tendency was to build smaller units and locate the schools in the neighborhood, so that no child would have a long way to go. But there are still distances of more than 2 km for many children. They receive a monthly pass for the public transportation system at a reduced rate (or even free, in some cases). Classes begin at 7:45 in summer (8:00 in winter). Each period goes for forty-five or fifty minutes, with a five-minute break after each lesson. After the second morning period, a thirty-minute pause allows for a snack which children bring along or which can be bought from a baker who comes to the school yard at this time. Everybody has to leave the classroom during a break, to move around and "get fresh air." The classroom will be aired in the meantime. The equipment is very much like that in American schools: large wall blackboards, movable seats and desks (but adjustable to the child's size), and cabinets. Most lower elementary classes have also a sandbox where models of landscapes, cities, castles, and so on can be made. It is often used in the *Heimatkunde* classes. Friendly colors prevail in the rooms: colorful drapes and pictures, flowers, and natural wood furniture create a pleasant atmosphere. Cleanliness is not only the responsibility of the janitors but of the teacher and the children.

The first morning hours are usually filled with the major subjects: arithmetic, spelling, and *Gesamtunterricht* (or *Heimatkunde*). Children use exercise books for each lesson. For writing, the lineation of these books is different for the first four years to aid the student in neat and accurate handwriting. (Cursive writing is used exclusively.) For arithmetic, quadrille paper with 5 mm squares is used. This also aids to develop concepts of metric measures. Exercise books contain the classwork and homework. They are kept in the classroom when filled, for evaluation, until the end of the school year. Neatness and organization are as important as correct results. Tests in all subjects are written in similar books. So a student has a whole year's mathematics tests or compositions, dictations, and so on in a respective book.

Textbooks are furnished by the school. They are well illustrated with pictures that depict events and items from the environment. Stories from older and contemporary writers, sometimes adapted to the age level of the respective grade, and the examples in all subjects (mathematics, science or whatever) deal with everyday experiences of children and adults.

Children do not wear uniforms but must appear in school neatly dressed and well kept.

As a rule, there are no classes in the afternoon. The teacher assigns homework which cannot require more than a half hour for first graders, an hour for second and third, and about two hours for the upper grades. No homework can be assigned over week-ends or holidays.

Discipline problems are handled by the teacher in the classroom. In most cases, an admonishing word is sufficient. Sometimes, a student is to stand near the teacher's desk for a while. In serious cases, the teacher has authority to apply corporal punishment. The parents and school principal are informed of this measure. If a child's behavior is not correctible, removal from class and transfer to special education is often used. In general, there are no serious problems due to a relaxed schedule (many breaks allow the children to "let off steam") and the positive attitude of most parents toward the school.

Evaluation of the students' achievements is continuous. Everyone has to show homework which is corrected. Part of a subject's grade is made up of the quality of homework. Regular tests (at least every two weeks) in all subjects allow the teacher and parents to monitor progress. During class, oral examinations (often unscheduled) or performance on the blackboard in front of class check on understanding and conceptualization. Report cards are issued at the end of the school year (summer vacation).

Vacations are spread over the year which begins in fall: about three weeks at Christmastime, two weeks for Easter, one week for Pentecost, and six weeks in summer. The long summer vacations are scheduled differently in the various states. Children in the northern part of Germany may have their summer vacation in late June to end of July, and those in the south, from early August to mid-September. Many religious and traditional holidays break up the long school year. Today many schools also close on Saturdays, ordinarily a school day.

Once a month, the elementary school teacher takes the class on an outing in the vicinity. It is usually a day's hike to some cultural or natural sight. Once a year, a longer excursion is scheduled for the whole school. These events are part of the curriculum and provide experiences that will be used in class afterwards.

Each child is examined by a school physician annually. Health defects are reported to the parents and have to be taken care of within a set time by a dentist or doctor of the parents' choice. All children are automatically insured for accidents during school hours, at no cost to the parents. Health insurance is compulsory for everybody in Germany. Children are always covered with their parents, for all medical expenses (including office visits and dental care).

## Secondary School

The diverse German secondary schools have only this in common: a highly structured curriculum that leads beyond the elementary school level, either to college (*Gymnasium*), or to technical-commercial institute (*Realschule*). The high schools are usually housed in large complexes, sometimes two or three different types under one roof. Students travel by public transportation (reduced rate monthly passes available to all who live farther than 2 km from school) and by bicycle or motorbike. School hours are normally from around 7:45 to 12:00 noon. One or two afternoons, with two periods (2 to 4 P.M.), may be scheduled, but never with major subjects. Class periods are longer than those in elementary school, but the same five-minute breaks apply after each lesson (and thirty minutes after the second morning period). Instruction is highly departmentalized, with many subjects taught in special rooms (laboratories, music room, workshop, and so on).

As in the elementary school, students use exercise books for each subject and keep them through the year. Tests are, however, written in special books and evaluated by the teachers. Textbooks are often furnished by the school, but most schools require that the students buy their own. No tuition is charged. Some of the *Gymnasien* are still sexually separated, especially private ones run by religious orders (all girls or all boys). *Realschulen* are all coeducational.

Discipline problems are usually handled through the homeroom teacher, who is responsible for a class through several years. Corporal punishment is virtually eliminated, but additional homework, which normally is quite heavy, and unscheduled examinations are the most effective measures. Persistent problems are brought to the attention of the Teachers Council of the school and usually result in dismissal. In contrast to the American high school, there are no significant occurrences of discipline or attendance problems. Schools are kept clean, and the classrooms are orderly. Students have a good relationship with their teachers.

Evaluation of achievement in the various subjects, many of which can be chosen by the student, is based on written and oral tests. The requirements of high grade averages, or number of "achievement points" for advancement into the next higher grade, make up most of the pressure that *Gymnasium* students complain about. So much time is spent on homework and studying for tests. It is virtually impossible (and also forbidden) for a secondary school student to have a job. Many students quit after the sixth grade *Gymnasium* and take on an apprenticeship. With the background that led them much higher than any elementary or even *Realschule* could lead, they have many advantages. The length of apprenticeship may be even reduced by a half year for them.

The others have to apply all their efforts to make it through the last three years to the *Abitur*, a comprehensive exam over nine years of studies. Not all subjects will be tested, but always the majors (German, two foreign languages, mathematics, two of the sciences), and some electives. Exams are both written and oral. Teachers of the school and commissioners from the state school authorities are present. The examination themes and questions are set by the state authorities, but graded by a committee of the local school.

Vacations are the same as for elementary schools. So are the regular excursions and the *Schul-Landaufenthalt*.

A student government exists at all secondary schools. It is represented at the Teachers Council, which mediates between students and faculty. It is more or less a formality because the homeroom teachers who know their students over several years represent the students' interests usually much more effectively when it comes to disputed issues or conflicts. The homeroom teacher takes the side of his class, not that of the faculty, whenever possible. This makes strong ties lasting over many years, sometimes for life. Class reunions held regularly (up to fifty years after graduation) always include the teachers when they are still around.

## PROSPECT

In a fast-changing society and economy, any prediction is to be made with caution. Too many variables prevent even an accurate assessment of the present situation. This is also true with education that is tied in with politics and economy. In Germany, the political factor has always been of decisive influence upon life because of the sharp ideological differences between the parties. At this time (1979) the Socialists rule with a majority that has been made possible through a coalition with the Liberals. If the Christian Democrats regain the majority, many political and economic structures will probably be changed again. This would affect many of the new developments and plans in education, especially in those states that had followed the socialistic trend during the last decade. On the other hand, the majority of the German population tends to be "conservative" and do not follow so fast when a government issues commands.

Reactions against the politicizing and bureaucratizing of the schools have gained momentum: many private schools are established, parents take initiative against unrealistic rules, and students still have strong positive ties with their parents and teachers. In academic circles, the critique of "curriculum theory" and of many planned reforms is increasing. Some educators demand a "reform of the reform" and insist on the return to the proven and successful principles that have produced better fruits than the recent "progress."

It may be predicted with some certainty that the German education system will again respond to the changing scenes and unchanging needs by a balance of carefully considered adjustments and well-established patterns. The theme that will pervade education in Germany (and other countries on the continent) during the next decade, is *Europa!* (Neumeister, 1970.) The unification of Europe is well underway: after the economic cooperative, the monetary, and eventually, the political union will become a reality. The schools have consistently been working toward this goal by systematic contacts with schools and students in other countries (regular exchange programs), teaching foreign languages (from fifth grade elementary), and a curriculum that follows the concentric circles pattern of a Pestalozzi from the *Heimat* to the greater European homeland.

In the vocational sector, the trend toward administrative and service occupations in industry and economy demands a more diversified offering of the schools. The planned reforms of the German school system will meet this trend, but also the growth of the "fourth track"—continuing and adult education. The shorter work week in industry opens up many opportunities for which the broad German education system already has a well-functioning base.

The goals for the future cannot be more "equal opportunities" but more "opportunities in its widest possible diversity." Though this "market" cannot and should not remain totally unregulated, in order to avoid the mistakes which have been made in America and in Germany the solution does not lie in a centrally controlled and regimented system where one ideology prevails, but in the cooperation of partners: church and state, theoreticians and practitioners, parents and professionals, students and schools. The present Constitution and the willingness of the German people to preserve freedom are the basis for continued work in this direction.

## GLOSSARY OF GERMAN TERMS

*Abitur:* Graduating examination (comprehensive) of Gymnasium; equivalent to
    B.A. (prerequisite for higher eduation).
*Abiturient* (pl. *Abiturienten*): One who passed the *Abitur.*
*Anschauung* (verb: *anschauen*): A view that involves the intellectual and emotional
    domains.
*Anschauungsmaterial:* Instructional aids that aim at the cognitive and affective
    domains.

*Arbeit:* Work.

*Arbeitsfreude:* Enjoyment of work.

*Arbeitslehre:* A subject in vocational schools dealing with materials, tools, and competencies.

*Arbeitsschule:* Kerschensteiner's idea of a work-oriented school.

*ASTA (Allgemeiner Studenten Ausschuss):* Student Government Association at universities in Germany.

*Aufbaugymnasium:* A specific form of Gymnasium allowing transition from vocational education to higher education.

*Ausbildung:* Training (in contrast to *Bildung,* education).

*Beamte* (pl. *Beamten*): Public servant, state official.

*Beamteneid:* Oath rendered at installation as public servant.

*Bildung:* Education, formation (contrast to *Ausbildung,* training).

*Bildungsideal:* Ideal, goal, objective of education.

*Bildungsplan* (-planung): Plans, planning of education.

*Bildungspolitik:* The governments' plans and policies concerning education.

*Bund:* The federation, federal government.

*Bund-Länder Kommission für Bildungsplanung:* A federal committee where representatives of the *Länder* (states) coordinate educational policies and planning.

*Elternbeirat:* Parents Council (advisory function in school matters).

*Fachhochschule:* College with specific orientation to various subjects (such as social work, adult education), mostly private institutions.

*Facharbeiter:* Skilled worker (diploma: Facharbeiterbrief) after passing an apprenticeship.

*Ganztagschule:* day-long school (normally, school is only held during morning hours).

*Ganzwortmethode:* Method in teaching reading that avoids phonetic attack of words emphasizing the "whole-word" attack.

*Gesamtschule:* Comprehensive school.

*Gesamtunterricht:* Comprehensive instruction that integrates all subjects in one unit.

*Gesellschaftskritik:* Critique of existing social conditions.

*Gestaltung:* Structuring, planning, developing instruction;

  *Unterrichtsgestaltung:* Structure of instruction and lessons.

  *Lebensgestaltung:* Directing, planning, deciding one's life.

*Grundgesetz:* The Constitution of the Federal Republic of Germany.

*Gymnasium:* Higher form of secondary education, college preparatory.

*Hauptfach:* Major subject; compulsory subject in *Gymnasium.*

*Hauptlehrer:* First (beginning) rank of elementary teacher.

*Heimat:* Homeland, home-world (ethnic roots).

*Heimatkunde:* Comprehensive subject in elementary schools dealing with all aspects of the home environment (natural sciences, history, current events, traditions, civics, field trips).

*Hitlerjugend:* Compulsory youth organization during the Hitler regime.

*Hochschule:* College, university.

*Hochschulrahmengesetz:* A law to regulate higher education.

*Kulturföderalismus:* Principle that allows the states authority over cultural matters.

*Kultusminister (Kultusministerium):* Head of department (ministry) of culture and education in the states' governments.

*Kultusministerkonferenz:* A standing conference of the ministers of culture of all states, coordinating cultural and educational affairs on the federal level.

*Land* (plural: *Länder*): State in the Federal Republic of Germany.

*Lehrfreiheit/Lernfreiheit:* Academic freedom, freedom to teach and to learn.

*Mittelschule:* Old name for *Realschule* (secondary education).

*Oberschulamt:* Regional school office.

*Pädagogische Hochschule:* Teachers college.

*Realschule:* Secondary school equivalent to American high school.

*Referendar:* Beginning rank (probationary years) of a secondary school teacher (in some states also for elementary teachers).

*Rektor:* The principal of a school; director of a university or college.

*Schulamt:* School office (superintendent's).

*Schulbezirk:* School district.

*Schullandheim:* Country school to accommodate classes from cities for their regular "outward-bound" weeks.

*Schulrat:* A superintendent of schools.

*Schulreifetest:* Test to determine readiness for school (age six or seven).

*Siedlungswerk:* An organization to help families to acquire property and an own home.

*Sozialdienst:* A volunteer year for young people to do social work (or in hospitals, nursing homes, and so on).

*Städtisches Schulamt:* Municipal school office (cities).

*Technische Hochschule:* Technical university; institute of technology.

*Volksbildungswerk:* Organization to foster adult education.

*Volkshochschule:* "People's academy" for adult education.

*Volksschule:* The elementary school (grades 1 through 8 or 9).

*Wandervogel:* Youth movement of the early twentieth century, emphasizing hiking and love of nature.

*Weltanschauung:* World view, philosophy, set of values (see also *Anschauung*).

*Wirtschaftswunder:* The economic miracle, recovery of postwar Germany.

## REFERENCES

Bartsch, Gunter. "Anarchismus-Nihilsmus-Terrorismus," in Kaltenbrunner, G. K., ed. *Wiedernehr der Wölfe*. Freiburg: Herder, 1978.

Bauer, Hans. *Das Ende des deutschen Gymnasiums*. Freiburg: Herderbücherei, 1974.

Boventer, Hermann. *Gebt uns die totale Schule*. Zürich: Edition Interfrom, 1975.

Brezinka, Wolfgang. *Erziehung und Kulturrevolution*. Munich: Ernst Reinhardt Verlag, 1974.

California State Board of Education. *Report of the Task Force on Early Childhood Education*. Sacramento, 1971.

Derbolav, Josef, ed. *Grundlagen und Probleme der Bildungspolitik*. Munich: Piper Verlag, 1977.

Hagenmaier, Theresia, Correll, Werner, and VanVeen-Bosse, Brigitte. *Neue As-*

*pekte der Reformpädagogik: Kerschensteiner, Dewey und Montessori.* Heidelberg: Quelle & Meyer, 1968.

Heisenberg, Werner. *Physics and Philosophy: The Revolution in Modern Science.* New York: Harper & Row, 1962.

Herbart, Johann Friedrich Wilhelm. *Science of Education.* Boston: Heath, 1902.

Kaltenbrunner, Gerd-Klaus, ed. *Klassenkampf und Bildungsreform.* Freiburg: Herder—Initiative, 1974.

Landeszentrale für Politische Bildung des Landes Nordrhein-Westfalen, ed. *Erziehungsnotstand.* Cologne: Verlag Wissenschaft und Politik, 1976.

Müller-Daehn, Claus. *Science and Research in the Federal Republic of Germany.* Bonn: Inter Nationes, 1969.

Neumeister, Hermann. "Education for International Understanding in the Federal Republic of Germany," in *Phi Delta Kappan,* January 1970, pp. 259.

Pestalozzi, Johann Heinrich. *Abendstunde eines Einsiedlers.* Transl. from Ulich, Robert, ed., *Three Thousand Years of Educational Wisdom.* Cambridge: Harvard University Press, 1954, pp. 481 ff.

von Rintelen, Fritz-Joachim. *Philosophie des lebendigen Geistes in der Krise der Gegenwart.* Göttingen: Musterschmidt, 1977.

————. *Der Europäische Mensch.* Vienna: UNESCO, 1957.

Robinsohn, Saul B. *Bildungsreform als Revision des Curriculums.* Neuwied: Luchterhand, 1973.

Rombach, Heinrich, ed. *Wörterbuch der Pädagogik,* 3 vols. Frieburg: Herder, 1977.

Schieser, Hans, "The Principle of Heimat in European Urban Education," in *Rethinking Urban Education,* ed. Herbert Walberg and Andrew Kopan. San Francisco: Jossey-Bass, 1972.

————. "The Original Idea of the 'Liberal Arts' and What Our Schools Made Out of It," *The Delphian Quarterly,* No. 4 (Autumn 1978): 11–20.

Simons, Diane. *Georg Kerschensteiner—His Thought and Relevance Today.* London: Methuen, 1966.

Stokes, William S., Jr. "Education in West Germany," *The Revue of Politics,* Vol. 42, No. 2 (April 1980), pp. 191–215.

Warren, Richard L. *Education in Rebhausen.* New York: Holt, Rinehart and Winston, 1967.

# Name Index

# Subject Index